20-Minute Watercolor

52 Projects Using 7 Paint Colors and 1 Brush

EMILY OLSON

Founder of Watercolor Mastery

QUARRY

Quarto.com

First Published in 2026 by Quarry Books, an imprint of The Quarto Group,
100 Cummings Center, Suite 265-D, Beverly, MA 01915, USA.
T (978) 282-9590 F (978) 283-2742

EEA Representation, WTS Tax d.o.o.,
Žanova ulica 3, 4000 Kranj, Slovenia.
www.wts-tax.si

10 9 8 7 6 5 4 3 2 1

ISBN: 978-1-57715-752-6

Digital edition published in 2026
eISBN: 978-1-57715-753-3

Library of Congress Cataloging-in-Publication Data

Names: Olson, Emily (Artist) author
Title: 20-minute watercolor : 7 paint colors, 1 brush, 52 projects / Emily Olson, founder of Watercolor Mastery.
Other titles: Twenty-minute watercolor
Description: Beverly, MA, USA : Quarry, 2026. | Includes index.
Identifiers: LCCN 2026010779 (print) | LCCN 2026010780 (ebook) | ISBN 9781577157526 trade paperback | ISBN 9781577157533 ebook
Subjects: LCSH: Watercolor painting--Technique | LCGFT: Handbooks and manuals
Classification: LCC ND2420 .O463 2026 (print) | LCC ND2420 (ebook)
LC record available at https://lccn.loc.gov/2026010779
LC ebook record available at https://lccn.loc.gov/2026010780
Design: Sporto

Printed in Guangdong, China TT052026

This book is dedicated to the wonderful members of my Watercolor Mastery School. Your curiosity, courage, and creativity inspire me every single day. Thank you for allowing me to be part of your artistic journey.

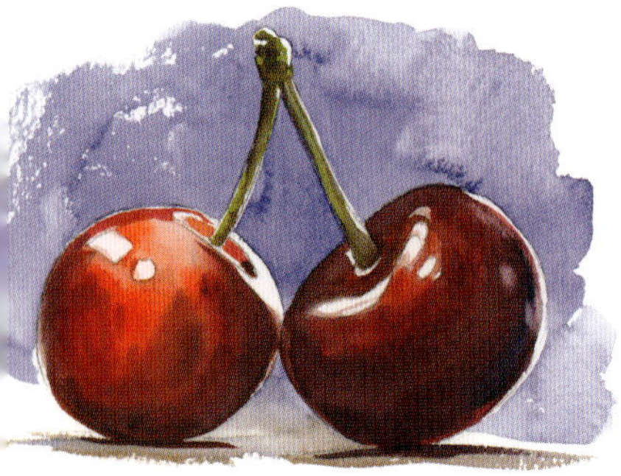

Contents

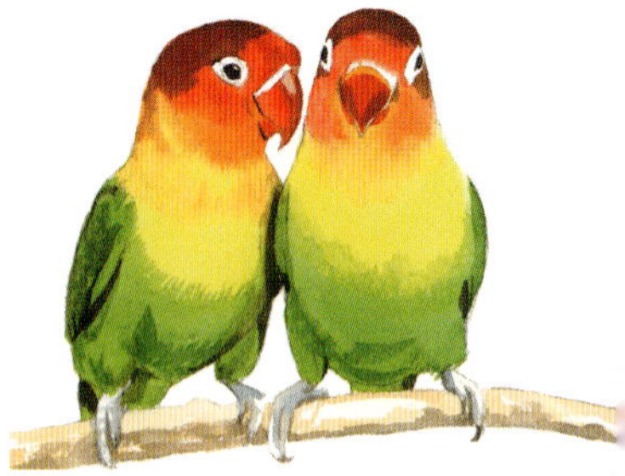

CHAPTER 4

20-Minute *Flowers* ... 77

CHAPTER 5

20-Minute *Birds* ... 99

CHAPTER 6

20-Minute *Still Lifes* ... 121

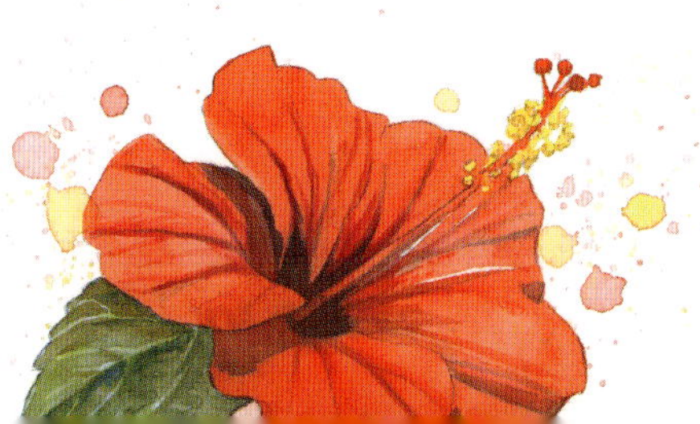

Introduction

Anyone can paint in watercolors! Yes, anyone—including you!

Maybe, like me, you once believed that watercolor was "the hardest medium." You looked longingly at art that you admired and said, "I could never do that!" But here's the truth: Watercolor is simply a skill, and like any skill it grows with practice, persistence, and a willingness to play.

My guess is that you picked up this book because you want two things: to improve your watercolor skills and to create paintings you genuinely love. You're in the right place. This book is about showing up consistently with brush in hand, making marks without pressure, and learning through joyful experimentation. The more you paint subjects that inspire you, the faster your skills (and your confidence) will grow.

Watercolor doesn't need to feel intimidating. It can be freeing, joyful, and deeply rewarding. Project by project, brushstroke by brushstroke, you'll find it becomes easier each time you paint. That's why I designed this book as a step-by-step guide: to help you build habits, learn techniques in bite-sized lessons, and experience the satisfaction of finishing paintings you'll be proud of.

How to Use This Book

This book is for anyone who wants to paint—whether you're a complete beginner or a more experienced artist returning to the essentials. Inside, you'll find:

- A clear, approachable introduction to watercolor basics
- Lessons on mixing any color from just seven paints
- Simple techniques that will help you grow comfortable with washes, layering, and brush control

From there, you'll dive into 52 unique projects, each designed to be completed in about 20 minutes. *That's one painting for every week of the year!* Paint them in any order, at your own pace—whether you're squeezing in a creative break on a busy day or settling in for a weekend session.

Each project includes step-by-step instructions right on the page, plus QR codes linking to short videos that demonstrate key techniques. At the back of the book, you'll find traceable sketches for convenience. You can also download or view full-sized sketches and reference photos.

Use these projects however you like. Practice exercises, framed art for your walls, handmade cards, or even gifts for friends. It only takes a brush, a bit of water, and some color to start creating without limits.

So, let's jump in! A year of watercolor adventures awaits!

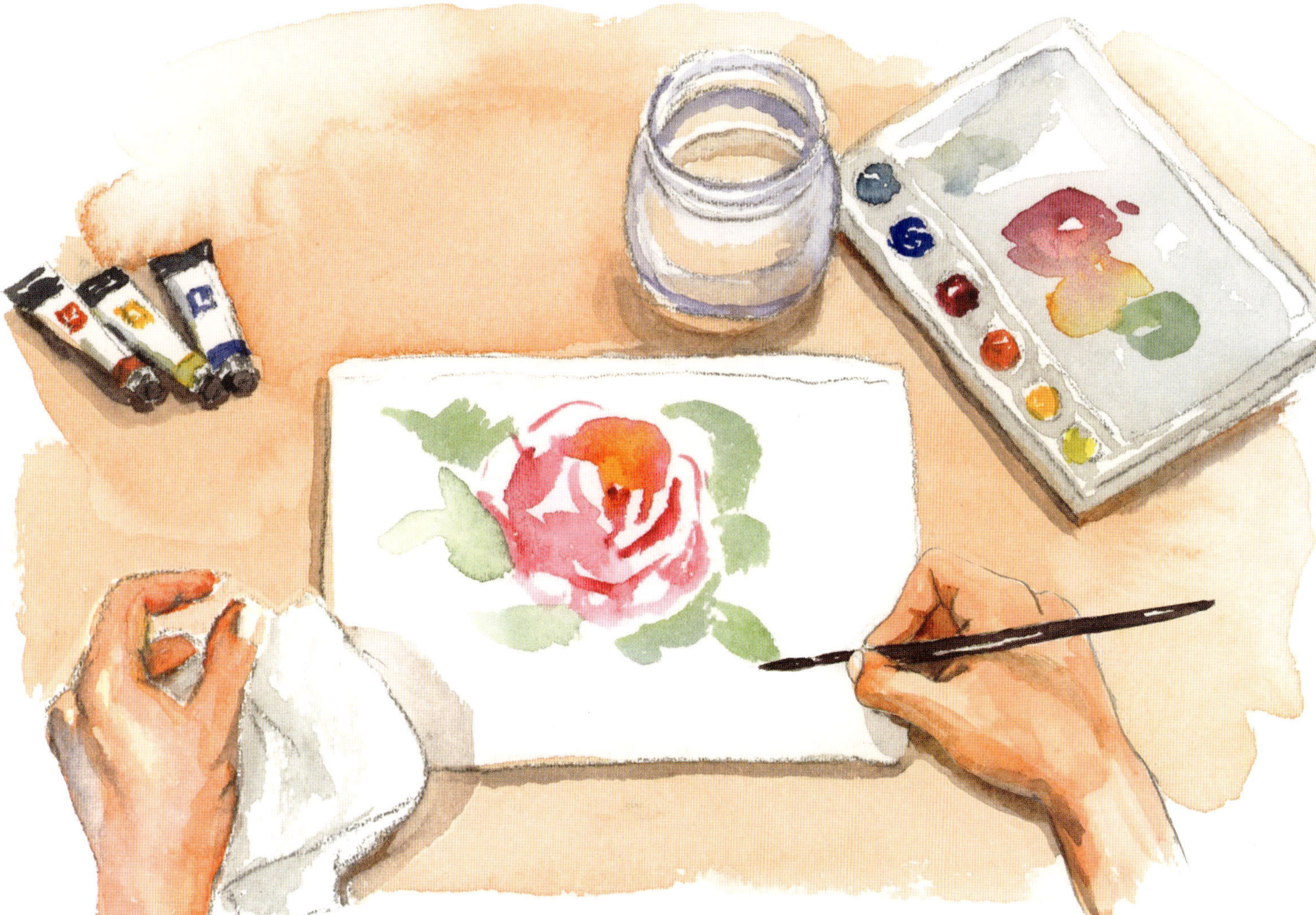

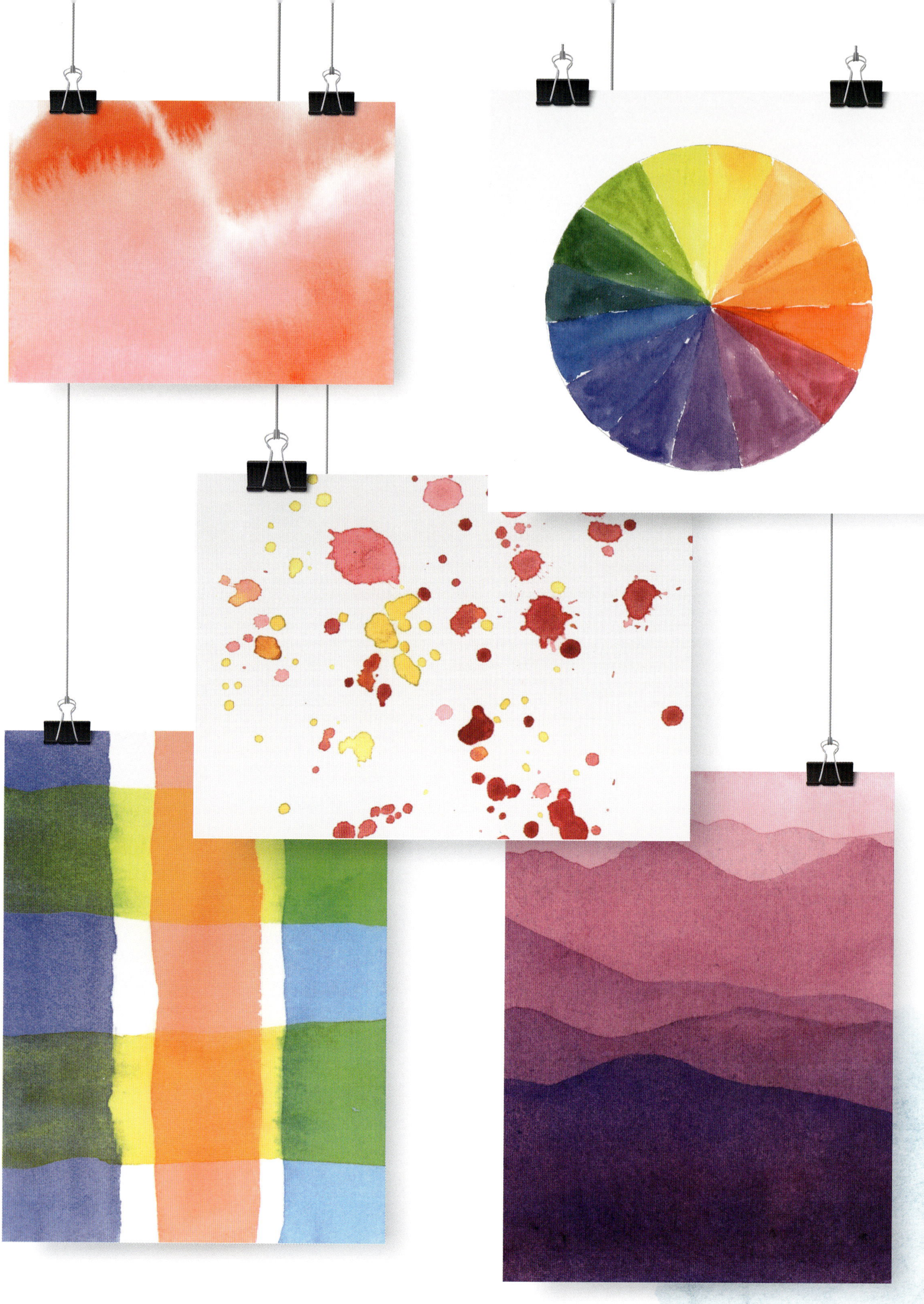

CHAPTER 1

Essentials for Success

In this chapter, we'll walk through the essentials—paper, brushes, and paints—and discover how primary colors can become your secret weapon for creating any color you dream of. You'll also get a chance to practice the foundational techniques that bring every painting to life. Whether you're brand new or a more experienced painter, this is your warm-up for the creative adventure ahead!

Materials

My goal with this book is to make watercolor painting as simple and approachable as possible. Part of that is using a limited number of supplies. Throughout the lessons, we'll be working with just seven carefully chosen paint colors, one trusty brush, and a single type of paper—because creating beautiful art shouldn't require a mountain of materials.

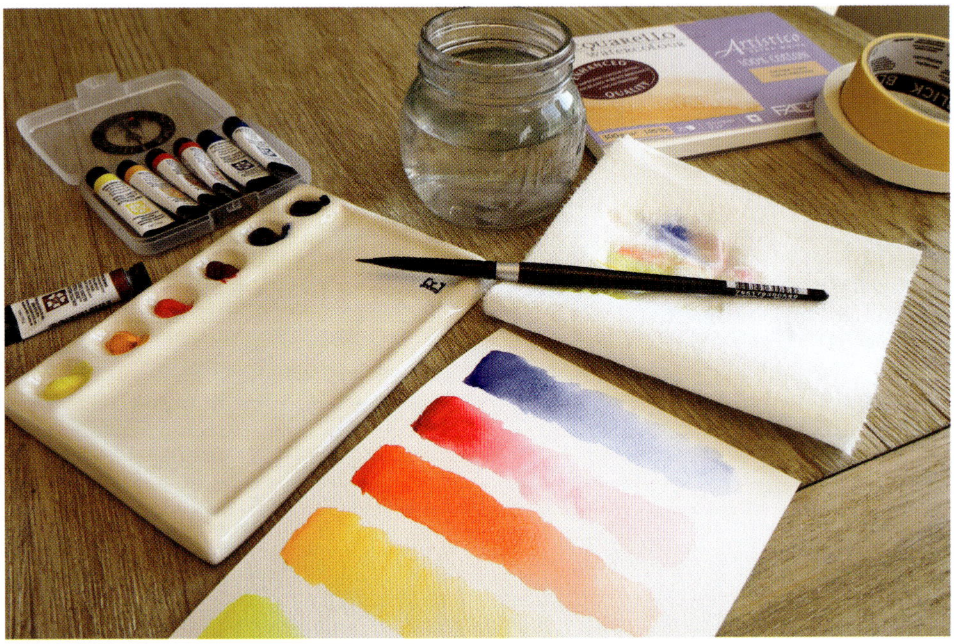

Paints

We'll be using a limited palette of warm and cool primary colors, plus one essential earth tone. I'm using the Daniel Smith Essentials Set, which includes:

- Hansa Yellow Light (cool yellow)
- New Gamboge (warm yellow)
- Pyrrol Scarlet (warm red)
- Quinacridone Rose (cool red)
- French Ultramarine (warm blue)
- Phthalo Blue Green Shade (cool blue)
- To complete the palette, I've added Burnt Sienna—a rich, reddish-brown that I reach for again and again.

Working with a smaller set of paints helps create natural color harmony in your work. It also teaches you how to mix your own colors from primaries, which builds confidence and gives you the freedom to paint just about anything with yellow, red, and blue. Less is more—and in this case, it's more creative too!

Brush

My go-to brush for all the projects in this book is the Silver Black Velvet round, size 8. It's made from a blend of synthetic and natural bristles, giving it the perfect balance of spring and softness. It's just the right size for laying down smooth washes and adding fine details—no need to switch brushes constantly!

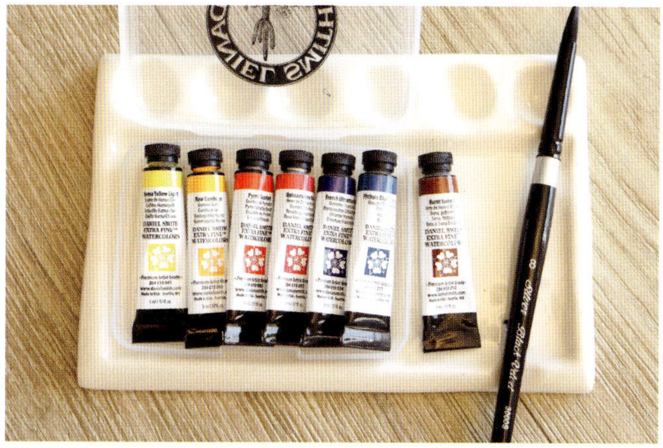

For the projects in the book, you only need seven paint colors and one brush.

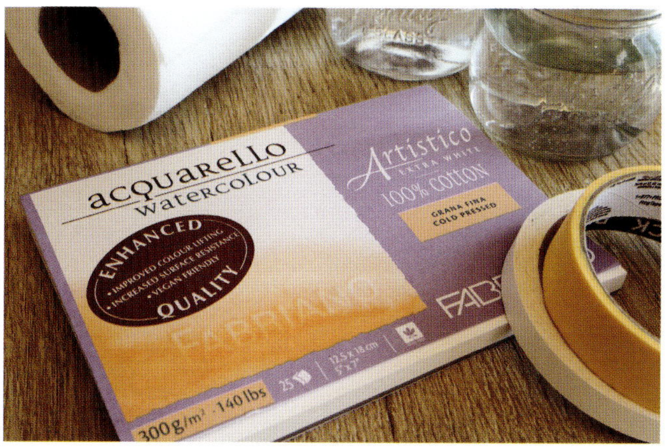

Using 100% cotton watercolor paper makes a difference in your painting results.

Paper

For all the tutorials, I'll be working on a 5" x 7" (12.5 x 17.75 cm) block of Fabriano Artistico, 140lb (300gsm) cold-pressed 100% cotton watercolor paper, extra white. You're welcome to use any brand you prefer, but I highly recommend 100% cotton paper for the best painting experience—it absorbs water beautifully and gives you vibrant, blend-able results.

Other Supplies

Here are a few more basics you'll need:

- A pencil and eraser
- A palette with plenty of space for mixing
- Two water containers (one for rinsing, one for clean water)
- Paper towel or a clean rag for controlling water on your brush
- Painter's tape to help create clean, straight edges

Ready to dive in? Awesome! Let's kick things off with some simple mixing exercises to get comfortable with your palette and set you up for all the exciting projects ahead!

The Magic of Primary Colors

Primary colors are special. They cannot be created by mixing other colors. They exist as self-sufficient pigments: red, yellow, and blue. All other colors are the result of mixing primary colors together.

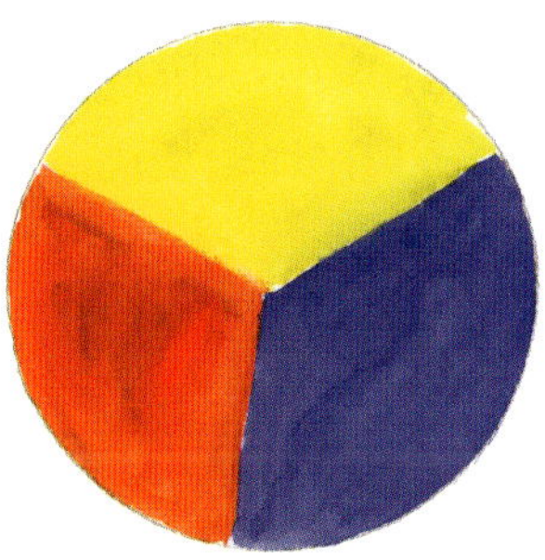

The Primary Colors: Red, Yellow, Blue.

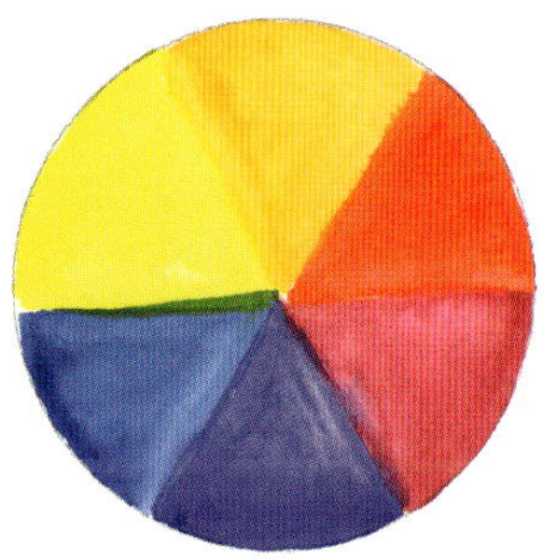

Daniel Smith Essential Primary Colors.

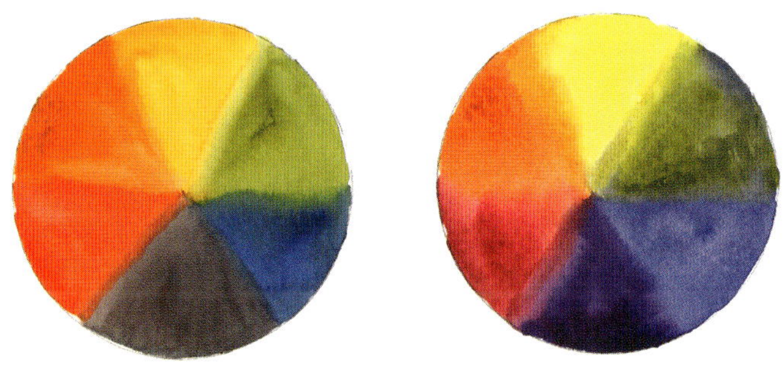

Here I've created two color wheels with secondary colors to show the difference: On the left, I used Pyrrol Scarlet, New Gamboge, and Phthalo Blue (GS). On the right, I used Quinacridone Rose, Hansa Yellow Light, and French Ultramarine.

But here's the fun part: there are many *kinds* of reds, yellows, and blues. Some are warmer, some are cooler, and this is why a good starter set of watercolors should include two sets of primaries—one warm and one cool.

Colors with more yellow in them are considered warm.

Colors with more blue in them are considered cool.

Of course, warmth and coolness are relative. A color may look warmer or cooler depending on what's around it. But understanding this basic idea helps us mix with confidence. Once you see what happens when warm colors mingle with cool ones, you'll realize that you can paint anything with just these six magical primaries!

When you mix two primary colors, you create the *secondary colors:* orange, violet, and green. And because you have both warm and cool versions of each primary, the variety of mixes is endless.

Exercise: Split Primary Color Wheel

A split primary wheel uses two of each primary—a warm and a cool. With secondaries and tertiaries added, you'll have a fifteen-slice wheel that shows the full range of your palette.

Essentials Set Colors

- Hansa Yellow Light (cool) and New Gamboge (warm)
- Quinacridone Rose (cool) and Pyrrol Scarlet (warm)
- Phthalo Blue (GS) (cool) and Ultramarine Blue (warm)

Steps

- Draw a circle and divide it into fifteen equal slices. Place your six primaries around the wheel, spaced evenly.
- Keep warm and cool versions of each hue family separated by a few slices (for example: cool yellow, warm yellow, then moving into oranges, etc.).
- Between each pair of primaries, mix them together to create the secondary colors (orange, green, violet).
- You'll now have six primaries + three secondaries = nine slices filled.
- Mix a primary with its neighboring secondary to create the tertiary colors (yellow orange, red orange, red violet, blue violet, blue green, yellow green).
- These go between the primaries and secondaries, giving you a smooth transition all the way around the wheel.

Observe the Difference

- The warm side of the wheel glows with fiery oranges and reds.
- The cool side leans into fresh greens and purples.
- Having both warms and cools and their tertiaries gives you a much richer picture of what your palette can do.

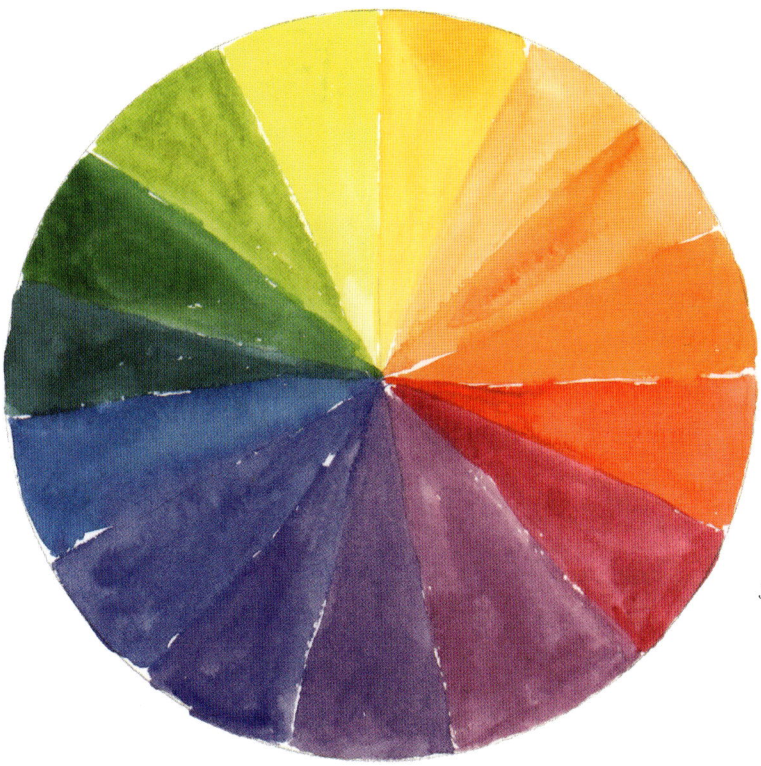

Split Primary Color Wheel.

Mixing 101:
Build a 7-Color Mixing Chart

Throughout this book we'll mix with primaries to make purples, greens, oranges, browns, and even rich near-blacks. If you have Burnt Sienna, it's a wonderful shortcut to warm browns, but every other secondary (and many neutrals) will come from your primaries.

One of the best ways to *really* get to know your paints is to create a color mixing chart.

Bonus: Scan the QR code or go to https://www.quarto.com/files/20MinuteWatercolor to download a printable 7-color mixing chart.

Scan for the template.

Step 1
Choose and Order Your 7 Colors

For this chart, we'll use the Essentials Set in this order (cool to warm within each hue family):

1. Hansa Yellow Light (cool yellow)
2. New Gamboge (warm yellow)
3. Pyrrol Scarlet (warm red)
4. Quinacridone Rose (cool red)
5. French Ultramarine (warm blue)
6. Phthalo Blue (GS) (cool blue)
7. Burnt Sienna (earth)

Step 2
Set Up the Grid

1. Draw a 7" × 7" (18 x 18 cm) grid on watercolor paper.
2. Label the top 1–7 and the side A–G, with each number and letter pair representing the same color.

- Example: 1 and A = Hansa Yellow Light, ,02 and B = New Gamboge, and so on.

3. This way, the square at 3B will be a mix of Pyrrol Scarlet (3) and New Gamboge (2).

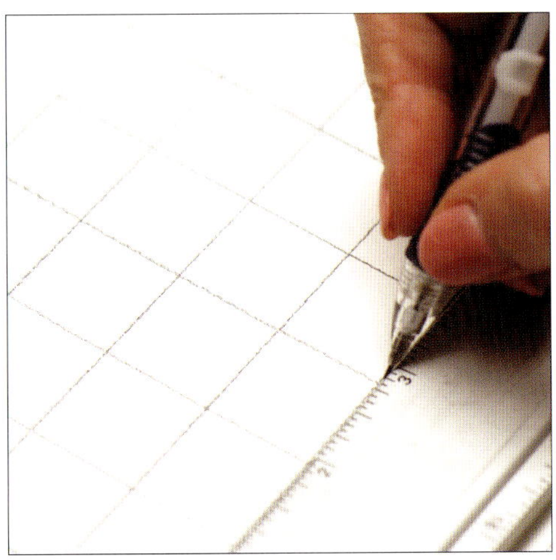

Sketch out your grid.

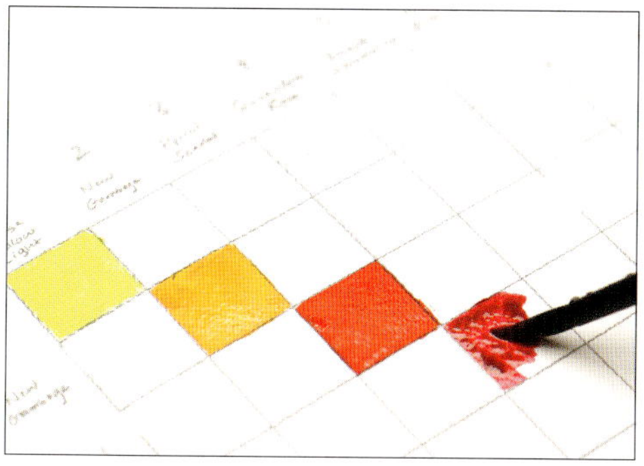

Fill the diagonal with pure color.

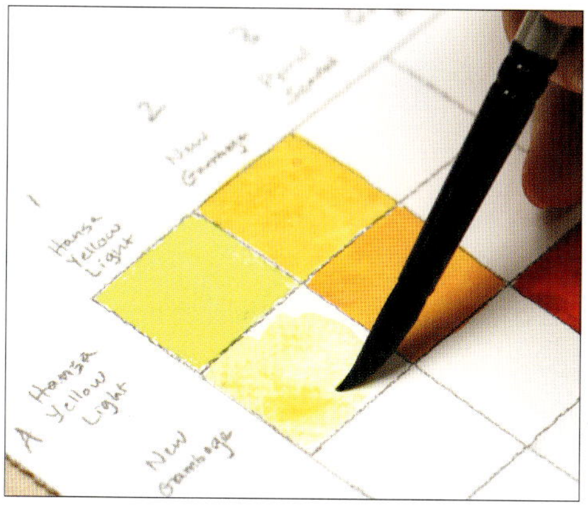

Remember right = rich and left = light.

Step 3

Fill the Diagonal with Pure Color

Paint each diagonal square (1A, 2B, 3C, 4D, 5E, 6F, 7G) with pure, undiluted color. These form your reference swatches.

Step 4

Mix the Off-Diagonals

1. Right of the diagonal → use a rich, dark mix (more pigment, less water).
2. Left of the diagonal → use the same mix but diluted for a light tint.
   - Example: 3B (right of diagonal) = Pyrrol Scarlet + New Gamboge, thick paint, deep orange; 2C (left of diagonal) = the same mix diluted with water, a light orange.
3. Repeat this for every pair until the chart is full.

Step 5

Observe

Which colors surprise you the most? You'll soon find yourself reaching for these favorites again and again. That fresh green in 6A will bring leaves and landscapes to life, while the deep black in 6C will be your secret weapon for shadows, fur, feathers, and dramatic details.

And remember, this chart only shows two-color mixes. Just imagine the magic that happens when you start blending three or more. With these foundations, your palette can take you anywhere—the possibilities are truly endless.

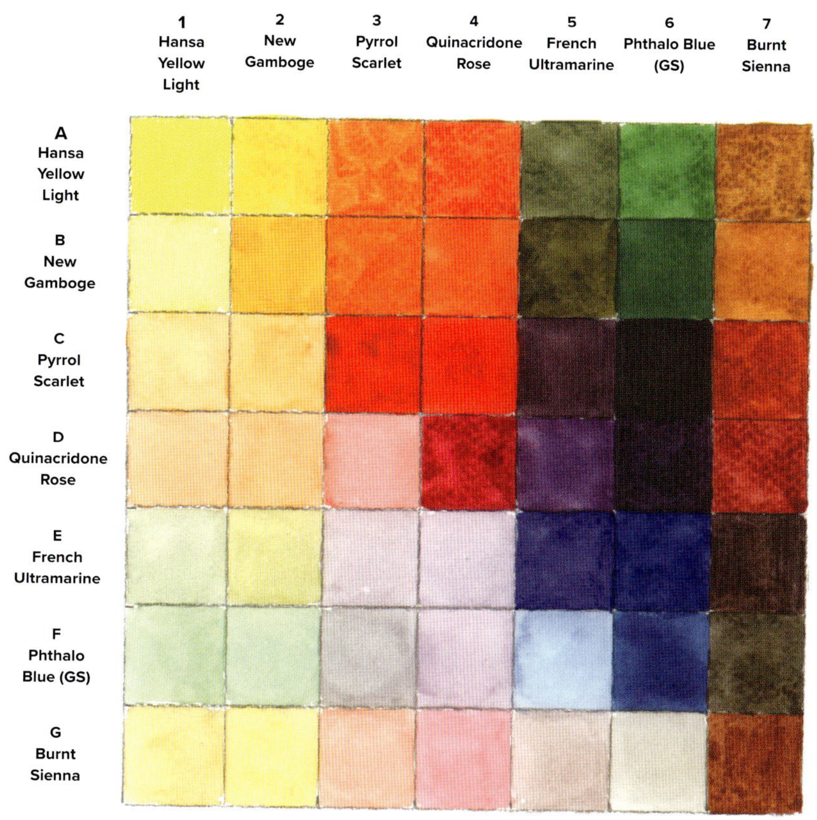

Basic Techniques

Now that you've explored your color palette, it's time to unlock the magic of watercolor itself. With just four simple ingredients—brush, paper, water, and pigment—you can create an incredible range of effects. This section is designed to introduce you to the essential techniques and terms that will become the foundation for every painting in the 52 projects that follow.

One of the biggest hurdles for beginners is learning water control. The question "How much water and how much pigment should I use?" comes up repeatedly, and for good reason. Once you understand how different consistencies of paint behave on wet versus dry paper, watercolor becomes not only easier but also much more enjoyable.

In the next pages, we'll break down these core skills step by step, so you can practice them with confidence before diving into full projects.

Paint Consistency

In this book, you'll often see me describe paint consistencies as watery, milky, or creamy. Each works best depending on the wetness of your paper.

- **Watery paint** is thin and flows easily. It's perfect for painting on dry paper when you want light washes that glide smoothly over the texture. However, on already wet paper, watery paint adds too much liquid, leading to puddles or backruns.
- **Milky paint** is a medium consistency and very versatile. On dry paper, it gives you medium to dark values with crisp, controlled edges. On wet paper, it softens beautifully, creating fuzzy edges and smooth blends.
- **Creamy (or thick) paint** is richer and more concentrated. It works especially well on wet paper, because it softens without spreading wildly, giving you stronger color while maintaining control. You can also use creamy paint for small dark details on dry paper, though it may catch on the texture and look rough. This rough effect is sometimes useful. When intentional, it's called the drybrush technique.

Rule of thumb: more water = less control, less water = more control.

Here you can see four different wetness levels of both paper and paint.

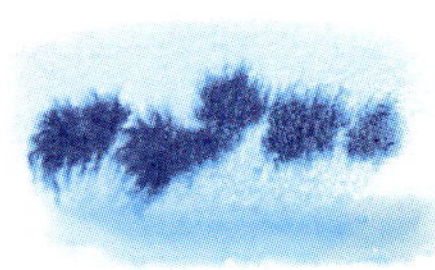

1. Watery paint on puddle

2. Milky paint on wet paper

3. Milky paint on damp paper

4. Creamy paint on dry paper (drybrush technique)

Wet-on-Dry

This is the easiest and most intuitive way to paint with watercolors. Simply load up your brush with watery or milky paint and apply it to dry paper. This technique is ideal for details and areas of strong contrast with hard edges because you have complete control of your lines.

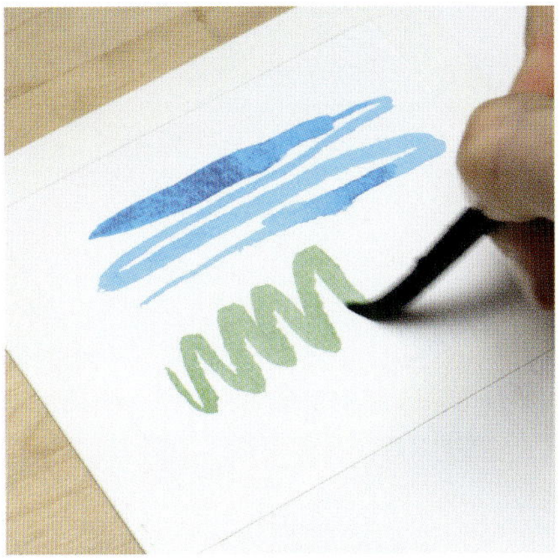

Create lines and shapes on the dry paper.

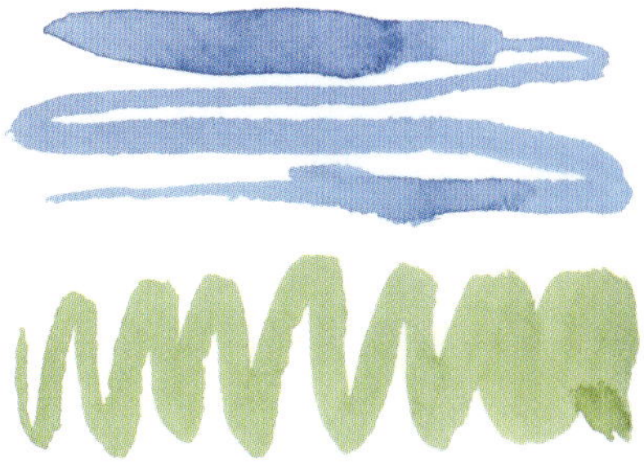

A very controlled result.

Wet-on-Wet

This technique involves painting wet paint onto an already wet surface. The surface can be pre-wet with clean water or already painted with another color. Use this technique whenever you want soft edges and natural color blends.

Wet the paper.

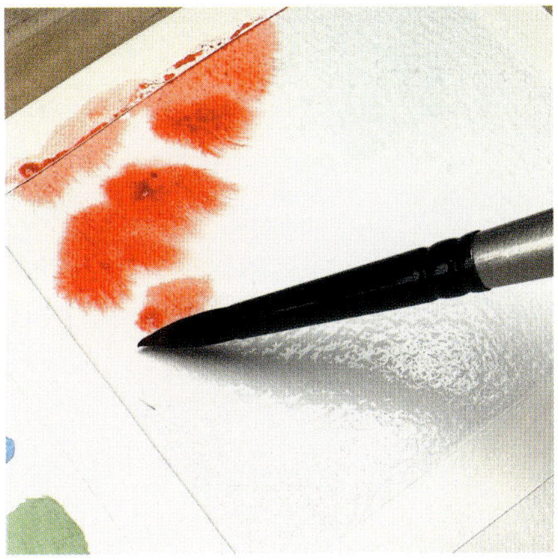

Drop in creamy paint.

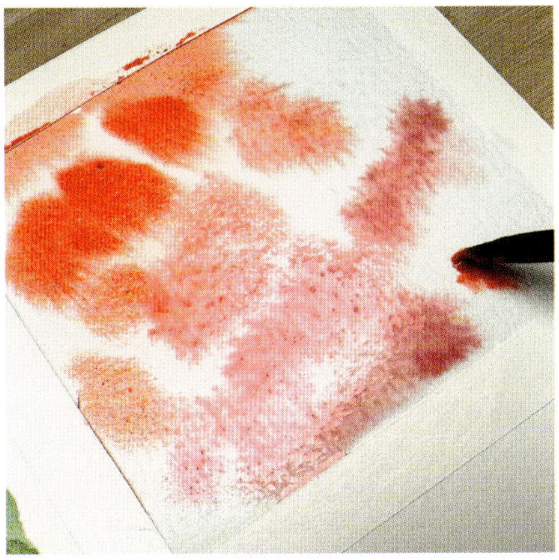

Add another color in a milky consistency.

Result.

Damp-on-Damp

This technique is useful when you want softened but not overly fuzzy edges. Your paper surface should be somewhat wet and your brush should be just damp with paint. A general guideline is to try to match your brush wetness level to the wetness level of your paper.

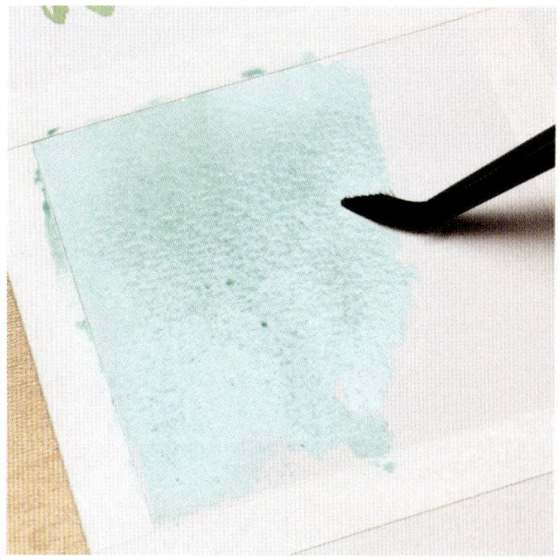

Fill an area with color.

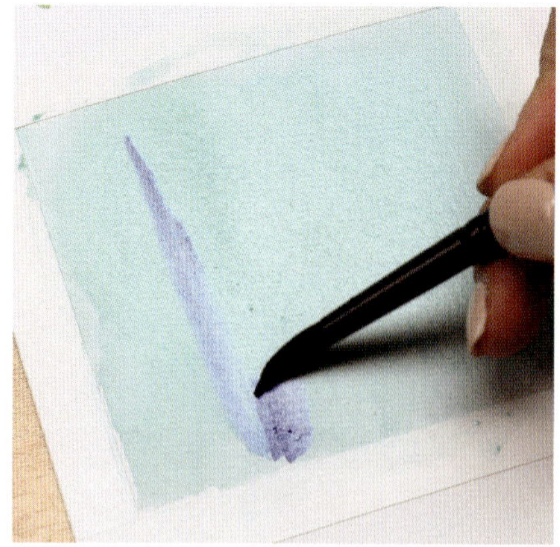

Load your brush with a second color; blot on rag to remove excess water.

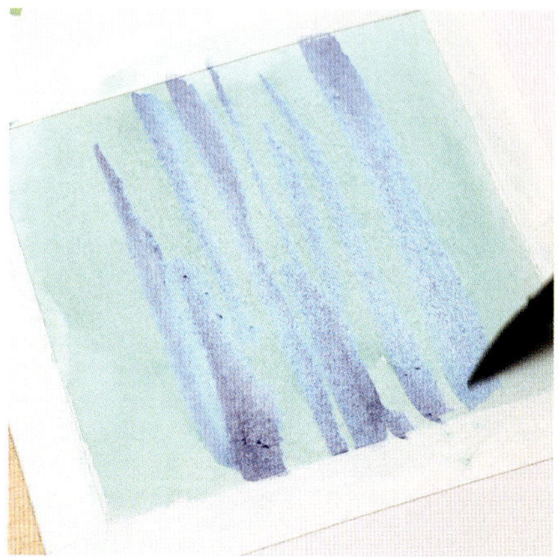

Paint damp into damp.

Result.

Adjusting Values

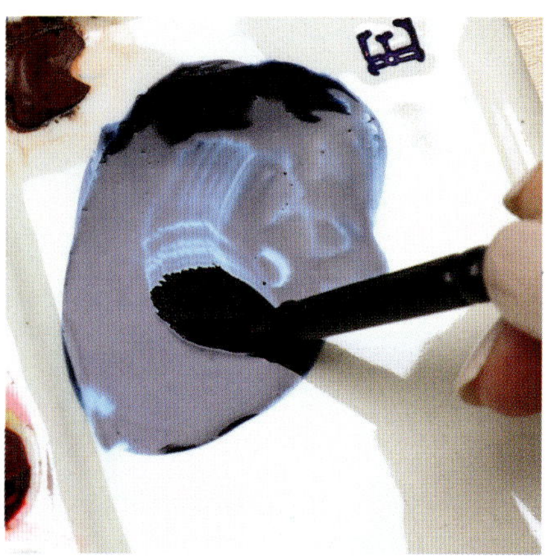

Watercolors are meant to be used with water. We rarely work with pigment straight out of the tube. To get a feel for how to adjust your pigment-to-water ratios so that you can achieve a variety of lights and darks, try creating a value scale with a single color.

Step 1

Prepare Your Pigment

Mix up a creamy puddle of your chosen watercolor on your palette. This will be your darkest, most saturated value.

Step 2

Paint the Darkest Square

On your paper, paint the first square (or section) with this creamy mix at full strength, making sure it's smooth and even.

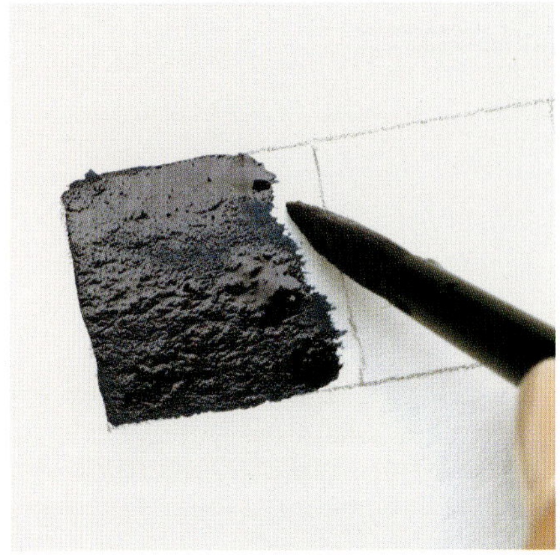

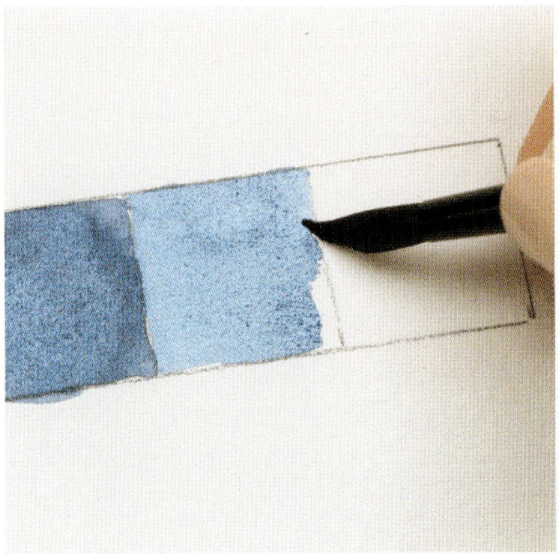

Step 3

Dilute Gradually

Rinse your brush slightly, then add more water to the pigment on your palette to create a lighter mixture. Paint the next square with this diluted version. Keep repeating—adding more water each time—to create a gradient of values.

A finished value scale.

Tip

Make a simple value scale for every color in your palette by painting swatches that range from the richest, creamy pigment to the palest tint. This not only shows you the full depth and delicacy each pigment can achieve but also helps you practice water control.

Glazing

When you apply wet paint over another painted area that is completely dry, this is called glazing. Glazing serves two purposes—it darkens an area and can also alter the color.

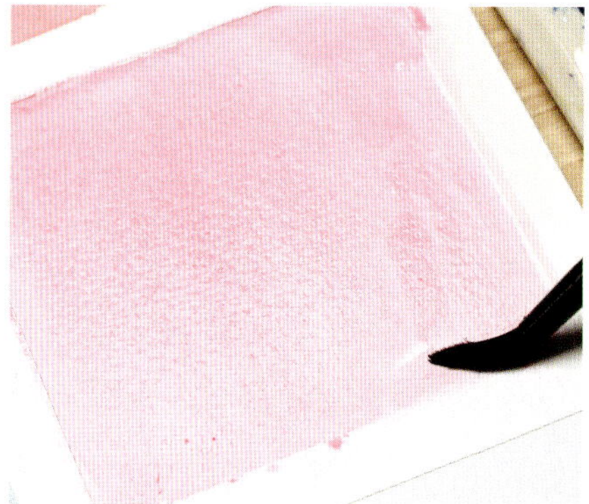

Paint a flat wash and let it dry completely.

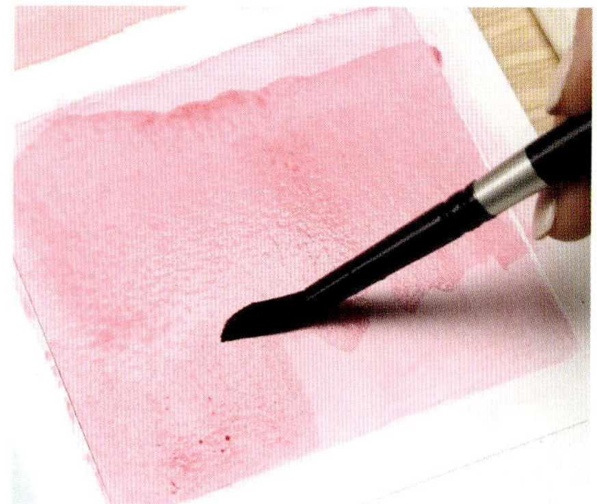

Paint a second layer. Let it dry.

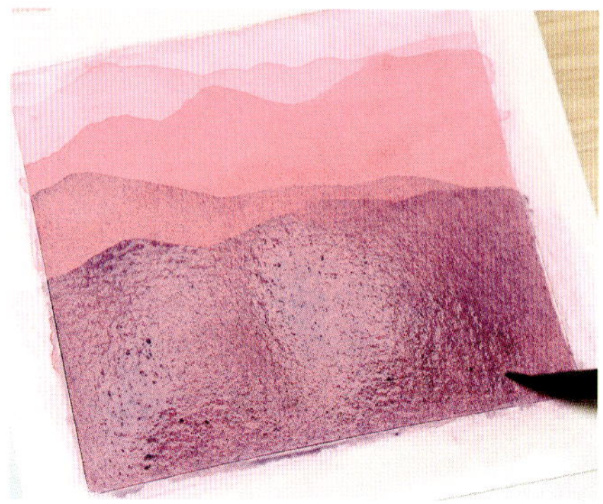

Repeat this process to create darker mountain layers.

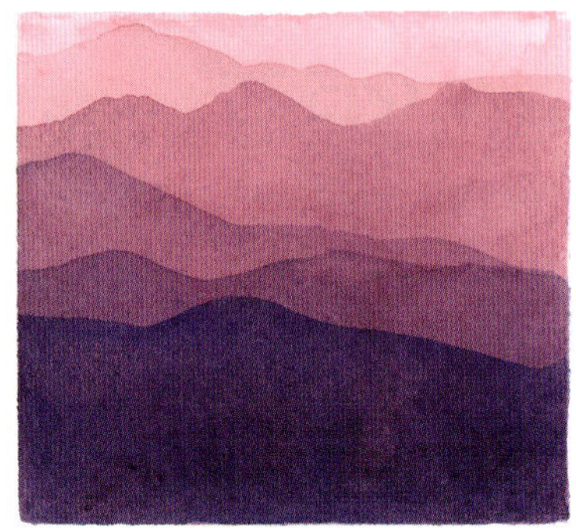

Result.

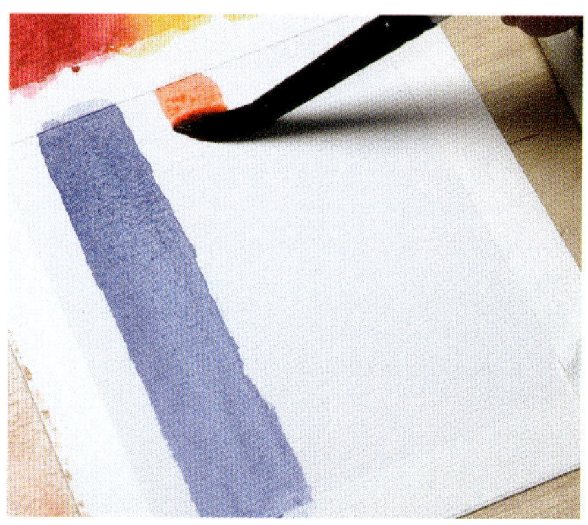

Paint milky paint on dry paper.

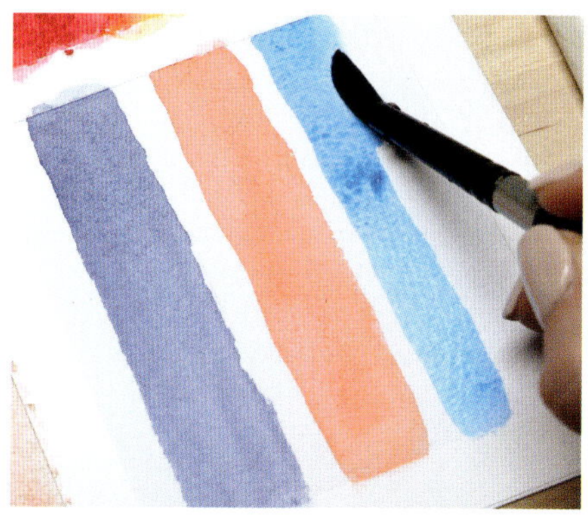

Vary the colors. Let it dry.

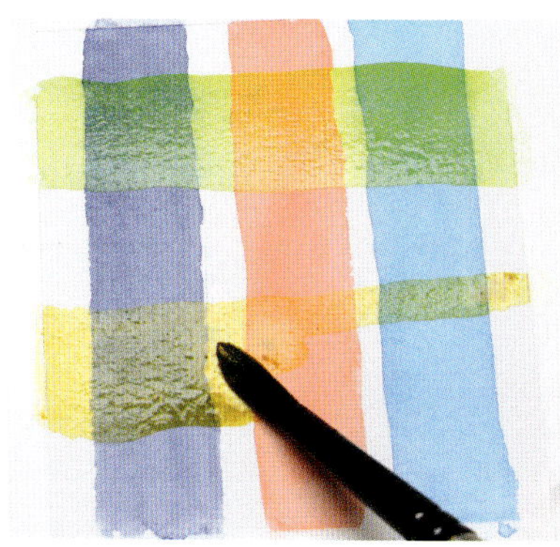

Apply a contrasting glaze for fresh color blends.

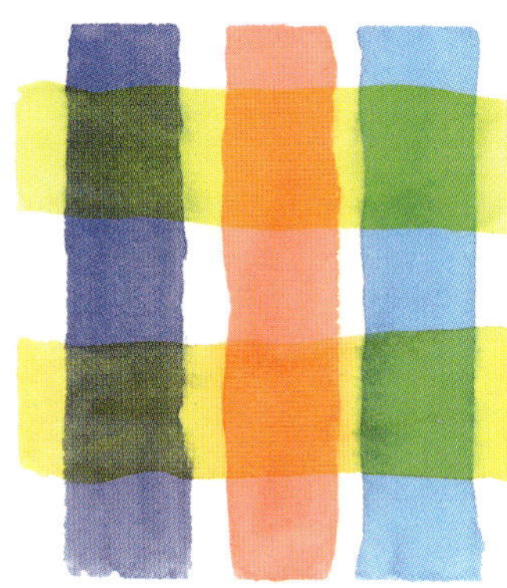

Result.

Drybrush

This technique is fabulous for achieving interesting textures. Use drybrush for bark, rocks, grasses, stubbly hair, and much more.

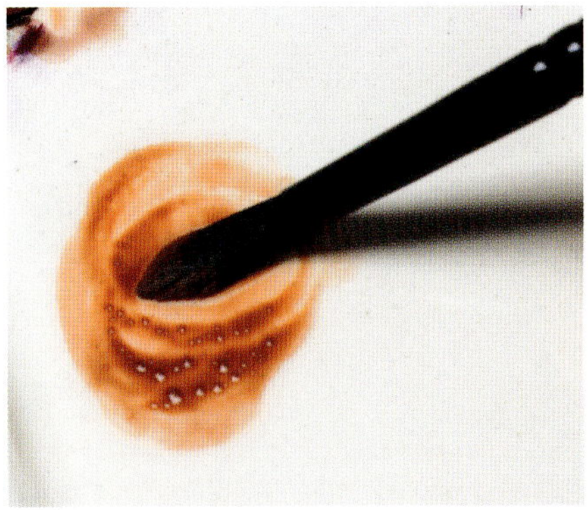

Mix up milky or creamy paint.

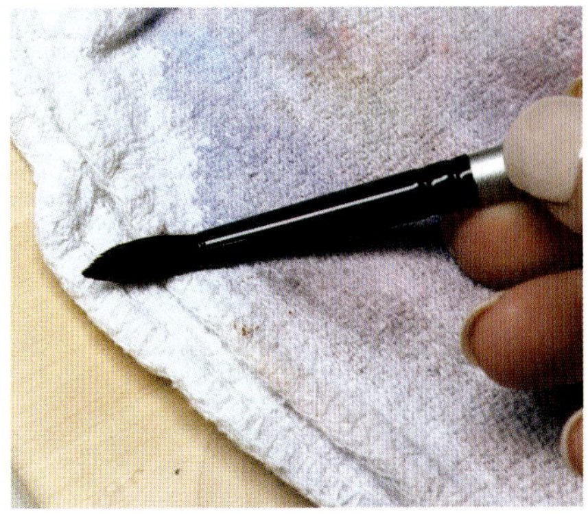

Remove any excess water on rag.

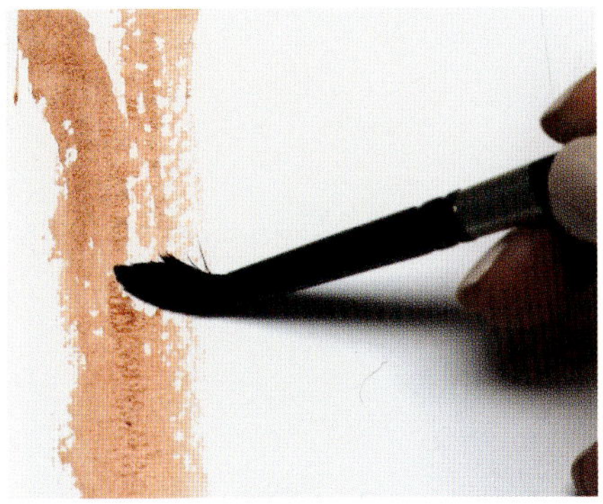

Scrape the brush along the surface of the paper.

The brush skips across the texture, catching only the raised areas.

Flat Wash

A flat wash is simply a single color applied in an even layer. You can create a wash either on dry paper or wet-on-wet.

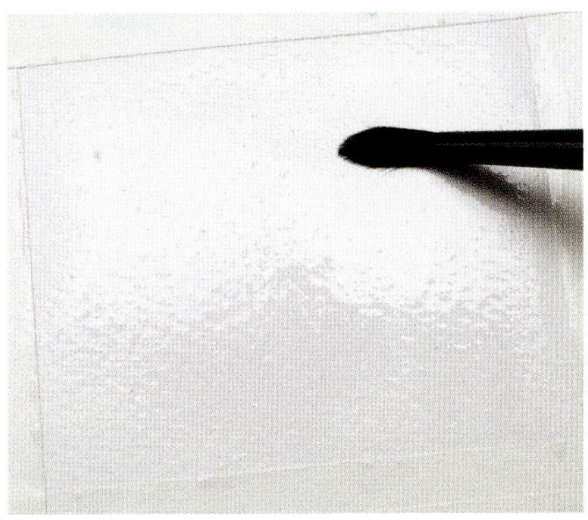

Wet the paper surface with clear water.

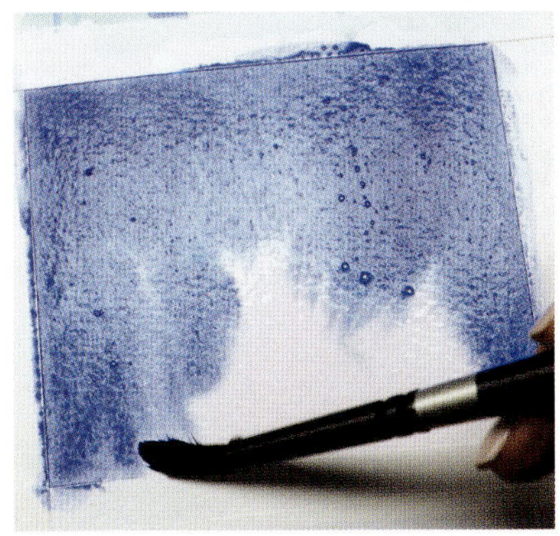

Paint with a single creamy color.

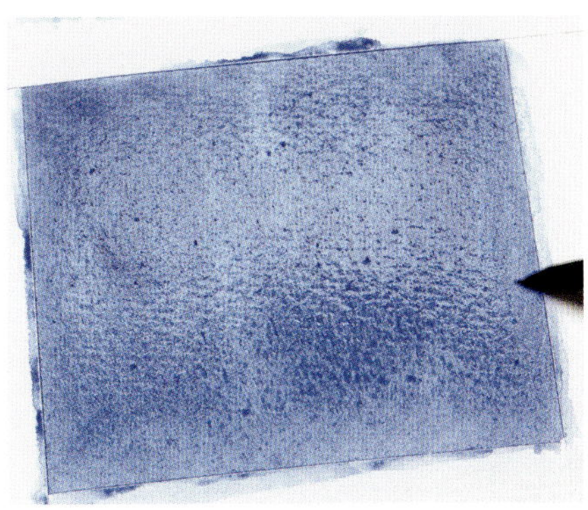

Fill the area quickly and evenly.

Result.

Gradated Wash

A gradated wash involves starting a flat wash with a creamy pigment and gradually diluting it so that you have a smooth gradient from dark to light.

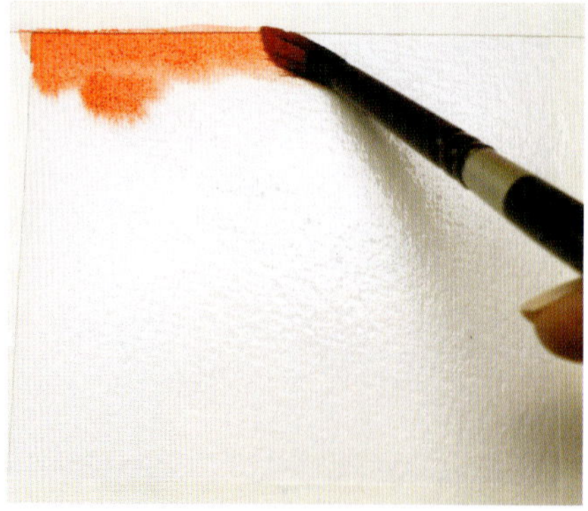

Apply creamy paint to pre-wet paper.

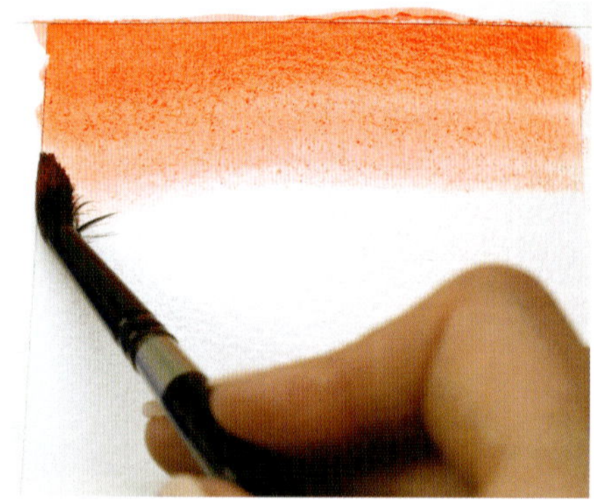

Paint gradually thins as you paint down the wash.

Dilute the color at the bottom.

Result.

Variegated Wash

This technique is a wash that shifts color while remaining seamless and fluid, useful for skies and water.

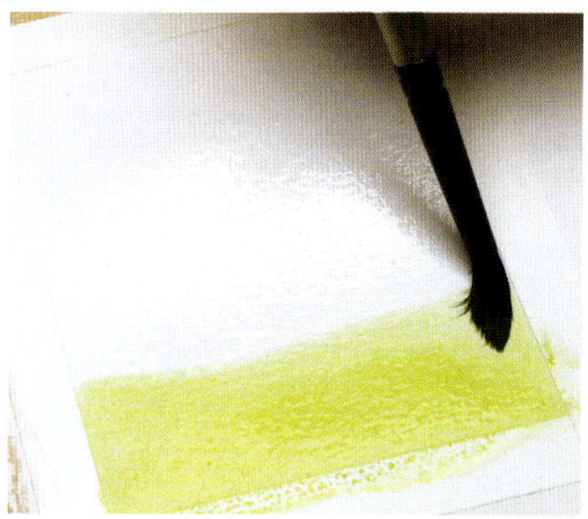

Lay creamy paint on the wet surface, fading it upward.

Quickly apply a second color at the top.

Blend in the middle.

Result.

Charging (Wet Next to Wet)

Charging involves adding a second color or a stronger value into a wet area of paint so the two merge naturally on the paper. This creates soft, organic blends.

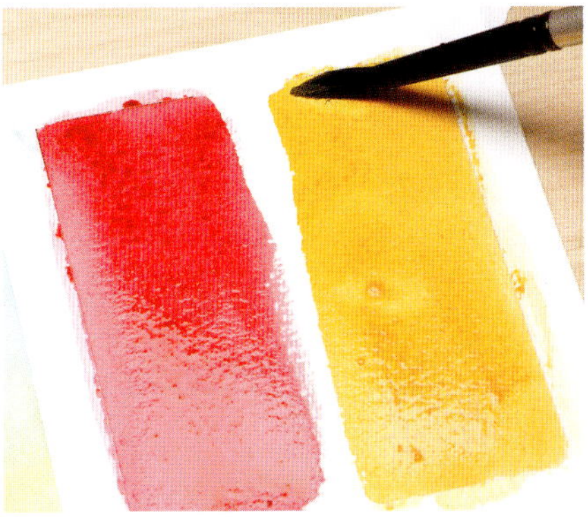

Paint two colors in the same consistency.

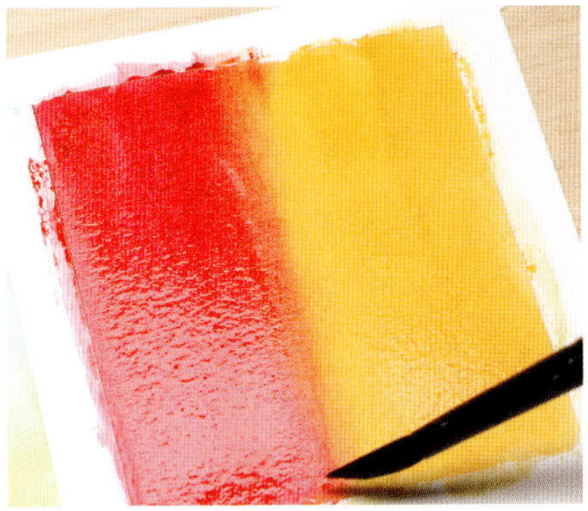

Let the paint touch in the middle.

Result.

Blending Hard to Soft Edges

This is a technique where you soften the edge of a painted shape by brushing clean water along one side, turning a crisp line into a gradual fade.

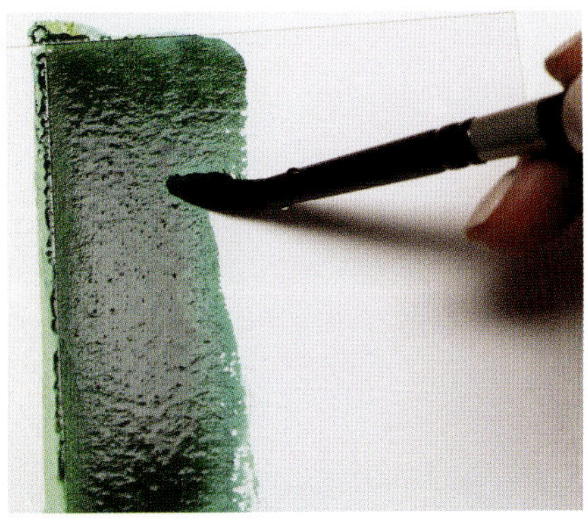

Start with a thick consistency of paint.

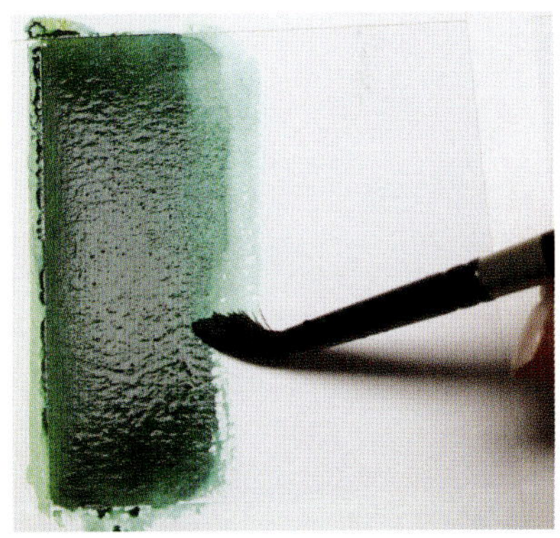

Pull the pigment.

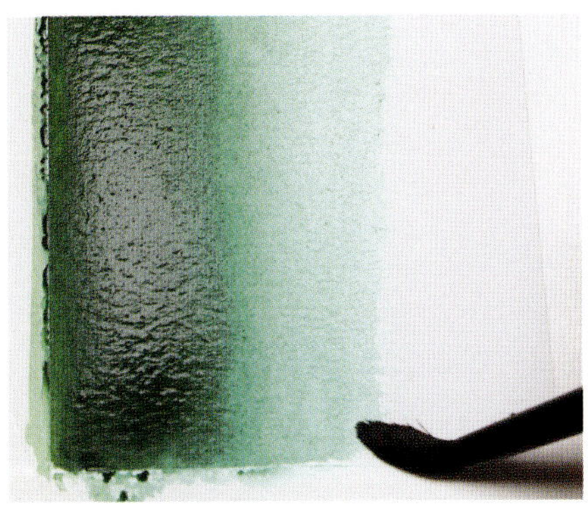

Blend with a damp brush.

Result.

Backruns, Blooms, or the "Cauliflower Effect"

These marks usually appear by accident when excess water lands on a drying wash. The added moisture pushes pigment outward, forming irregular blooms with soft, uneven edges. Once you understand the process, though, you can also use it intentionally to create interesting textures and atmospheric effects.

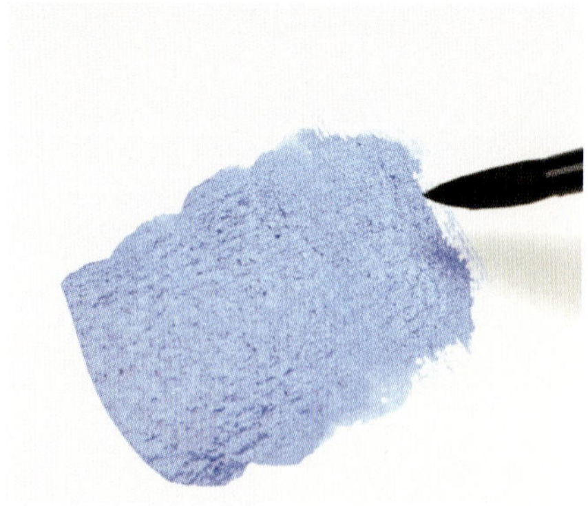

Paint a milky wash.

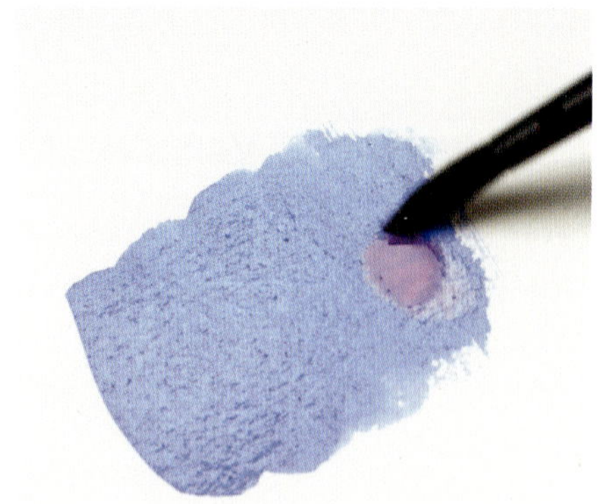

Let watery paint touch the wash.

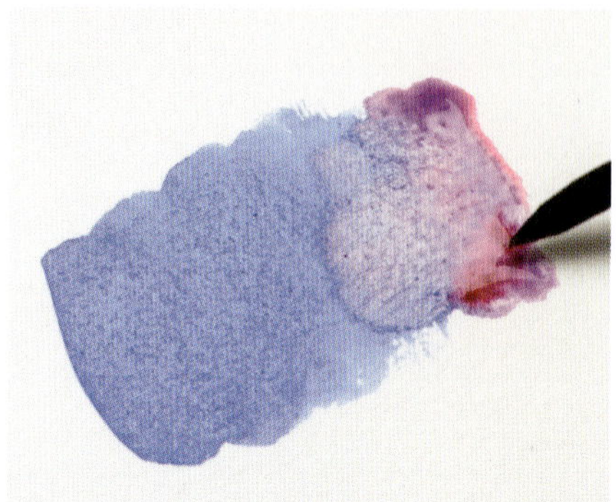

The extra water pushes the pigment aside.

Result.

Spatter

This is a fun texture technique where you flick or tap a loaded brush to scatter droplets of paint across the paper, creating random speckles.

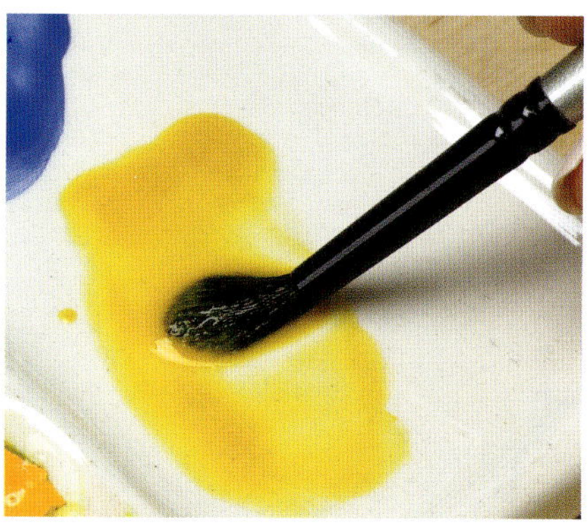

Load the brush with dripping paint.

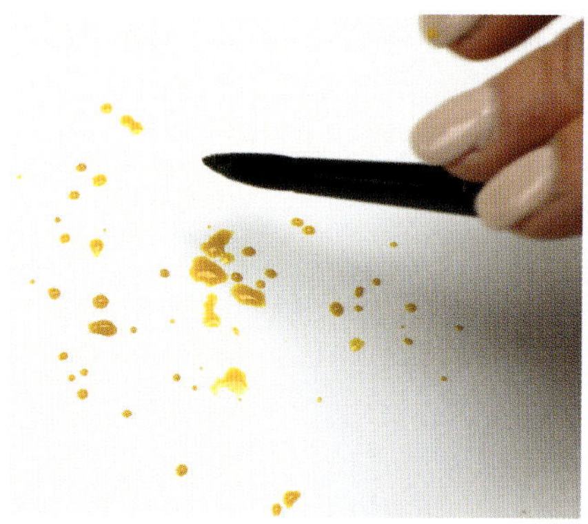

Tap the brush over your paper.

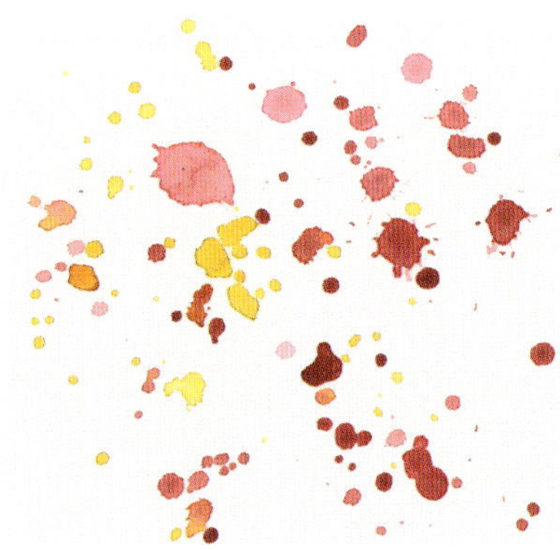

Result of spattering two different colors.

White in Watercolor

White areas are the brightest highlights in a watercolor painting, bringing sparkle and contrast to the scene. To preserve this freshness, we must plan ahead, leaving portions of the paper untouched so the natural white surface can shine through. There are several ways to preserve and create white in watercolor. In this book, we'll explore techniques such as negative painting, lifting, and using opaque white.

Negative Painting

Negative painting is when you paint around a subject, rather than painting the subject itself. By applying darker washes around lighter shapes, the unpainted (or lightly painted) areas are revealed as the subject.

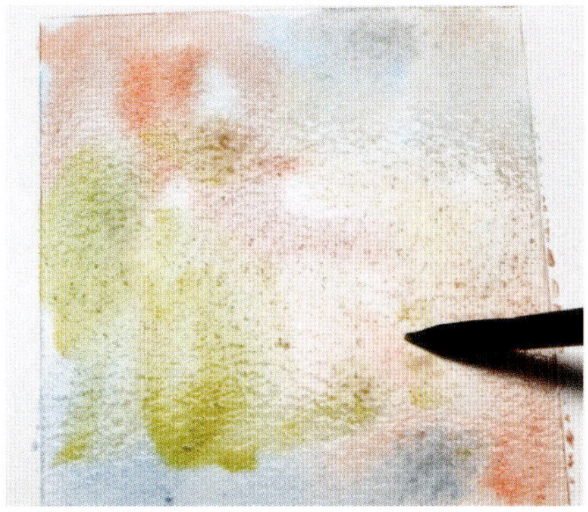

Apply a light wash of color and let it dry.

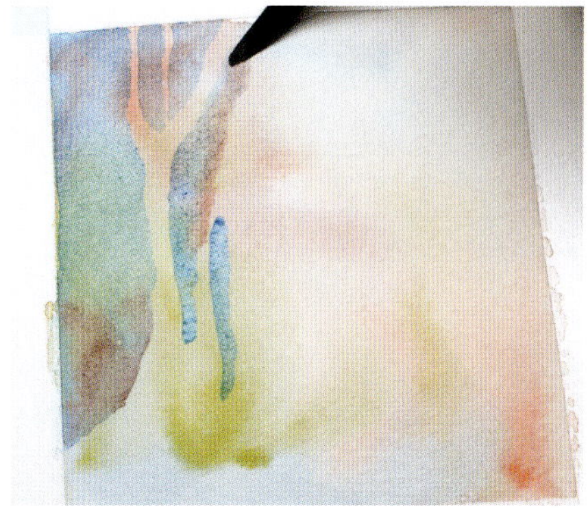

Paint a darker wash around the shapes you want to highlight.

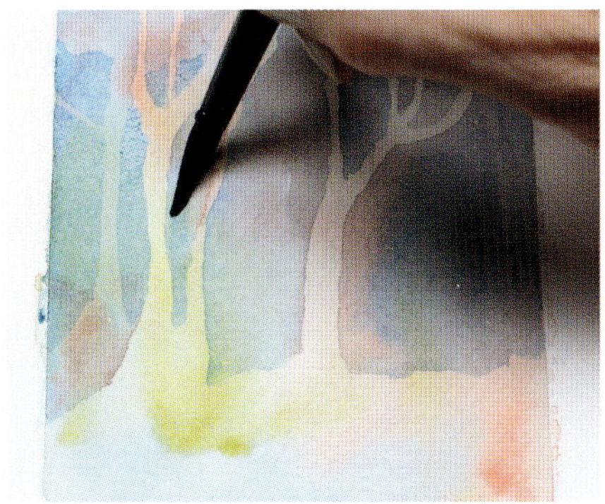

Add more wet-on-dry layers for depth around and in-between your light shapes.

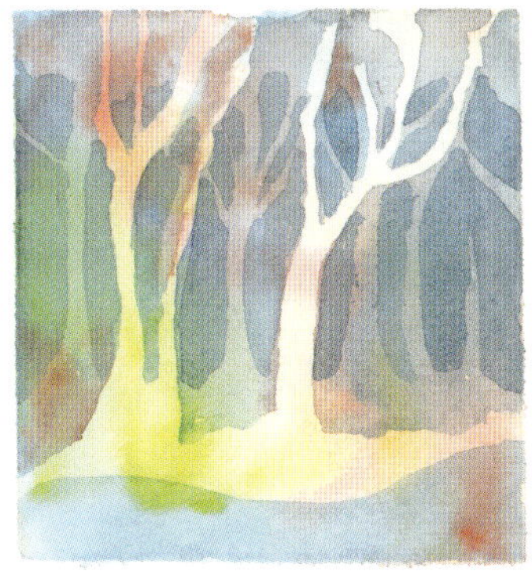

Result.

Lifting

Lifting is the process of removing paint from the paper to create highlights, correct mistakes, or soften edges. This can be done while the paint is still wet (using a damp brush, tissue, or sponge) or after it's dry by scrubbing gently with a damp brush.

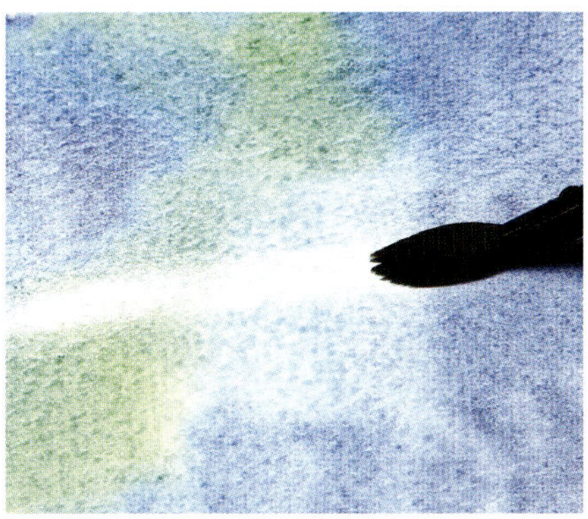

Lift paint with a clean damp brush.

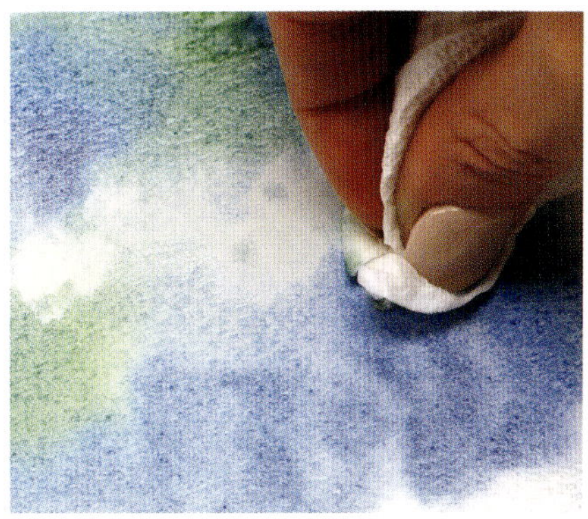

Lift paint with a damp paper towel.

Opaque White Watercolor

Using an opaque white watercolor is a handy way to add tiny splashes, sparkling highlights, or stars. I recommend using it sparingly, since it creates a heavier look compared to the natural freshness of leaving the paper white.

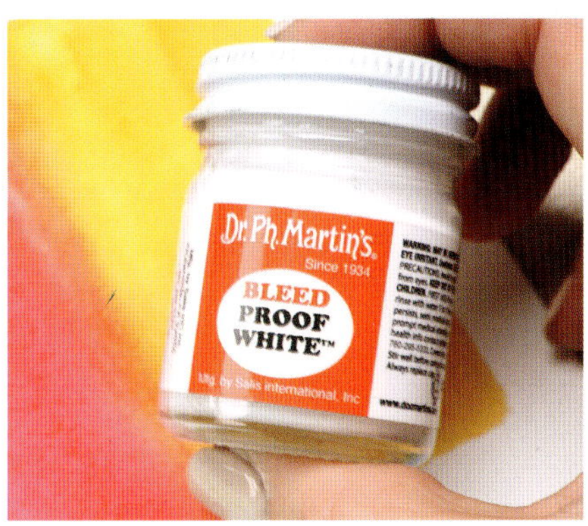

My favorite opaque white paint.

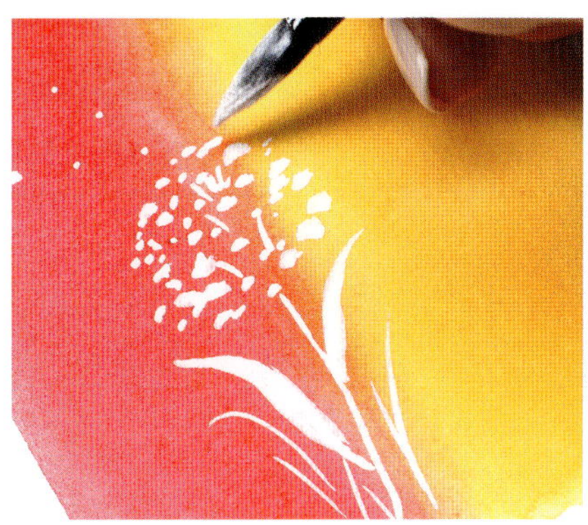

Result.

Tracing and Sketching: Your First Step into Painting

Before we dive into the 52 painting projects, let's talk about how we'll begin each one: with a drawing.

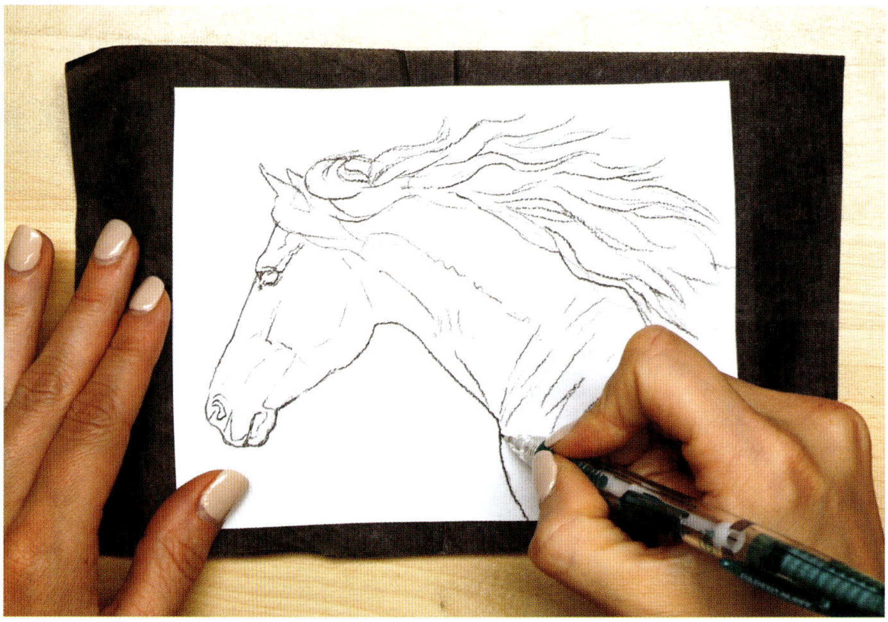

Transferring an image with transfer paper.

Don't worry. You don't need to be a master sketch artist to create beautiful watercolors! Every project in this book comes with a traceable outline so you can get started quickly and focus on the joy of painting.

Transferring the Images

If you'd like to use the traceables, transfer paper is the easiest method. Simply place a sheet of graphite transfer paper between your watercolor paper and the printed outline, shiny side facing down. Trace over the lines of the outline with a pencil or pen, applying gentle pressure. When you lift the papers, you'll have a clean, light drawing ready to paint on your watercolor paper.

Tip

Keep your pressure light so the lines don't become too dark. Watercolor is transparent, and heavy lines can show through the paint and cause indents in the paper.

Sketching the Images

If you'd like to sketch freehand, treat it as a *warm-up*, not a test. Begin with the largest, simplest shapes—think circles, ovals, and triangles—to block in the structure. From there, gradually refine the smaller details. Keep your pencil lines light and loose so they're easy to adjust as you go, and have a kneaded eraser handy to lift away extra marks. Remember, your sketch isn't the finished artwork; it's simply a roadmap to guide your brush once the painting begins.

Whichever method you choose—tracing, sketching, or a mix of both—keep your lines delicate, embrace a little imperfection, and remember that the real magic happens once the paint hits the paper. With your drawing in place, you're ready to jump into the painting projects ahead!

Scan to download reference photos and traceable templates for all of the projects in the book.

You can also go to https://www.quarto.com/files/20MinuteWatercolor to access the download.

Scan for the reference photos and templates.

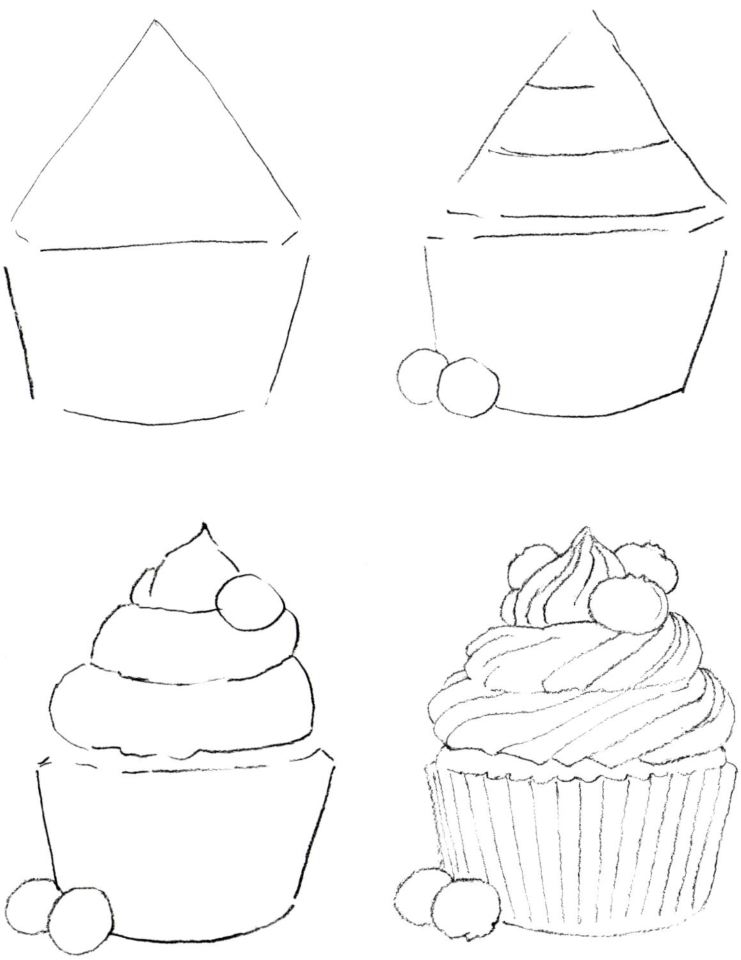

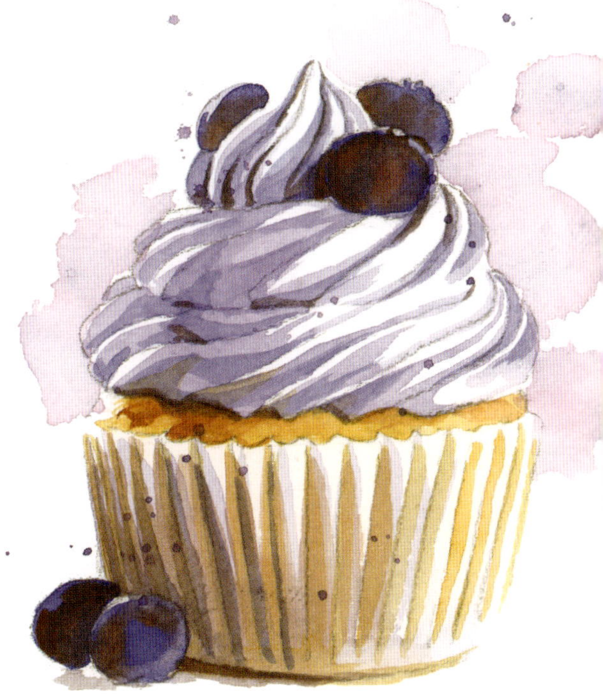

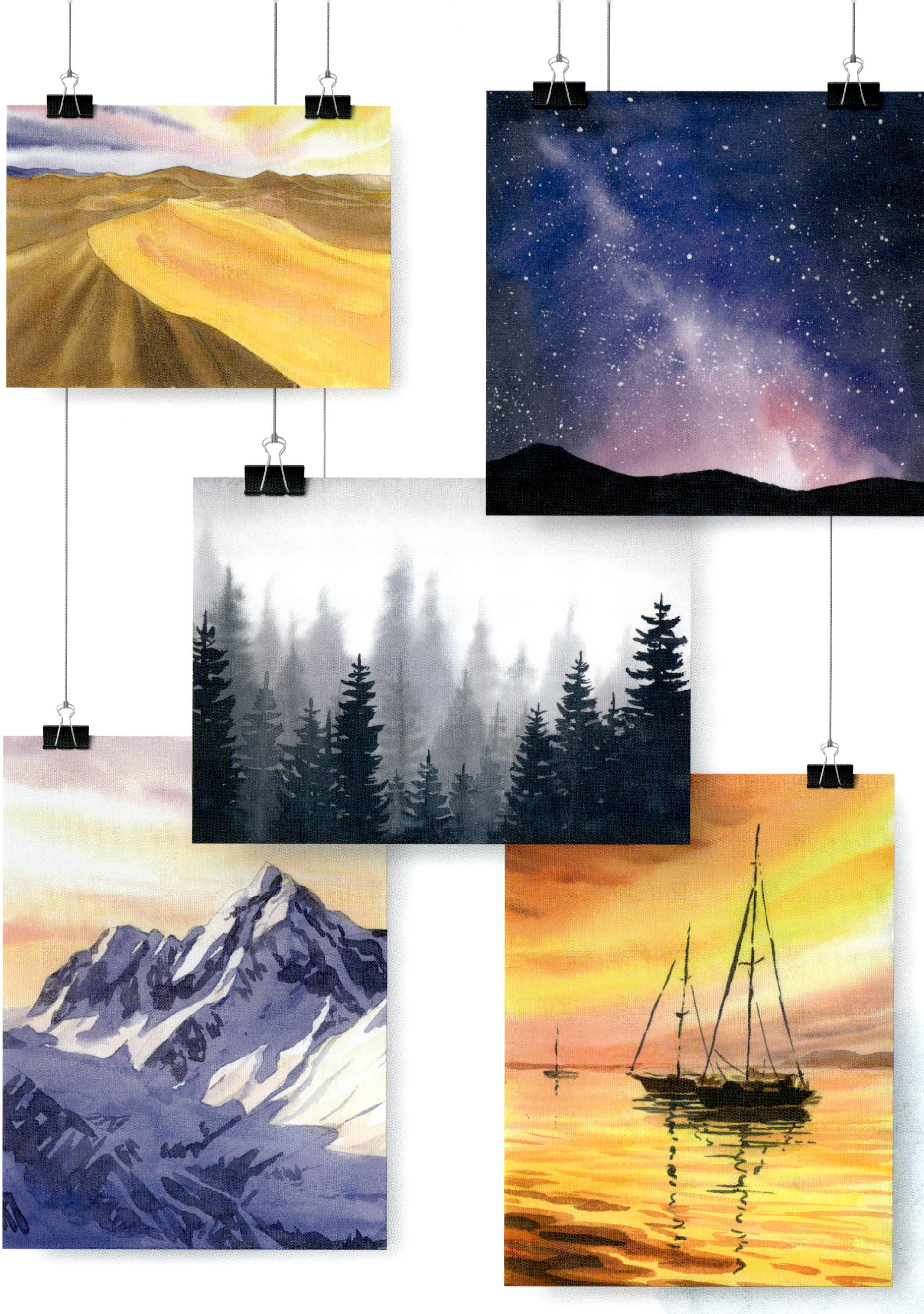

CHAPTER 2

20-Minute Landscapes

A landscape is more than scenery—it's a boundless canvas where shapes can bend, colors can sing, and imagination reigns. In this chapter, we'll journey through diverse vistas, discovering how to capture the character of the land while letting creativity guide every brushstroke.

Desert Dunes

This desert scene celebrates the beauty of complementary colors—a soft violet sky glowing above warm golden sands. You'll explore the play between gentle textures and sharp edges, building depth and drama through subtle glazes.

COLORS

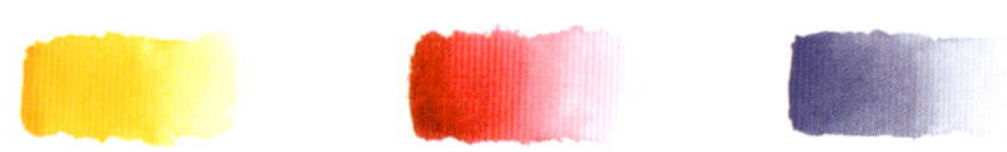

New Gamboge | Quinacridone Rose | French Ultramarine

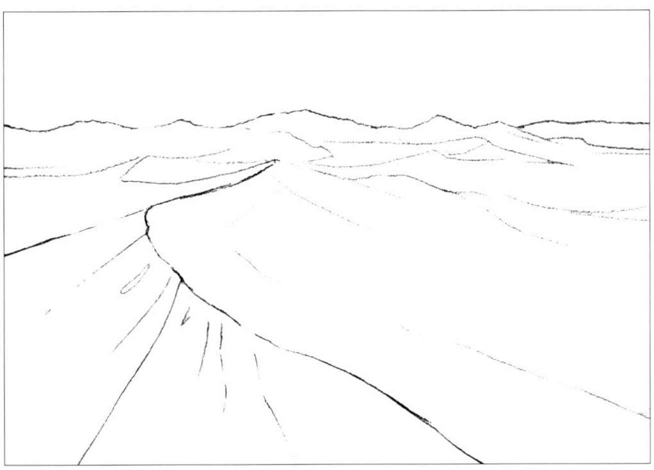

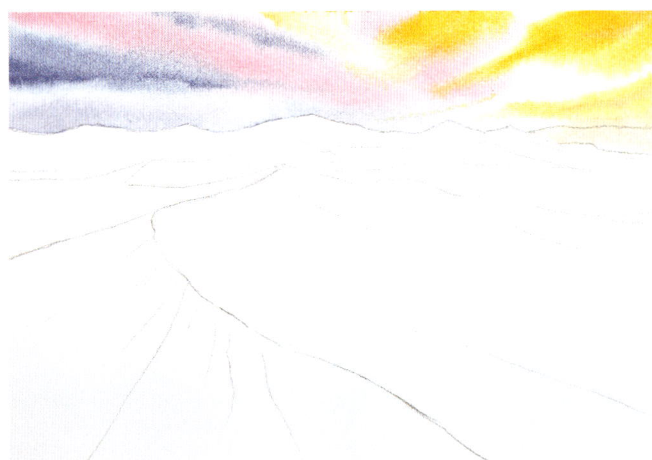

Step 1

Sketch the Desert

Begin with a bumpy horizontal line at the top fourth of your paper to indicate the vast sandy horizon. Draw a serpentine line marking the curve of the largest dune and add some sloped lines to show the peaks and valleys of the dunes.

Step 2

Paint a Colorful Wet-on-Wet Sky

Wet your paper in the sky area with clean water to create a damp, shiny surface. While it's still wet, paint gentle angled brushstrokes of creamy Quinacridone Rose, French Ultramarine, and New Gamboge, cleaning your brush in-between each color. Leave gaps of white showing between your colored strokes to suggest the sunlight shining through the clouds. Allow this to dry.

Scan to watch a video.

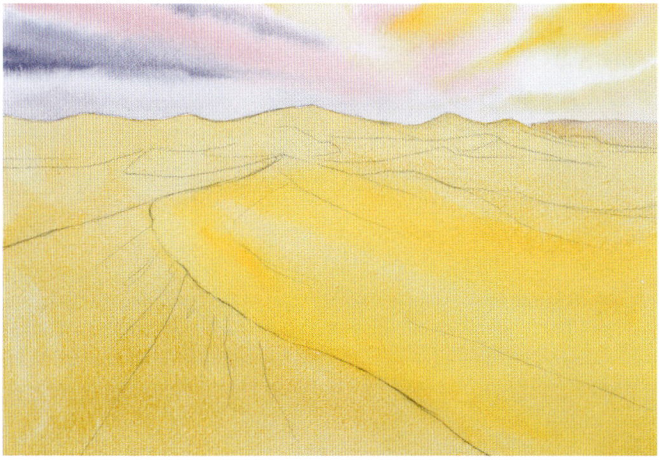

Step 3

Paint a Glowing Base Wash on the Sand

Mix up a large milky puddle of New Gamboge and paint a flat wash across the entire landscape. Don't be afraid to paint this with loads of paint. Remember that watercolor dries lighter!

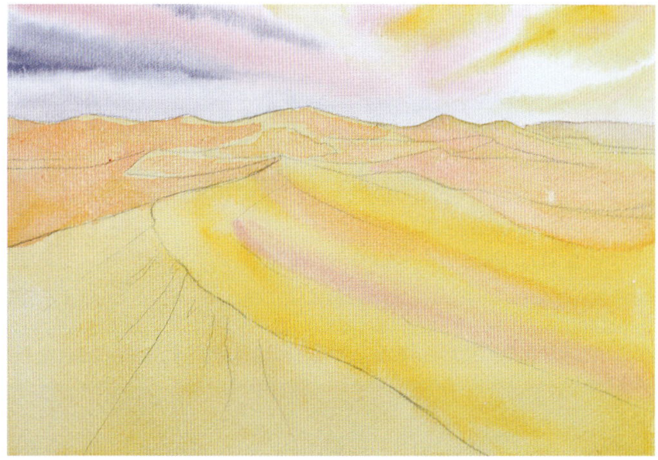

Step 4

Sculpt Sunlit Dunes

Mix a milky blend of Quinacridone Rose and New Gamboge with just a touch of French Ultramarine to create a warm orangey tan. Gently negative paint around the dune peaks to leave them glowing in sunlight. On the largest foreground dune, add sweeping pinkish strokes to suggest subtle ridges and contours in the sand.

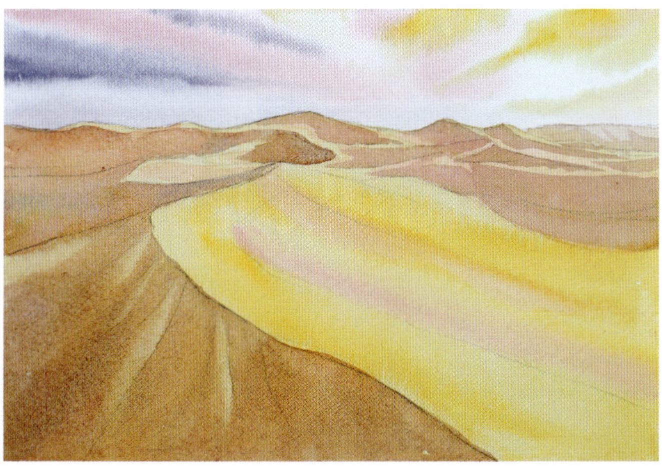

Step 5

Carve Out Dimensional Shadows

For rich shadows, blend all three primaries until you achieve a deep chocolate brown. Paint this into the shaded sides of the dunes to enhance depth and form. On the largest dune, softly lift out some pigment with a clean, damp brush to reveal delicate slopes and sandy furrows.

Scan to watch a video.

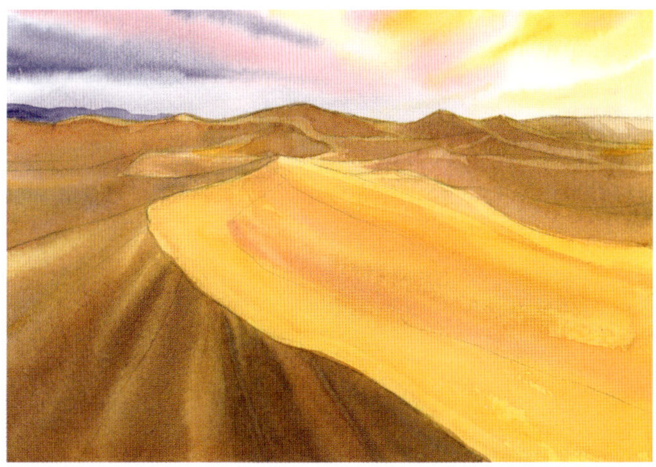

Step 6

Layer Depth and Distant Horizons

Mix a creamier, darker brown from your same trio of pigments, and use gentle strokes to deepen the shadow areas on the foreground dune. Rinse your brush, then load it with milky French Ultramarine to delicately paint the distant flat mountain on the horizon, giving the scene a soft backdrop and atmospheric perspective.

Beach Getaway

This easy ocean scene invites you to blend vibrant colors into tranquil waves. It's a beginner-friendly project that feels like a mini vacation with your brush in hand.

COLORS

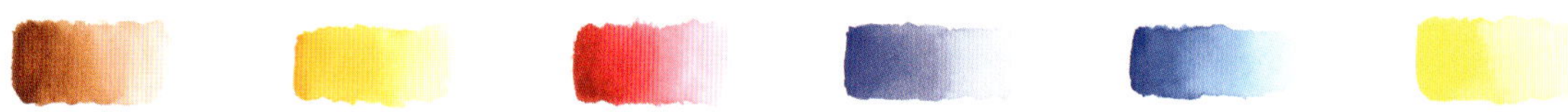

Burnt Sienna	New Gamboge	Quinacridone Rose	French Ultramarine	Phthalo Blue (GS)	Hansa Yellow Light

Step 1

Set the Shoreline with a Warm Base Wash

You don't need to start with a drawing, but if you'd like a guide for where the water ends, lightly sketch an uneven line across the bottom third of your paper. Mix a milky blend of Burnt Sienna and New Gamboge, and quickly lay down a flat wash. While the wash is still wet, create a warm violet by mixing Quinacridone Rose with Ultramarine, and gently brush it in with light, horizontal strokes to add depth and interest.

Scan to watch a video.

Step 2

Paint the Sky and Sea Gradient

Mix a generous puddle of Phthalo Blue (GS) to a milky consistency. Tilt your paper slightly to let gravity help as you use quick, horizontal brushstrokes to paint the top half of the page. As you near the middle third, pick up some Hansa Yellow Light with your brush and blend it into the blue, creating a soft turquoise green as you move downward. Stop just before reaching the white foam area.

Scan to watch a video.

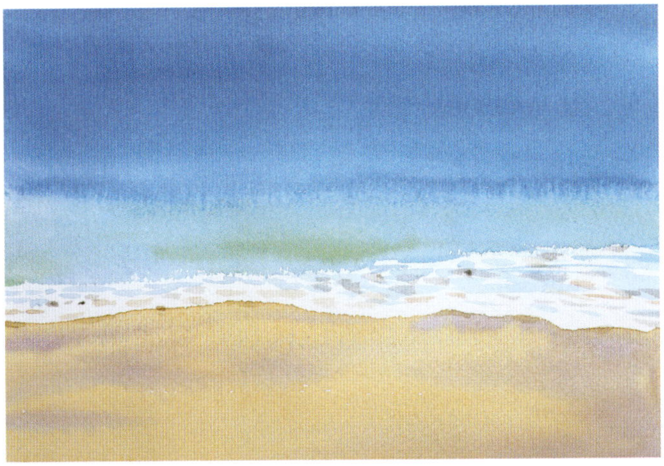

Step 3

Add Texture to the Shoreline Foam

While your washes are drying, this is the fun part! Add blobs of soft tan using your original mix for the sand, and Phthalo Blue (GS) to the foamy water's edge. Make sure your values are light and that you leave plenty of the white of the paper still untouched. Let the painting dry completely.

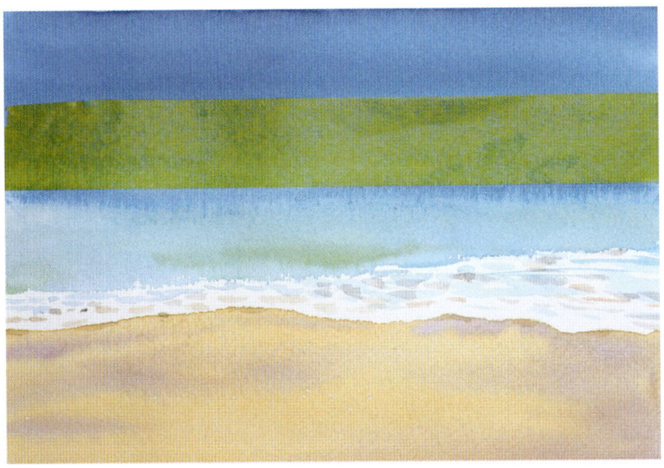

Steps 4 and 5

Define the Horizon with Drybrush Texture

Use a strip of washi or artist's tape to mask off a clean, straight horizon line. Then, mix French Ultramarine to a milky consistency and apply it to the distant water using horizontal strokes. Let your brush lightly skim the surface of the paper to create a drybrush effect, adding beautiful texture to the ocean. Once you're done, carefully peel off the tape to reveal a crisp horizon.

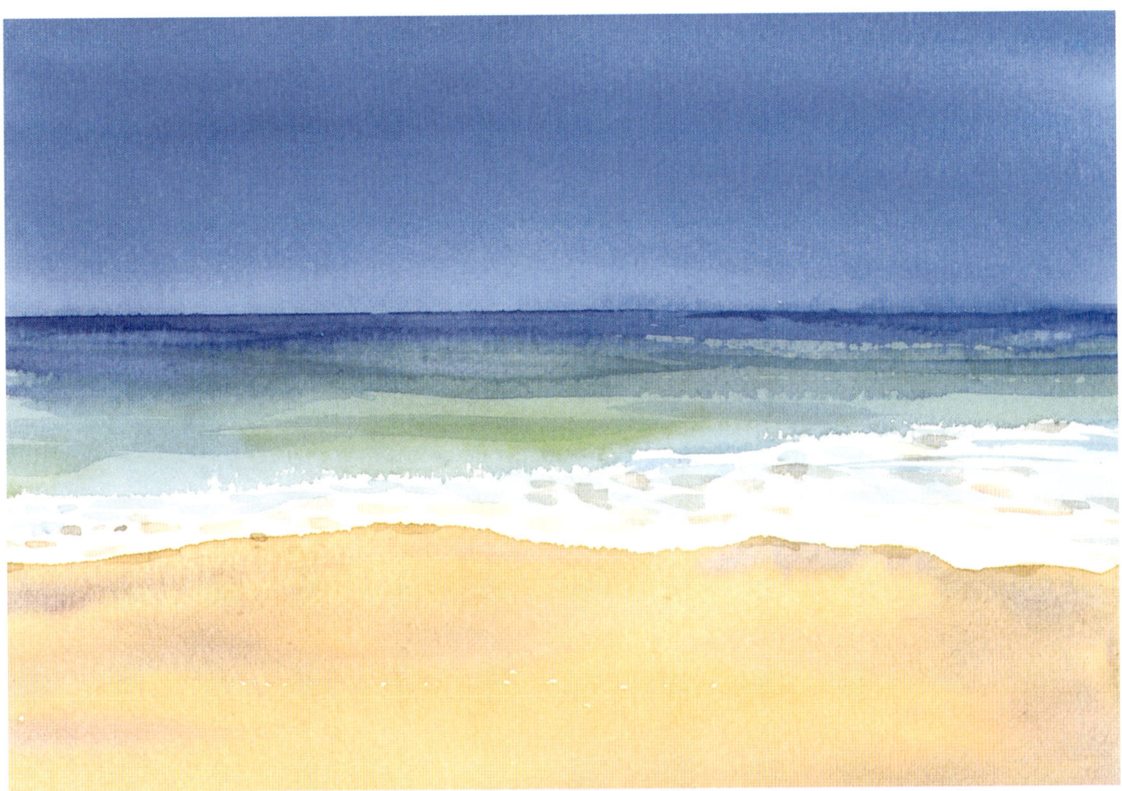

Deep in the Jungle

Discover the magic of light in this mysterious jungle scene. Use your imagination to shape trees and hanging vines silhouetted against brilliant sunlight as it filters through the canopy and dances across the stream below.

COLORS

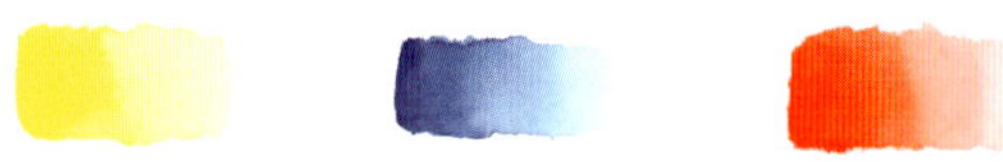

Hansa Yellow Light	Phthalo Blue (GS)	Pyrrol Scarlet

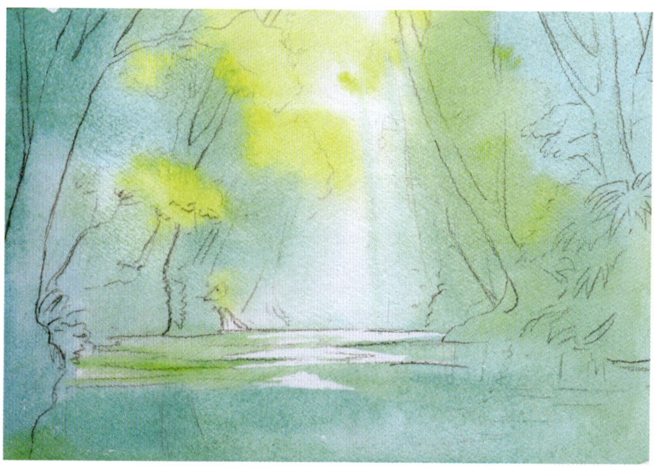

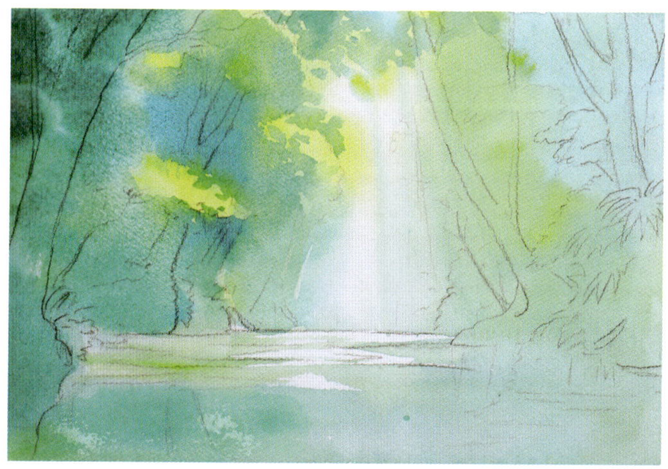

Step 1

Lay Down the Glowing Base Wash

Sketch the scene. Lightly wet your paper, skipping a few narrow streaks near the top of the river. With the surface evenly damp and glossy, brush in creamy Hansa Yellow Light wherever sunlight will filter through the foliage. Then, mix Phthalo Blue (GS) with your yellow to create a vibrant turquoise, and blend this into the treetops and background. Leave the center of the river untouched to mimic shimmering light.

Scan to watch a video.

Step 2

Soften and Shape the Scene

While the background is still damp, deepen the colors by dropping in thicker mixes of your turquoise (Phthalo Blue + Hansa Yellow Light). Keep your brush damp—not drippy—to avoid backruns. As the paper continues to dry, begin forming suggestive clumps of leaves or vines, especially near the focal point. Let the paint flow and create organic edges.

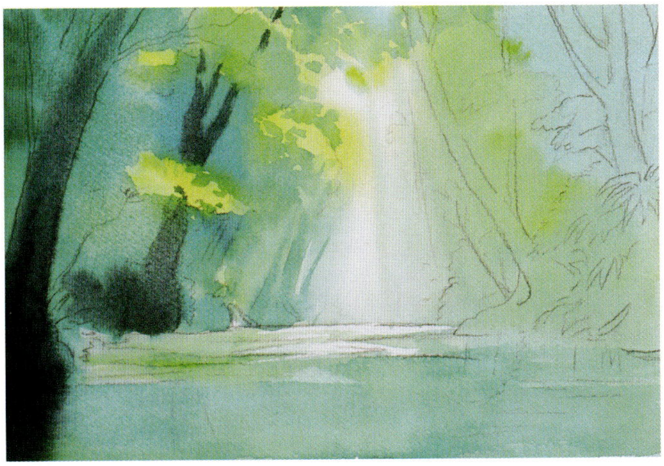

Step 3

Draw Out Silhouettes

Time to introduce bold shapes! Mix a deep black using Phthalo Blue (GS) and Pyrrol Scarlet, and use it to paint silhouetted trees. Let some yellow-green areas peek through so the dark trees appear layered behind sunlit foliage. Use varied brush pressure to keep your shapes interesting.

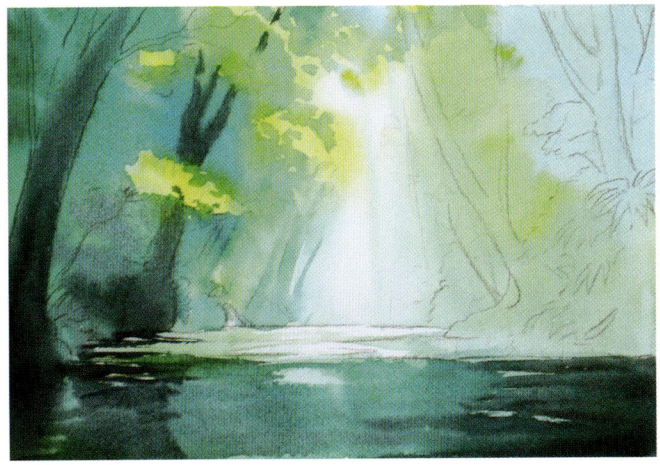

Step 4

Reflect and Ripple

Using the same dark mix, begin mirroring the tree shapes on the river's surface. Use light, horizontal strokes to suggest subtle ripples in the water. A slightly damp surface is perfect for this. It allows the paint to soften just enough for a dreamy, atmospheric effect.

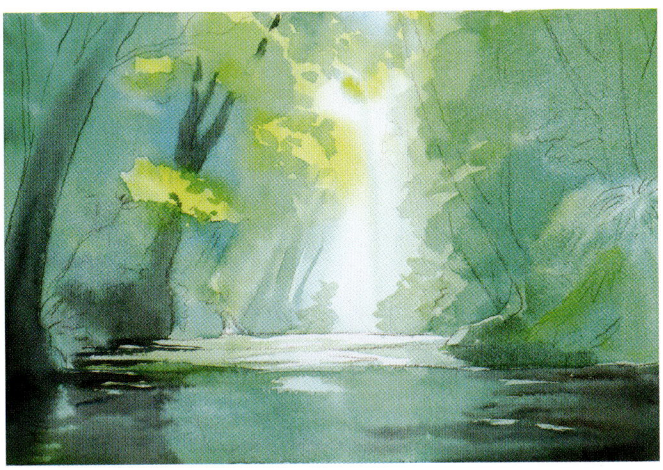

Step 5

Layer the Lushness

Rewet the foliage with clean water, then build believable plant textures. Use mixes of Phthalo Blue and Hansa Yellow Light in quick, blobbing brushstrokes to define ferns and tree clusters. Alternate cool turquoise and warm yellow greens.

Scan to watch a video.

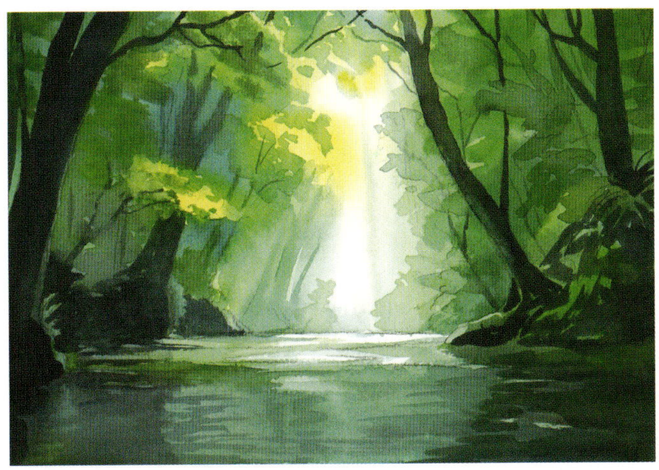

Step 6

Texture and Final Details

Once the base layers are dry, refine tree trunks and foliage with a dark neutral mix, using negative painting to shape grasses and backlit leaves. Add soft horizontal river reflections with watery black, then finish with branches and fern silhouettes.

Scan to watch a video.

Galaxy Sky

Dive into bold wet-on-wet washes of deep blues and violets for a no-sketch, high-impact nightscape that feels both dramatic and effortless.

COLORS

Quinacridone Rose — French Ultramarine — Phthalo Blue (GS) — Pyrrol Scarlet — Opaque White

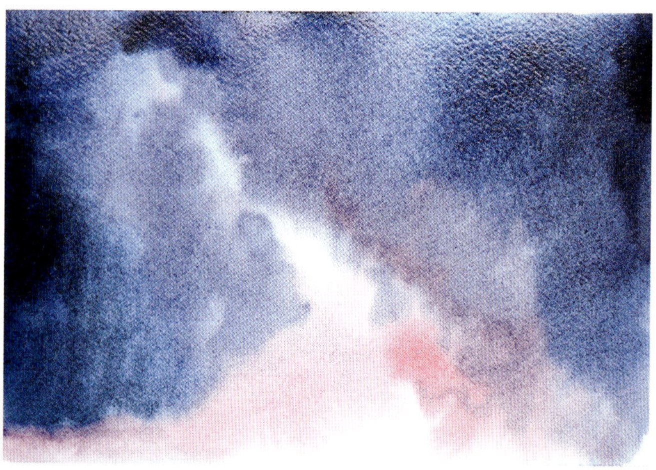

Step 1

Lay Down Your First Galaxy Wash

Soak your paper edge-to-edge with clear water until it's evenly glossy, no puddles. Working quickly, drop in creamy Quinacridone Rose at the galaxy's center, leaving a few untouched specks of paper for natural highlights. Next, blend in creamy French Ultramarine, then push a dark, moody mix of Phthalo Blue (GS) and Pyrrol Scarlet into the outer edges for a soft vignette. Don't overthink it. The thicker the paint, the richer your darks will be, and speed is key to keeping the colors fluid and luminous. Let it dry completely.

Scan to watch a video.

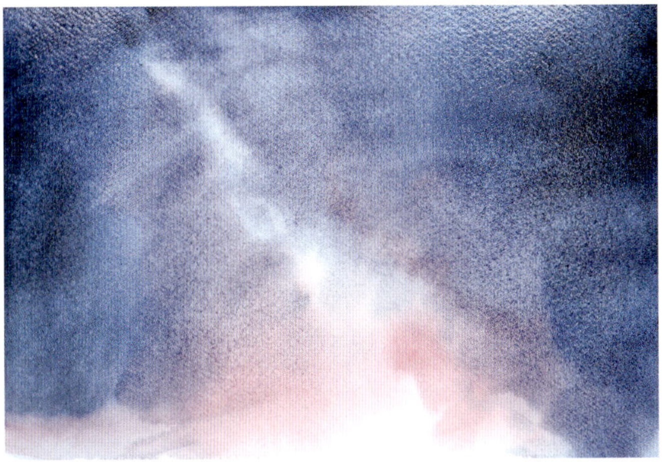

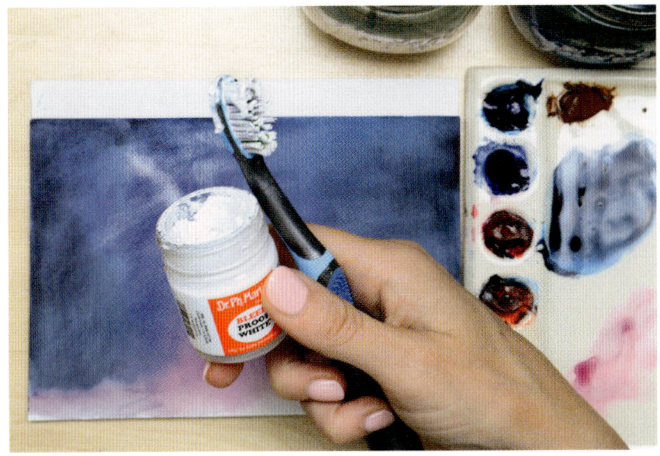

Step 2

Rewet to Smooth and Deepen

If your first wash dried a little streaky or lighter than you hoped, this is the fix. Gently rewet the entire sky, letting your brush lightly reactivate and smooth the existing pigments. While the paper is still damp, you can strengthen colors by adding more pigment where needed. Let dry again before moving on.

Scan to watch a video.

Step 3

Spatter in the Stars

With your sky fully dry, load up an old toothbrush (or a round brush) with opaque white paint—gouache, acrylic, or Dr. Ph. Martin's Bleed Proof White all work well. For a fine starfield, pull your thumb across the toothbrush bristles to release a controlled spatter. Using a round brush? Tap gently for dots or hand-paint individual bright stars. Vary the sizes for a more natural look. Let the white paint dry completely.

Scan to watch a video.

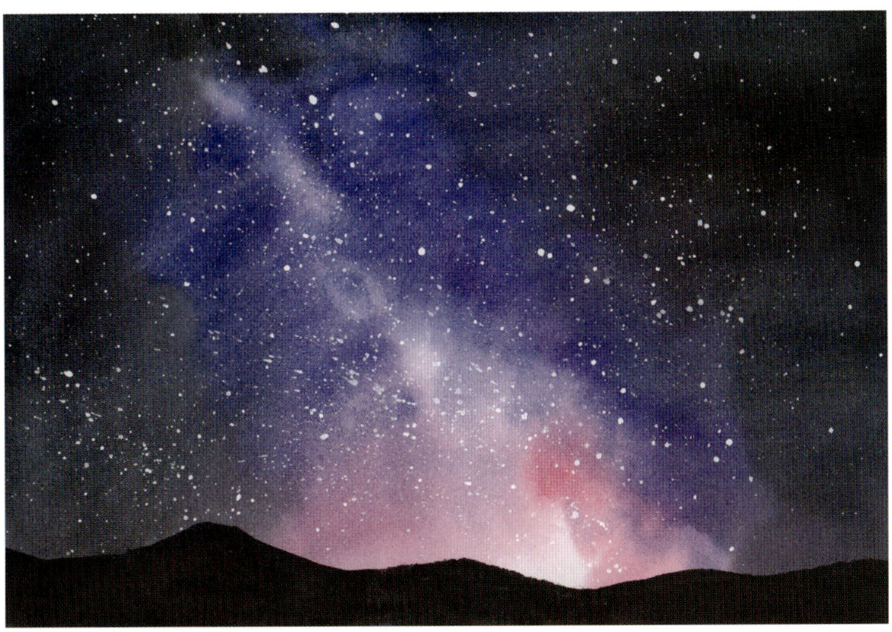

Step 4

Add a Striking Foreground Silhouette

For instant drama and depth, paint a silhouette over the lower edge of your sky. It could be jagged mountain ridges, tall pines, a distant city skyline—anything that suits your mood. Mix Phthalo Blue (GS) and Pyrrol Scarlet into a creamy, opaque black and apply with confident strokes. This contrast will make your galaxy sky glow even brighter.

Lighthouse

In this tranquil lighthouse project, you'll explore soft washes for sky and sand while developing depth and texture in the structure and grasses. It's a great way to practice balance—keeping broad areas simple while refining your main focal point.

COLORS

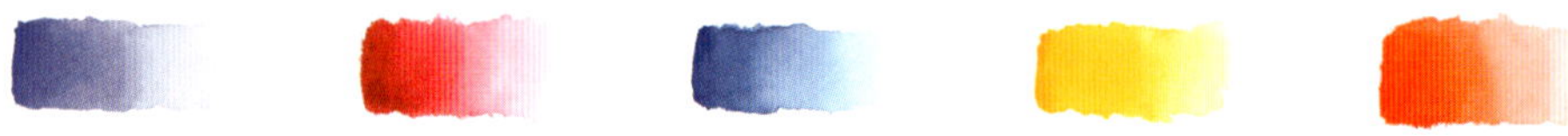

French Ultramarine | Quinacridone Rose | Phthalo Blue (GS) | New Gamboge | Pyrrol Scarlet

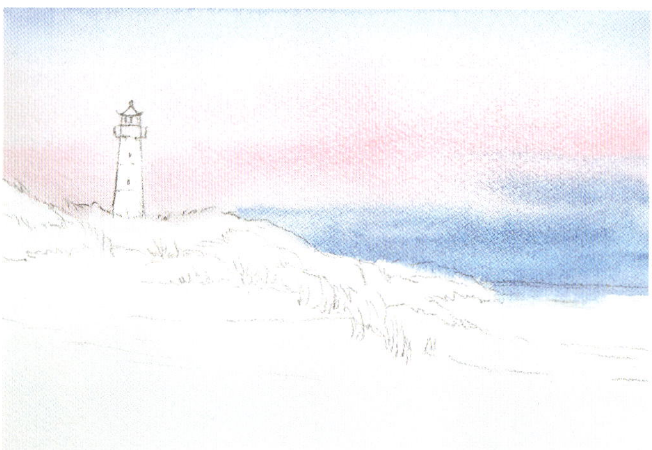

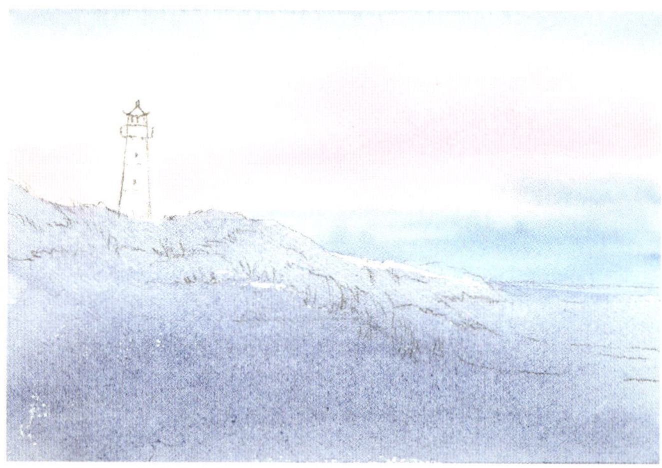

Step 1

Paint a Soft Sky Gradient

Sketch the scene, then dampen the sky evenly with clean water until glossy, not dripping. Using a milky French Ultramarine, sweep strokes across the top for a hint of blue. Rinse your brush, then blend gentle streaks of Quinacridone Rose into the middle. For clouds near the horizon, mix the two blues to a slightly creamier consistency and paint soft shapes.

Scan to watch a video.

Step 2

Lay in a Cool Ground Wash

Mix mostly French Ultramarine with just a touch of Quinacridone Rose and New Gamboge to create a muted slate gray. Using wet-on-dry, paint a smooth wash over the ground area, keeping your brush evenly loaded so the wash stays streak-free.

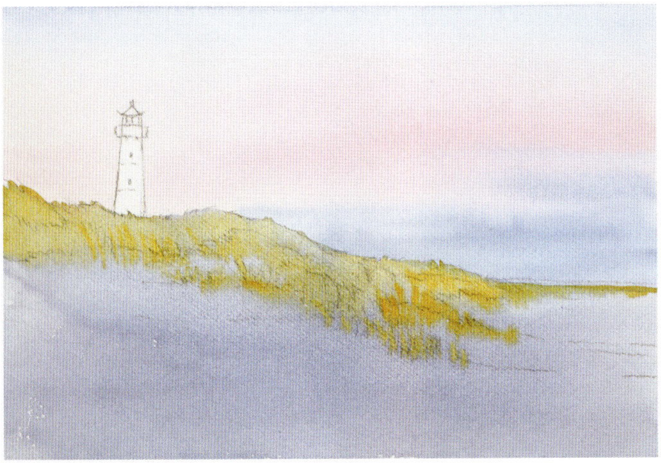

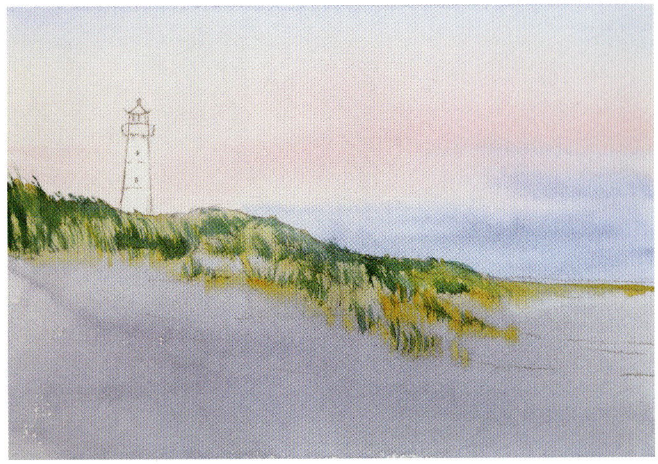

Step 3

Add Golden Warmth to the Grass

While the ground wash is still damp, drop in creamy New Gamboge wherever the grass will be. Keep your brush only damp—not dripping—to avoid blooms or uneven edges. Let the yellow mingle softly with the cooler base.

Step 4

Glaze in Lively Green Grass

Mix Phthalo Blue (GS) and New Gamboge to a fresh, vibrant green. In a milky consistency, and with your bristles gently fanned out, make quick vertical strokes over the grass. Vary your stroke length and pressure to keep it looking natural.

Scan to watch a video.

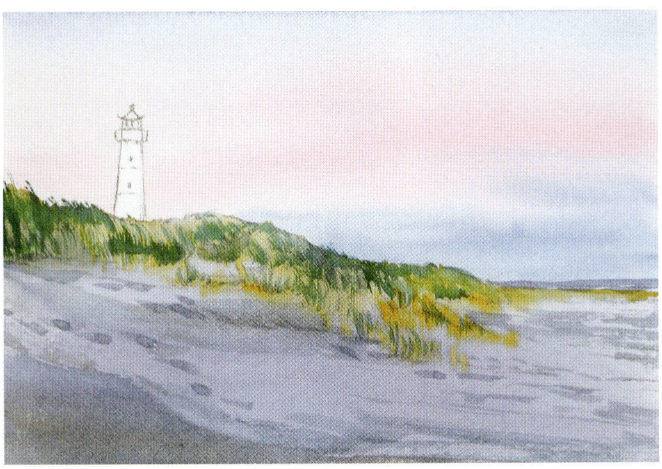

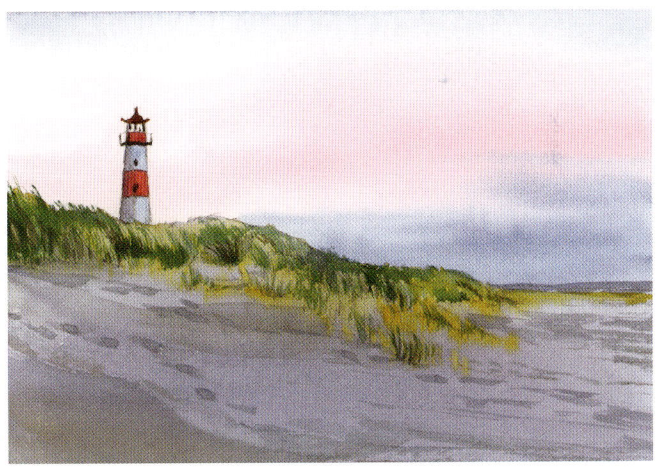

Step 5

Suggest Footsteps in the Sand

With your muted blue-gray mix from Step 2, paint a few gentle, meandering footprints leading toward the lighthouse. Add a soft, darker vignette in one corner to subtly guide the viewer's eye toward your focal point.

Step 6

Bring the Lighthouse to Life

Use pale French Ultramarine to shade the "white" areas of the lighthouse, adding form without dulling the brightness. Let dry, then paint the red sections with milky Pyrrol Scarlet. Add a soft gray shadow on the left for roundness, and finish by mixing Pyrrol Scarlet and Phthalo Blue to paint the windows and railings.

Misty Trees

Fog might look complicated, but watercolor makes it surprisingly easy. By layering from background to foreground, wet to dry, we can create an atmospheric forest full of depth.

COLORS

Phthalo Blue (GS)

Pyrrol Scarlet

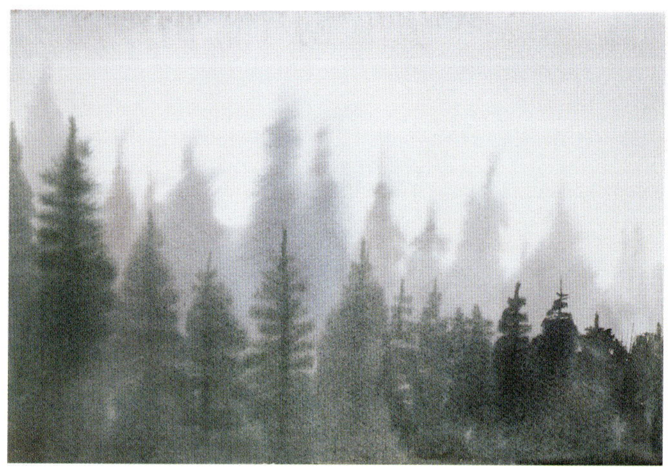

Step 1

Create a Foggy Base (Wet-on-Wet)

No sketching needed. Wet your entire paper until it's evenly glossy, no puddles. Mix a pale cool gray with Phthalo Blue and Pyrrol Scarlet, then wash it in a soft vignette at the top and corners of your paper. While it's still damp, load a slightly thicker gray and loosely suggest distant trees with squiggly vertical strokes. Vary your grays—some warmer, some cooler.

Scan to watch a video.

Step 2

Add Middle-Ground Trees (Damp-on-Damp)

If the surface is still slightly damp (not glossy wet, not bone dry), you're in the sweet spot. Mix a milky gray and paint a second layer of trees, darker than the first. Be sure your brush has pigment but not excess water; blot at the ferrule if needed. These trees should look a bit sharper than the background but still softened by the damp paper. Let the whole layer dry fully before moving on.

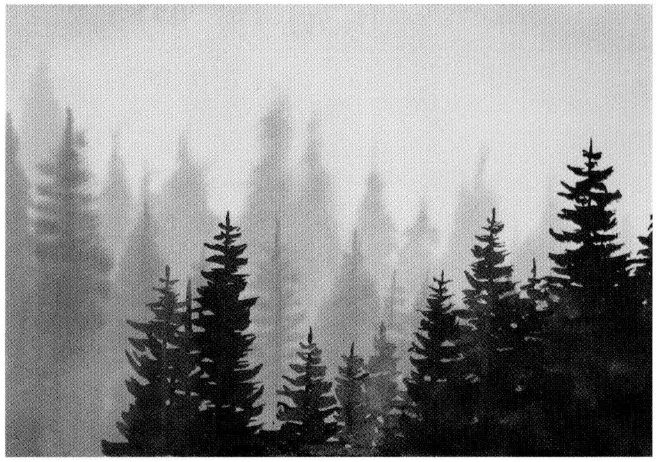

Step 3

Paint Foreground Silhouettes (Wet-on-Dry)

Now switch to drama! Mix a deep greenish-black from your red and blue in a creamy consistency. Paint the strong vertical trunks first, then add short, curved brushstrokes branching out from the sides. Leave gaps to suggest sky peeking through and avoid making the shapes too uniform.

Step 4

Build Variety in the Foreground

Continue adding trees, keeping them irregular in height, spacing, and shape. For some variety, dilute your dark slightly and paint a few shorter or paler trees in the middle distance. This layering makes the forest feel deeper and more dense.

Scan to watch a video.

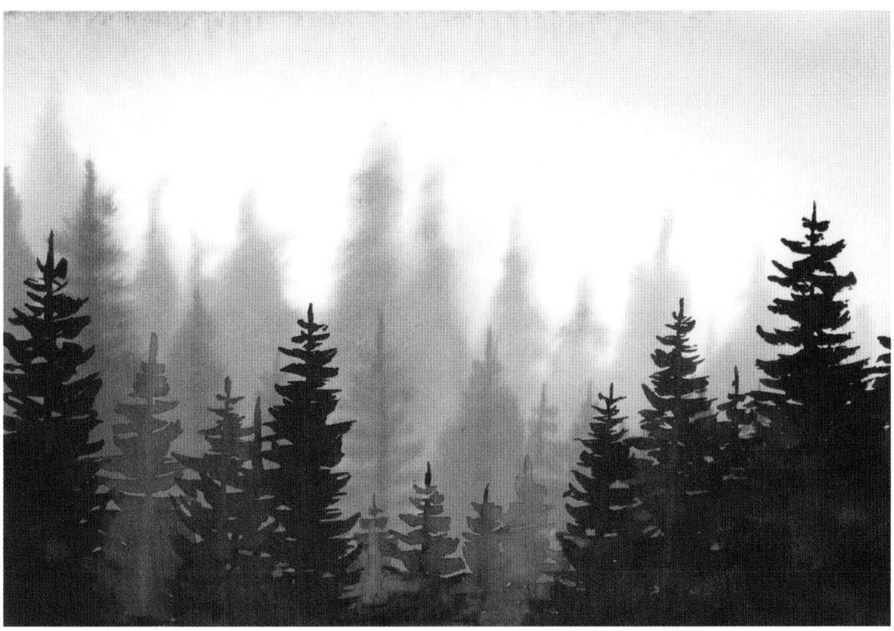

Step 5

Finish the Forest

Finish with a few more bold evergreens or strong silhouettes, staggering their placement so they aren't lined up like soldiers. The irregular spacing and depth of tone are what make the composition pleasing.

Mountain Flowers

Capture the serenity of a mountain meadow with soft washes of green, distant peaks, and blooming wildflowers. This project focuses on layering and blending to create depth and a tranquil natural scene.

COLORS

Phthalo Blue (GS)	Quinacridone Rose	New Gamboge	French Ultramarine	Pyrrol Scarlet

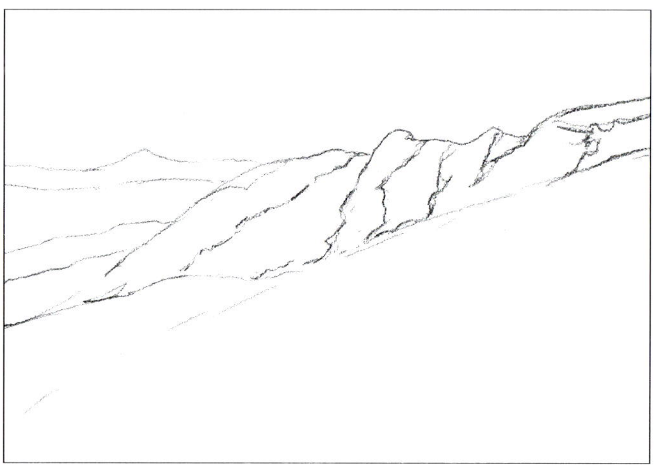

Step 1

Sketch a Balanced Landscape Composition

Start by lightly sketching the main elements of your landscape. Pay close attention to the angle of the hill in the foreground and the distinct shadow shapes on the mountain. Keep your composition balanced by making sure the sky fills the top third of your paper.

Scan to watch a video.

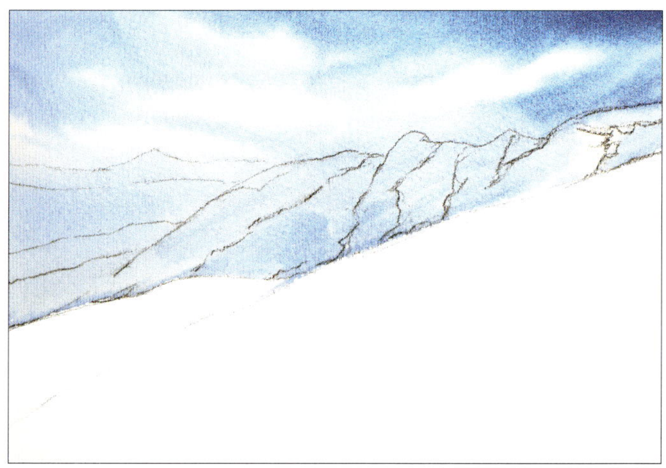

Step 2

Paint a Luminous Sky and Soft Mountain Base

Using clean water, pre-wet the top portion of your paper—everything above the foreground field. Mix a generous puddle of Phthalo Blue (GS) to a milky consistency. Paint this across the sky and mountains, leaving bits of white paper showing through to suggest soft, fluffy clouds. To add depth, use slightly thicker paint near the top edge, creating a subtle vignette effect.

Scan to watch a video.

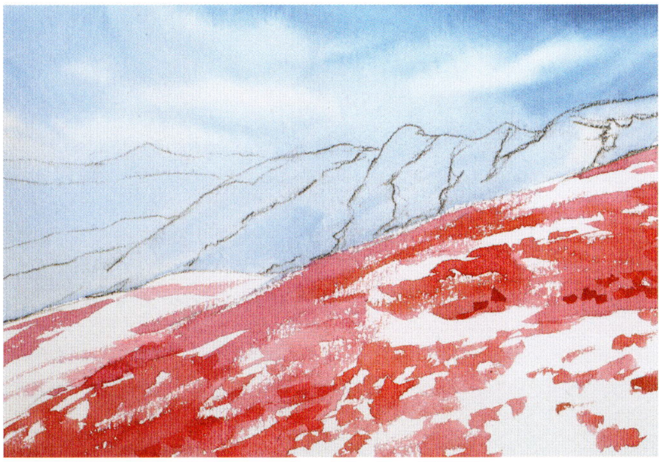

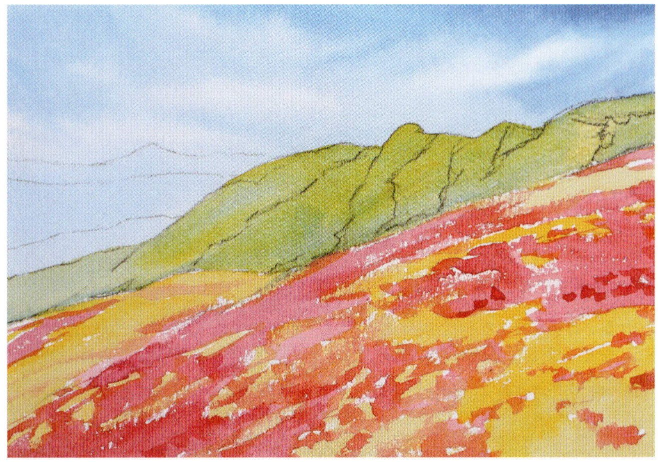

Step 3

Add Pops of Pink with Flower Clusters

While the blue is drying, prepare a milky mix of Quinacridone Rose. Use a quick, dabbing motion with your brush to paint clusters of pink flowers in the field, working wet-on-dry. Be sure to leave gaps for green foliage, which you'll add in the next steps.

Step 4

Warm the Scene with Golden Sunshine

Using a milky mix of New Gamboge, paint over the central mountain to warm it up. Then, lightly brush the same color between the pink flower clusters to begin building up the sunny meadow tones.

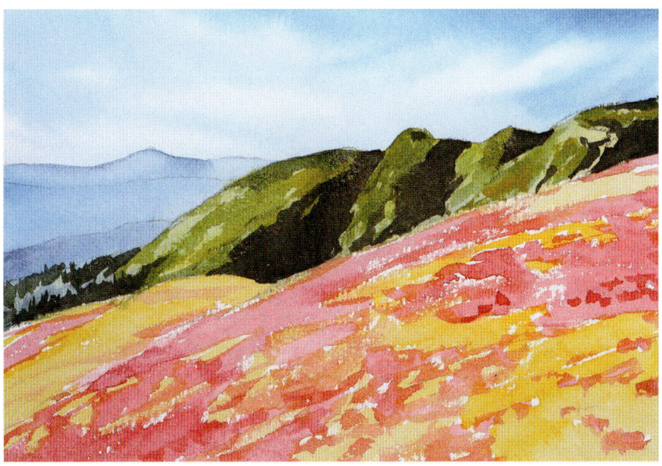

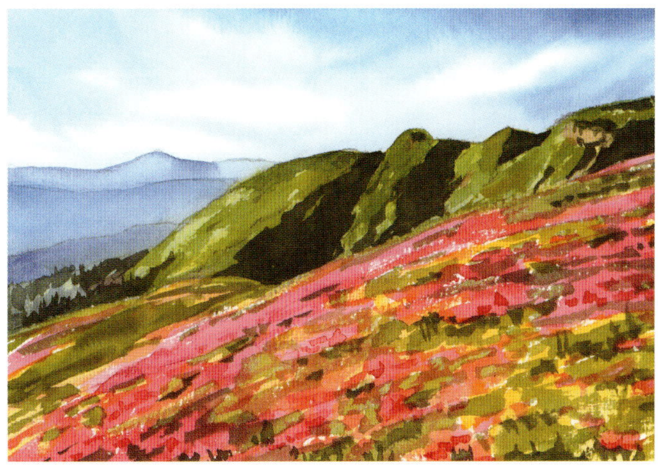

Step 5

Build Contrast with Mountains and Trees

Glaze another layer, of French Ultramarine this time, over the distant mountains to deepen them. Mix a creamy dark green with Phthalo Blue (GS), New Gamboge, and a touch of Pyrrol Scarlet. Use it to paint scrubby trees on the left and the shaded areas of the green slope. For sunlit sections, thin the mix with water and add light brushstrokes across the brighter parts of the mountain.

Step 6

Foliage, Flowers, and Finishing Touches

With the lighter green still on your brush, add scattered blobs of foliage between the pink flower patches to suggest depth and variety. For a final touch, dot in a few deeper dabs of Quinacridone Rose or Pyrrol Scarlet to create the illusion of shadowed blooms and give your vibrant field more dimension.

Scan to watch a video.

Rocky Shore

Capture the drama of a rugged coastline by combining soft wet-on-wet skies, rippling ocean water, and strong rocky textures—all with just three colors!

COLORS

Phthalo Blue (GS)	French Ultramarine	Burnt Sienna

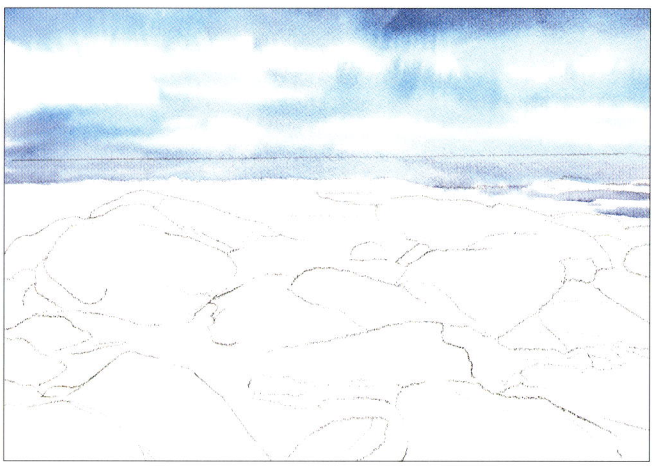

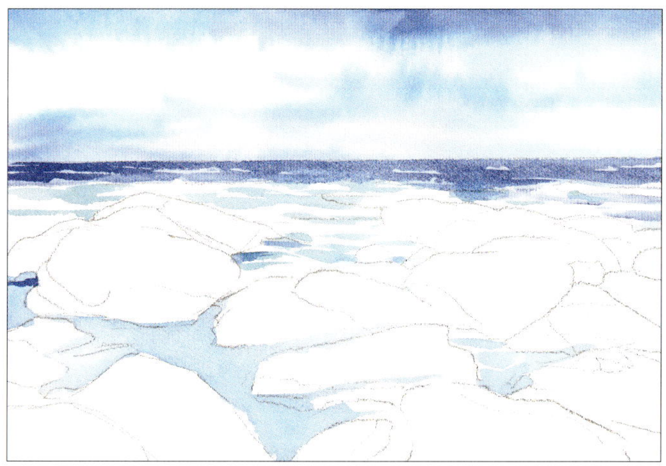

Step 1

Paint the Sky and Distant Sea

Sketch the scene then wet the entire sky and ocean area so the surface is glossy damp. Drop in milky Phthalo Blue (GS) for a soft blue sky, leaving white gaps for clouds. As you reach the horizon, transition into deeper French Ultramarine for the ocean. Preserve a few white streaks for wave caps. Let this layer dry before continuing.

Scan to watch a video.

Step 2

Paint the Water Between the Rocks

Use watery Phthalo Blue to fill in the pools and channels between rocks, leaving areas of untouched paper for foamy ripples. Strengthen the horizon with another pass of French Ultramarine for depth and distance.

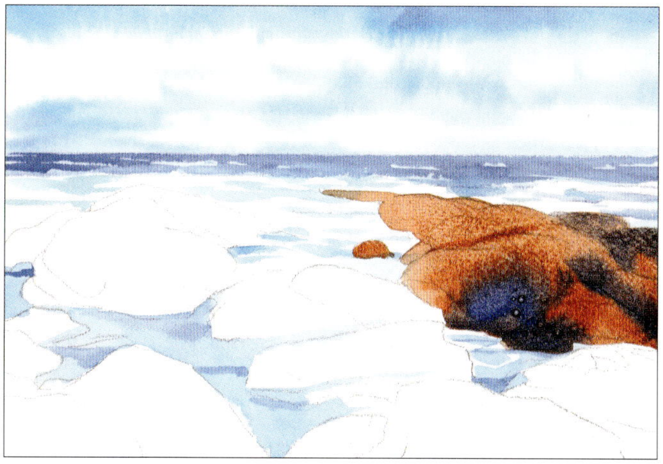

Step 3

Block in Rock Colors

For each rock, start with a wash of milky Burnt Sienna. While it's still wet, blot creamy French Ultramarine into the shadow side. Watch as the reddish brown and cool blue merge into a natural stony texture.

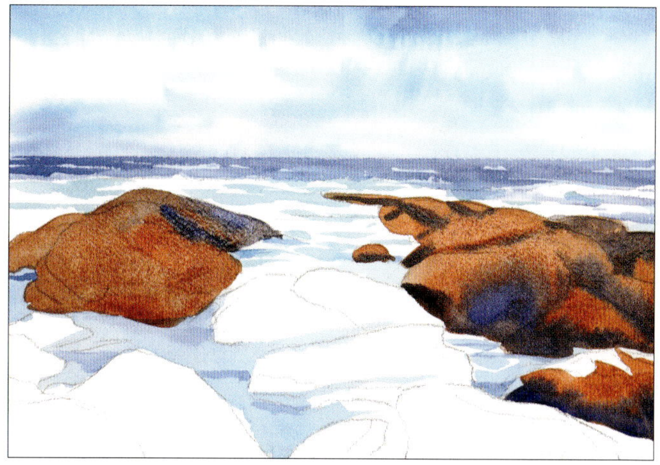

Step 4

Build Up the Rock Forms

Continue painting one rock at a time with the same wet-on-wet method. Vary the balance of Burnt Sienna and Ultramarine so that no two rocks look alike. The layering of warm and cool tones will give them instant depth.

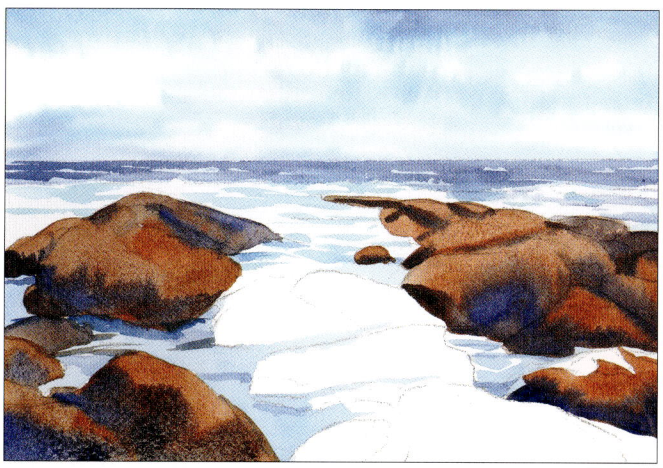

Step 5

Frame the Composition

Anchor the corners of your painting with dark foreground rocks. Add deeper shadows in the water close to the boulders by glazing French Ultramarine with a few horizontal strokes.

Scan to watch a video.

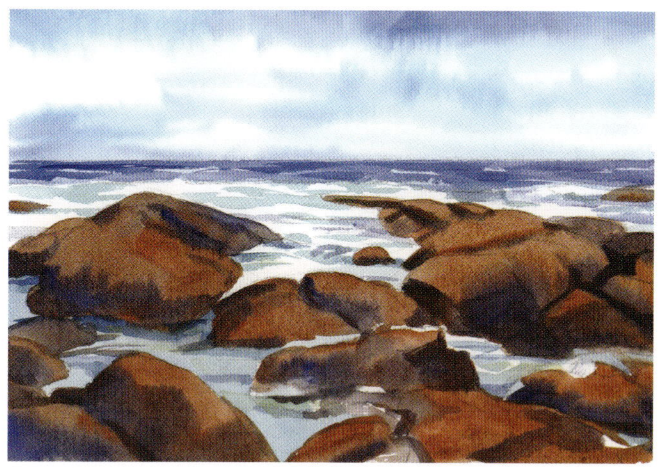

Step 6

Add Final Darks

Finish by painting the last rocks along the shoreline, leaving bright channels of white paper where water snakes between them. Mix a creamy dark from Burnt Sienna and Ultramarine to paint cracks, crevices, and the deepest shadows. These bold accents will give the scene structure and drama.

Snowy Peaks

Capture the drama of a sunlit mountain using just a few simple washes and carefully placed dark details. You'll create the illusion of rich depth and atmosphere with minimal layers—proof that simplicity can be powerful.

COLORS

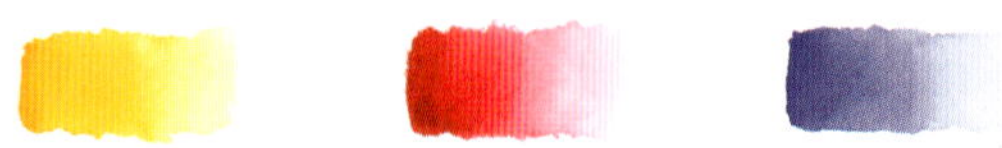

New Gamboge | Quinacridone Rose | French Ultramarine

Step 1

Sketch Your Mountain Composition

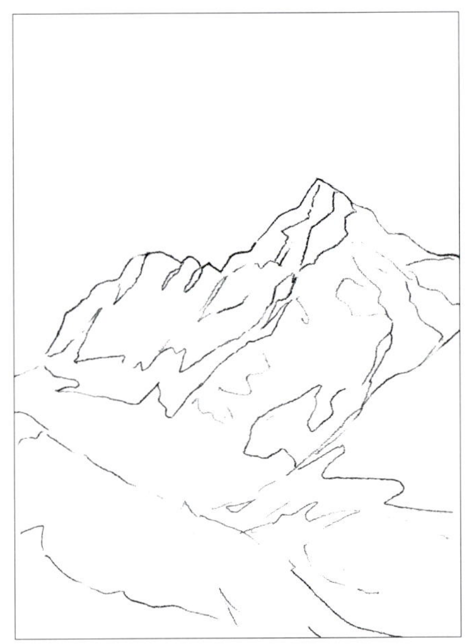

You've got creative freedom here—go vertical or horizontal, and feel free to adjust the slope lines to suit your style. The most important thing is to define clear light and shadow shapes, which will make the painting process much easier later on. I placed the tallest peak along the rule of thirds to create a strong, balanced composition, but you can make it your own.

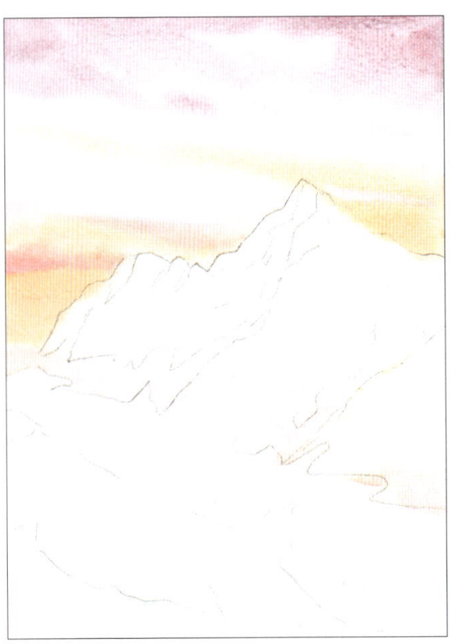

Step 2

Paint a Soft, Glowing Sky

For a dreamy wet-on-wet sky, first brush clean water over the area until it has a soft sheen. Sweep in a New Gamboge–Quinacridone Rose orange near the mountain base for warmth. Then add a light Quinacridone Rose–French Ultramarine purple to the upper sky, leaving gaps for wispy clouds. Finish with a light orange wash to tint the sunlit mountain slopes.

Scan to watch a video.

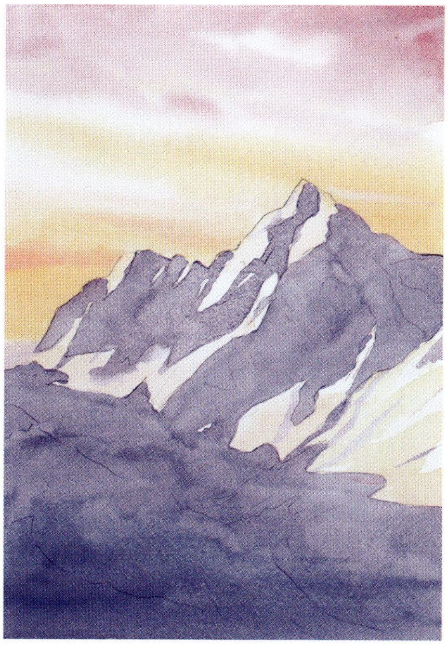

Step 3

Block in the Mountain Shadows

This part feels a bit like coloring in a mountain-themed coloring book—and it's super satisfying! Mix a milky puddle of French Ultramarine for a medium-dark value, and tone it down slightly with touches of New Gamboge and Quinacridone Rose for a more natural, less saturated look. Using a flat wash, paint in all the shadow shapes on the mountains, carefully working around the sunlit snow using negative painting. Aim for clean, confident brushstrokes to keep the shapes crisp and bold.

Step 4

Add Rock Texture in the Shadows

Now it's time to bring those shadow areas to life with texture and structure. Mix a dark blend of all three primaries—Ultramarine, Quinacridone Rose, and New Gamboge—keeping blue as the dominant color. With the fine tip of your brush, suggest rock formations breaking through the snow using quick, varied strokes. Keep it loose and expressive, and don't overwork any one area. This step is about impression, not precision.

Scan to watch a video.

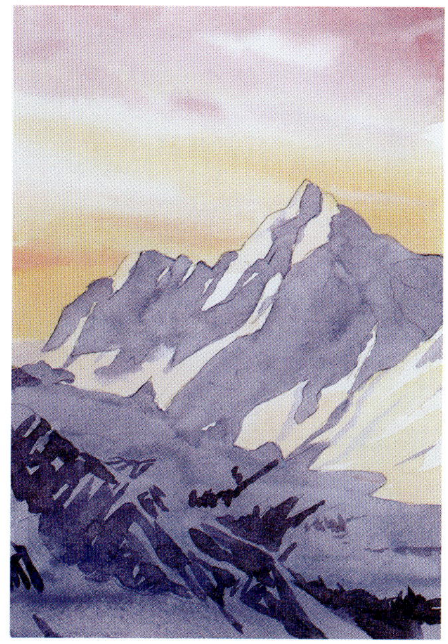

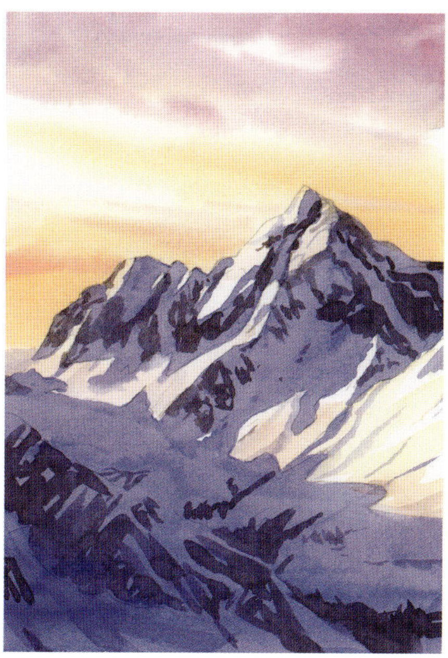

Step 5

Refine and Focus Your Details

Continue developing the rocky textures, but slow down as you near the focal point—the mountain peak. This is where you can add a little extra contrast and care. Use your darkest tones sparingly to draw the eye upward, and remember: Less is more. Avoid overworking the details so your painting stays fresh and full of energy.

Verdant Hills

Create a glowing summer landscape in just three simple washes. In this beginner-friendly project, you'll learn to mix vibrant greens from your primary colors and build a scene that radiates warmth, light, and the joy of a summer evening.

COLORS

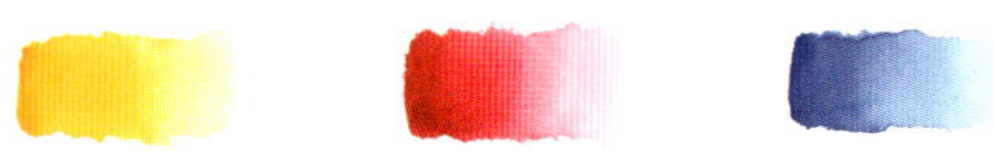

New Gamboge | Quinacridone Rose | Phthalo Blue (GS)

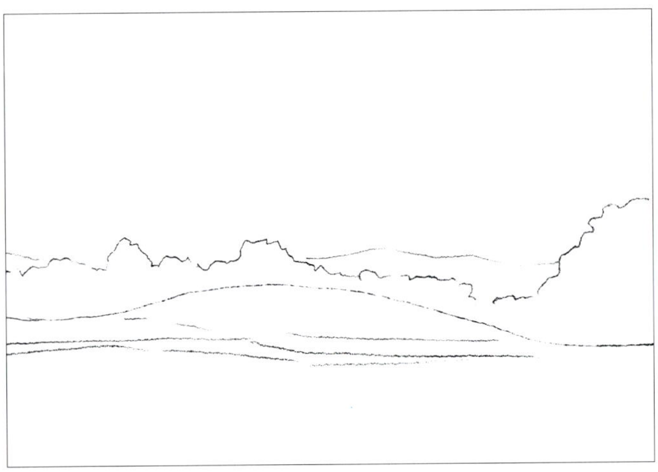

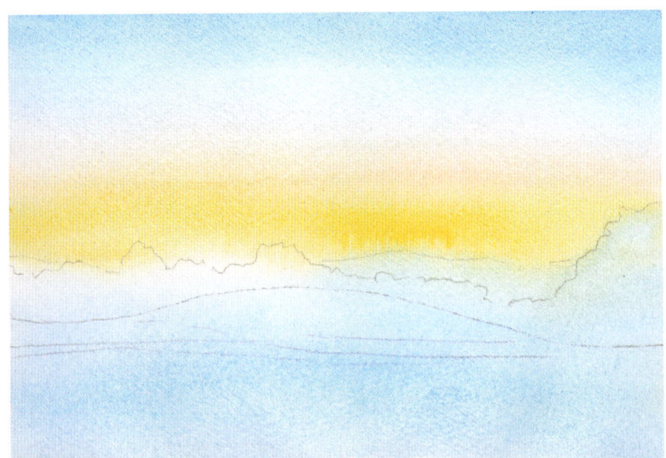

Step 1

Sketch a Simple Landscape

Begin with a soft curved line about one-third up from the bottom of your paper to mark the hill. Above this line, sketch a few bumpy tree shapes and a distant bluff. Keep your lines loose and simple. This is more about shape and flow than detail!

Step 2

Create a Glowing First Wash

Wet the paper until it's evenly glossy. While damp, brush creamy New Gamboge into the center for a warm glow. Add milky Quinacridone Rose above it with soft horizontal strokes. Then apply Phthalo Blue (GS) to the top of the sky and bottom of the field, letting the colors transition naturally. Avoid over-blending the pink and blue. Let dry completely.

Scan to watch a video.

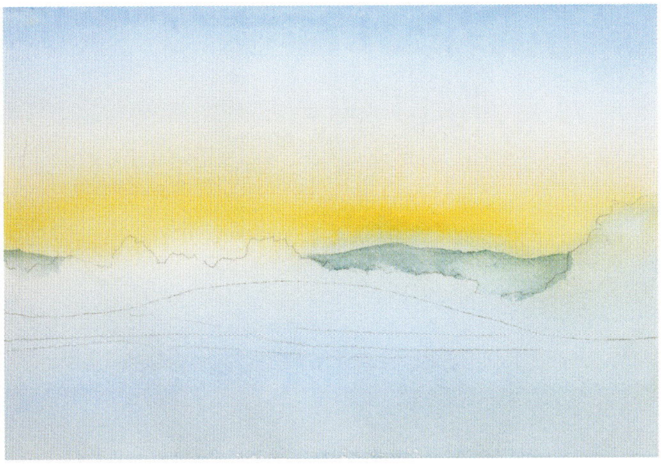

Step 3

Add the Distant Bluff

Mix a watery blend of Phthalo Blue and New Gamboge to create a soft, bluish-green. Use this to paint the distant bluff, keeping it light in value to push it back into the distance and enhance your atmospheric perspective.

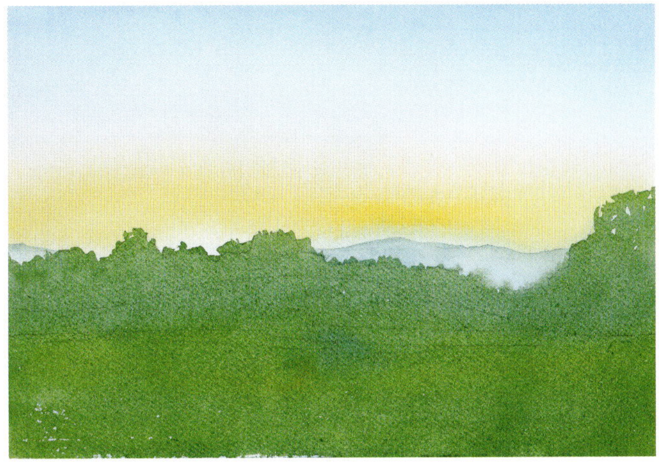

Step 4

Paint the Foreground and Tree Line

Create a medium-value green using Phthalo Blue and New Gamboge. Using the tip of your brush, paint the jagged edges of the tree line, then quickly fill in the grassy foreground below. Add more yellow into the bottom of the field for a sunlit effect.

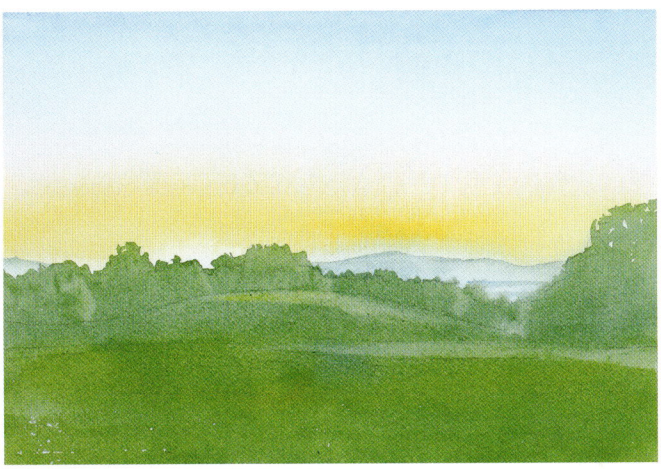

Step 5

Lift Highlights While Damp

Before the green dries completely, use a clean, damp brush to gently lift out color along the tops of the hill slopes. This creates soft highlights and enhances the sense of sunlight hitting the land.

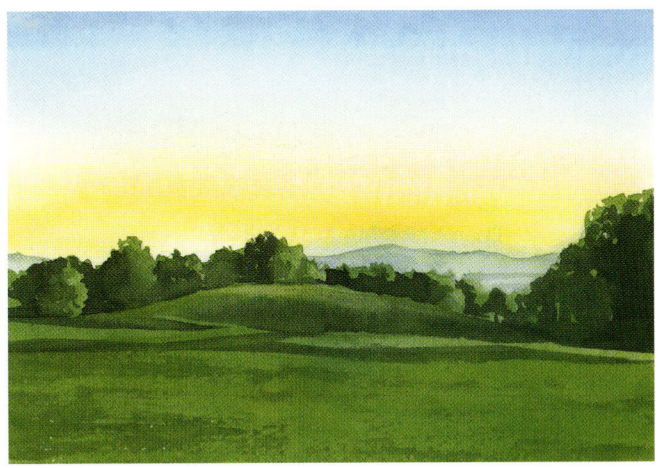

Step 6

Add Shadows and Finishing Texture

Mix a deep green with Phthalo Blue, New Gamboge, and a touch of Quinacridone Rose. Use soft dabbing strokes to add shadows to the left side of the tree clusters, varying the values for depth. Thin the mix for a midtone to transition from shadow to light. Finish with light, dry brushstrokes across the field to suggest grass and subtle texture.

Sunset Sailboat

This lesson will guide you through painting a radiant sailboat scene at sunset, focusing on warm hues and luminous reflections.

COLORS

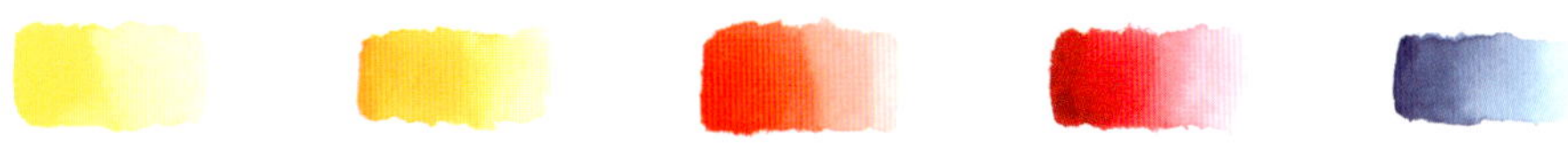

Hansa Yellow Light | New Gamboge | Pyrrol Scarlet | Quinacridone Rose | Phthalo Blue (GS)

Step 1

Lay Down the Golden Glow

Sketch the scene then brush clean water over the entire sheet until the surface is evenly damp and glossy but not puddling. Load your brush with creamy Hansa Yellow Light and paint soft streaks across the top and bottom of the paper, leaving a white diagonal opening in the center for brightness. Layer New Gamboge on top in creamy consistency to suggest glowing movement in both the sky and water.

Scan to watch a video.

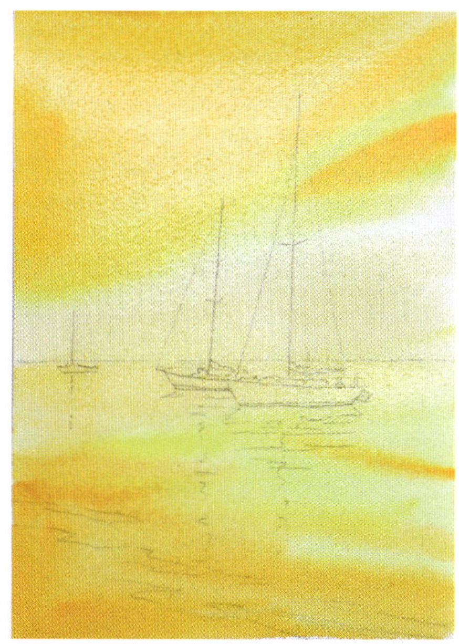

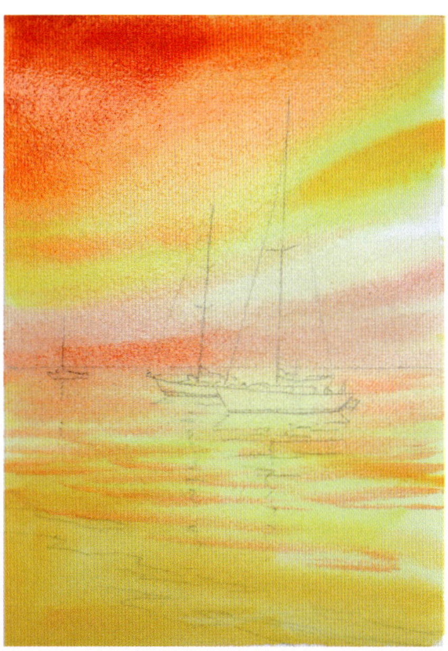

Step 2

Infuse the Sky with Warm Reds and Pinks

While the yellow base is still damp, drop in rich Pyrrol Scarlet and softer Quinacridone Rose. Concentrate stronger Pyrrol Scarlet in the upper left corner to frame the scene with warmth. Sweep in lighter, wispy Rose near the center, and pull some horizontal streaks into the water to suggest rippling reflections.

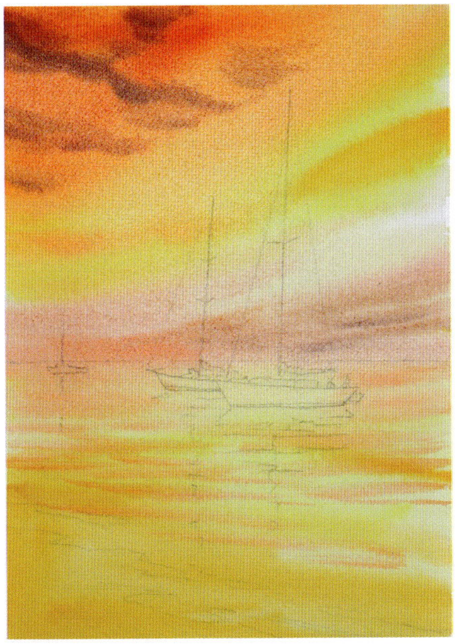

Step 3

Shape the Clouds

Mix a deep earthy purple by combining Pyrrol Scarlet with a touch of Phthalo Blue (GS). Apply this in soft, irregular shapes while the sky is still slightly damp so the edges feather naturally. Avoid painting too many clouds; a few bold forms will create more drama.

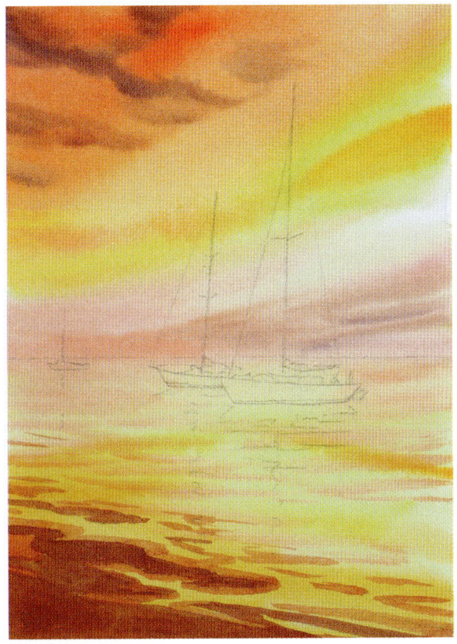

Step 4

Deepen the Water with Bold Reflections

Using a creamy mix of Pyrrol Scarlet and a hint of Phthalo Blue, paint the darkest ripples in the foreground. Then edge a few of these shapes with glowing New Gamboge, which will give your water dimension.

Scan to watch a video.

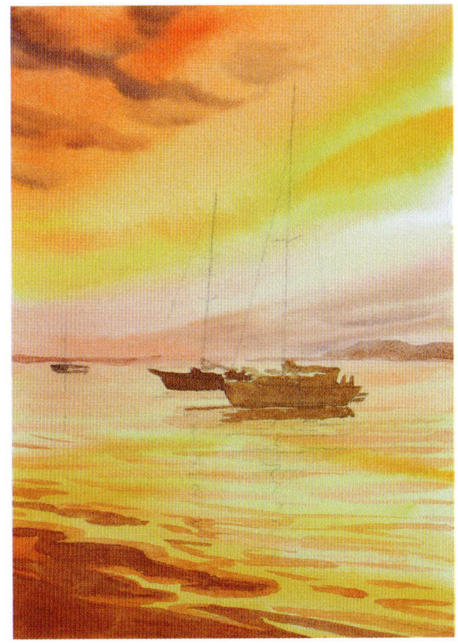

Step 5

Block in the Boats and Shoreline

Mix a muted brown from Pyrrol Scarlet, Phthalo Blue, and a hint of New Gamboge. Use this to underpaint the boats and distant landscape. As you work, negative paint around a few small boat-top shapes to leave light highlights, suggesting sunlit edges.

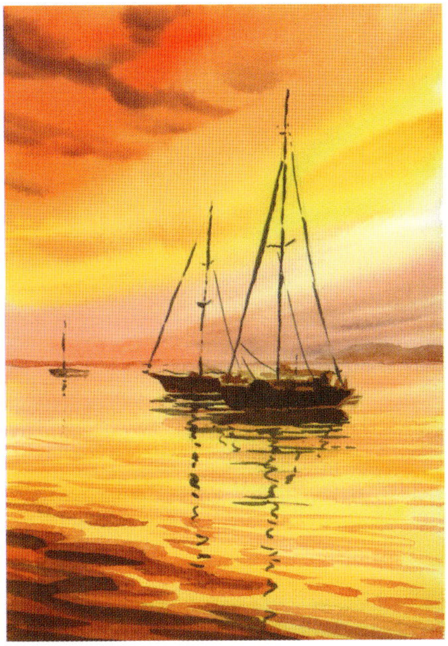

Step 6

Add Final Silhouettes and Strong Details

Mix a rich black with Phthalo Blue and Pyrrol Scarlet. With confident brushstrokes, darken the boats, complete the masts, and extend their reflections in the water. Add a few last dark ripples in the foreground to anchor the composition and create depth.

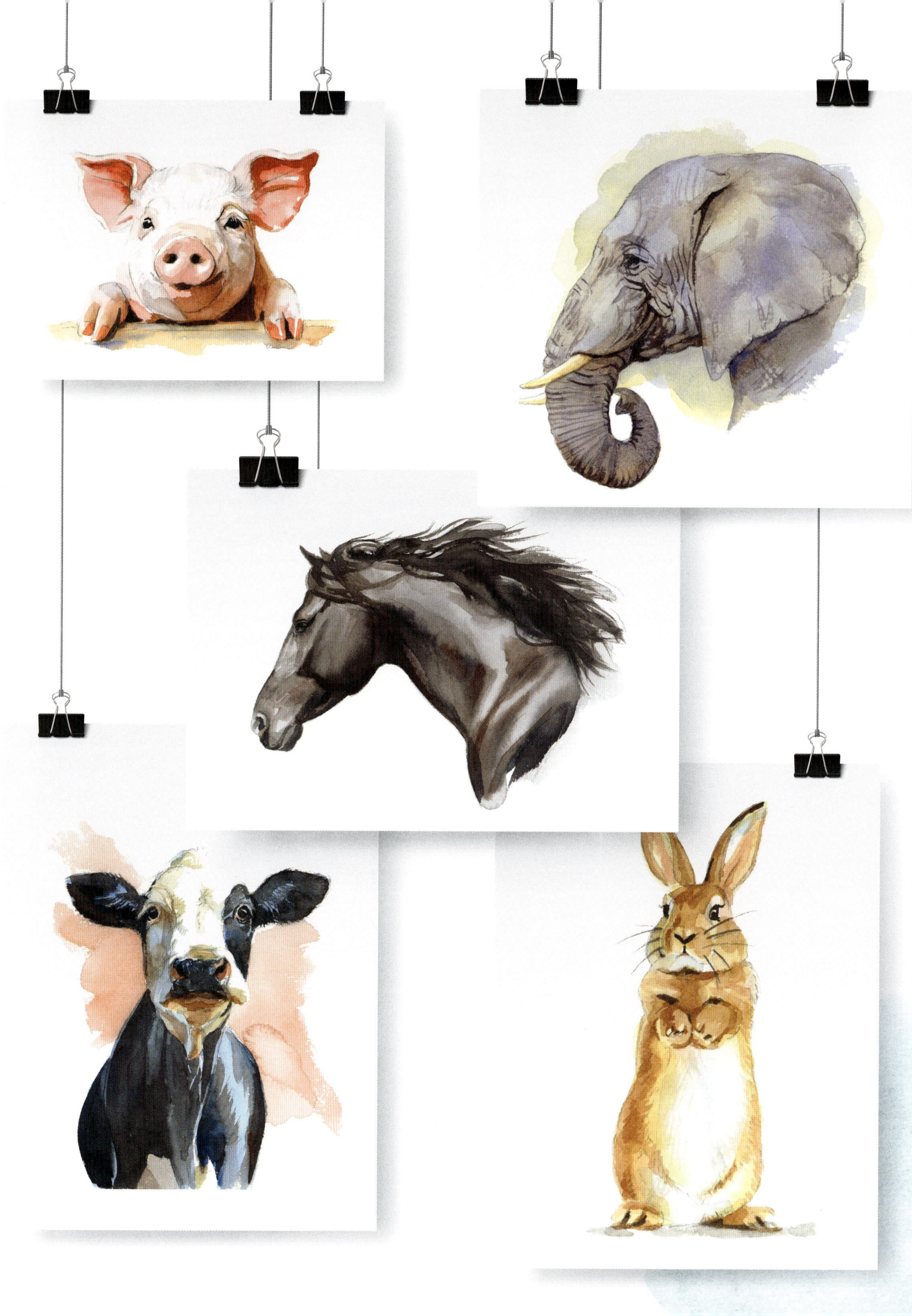

CHAPTER 3

20-Minute Animals

When I first started painting professionally, I did pet portraits, and painting animals has always been a passion of mine. In this chapter you'll learn to paint a variety of animals and, in the process, create a range of interesting textures!

Corgi with a Bow Tie

This dapper little corgi is the perfect subject for practicing soft tan washes and bold, dark accents. Capture its lively personality and those unmistakable features—and don't be surprised if your finished portrait melts a few hearts.

COLORS

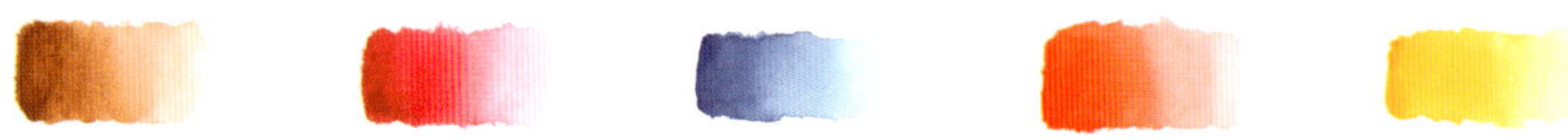

Burnt Sienna	Quinacridone Rose	Phthalo Blue (GS)	Pyrrol Scarlet	New Gamboge

Step 1

Paint Soft Fur on the Face and Ears

Sketch the corgi, then brush clean water over the head and ears, avoiding the eyes and white center stripe. While the surface is still damp, apply creamy Burnt Sienna to the tops of the ears, sides of the face, and across the head. Dilute your color slightly to paint around the eyes and along the cheeks. Drop in a little Quinacridone Rose into the inner ears for warmth. Let those edges stay soft and feathery to mimic fur.

Scan to watch a video.

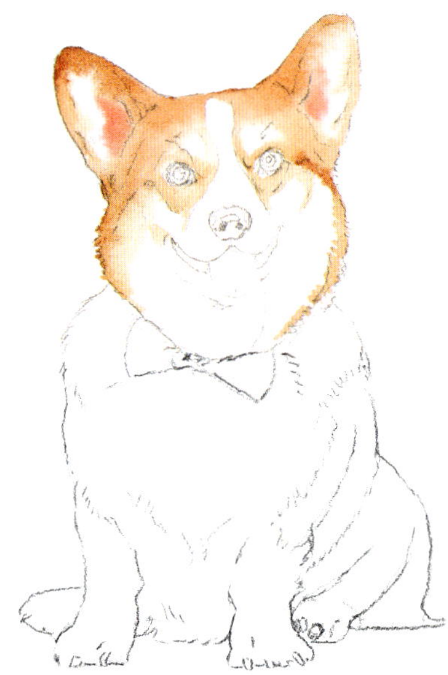

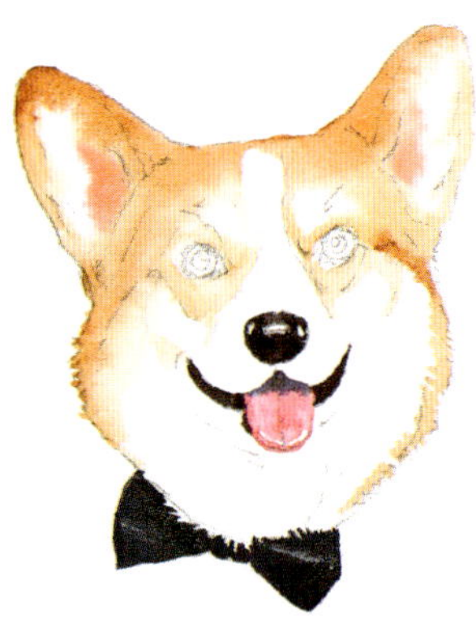

Step 2

Paint the Facial **Features and Fancy Accessories**

Mix a deep black using Phthalo Blue (GS) and Pyrrol Scarlet. With a fine point, paint the shiny nose, leaving small highlights for a wet look. Add the curved mouth lines, and use the same mix to paint the bow tie, leaving a narrow unpainted stripe across the center for a satinlike shine. Gently soften this area with a clean, damp brush. Paint the tongue with Quinacridone Rose, keeping the highlight curved along the edge.

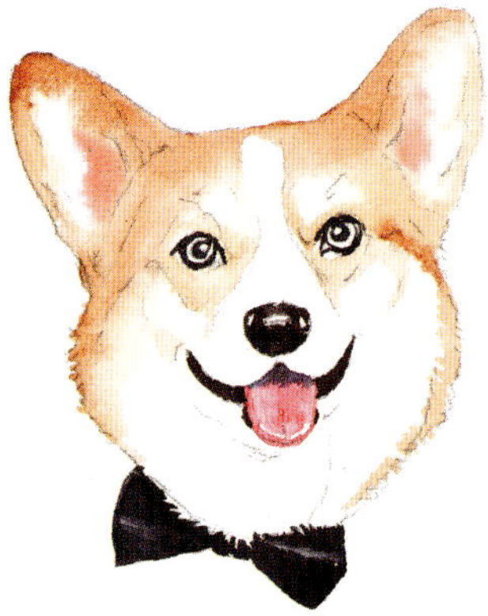

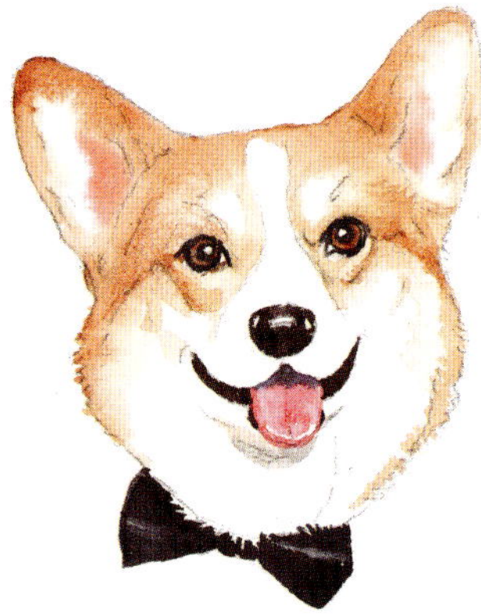

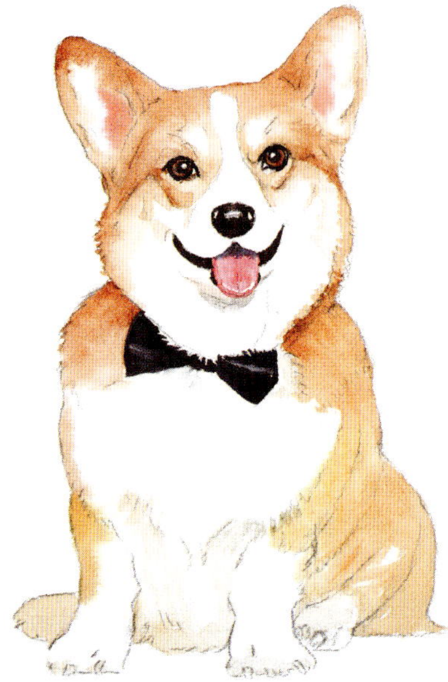

Step 3

Outline the Eyes

Use your black mix to outline each eye and fill in the pupils, making sure to preserve tiny white highlights in the center. Let this layer dry fully before moving on.

Step 4

Bring the Eyes to Life

Once the eyes are dry, fill them with Burnt Sienna to warm them up. While you have that color on your brush, use it to deepen fur creases around the eyes and add texture to the forehead. Mix a light gray (diluted black mix) to paint a soft shadow under the chin.

Step 5

Paint Glowing Golden Fur on the Body

Just like you did for the head, wet the body area with clean water. Apply a mix of New Gamboge and Burnt Sienna for a golden-brown coat, placing more yellow on the back and more sienna on the shoulders. Use a very diluted black to gently shade the belly and paws.

Scan to watch a video.

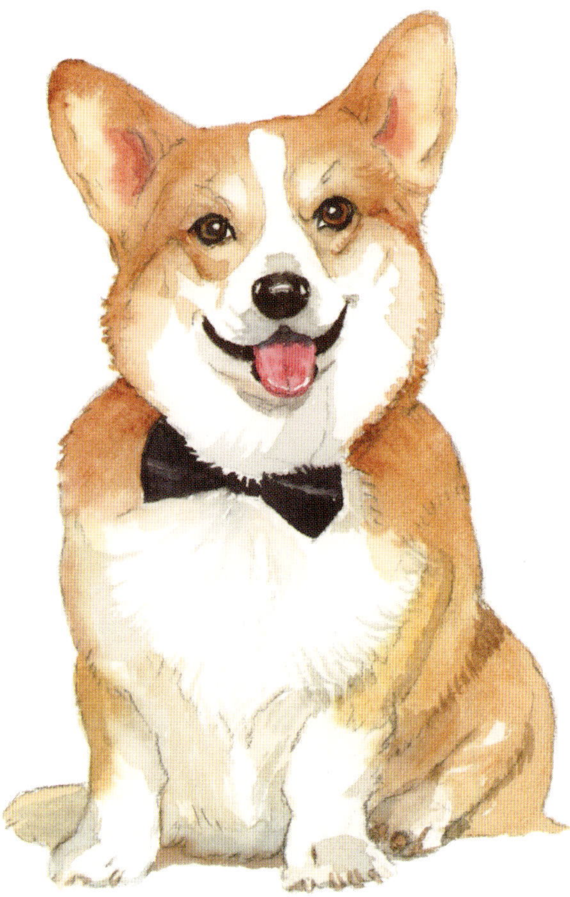

Step 6

Add Final Fur Touches and Shadows

Once the head is dry, glaze over it with a light wash of New Gamboge, but avoid the white center fur. Then, using a diluted gray (your black mix with extra water), splay your brush bristles and add soft, parallel fur strokes to the white chest and neck, curving them outward for realism. Finally, paint a soft brown shadow beneath the corgi so he feels grounded and complete.

Curious Rabbit

Bring this curious tawny rabbit to life with gentle, layered washes. Practice glazing to create rich depth and texture, while reserving your whites to capture the softness of fur and the sparkle of alert, expressive eyes.

COLORS

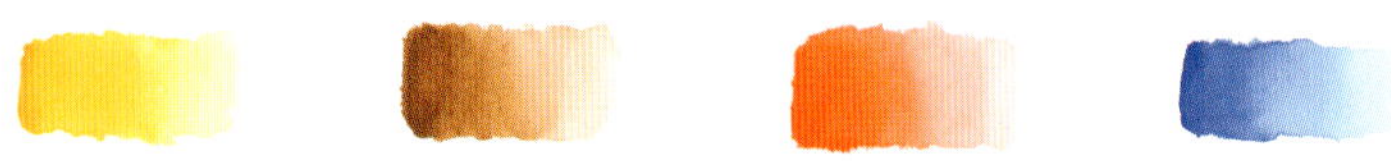

New Gamboge	Burnt Sienna	Pyrrol Scarlet	Phthalo Blue (GS)

Step 1

Sketch Your Quirky Standing Bunny

Let's start by sketching our funny little bunny! To get the proportions right, notice that the distance from the bottom of the feet to the front paws is about halfway up the bunny's body. The top half of the bunny can be roughly divided into thirds: ears, head, and chest with forefeet. Lightly sketch the shape of the white belly so you'll remember to keep it paint-free later.

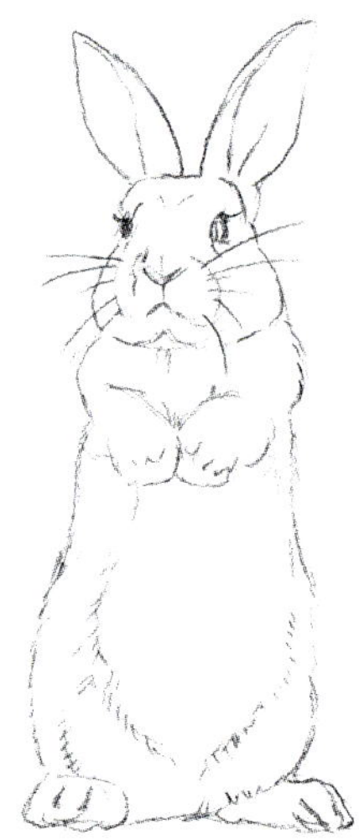

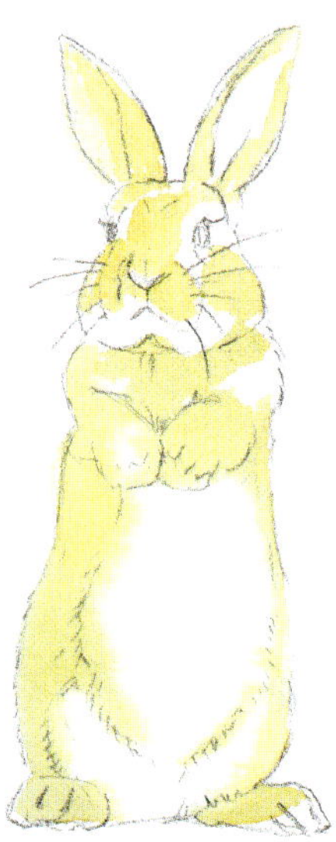

Step 2

Create a Glowing Yellow Base Coat

First, paint clean water inside your bunny's pencil lines to prepare the paper for a soft wet-on-wet effect. While the paper is still damp—but not dripping—load your brush with New Gamboge and apply it to the outer edges of the body. Let the color naturally fade inward toward the belly for a soft, fluffy fur look. Paint the head and feet as well, but leave the white areas untouched, like the inner ears, around the eyes, and below the mouth.

Scan to watch a video.

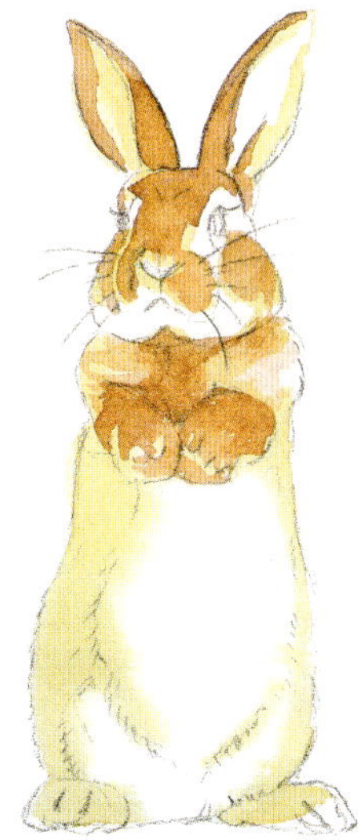

Step 3

Add Warm Brown Fur

It's perfectly fine if your yellow base is still damp for this step! Mix a milky Burnt Sienna and brush it onto the outer parts of the ears, center of the face and cheeks, chest, and feet. Use negative painting around the tiny toes to keep those delightful little details visible and whimsical.

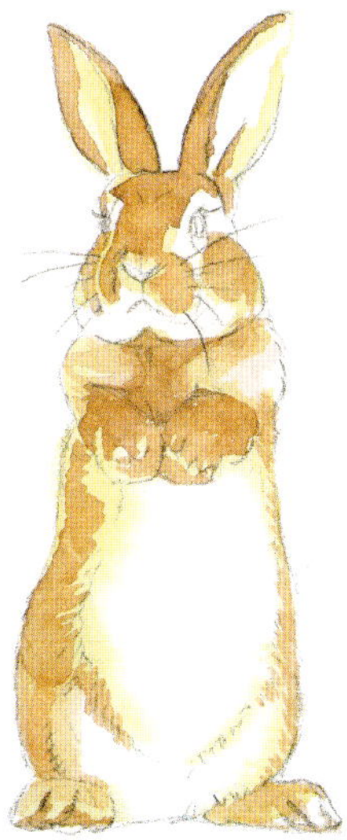

Step 4

Build Texture Around the Belly and Feet

Keep layering soft fur textures using Burnt Sienna. Carefully negative paint around the white belly and toes, preserving their brightness. Use the fine tip of your brush to create feathery strokes where the darker fur blends into the light belly. Vary your paint's value so the tops of the feet stay lighter, while the spaces between the toes are painted darker for depth.

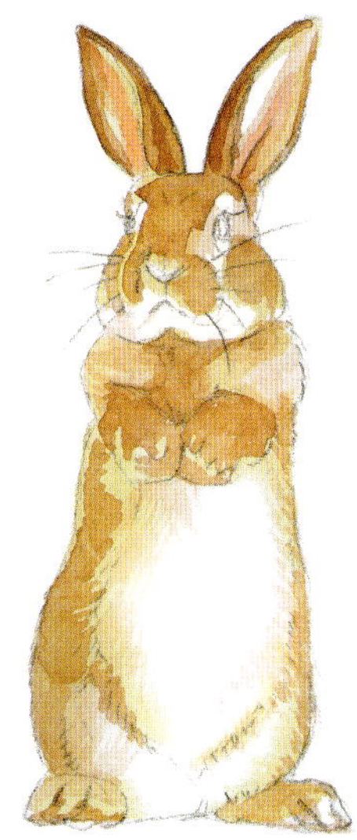

Step 5

Paint Pink Ears and Delicate Fur Texture

Mix a light Pyrrol Scarlet wash and add quick strokes to the inner ears and around the eyes for a soft pink. Then dilute Burnt Sienna, splay the brush bristles on the palette, and lightly stroke toward the belly to create soft, realistic fur. Keep the layer subtle.

Scan to watch a video.

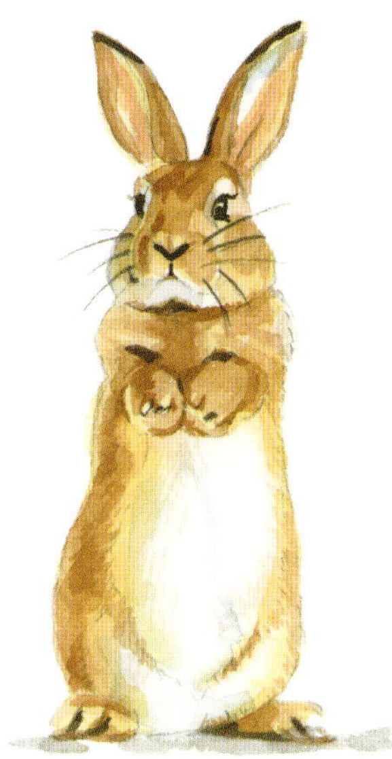

Step 6

Add Charming Facial Features and Final Shading

Now for the details that bring your bunny to life! Mix Burnt Sienna and Phthalo Blue (GS) to create a rich, velvety black. With a fine-tipped brush, carefully paint the bunny's eyes, nose, slender whiskers, and subtle shadows, tiny V shapes under the chin, on the ears, and around the toes. For the finishing touch, mix a super light wash of Phthalo Blue and glaze it softly across the ears, chin, and belly to add a hint of cool shading and extra dimension.

Scan to watch a video.

Gentle Elephant

With only three colors, you'll create a lifelike elephant portrait rich in depth and character. Layer soft glazes of warm and cool tones to suggest the complex texture of weathered skin and the quiet majesty of this gentle giant.

COLORS

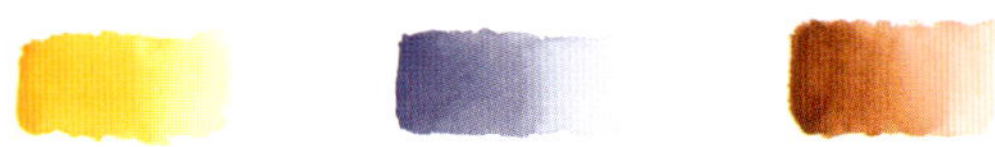

New Gamboge	French Ultramarine	Burnt Sienna

Step 1

Sketch the Elephant with Bold, Simple Shapes

If you choose to sketch the elephant freehand, begin by blocking in the largest shapes first, like the teardrop-shaped ear, the gentle slope of the head, and the sweeping curve of the trunk. Start broad and general, focusing on getting the overall proportions right before refining with details.

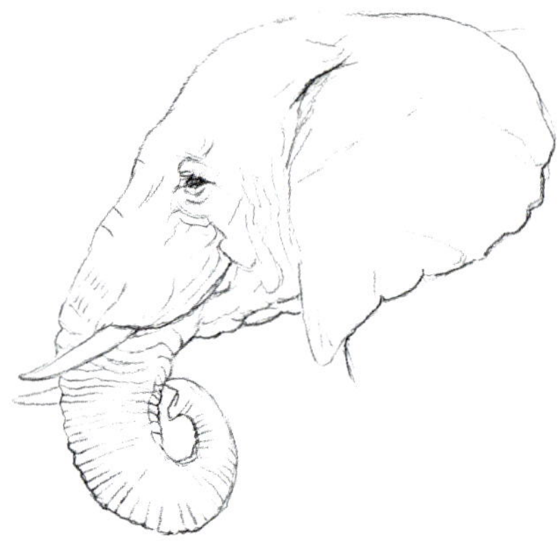

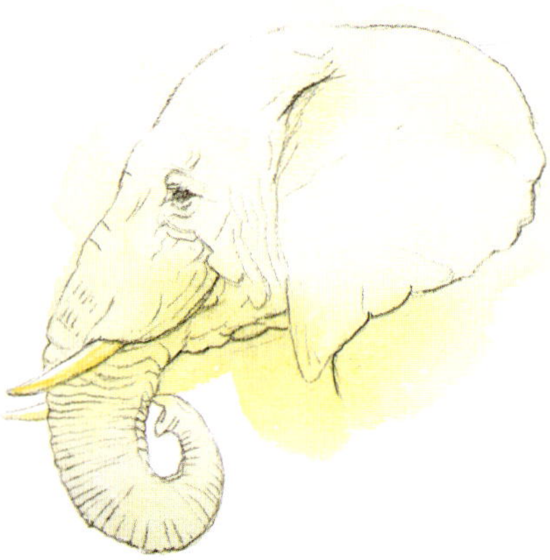

Step 2

Lay Down a Warm Golden Base

Mix a watery puddle of New Gamboge and brush it over the entire elephant, allowing the color to flow even slightly beyond your pencil lines. This warm base wash will set the tone for the layers to come. Leave highlights along the tops of the tusks. Let this dry completely.

Step 3

Add Blue Shadows and Form

Mix a generous puddle of French Ultramarine and carefully paint the entire elephant's head, leaving the tusks untouched. Use slightly thicker paint in areas meant to be darker, such as the trunk, and the shadowed spots beneath the mouth and ear. You can move on to the next layer while this wash is still damp to create soft blends.

Scan to watch a video.

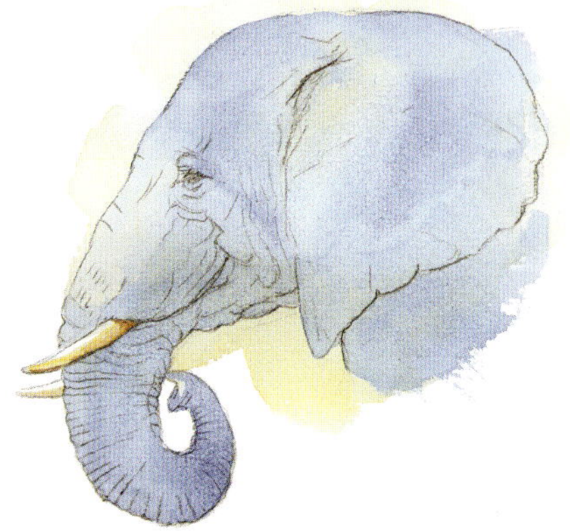

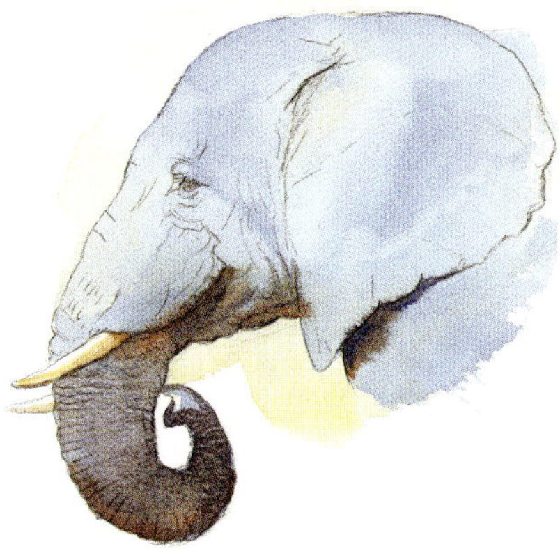

Step 4

Create Lively Grays with Pigment Mixing

Burnt Sienna and French Ultramarine combine beautifully to create a rich, natural gray. Use this mix to begin building warmth and depth in the trunk, mouth, and ear. For added interest, don't just pre-mix the color on your palette; try dropping the two pigments directly onto the paper and let them mingle. This creates a lively dance between warm and cool tones within your grays.

Step 5

Sculpt with Midtones

Use a watery wash of Burnt Sienna to brush in some medium dark shapes on the head and ear. These marks are beginning to describe the anatomy.

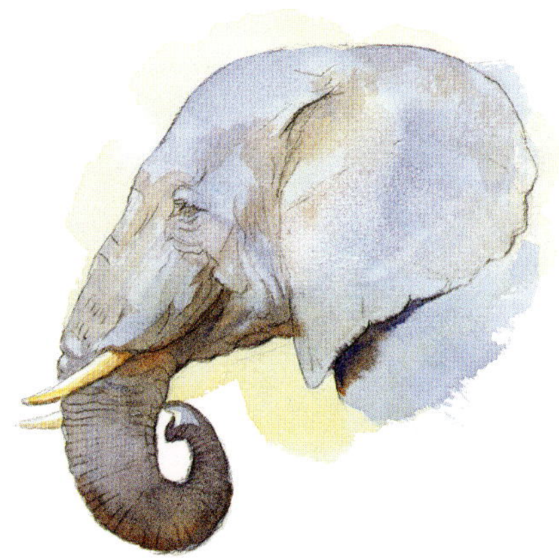

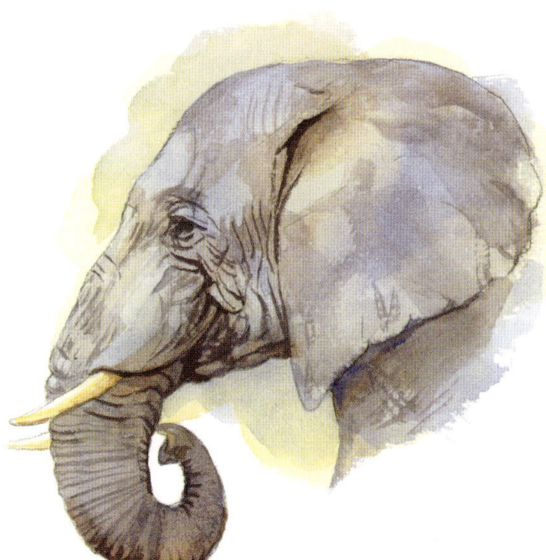

Step 6

Define Wrinkles and Deep Shadows

Keep building up the gray details, especially the wrinkles along the trunk and head. For the deepest shadows, mix equal parts French Ultramarine and Burnt Sienna to create a rich, near-black with a creamy consistency. Use the fine point of your brush to carefully place those final dark accents, like the eye and the deepest creases.

Scan to watch a video.

Friendly Cow

This fun Holstein cow portrait is a great way to explore light and shadow. Learn to mix vibrant blacks from your primaries and create lively contrasts that shift beautifully from cool shadow to sunlit warmth.

COLORS

Phthalo Blue (GS) | Burnt Sienna | Pyrrol Scarlet | New Gamboge

Step 1
Paint Soft Shadows on the Face

Sketch the cow. For beautifully blended shadows, use the wet-on-wet technique. Begin with a light wash of Phthalo Blue (GS) over the shadow areas of the head. While it's still damp, gently dab in watery Burnt Sienna with a hint of Pyrrol Scarlet around the eye, along the jawline, and under the chin. Then, switch to a creamier Burnt Sienna mix to "draw" the mouth line and lower lip for subtle definition.

Scan to watch a video.

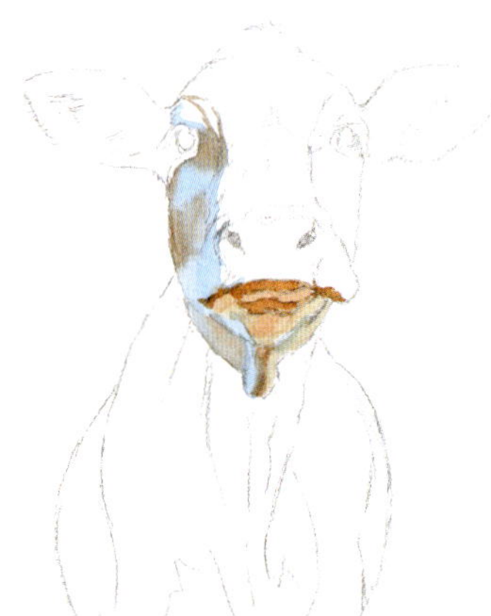

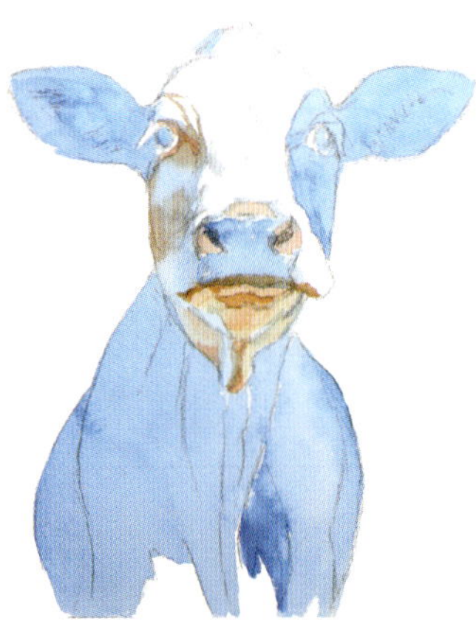

Step 2
Create a Blue Underpainting

Next, lay down a flat wet-on-dry wash of Phthalo Blue (GS) over all the cow's black markings and nose, leaving the white center of the face, whites of the eyes, and eyelashes untouched. Don't worry if it looks a bit blotchy, that texture adds character! Drop in some watery Pyrrol Scarlet into the nostrils and across the top of the muzzle for warmth. Let everything dry completely.

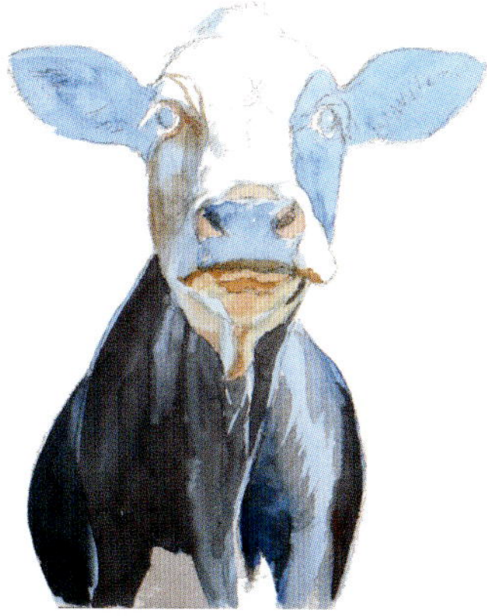

Step 3

Start Defining the Black Markings

Mix up a rich, deep black using a creamy 50/50 blend of Pyrrol Scarlet and Phthalo Blue (GS). Paint this darker mix into the deep shadows on the cow's body. For areas like the neck and the shiny right side of the cow, dilute your mix slightly to create a softer, grayed-down black that suggests reflected light and glossy fur.

Step 4

Bring the Left Ear and Eye to Life

Use your black mix to carefully paint the left ear and the eye, leaving the highlight and delicate eyelashes untouched. For a touch of realism, allow some of the blue underpainting to peek through, especially on the sunlit edges of the ear, neck, and right shoulder. This creates a lively shimmer in the fur.

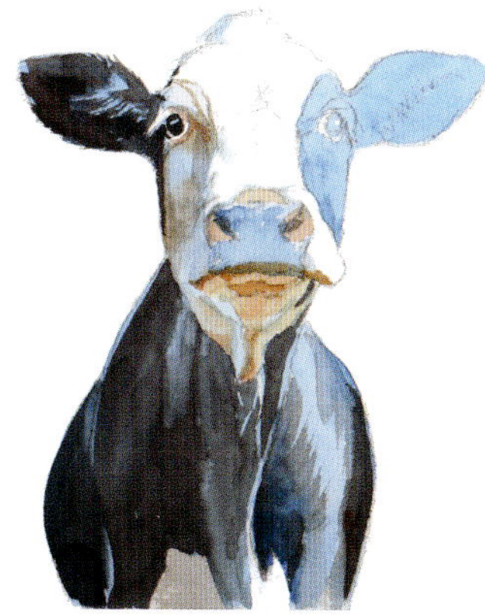

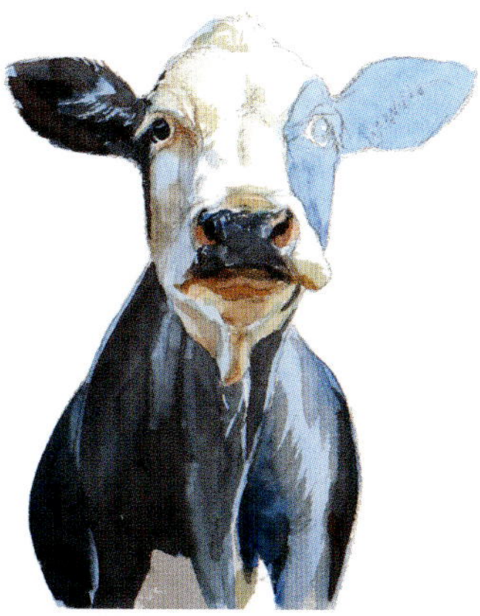

Step 5

Paint a Glossy Wet Nose

Reload your brush with a milky consistency of your black mix. To mimic the wet, textured look of a cow's nose, try a drybrush technique: Gently scrape the brush across the surface so little flecks of the light blue underpainting show through, suggesting glistening moisture. Use watery New Gamboge to add hints of warmth to the cow's white facial markings.

Step 6

Shadows and Background

Paint the right side of the cow's head with your black mix, keeping the layer lighter and more transparent near the eye and deepening the tone toward the muzzle to create a rounded, illuminated look. Then add a bold pop of background color—Pyrrol Scarlet or any bright hue you love—splashing it around the cow's head to make the portrait stand out with a lively, expressive finish.

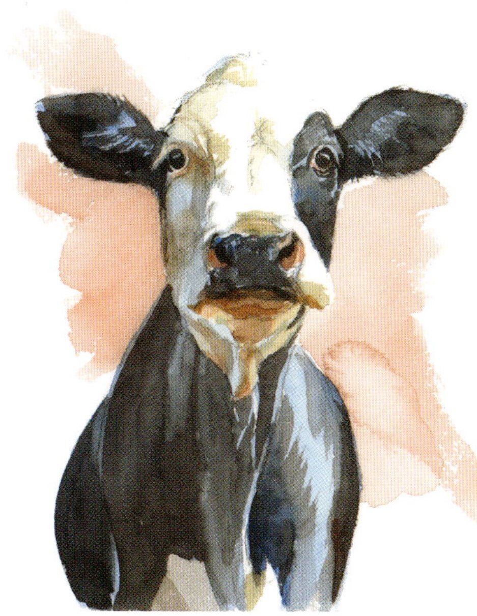

Gazing Giraffe

In this lesson, we'll combine soft wet-on-wet washes with crisp wet-on-dry details to bring a giraffe to life. Warm Burnt Sienna spots meet cool Phthalo Blue shadows, creating a striking balance of color and form.

COLORS

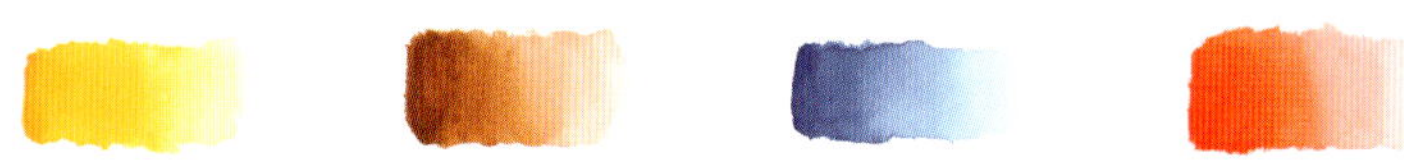

New Gamboge	Burnt Sienna	Phthalo Blue (GS)	Pyrrol Scarlet

Step 1

Create a Golden Base

Sketch the giraffe, then brush clean water inside the giraffe's outline until the paper is evenly glossy. Drop in creamy New Gamboge on the underside of the neck, muzzle, and center of the head. Use a paler yellow for the ears so they don't overpower the face.

Scan to watch a video.

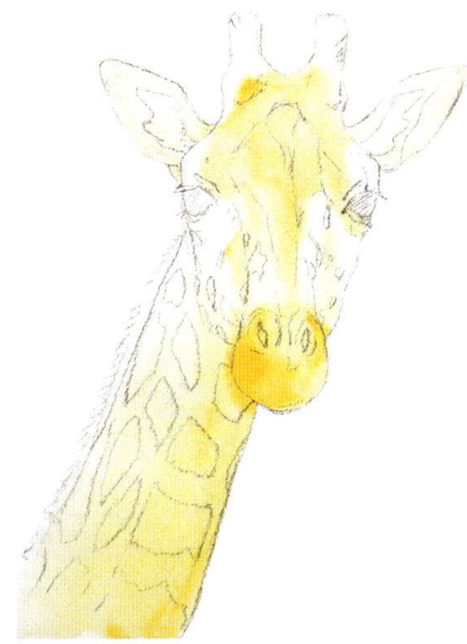

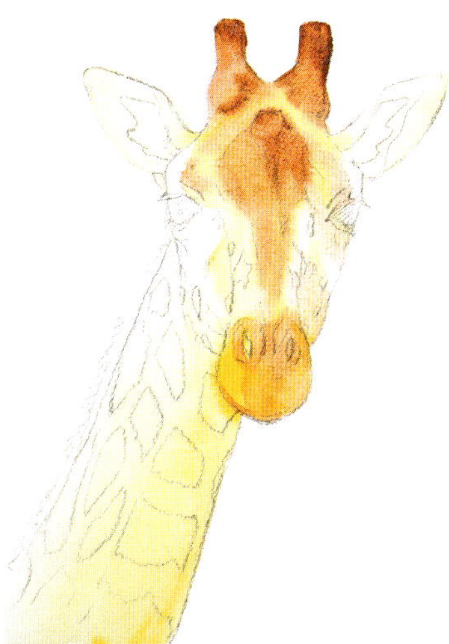

Step 2

Warm the Face with Burnt Sienna

While the yellow is still damp, add milky Burnt Sienna to the ossicones, the bony ridge between the eyes, and the velvety muzzle. Strengthen the ossicones once more with thicker sienna so they stand out.

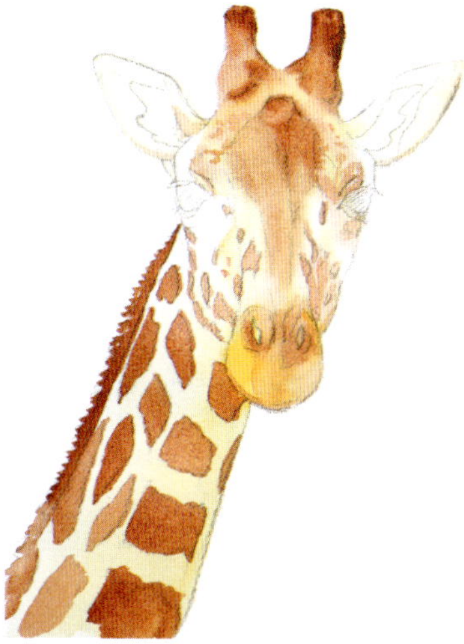

Step 3

Add Smaller Facial Spots

Using a milky Burnt Sienna mix, paint the mane and larger body spots, softening the mane's edge with the tip of your brush. Then dilute the sienna slightly and add the smaller facial spots around the crown and cheeks, keeping them light so the giraffe's gentle expression comes through.

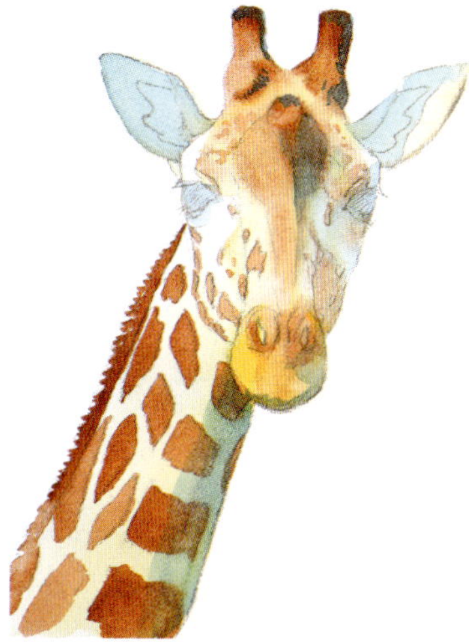

Step 4

Cool the Shadows with Blue

Glaze watery Phthalo Blue (GS) over the ears, around the eyes, and along the right side of the face and neck to suggest light direction. Add a slightly darker streak of blue down the shadow side of each ossicone. This interplay of warm and cool keeps the giraffe dimensional.

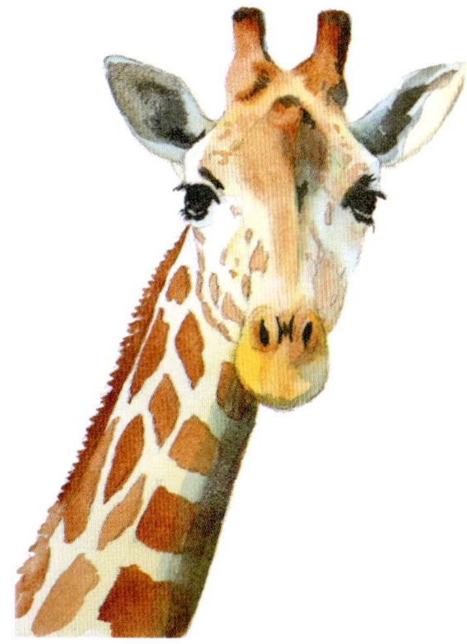

Step 5

Define the Features

Mix Phthalo Blue and Pyrrol Scarlet into a deep black. With a fine brush point, carefully paint the eyes, lashes, nostrils, and the dark inner ear shadows. Be mindful to leave small highlights in the eyes for life and sparkle.

Scan to watch a video.

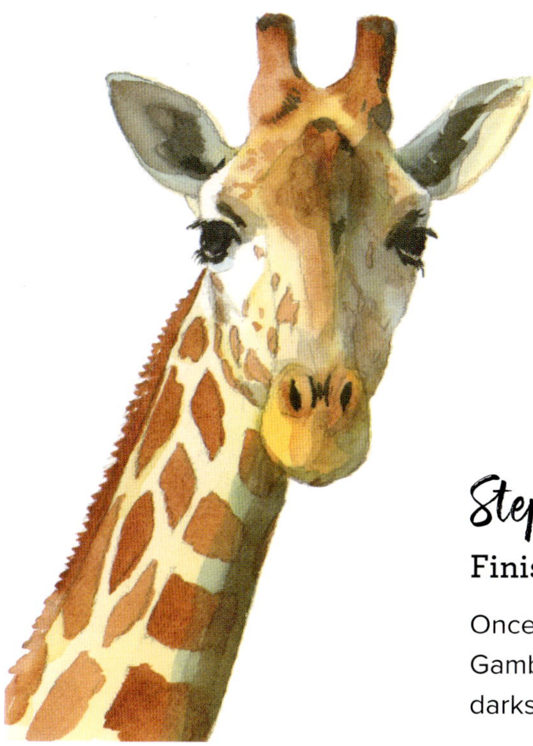

Step 6

Finish with Warmth and Balance

Once everything is dry, glaze a final transparent layer of watery New Gamboge across the head and neck to unify the warm tones. Adjust any darks as needed and step back to admire your gentle, gazing giraffe.

Graceful Dolphin

Bring this playful dolphin to life with shimmering washes of warm and cool tones. You'll explore contrast and movement, balancing sharp dark accents against luminous "lost" edges that dissolve into light and water.

COLORS

Phthalo Blue (GS)	Burnt Sienna	Pyrrol Scarlet	French Ultramarine

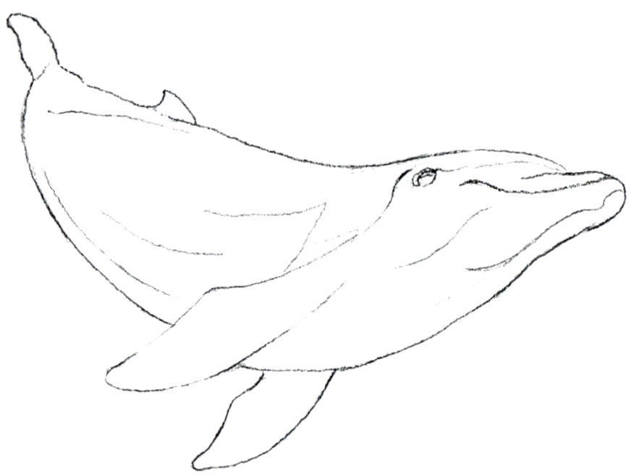

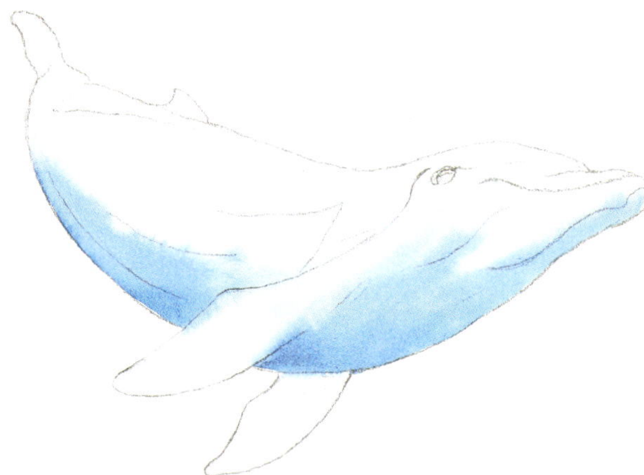

Step 1

Sketch with Movement in Mind

Think of the dolphin as an upside-down triangle shape. This helps you capture the gesture and motion right from the start. From there, refine the lines into soft, flowing curves, and sketch in the fins, head, and key facial features.

Step 2

Lay Down a Cool Blue Base

Using a clean brush, wet the entire dolphin with clear water, staying carefully inside your pencil lines. The surface should look evenly glossy, not puddly. Mix a milky wash of Phthalo Blue (GS) and paint it along the belly and midsection of the dolphin, letting it gently diffuse. If too much paint creeps into the forward fin, just lift it out with a damp brush.

Scan to watch a video.

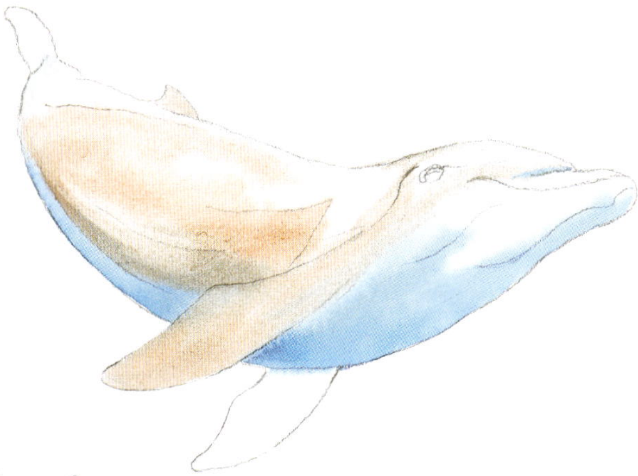

Step 3

Add a Touch of Warmth

While the blue layer is still damp, drop in Burnt Sienna along the belly to create a soft, warm transition. Gently blend where the two colors meet, keeping the top of the dolphin free of paint to preserve the highlight and light source from above.

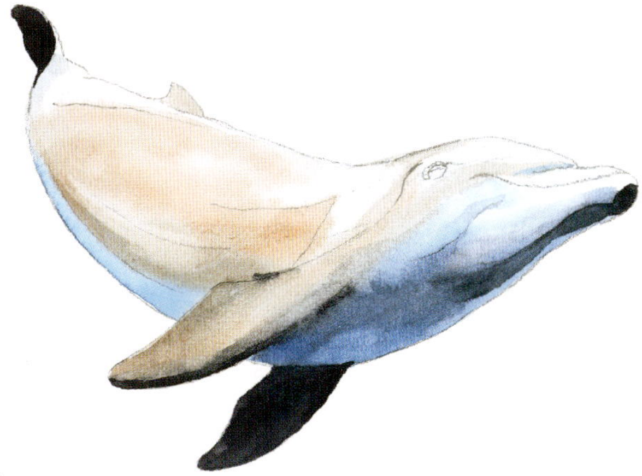

Step 4

Carve Out the Shadows

Mix a rich black by combining Phthalo Blue (GS) with Pyrrol Scarlet to a creamy consistency. Use this bold color to define the tail fin, shadowed front fin, and darker areas beneath the head and along the belly. To soften the transition into the blue, use a diluted French Ultramarine wash to gently blend the edges of your shadows into the midtones.

Scan to watch a video.

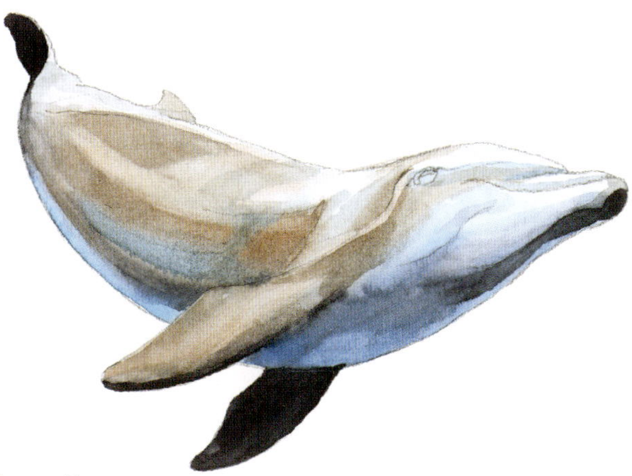

Step 5

Shape the Body with Soft Brushstrokes

Create a soft gray brown by mixing French Ultramarine with Burnt Sienna. Use this muted color to paint subtle curved streaks across the body and head, helping to define the dolphin's form and rounded shape without overworking it.

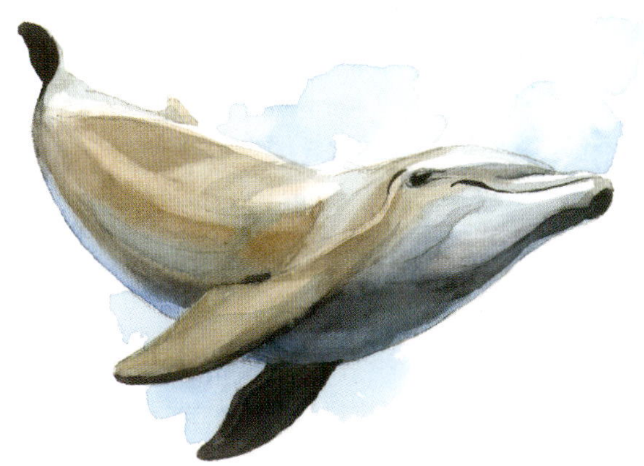

Step 6

Add Character and a Splash of Fun

Use your black mix to carefully paint the eye and smiling mouth, giving your dolphin expression and charm. For a playful finishing touch, splash watery Phthalo Blue around the background, suggesting the dolphin's ocean home with a burst of color and movement.

Spirited Horse

Create a horse portrait alive with energy and grace using only two colors. Explore luminous shifts from warm to cool and delicate blends of light and shadow that convey the animal's strength, beauty, and motion.

COLORS

Phthalo Blue (GS)

Pyrrol Scarlet

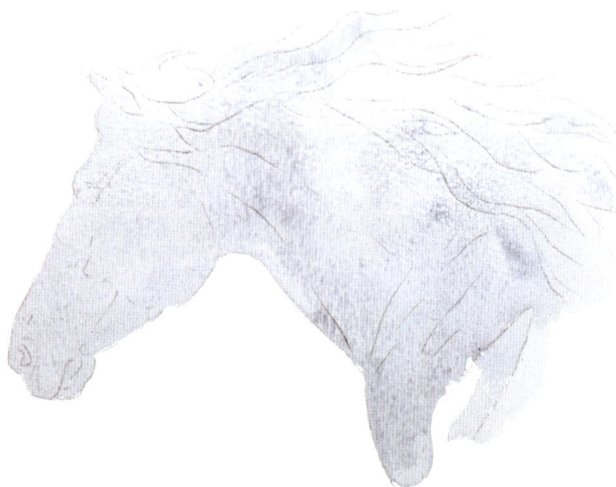

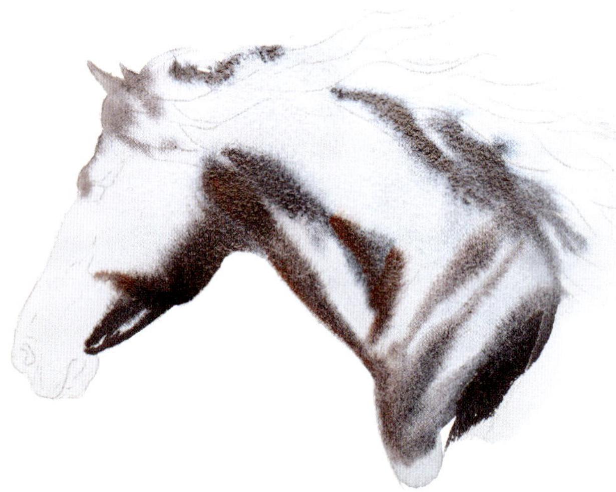

Step 1

Lay the Gray Base Wash

Working with just two primaries—Phthalo Blue (GS) and Pyrrol Scarlet—we'll control values by varying paint consistency. Pre-mix a few puddles in different viscosities. For the base layer, use a very watery 50/50 blue-red mix to create a soft neutral gray, covering the entire horse head. Keep brushwork loose and expressive, especially where the neck and mane fade out.

Scan to watch a video.

Step 2

Add Wet-on-Wet Shadows

While the base layer is still damp, use a creamy, thicker version of your red-blue mix to drop in the darkest shadows, along the jaw, beneath the mane, and down the neck. To add visual interest, vary your red-blue ratios slightly to shift between warmer and cooler tones in the shadows.

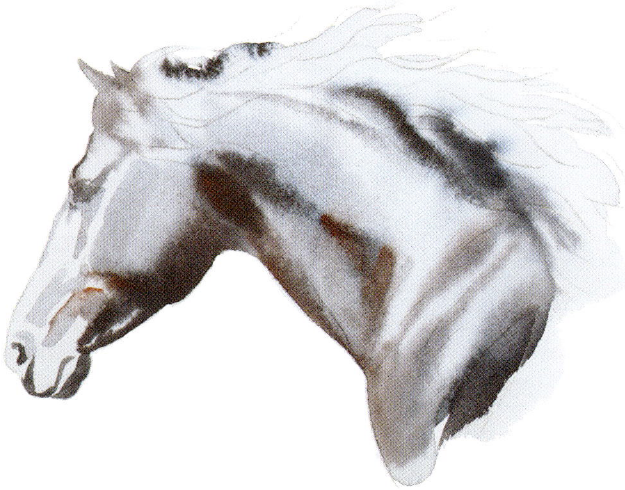

Step 3

Build the Form

As the first layer begins to dry, watch your water content. Your brush should be damp, not wet. Begin layering a lighter consistency of your red-blue mix to define the horse's structure: cheekbones, eye socket, forehead, and muzzle. Think sculpturally and build up those planes with care.

Scan to watch a video.

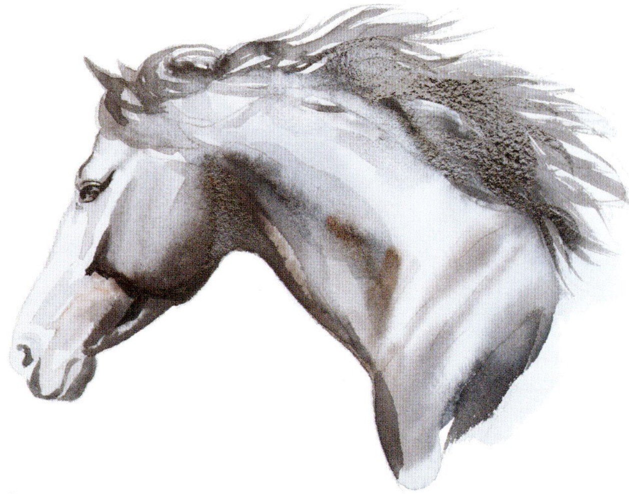

Step 4

Paint the Deepest Darks

Mix up your darkest value using equal parts Phthalo Blue and Pyrrol Scarlet in a thick, creamy consistency, just enough water to keep it flowing. This rich, near-black mix is perfect for the mane, eye, and the deepest shadow areas. Use the tip of your brush to suggest hair texture in the mane. Pull curved strokes in the direction of the hair growth, and lift your brush gently at the end of each stroke to create a soft, feathered look.

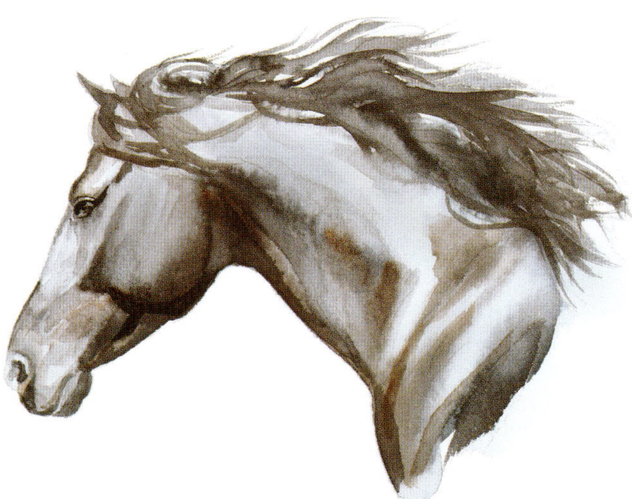

Step 5

Refine with Subtle Layers

Add soft gray glazes to the muzzle, jaw, and neck to deepen form. If you'd like warmer tones in these areas, simply lean a little heavier on the red in your mix to create a soft brownish gray.

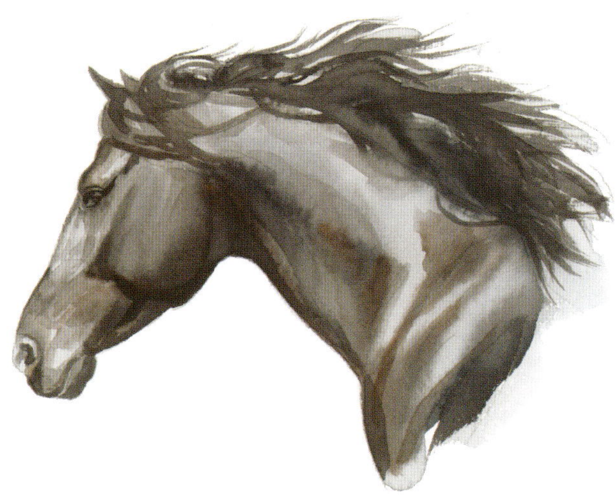

Step 6

Soften and Blend

Continue developing midtones and refining the anatomy. To soften transitions, lay down a stroke, then dip your brush in clean water (without fully rinsing), blot lightly, and drag it along the damp edge to create seamless blends.

Orange Goldfish

Dive into the warm, glowing side of your palette with this radiant goldfish project. You'll practice controlling paint consistency to create shimmering depth and the illusion of light beneath the water.

COLORS

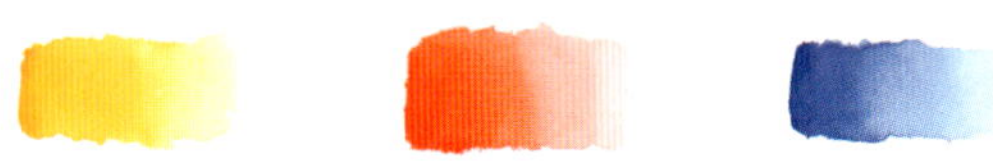

New Gamboge | Pyrrol Scarlet | Phthalo Blue (GS)

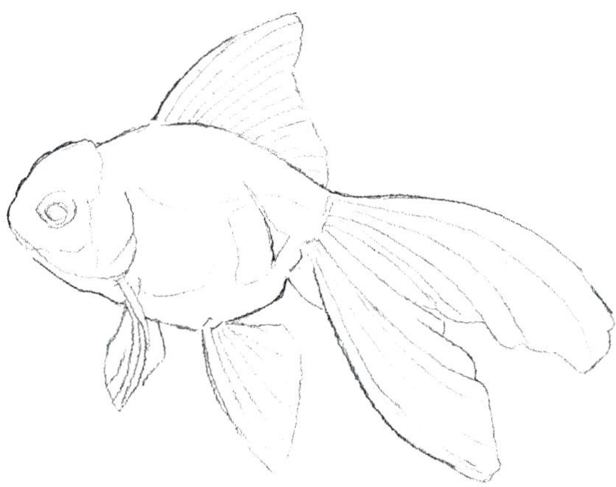

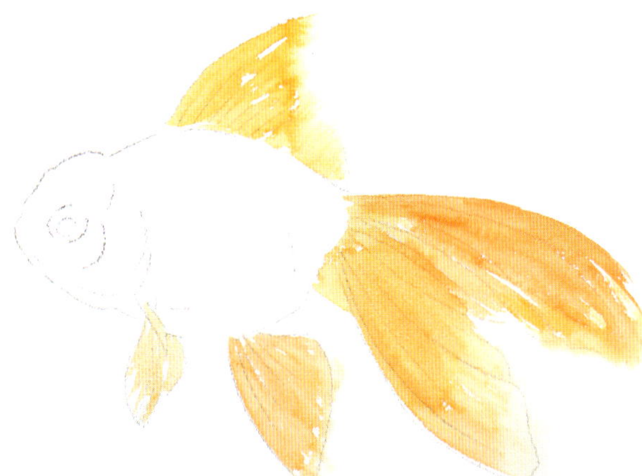

Step 1

Sketch Your Fishy Friend

Begin by sketching or tracing the shape of your fish. Notice how the body and tail are roughly the same length. Don't forget to add key features like the eye, and gently sketch the lines of the fins to guide your brushstrokes later.

Step 2

Paint the Flowing, Delicate Fins

Wet a finger-width area beyond each fin to give space for soft edges and movement. Brush in New Gamboge along the fin direction, letting it fade into the damp paper and leaving small gaps for a translucent look. Drop in a touch of Pyrrol Scarlet for a warm orange glow. Repeat for each fin.

Scan to watch a video.

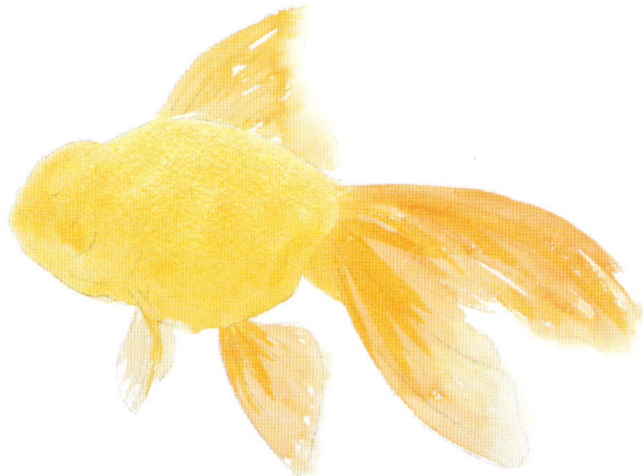

Step 3

Lay a Golden Base for the Body

While the fins dry, switch to the body. Use a milky mix of New Gamboge and paint the full body of the fish wet-on-dry, keeping your strokes smooth and even. This sets a warm, luminous foundation.

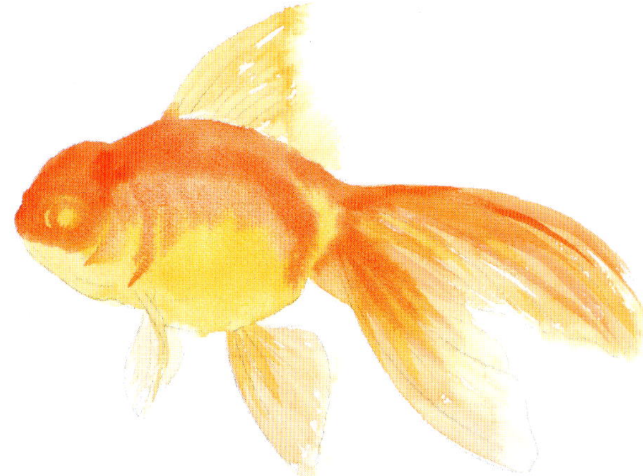

Step 4

Add Rich Reds for Depth

While the yellow is still damp, grab some creamy Pyrrol Scarlet and apply it along the top of the head and spine to create depth and dimension. To soften the red, dip your brush in water, blot slightly, and pull curved strokes downward, mimicking the rounded shape of the fish's body. Add a few soft red lines to the tail fin, and carefully paint around the eye and gills, leaving those areas untouched for now.

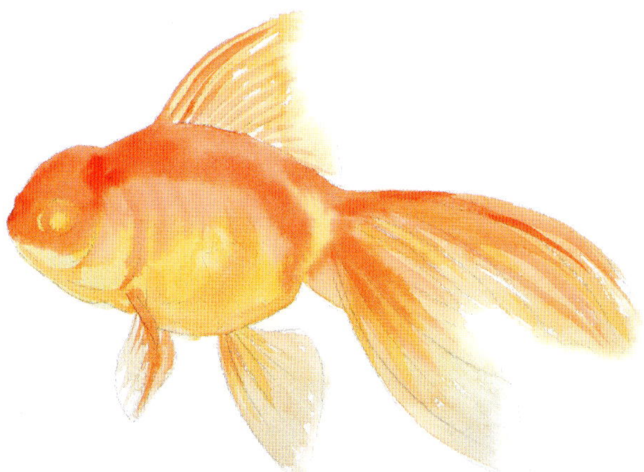

Step 5

Define Fins and Form

Using a slightly thinned version of Pyrrol Scarlet, begin adding curved, flowing lines inside each fin. Feather the lines outward so they naturally disappear at the edges, maintaining that airy, delicate look. Then, glaze a light red wash over the belly to suggest roundness and soft shadow. Let everything dry completely before moving on.

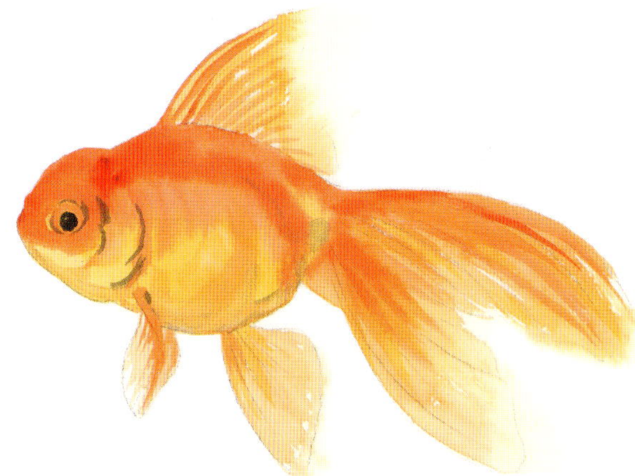

Step 6

Bring It to Life with the Eye

To mix a natural-looking black, combine Phthalo Blue (GS) and Pyrrol Scarlet in equal parts for a rich, creamy consistency. With your brush at a fine point, carefully paint the round eye, leaving a tiny white highlight if desired. Water down the black mix to make a gentle gray and use it to add curved shadows around the eye and head, giving your fish a realistic, lively expression.

Hungry Pig

Bring personality to life with a playful watercolor pig! Learn to paint expressive features and soft textures, while practicing color mixing for natural-looking pinks and grays.

COLORS

Pyrrol Scarlet	Quinacridone Rose	Burnt Sienna	New Gamboge	French Ultramarine

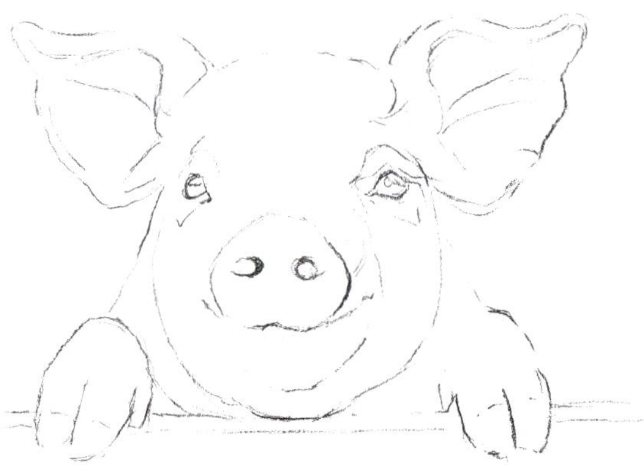

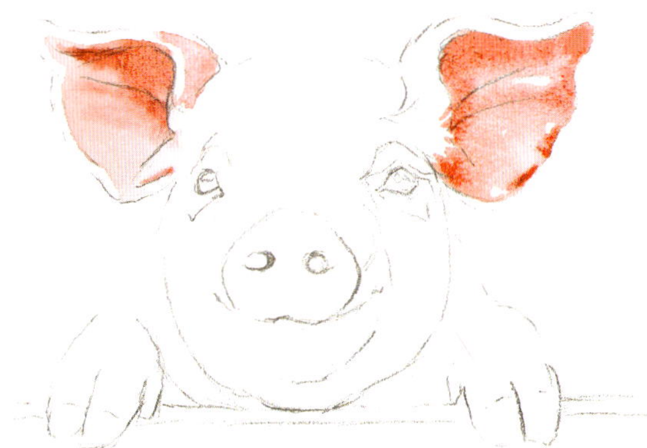

Step 1

Sketch the Pig

Sketch or trace the pig, paying attention to the slight turn of its head. This subtle angle makes one eye appear smaller than the other. Gently erase any extra or overly dark lines to keep the drawing clean and soft.

Step 2

Build Warmth in the Ears

Mix a light, watery blend of Pyrrol Scarlet and Quinacridone Rose to paint the ears. While the paint is still wet, switch to a creamier version of the same red mixture and dab it into the inner ears to deepen the color and add dimension.

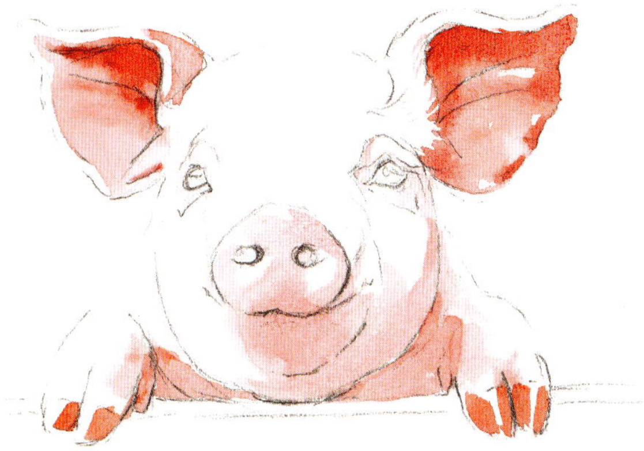

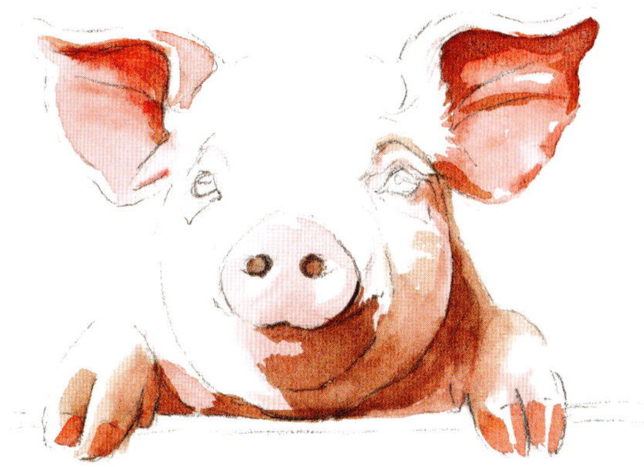

Step 3

Paint the Snout, Shadows, and Feet

Continue adding pink to the pig by painting the snout, the shadow beneath the head, and the feet. Use negative painting to define the brightest spots, leaving the areas just below each nostril and along the hooves untouched, letting the white of the paper create natural highlights.

Step 4

Deepen the Shadows with Warm Tones

Use Burnt Sienna with a touch of New Gamboge in a milky consistency to add deeper shadows to the ears and below the head.

Scan to watch a video.

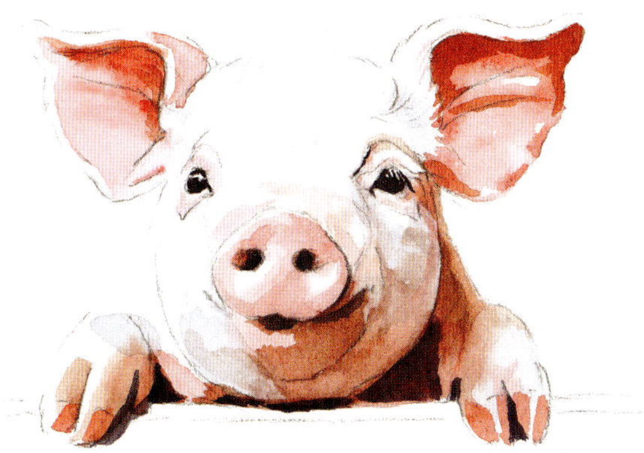

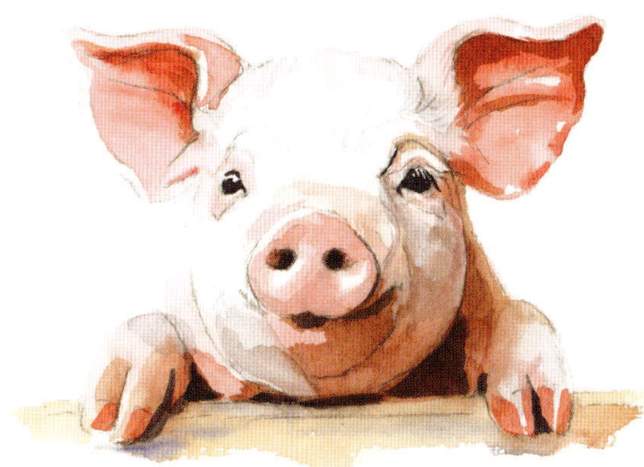

Step 5

Define the Darks and Add Detail

Mix Pyrrol Scarlet and Ultramarine into a creamy black, then use a fine point to add dark accents to the feet, nostrils, mouth, and neck. Paint around the eye highlights, and on the right eye, use the brush tip to suggest white lashes. For cooler shadows, apply a light gray wash of French Ultramarine and Burnt Sienna to the feet and right side of the face. To imply fine forehead fur, splay the bristles and make quick upward strokes.

Step 6

Finish with a Rustic Fence Base

To finish, paint the wooden fence beneath the pig using a watery mix of New Gamboge and Burnt Sienna, applying it in horizontal strokes. While the paint is still damp, swipe in a touch of French Ultramarine to add a bit of texture and color variation for a more natural, weathered look.

Regal Lion

In this lesson, you'll layer warm browns and glowing golds with cool shadow tones to bring the king of the jungle to life. By combining soft wet-on-wet washes with crisp wet-on-dry details, you'll capture both the majesty and gentle expressiveness of this big cat.

COLORS

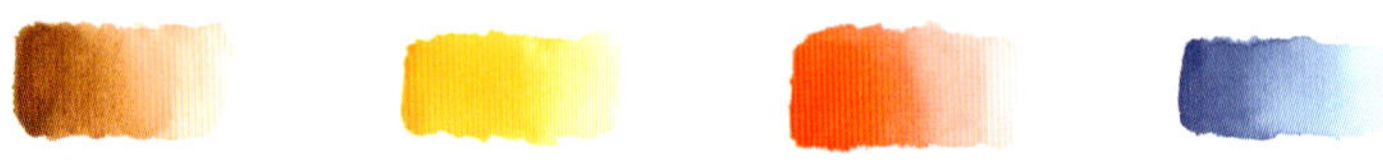

Burnt Sienna	New Gamboge	Pyrrol Scarlet	Phthalo Blue (GS)

Step 1

Paint the First Wash

Wet everything inside the lion's outline except the eyes, nose, and white muzzle. Apply a milky wash of Burnt Sienna, concentrating more pigment in the outer mane and across the top of the head for subtle variation.

Scan to watch a video.

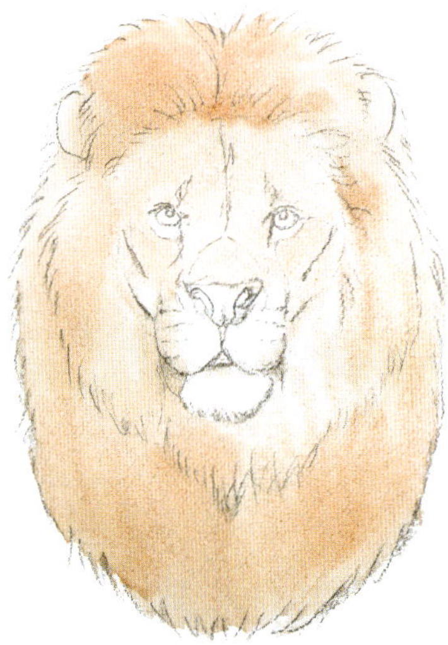

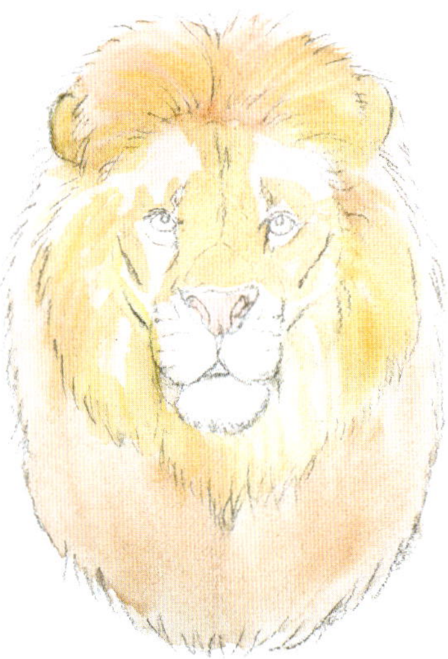

Step 2

Add a Touch of Warmth

While the first layer is still damp, drop in New Gamboge around the ears and face to warm the fur. For the pink nose, paint watery Pyrrol Scarlet wet-on-dry.

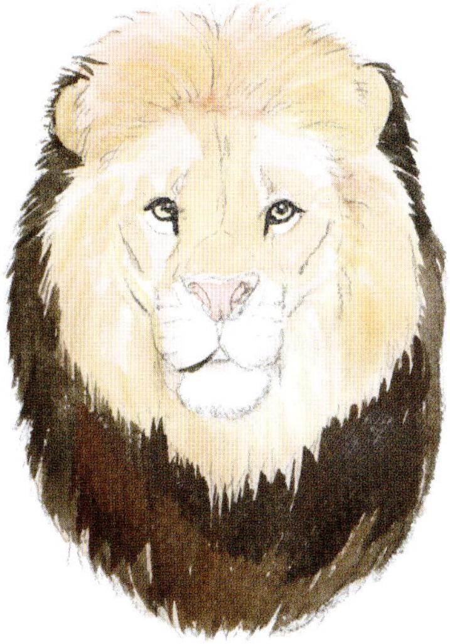

Step 3

Begin the Dark Details

Mix Burnt Sienna and Phthalo Blue into a creamy, rich dark brown. Use separated bristles to paint the mane with loose, hair-like strokes, leaving gaps for lighter tufts to overlap. Bring your brush back to a fine point to outline the eyes and pupils, leaving tiny highlights of paper white for sparkle.

Scan to watch a video.

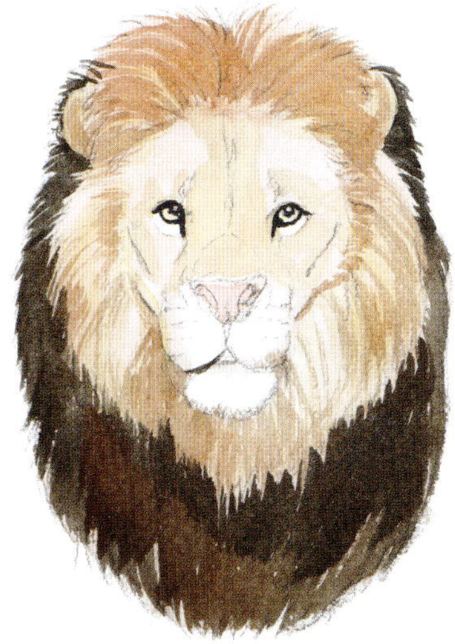

Step 4

Add Fur Texture

Load a milky Burnt Sienna and layer soft strokes around the face, curving them in the direction of growth. Leave small gaps to create the illusion of lighter and darker strands intermingling.

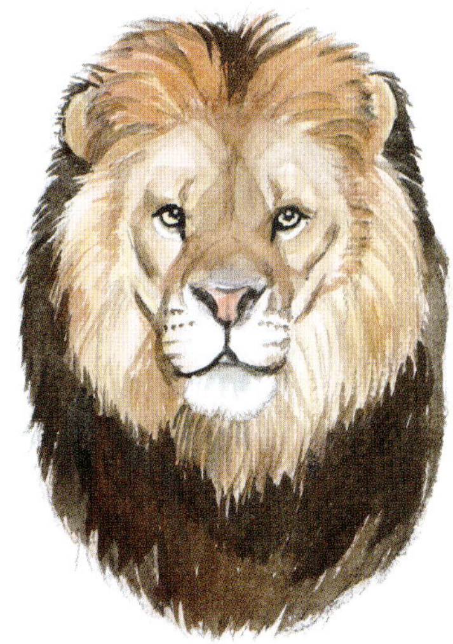

Step 5

Refine the Nose and Mouth

With a diluted brown from Step 4, darken the center of the face in a soft triangle between the eyes and down to the nose, and use the same mix to define creases above the eyes and along the cheeks. Add cooler accents with a gentle gray made from Phthalo Blue and Burnt Sienna. Then use your dark mix to refine the nostrils, mouth, whisker dots, and deepen shadows inside the ears, beneath the chin, and in the mane's darkest areas.

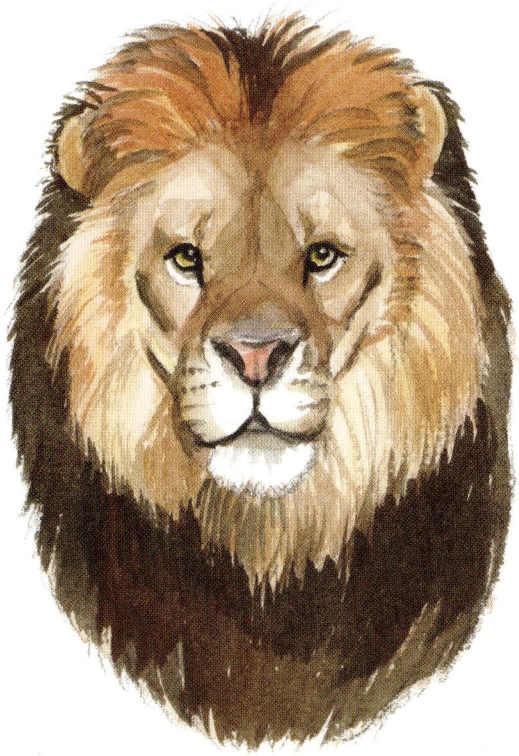

Step 6

Finish the Lion

Glaze a light brown wash over the sides of the muzzle to round out its form. Then step back and selectively darken any areas that need extra contrast to bring out the lion's commanding presence.

Snoozing Red Panda

Paint a cozy red panda and master soft fur textures, warm shadows, and the gentle features of this sleepy little creature.

COLORS

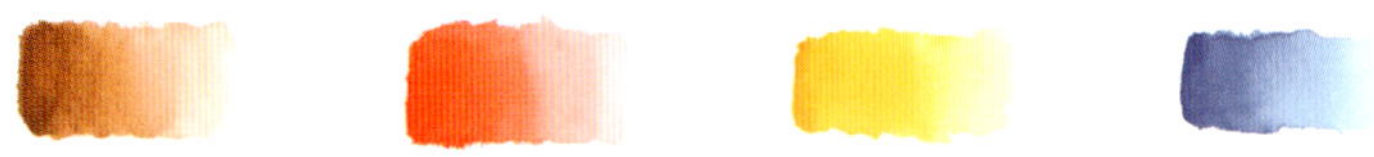

Burnt Sienna	Pyrrol Scarlet	New Gamboge	Phthalo Blue (GS)

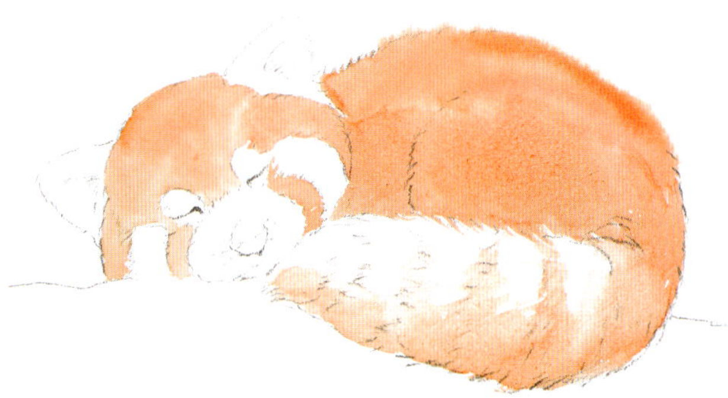

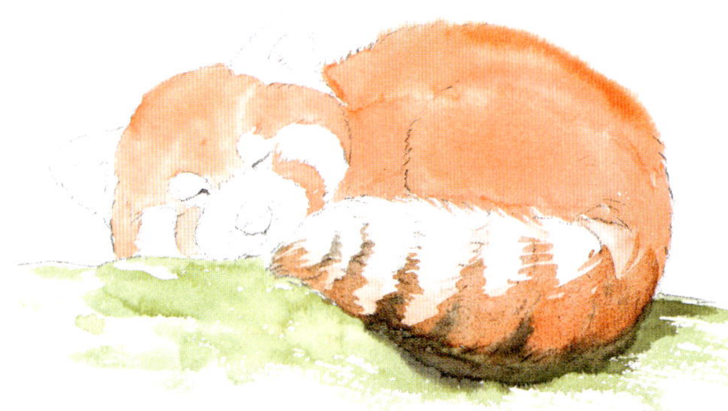

Step 1

Lay in the Red Fur

Brush clear water over the back, head, and tail, extending slightly beyond your pencil marks to avoid hard edges. Mix a warm red orange from Burnt Sienna, Pyrrol Scarlet, and New Gamboge, and drop it into the damp areas, letting it soften outward. Use the same mix for the head markings and underside of the tail.

Scan to watch a video.

Step 2

Paint the Tree and Tail Base

Create a mossy green from Phthalo Blue (GS) and New Gamboge and brush it loosely across the branch. For shadows beneath the tail, shift that green toward brown by adding Pyrrol Scarlet. Begin hinting at tail rings with soft strokes that follow the fur's direction.

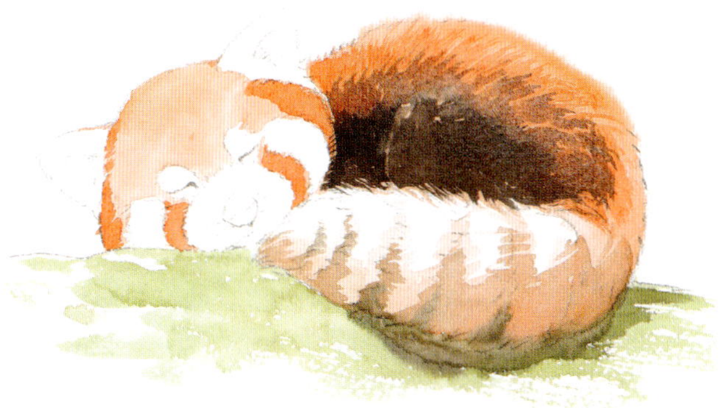

Step 3

Darken the Body

Glaze a second layer of your warm red mix over the back and head, concentrating on shadowed areas and using splayed bristles to suggest fur texture. Then mix a nearly black brown from Burnt Sienna and Phthalo Blue to darken the shaded body behind the tail, leaving a slightly lighter patch to hint at the tucked hind leg.

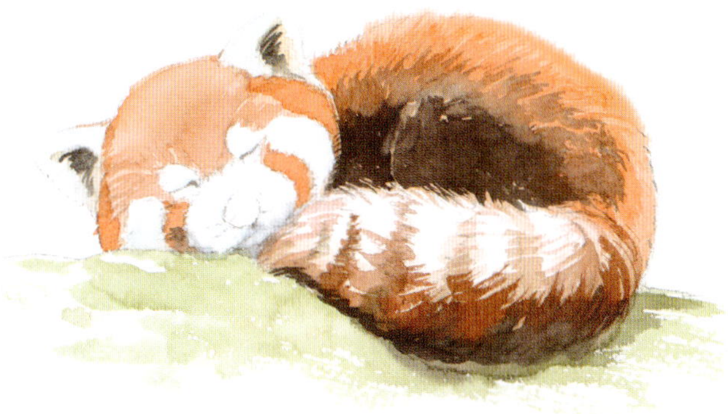

Step 4

Add Texture and Subtle Shadows

With your reddish-brown mix, deepen the tail stripes and add another soft wash across the head. Use your darkest mix for the inner ears and shadows under the tail. For the white face areas, glaze a faint tint of Phthalo Blue for natural-looking shadows, avoid the snout and eyelids to keep them bright.

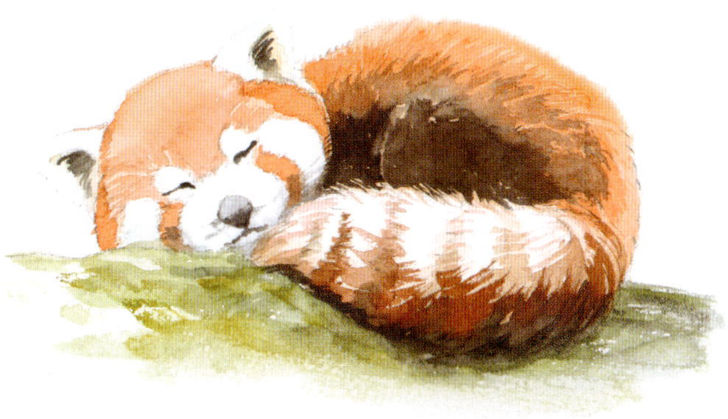

Step 5

Define the Facial Features and Tree Bark

With a fine point and black mix made with Phthalo Blue (GS) and Pyrrol Scarlet, carefully paint the eyes, nose, and mouth. Lightly tint the nose top and whisker pads with watery gray. For bark texture, drag a dry brush loaded with New Gamboge (dirtied slightly with your palette colors) across the paper to suggest rough mossy texture.

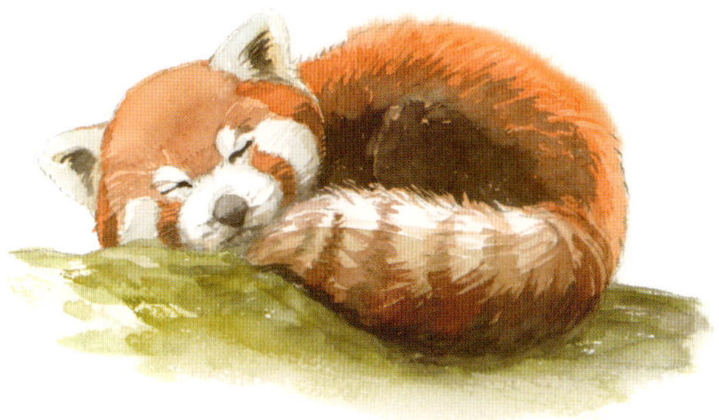

Step 6

Add Final Touches

Glaze a few warm shadows across the cheeks, snout, and tail to round out the form. Adjust any details to bring your sleepy red panda to life.

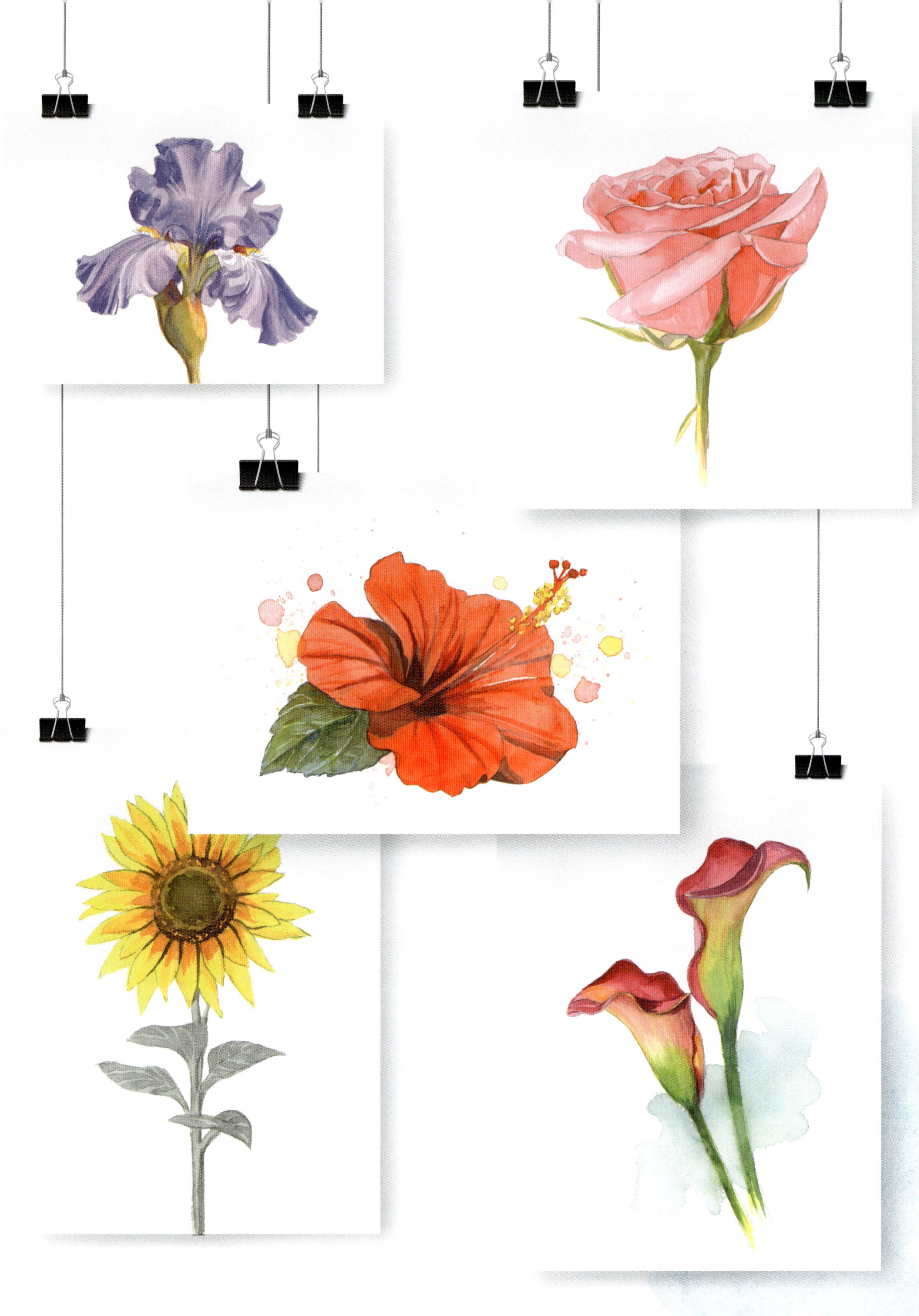

CHAPTER 4

20-Minute Flowers

No two flowers are alike, and that's what makes them such joyful subjects. In this chapter, we'll paint everything from bold garden blooms to wild meadow blossoms, learning how to express their unique character through color, light, and brushwork.

Calla Lilies

Celebrate the elegance of calla lilies in this luminous botanical study. Through gentle, layered washes, you'll build transparent color and subtle dimension, revealing the graceful curves and quiet charm of these timeless blooms.

COLORS

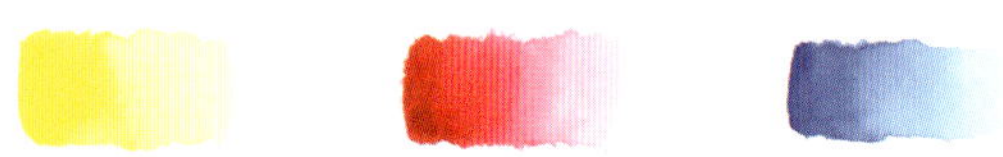

Hansa Yellow Light	Quinacridone Rose	Phthalo Blue (GS)

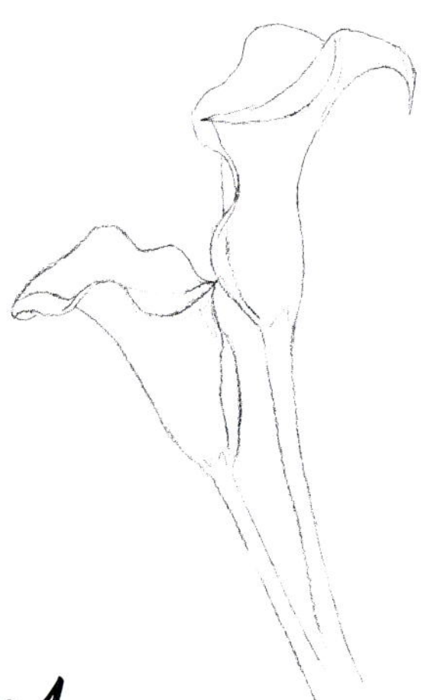

Step 1

Sketch Your Lovely Lilies

Start by lightly sketching or tracing your lilies. Pay attention to the tilt of the stems and the wavy, delicate edges of the flower openings. Try making one flower a bit taller than the other. It creates beautiful asymmetry and adds visual interest!

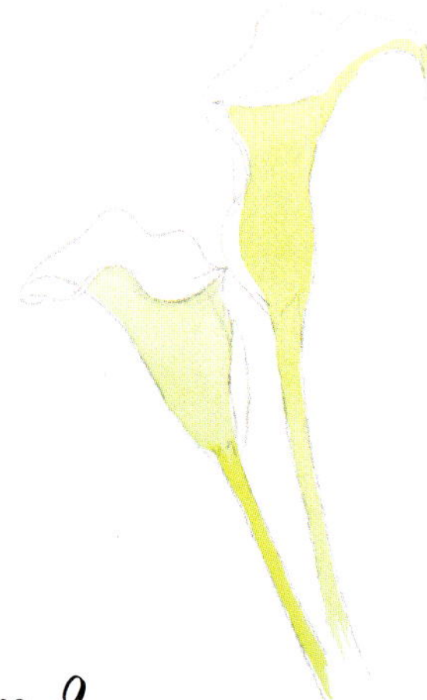

Step 2

Lay Down a Sunny Yellow Base

On your palette, mix a milky puddle of Hansa Yellow Light. (Mine was tinted green.) Paint this yellow wet-on-dry into the stems and the base of each flower. Quickly mix up some Quinacridone Rose so you're ready for the next step!

Scan to watch a video.

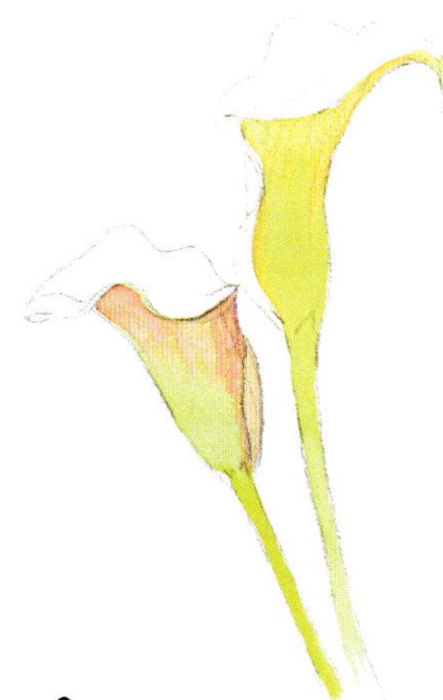

Step 3

Add Soft Pink to the Spathes

While the yellow is still damp, dip your brush into milky Quinacridone Rose and gently sweep downward strokes onto the leafy spathes of each flower. Concentrate the color beneath the wavy openings, where the shadows are deepest, to give them shape and depth.

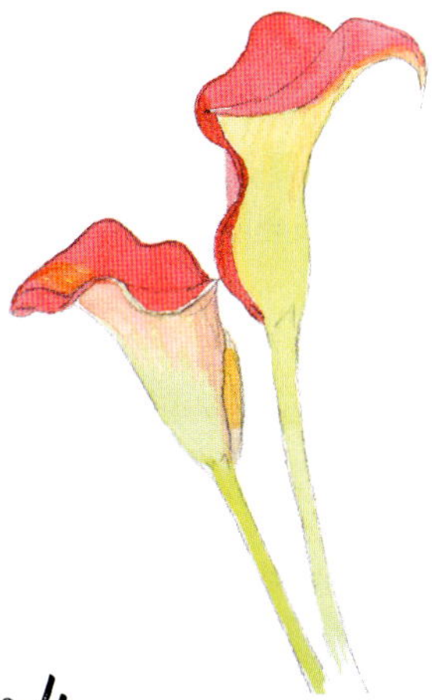

Step 4

Paint the Pink Flower Interiors

Use creamy Hansa Yellow Light to brighten the folded parts of the first flower and a small section of the inner spathe. Next, fill in the entire interior of both flowers with medium-value Quinacridone Rose (aim for a consistency that's milky, almost creamy!). This vibrant pink will make your lilies glow!

Scan to watch a video.

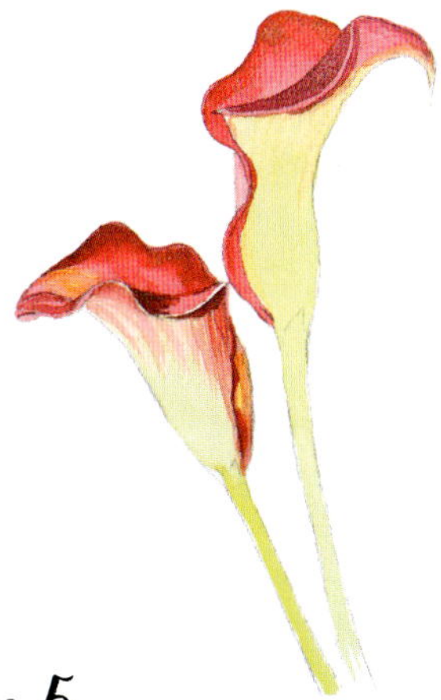

Step 5

Add Depth with Dark Details

Now let's make your lilies pop! Mix a creamy blend of Quinacridone Rose and a touch of Phthalo Blue (GS) for a gorgeous, rich dark that complements your pink petals. Paint this mixture into the folds and shadows of the spathes, especially underneath the parts that flatten at the top. Add subtle texture by gently dragging downward pink brushstrokes across each flower for delicate shading.

Scan to watch a video.

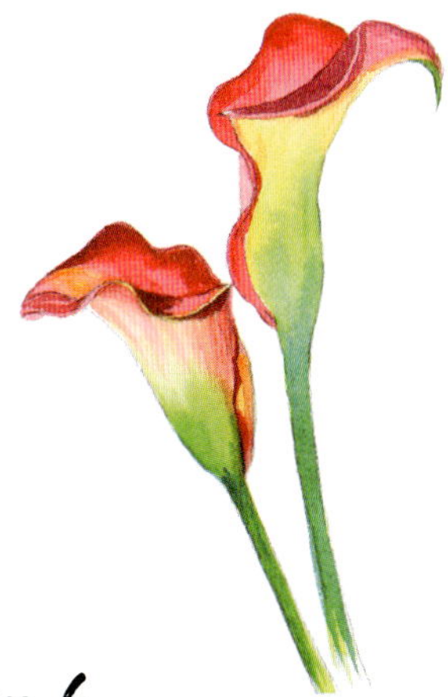

Step 6

Create Gorgeous Green Stems

Time to turn those stems green! Rewet one stem at a time with clean water. While it's damp, drop in milky Phthalo Blue, adjusting with a bit of yellow if the blue is too intense. Use more watery blue toward the tops of the stems so they gradually fade into the bright yellow you painted earlier. The result? A brilliant, lively green created by glazing blue over yellow.

Step 7

Add a Playful Splash of Background Color

For a fun finishing touch, load your brush with any leftover watery Phthalo Blue and wash it into the background, right over and around the stems. This cool blue pushes your warm flowers forward in the painting and adds a whimsical, carefree vibe to your composition.

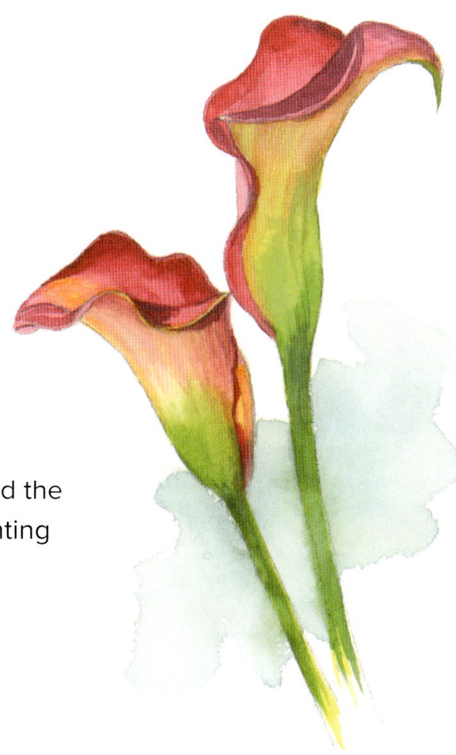

Cheery Sunflower

Capture pure sunshine on paper with this joyful sunflower project. You'll explore how brilliant yellows glow against soft greens, using simple layers and lively brushwork to create a flower that radiates warmth and happiness.

COLORS

Hansa Yellow Light

Pyrrol Scarlet

Phthalo Blue (GS)

New Gamboge

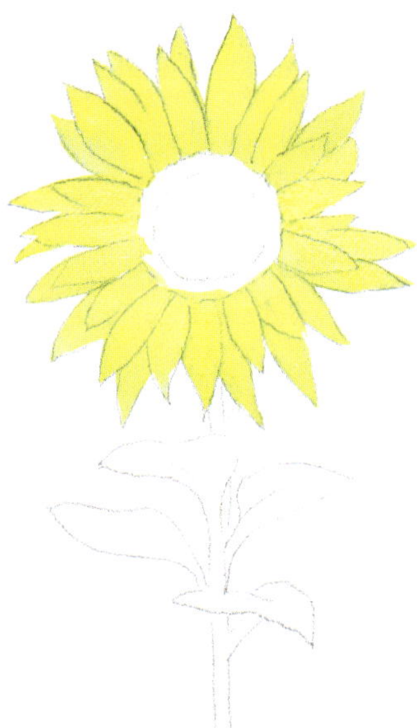

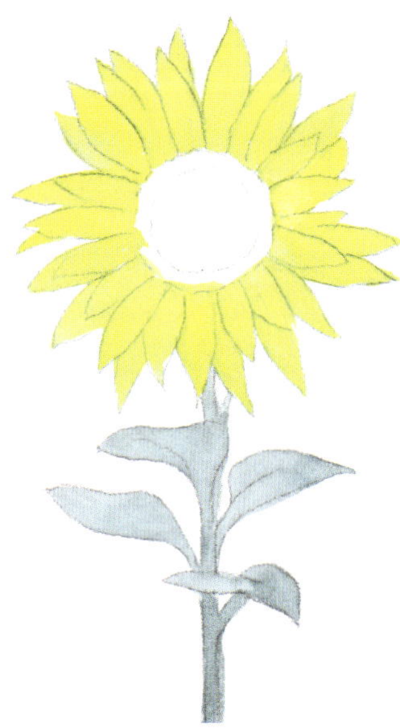

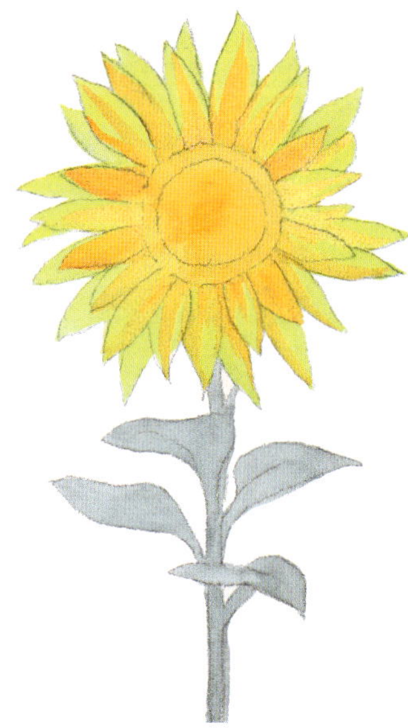

Step 1

Paint the Bright Petal Base

Paint a fresh first layer using pure Hansa Yellow Light across all the sunflower petals. Keep the brushstrokes light and clean. This sets the stage for those glowing petal layers.

Step 2

Paint the Stem and Leaves

Mix a cool slate green with mostly Phthalo Blue (GS) and a hint of Pyrrol Scarlet. Use this watery mix for the stem and leaves, painting carefully around the flower base.

Scan to watch a video.

Step 3

Warm Up the Flower

Now mix a milky New Gamboge and layer it over the center of the sunflower and a few selected petals. Leave some of the outer petals with just the initial yellow. This variation gives your flower depth and glow.

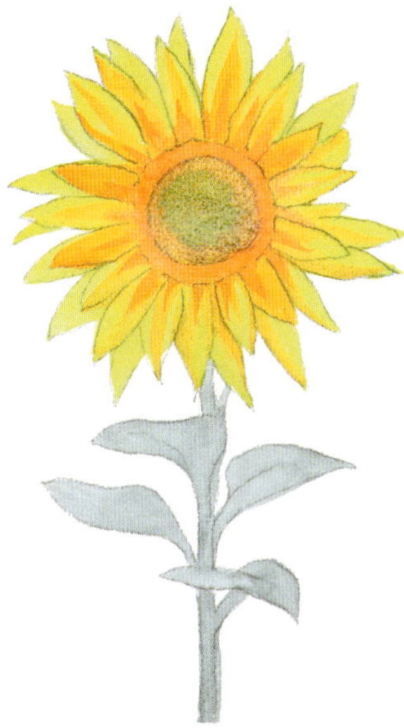

Step 4

Define Disk, Shadows, and Center

Use watery Pyrrol Scarlet to paint the warm reddish ring around the center disk, then pull a few loose, sunbeam-like strokes across selected petals to suggest gentle shadows and folds. Follow with a thin wash of watery Phthalo Blue (GS) over the yellowed center to create a natural, earthy green in the middle of the bloom.

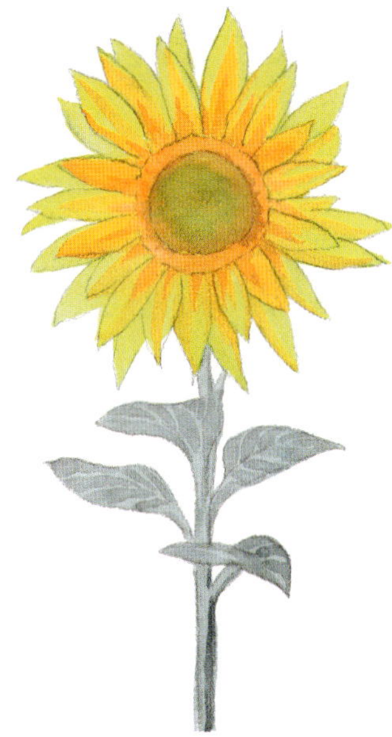

Step 5

Leaf Details with Negative Painting

Revisit your green-gray mix (Phthalo Blue and a touch of Pyrrol Scarlet), and use it to add detail to the leaves. This time, negative-paint around the veins, letting the lighter underlayer peek through for a realistic, textured leaf look.

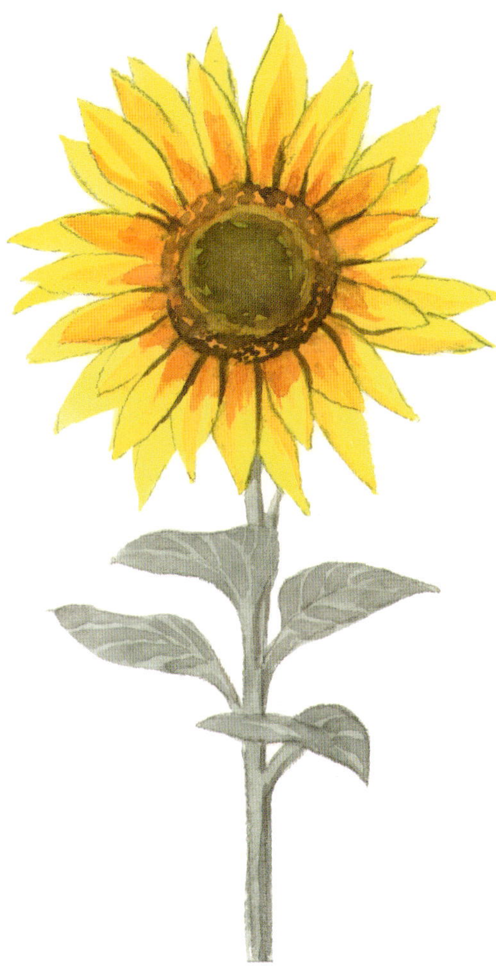

Step 6

Final Rich Darks and Finishing Touches

Mix a deep, rich brown using your three primaries (Phthalo Blue, Pyrrol Scarlet, and New Gamboge) in a creamy consistency. Dot this into the outer ring of the disk to suggest seeds. Use a thinner version to darken the center and lightly define petal shadows and creases. Finally, darken the base of the stem and leaves to complete your sunflower with beautiful depth and contrast.

Scan to watch a video.

Coneflower

This cheerful garden favorite is a great way to practice glazing techniques. You'll layer both thin transparent washes and deeper darks, learning how to balance luminosity with contrast.

COLORS

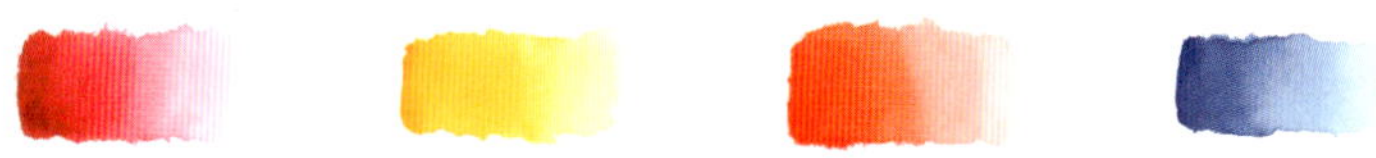

Quinacridone Rose | New Gamboge | Pyrrol Scarlet | Phthalo Blue (GS)

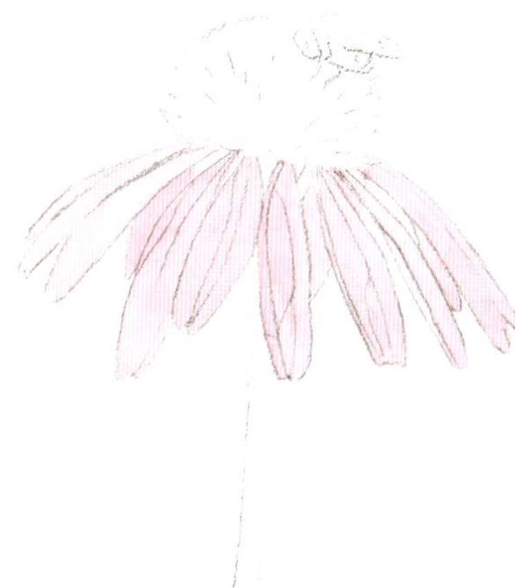

Step 1

Paint the Petal Wash

Lay down a very watery wash of Quinacridone Rose over each petal, wet-on-dry. Keep it light. You'll deepen the colors in later steps.

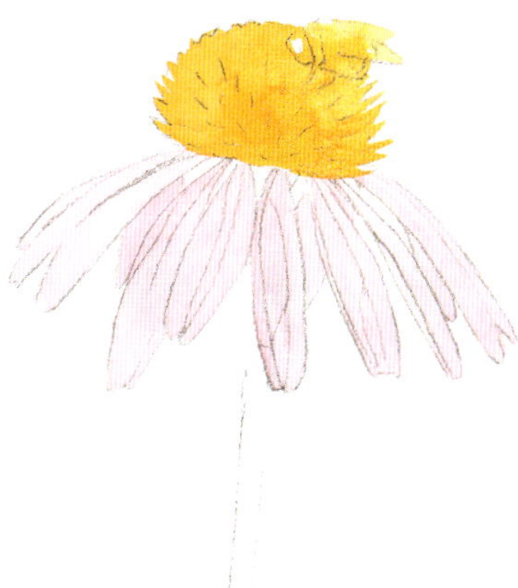

Step 2

Paint the Golden Cone

Rinse and blot your brush, then load it with creamy New Gamboge. Fill in the cone and give the bee its first layer of yellow, leaving a tiny highlight on the bee's head untouched.

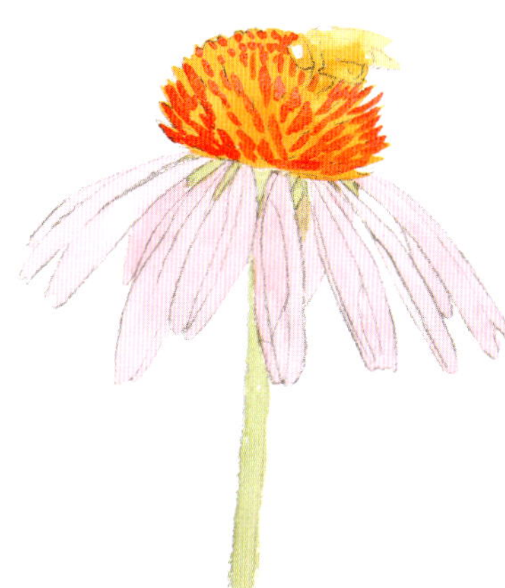

Step 3

Add Red Speckles and a Stem

With Pyrrol Scarlet, use short, upward strokes radiating out from the center of the cone, letting bits of yellow peek through for texture. Mix a muted green with diluted New Gamboge and Phthalo Blue, and carefully paint the stem. Use this same green between the petals at the flower's base for extra depth.

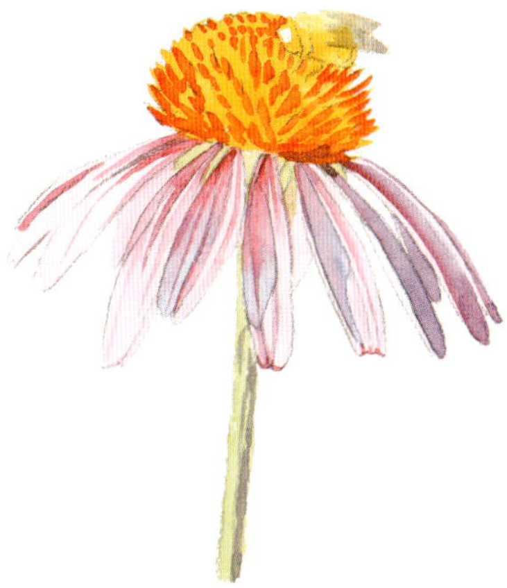

Step 4

Begin Adding Cool Shadows

Set up two puddles on your palette: one milky Quinacridone Rose, the other diluted Phthalo Blue. Work one petal at a time. Glaze a pink base, then brush in the blue alongside it. The wet-on-wet blending will create luminous, natural-looking shadows.

Scan to watch a video.

Step 5

Finish Petals and Paint the Bee

Strengthen the petals with your rose-blue mix, deepening purples in the shadowed areas. Use the same mix, diluted to a soft gray, for the stem shadow and a light wash over the bee's wings to keep them transparent. Then mix a creamy near-black with Phthalo Blue and Pyrrol Scarlet, and with the fine tip of your brush paint the bee's head and body, preserving the tiny highlight.

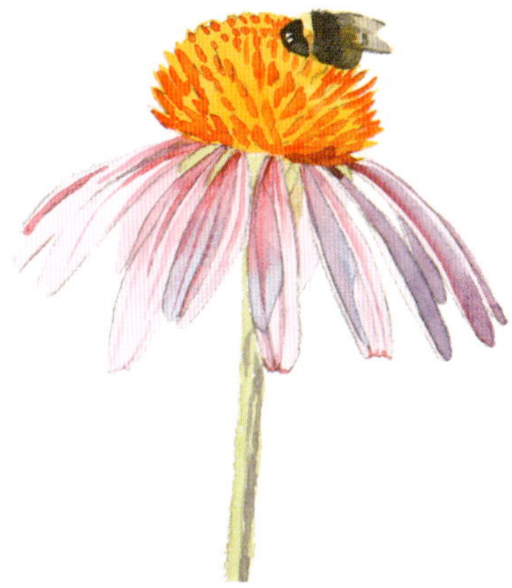

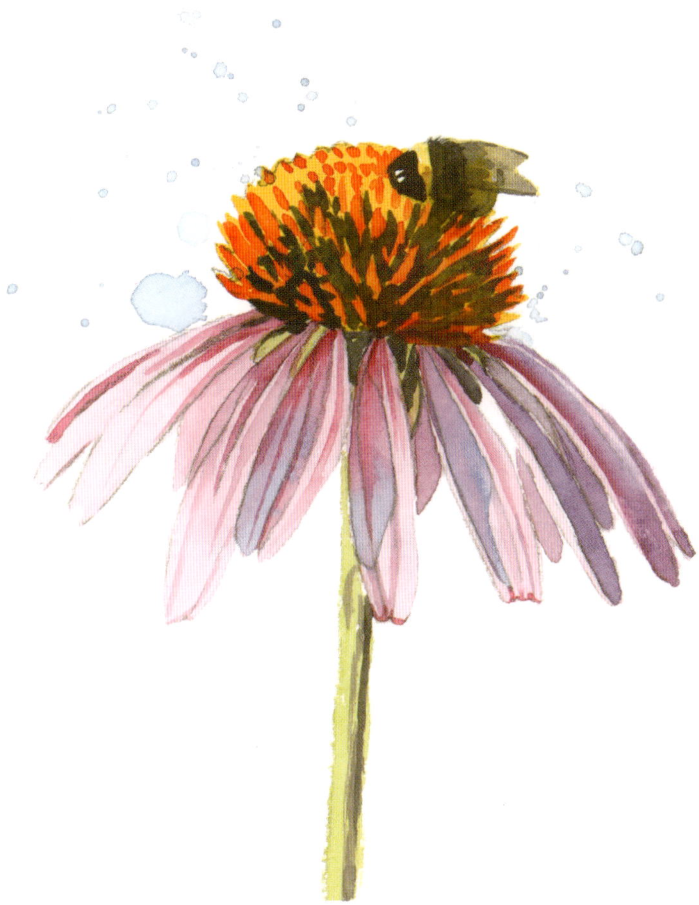

Step 6

Final Darks and Spatter

Finish the flower with the black base of the cone, negative painting around your reds and leaving the top of the flower glowing yellow. Reload your brush often and twist it to a point for crisp details. Strengthen any needed shadows in the petals or stem. For a playful finishing touch, spatter watery Phthalo Blue around the flower.

Scan to watch a video.

Hibiscus

Dive into your richest reds with this vibrant tropical hibiscus project. You'll practice subtle negative painting to suggest realistic leaf and petal details while keeping the composition bold, modern, and full of island energy.

COLORS

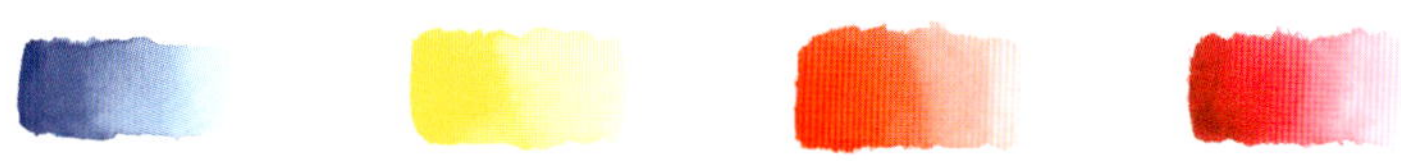

Phthalo Blue (GS) | Hansa Yellow Light | Pyrrol Scarlet | Quinacridone Rose

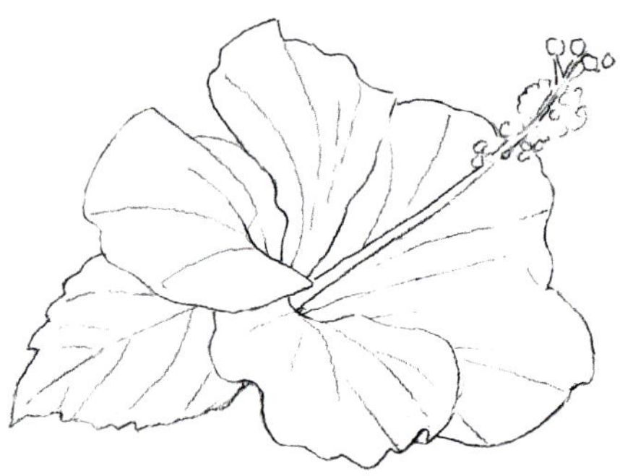

Step 1

Sketch the Flower

Begin by sketching or tracing the flower outline. Pay close attention to the shape and direction of each petal, and note the gentle curve of the leaf. Lightly mark the stamen's 45-degree tilt as it rises from the flower's center. This angle adds a sense of natural movement and elegance to your composition.

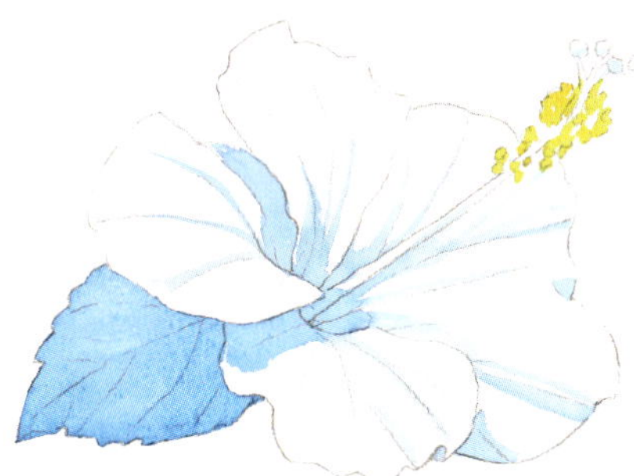

Step 2

Create a Blue Underpainting

Mix Phthalo Blue (GS) to a milky consistency, and use it to gently paint in the leaf and the slender shadows that define the form inside the flower.

Next, switch to creamy Hansa Yellow Light and carefully paint the bright anthers on the stamen to set their glow. Let the entire underpainting dry completely before moving on to the reds.

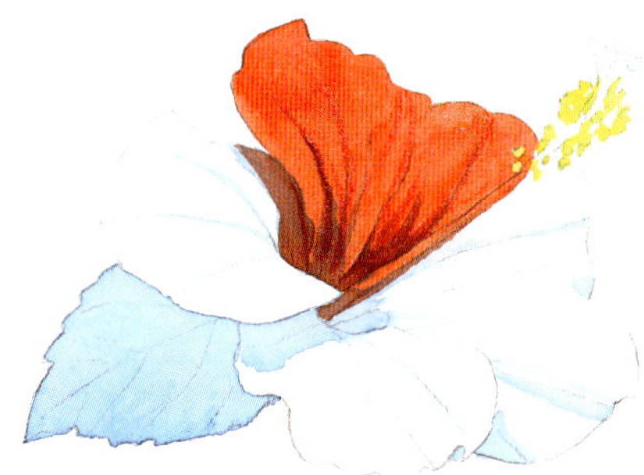

Step 3

Start Painting the Red Petals

Load a milky Pyrrol Scarlet mix and, with a sharp tip, carefully fill the first petal, avoiding the yellow anthers. While the red is damp, use a slightly drier brush to glide in Quinacridone Rose along shadows and natural creases, adding soft dimension and delicate texture.

Scan to watch a video.

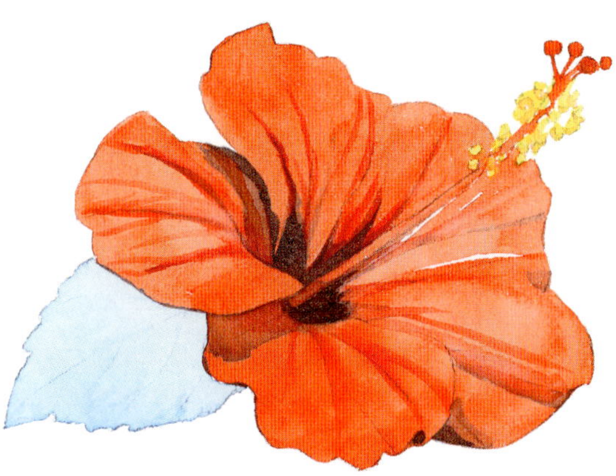

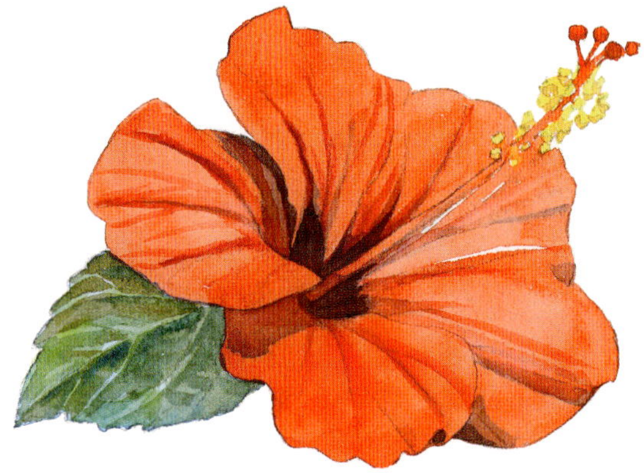

Step 4

Build Petal Depth and Vibrance

Paint each petal with warm Pyrrol Scarlet, staying within the lines. Use thinner paint toward the center to suggest curvature and gloss, and richer pigment at the base. Add Quinacridone Rose in the creases for depth. Paint the red stamen, avoiding the yellow anthers. For deep center shadows, mix Pyrrol Scarlet and Phthalo Blue (GS) into a dark purple and drop it in gently.

Step 5

Bring the Leaf to Life with Layers

To complete the leaf, mix Hansa Yellow Light, Phthalo Blue (GS), and a tiny touch of Pyrrol Scarlet to create a soft, earthy yellow green. Glaze this over your existing blue underpainting, negative painting around the veins to let them shine through naturally. While the glaze is still damp, drop in a darker blue-green (Phthalo Blue and Hansa Yellow Light) just beneath the flower and at the center of the leaf to deepen the shadows and suggest subtle folds and contours.

Scan to watch a video.

Step 6

Add a Playful Spatter Finish

For a fun and expressive final touch, create a spatter effect using watery mixes of your reds and yellow. Load your brush with very wet pigment, then gently tap it over the paper in areas where you want a bit of loose energy. For bolder droplets, lightly touch the brush tip to the paper to create larger manual "drips." This playful technique adds spontaneity and a modern twist to your floral painting.

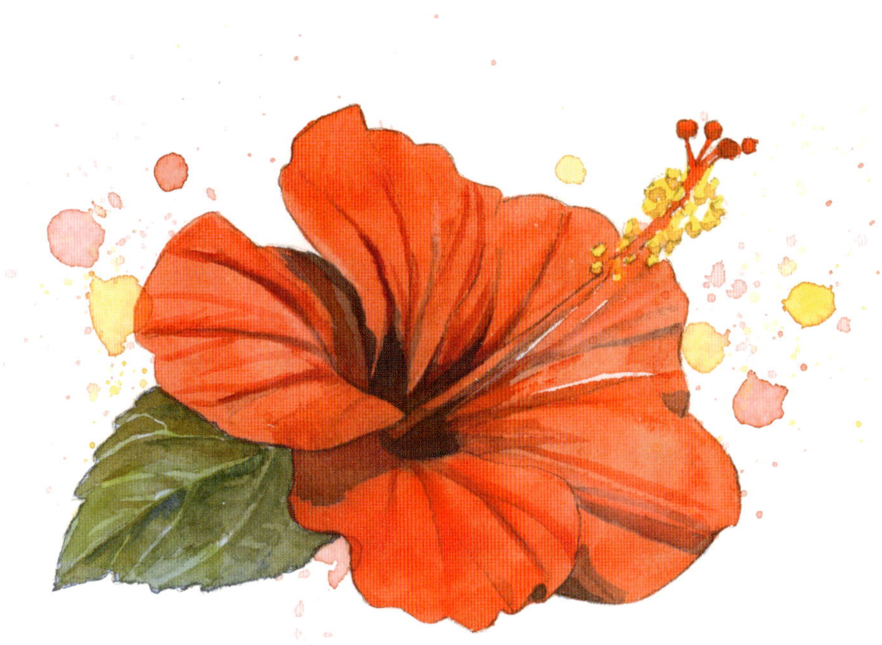

Lavender

Paint the gentle elegance of lavender in this fun, beginner-friendly project. With sweeping strokes for the leaves and bold, dotted textures for the blossoms, you'll create a delicate yet lively study that captures the essence of this fragrant flower.

COLORS

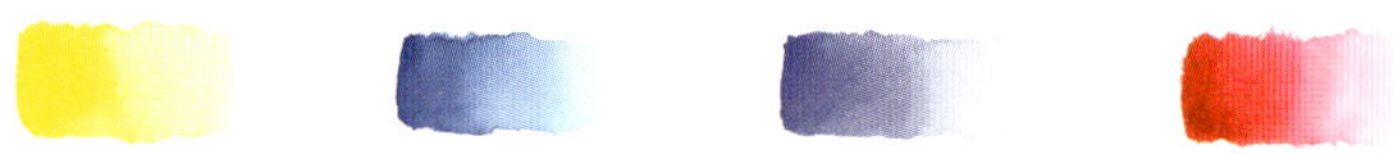

Hansa Yellow Light

Phthalo Blue (GS)

French Ultramarine

Quinacridone Rose

Step 1

Sketch the Flower Clusters

Start by drawing a central stem, then branch out with three curving "finger" shapes topped with bumpy edges. These will become your flower clusters. Vary their heights for a natural look. Add a few slender, upward-turning leaves. No need to fuss with tiny flower details; we'll let the brush do that magic later.

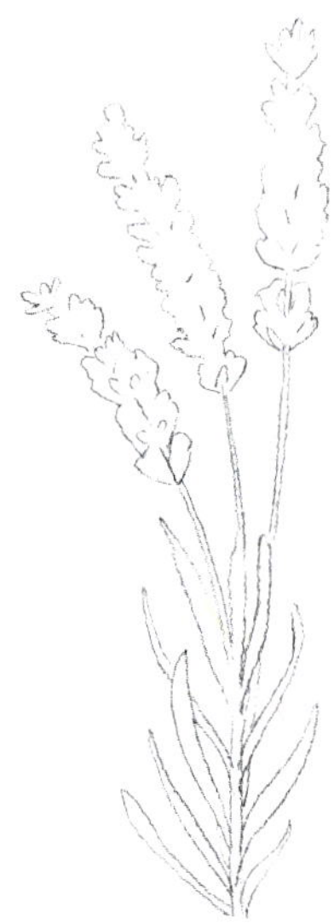

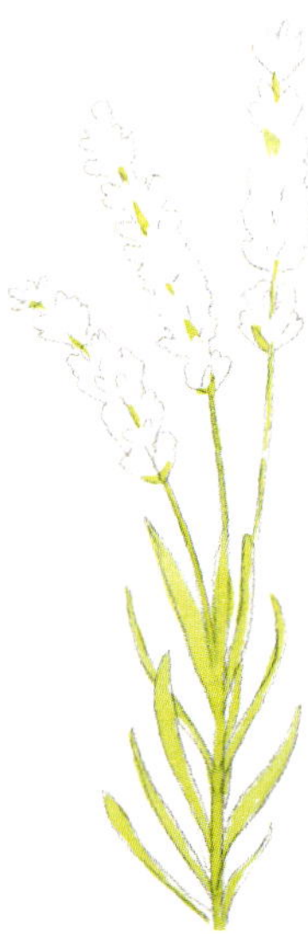

Step 2

Lay Down a Sunny Yellow Base

Load your brush with creamy Hansa Yellow Light and fill in the leaves, stems, and a few bright spots between the flower clusters. This cheerful yellow will set the stage for some glowing greens.

Scan to watch a video.

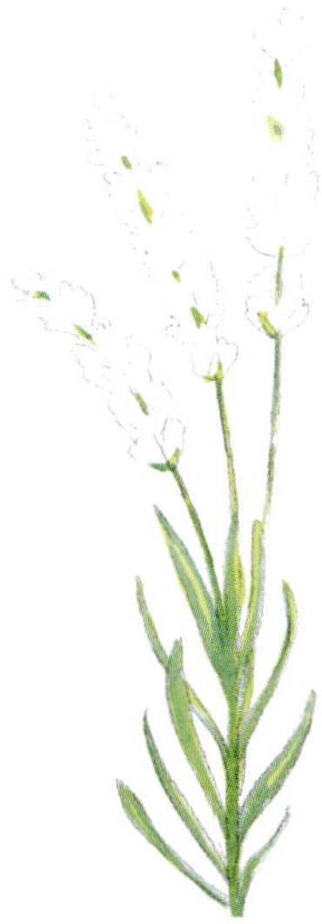

Step 3

Glaze on the Green

Now for the color alchemy! Mix up a watery Phthalo Blue (GS) and glaze it right over your yellow stems and leaves. Watch the magic happen as it transforms into a vibrant green. Leave a few slivers of yellow peeking through for extra luminosity.

Step 4

Dot in a Lavender Base

Time to bring those blossoms to life! Mix French Ultramarine with Quinacridone Rose to get a soft, watery violet. With the tip of your brush, gently dab tiny blobs where the flowers go. Let gaps peek through to create a light, airy effect. Keep it loose and playful.

Scan to watch a video.

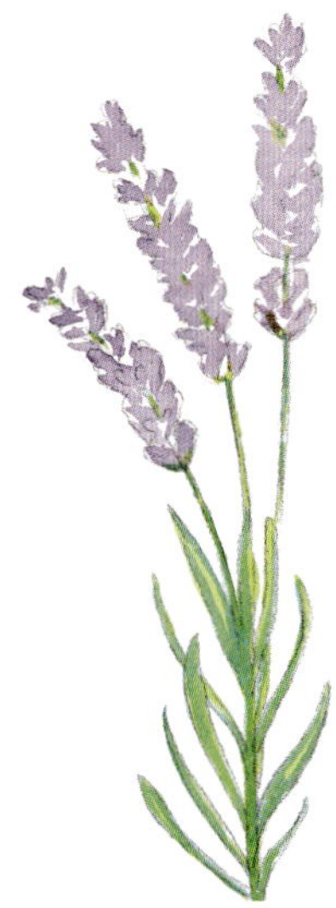

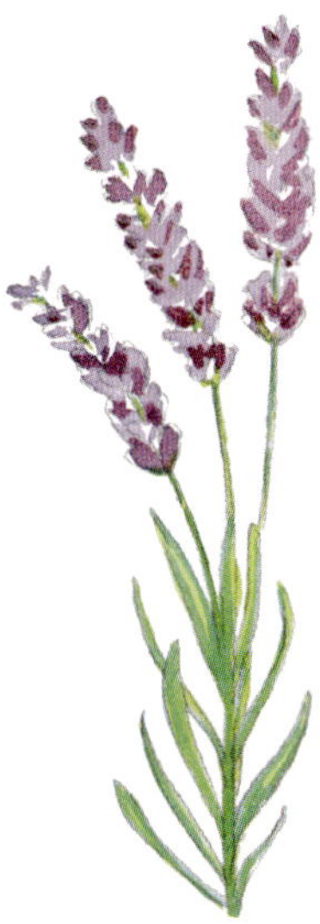

Step 5

Layer in a Pop of Red Violet

Now mix a warmer, rosier purple by using more Quinacridone Rose than blue. You want a milky red-violet shade. Add smaller dots over your first layer, creating dimension and variety. It's starting to bloom beautifully!

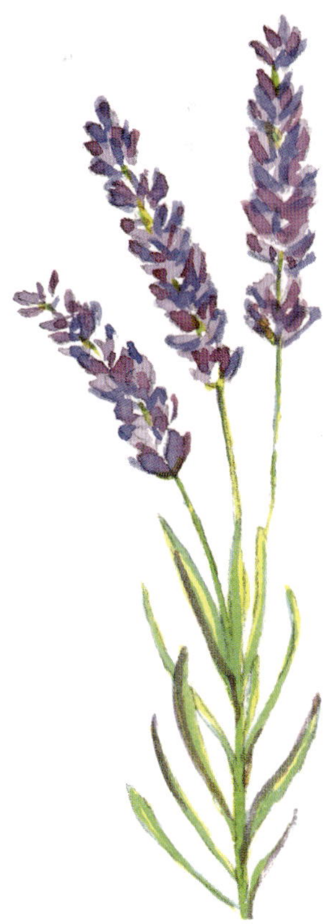

Step 6

Add Blue Violet and Finishing Touches

Balance things out with a cooler blue violet. This time, lean heavily on French Ultramarine. Dab this in and around your existing petals, letting the previous colors peek through. Finally, use this same mix to add soft shadow touches to the leaves and stems for subtle contrast and a hint of realism.

Scan to watch a video.

Pansy

Paint a realistic pansy while learning to mix beautiful purples, spring greens, and rich blacks using only primary colors. Focus on layering subtle washes to capture the velvety petals and delicate contrast that make this flower so striking.

COLORS

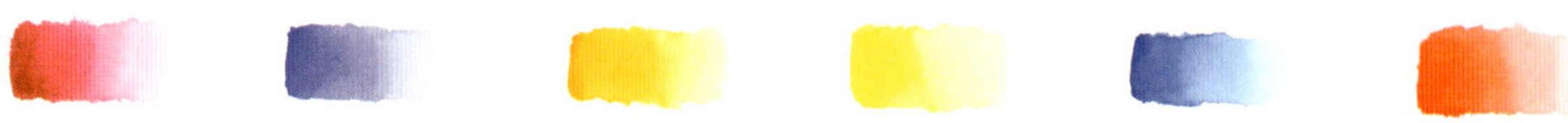

Quinacridone Rose	French Ultramarine	New Gamboge	Hansa Yellow Light	Phthalo Blue (GS)	Pyrrol Scarlet

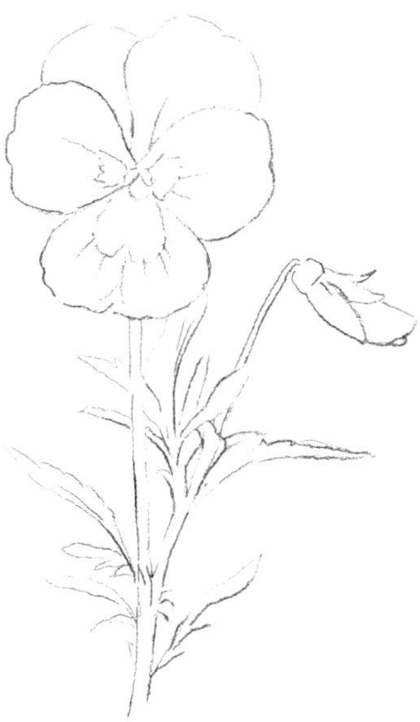

Step 1

Sketch the Flower with Guiding Shapes

Begin by sketching or tracing the flower along with its stem and leaves. Mark the center point of the bloom and lightly outline any areas where the color will shift or change.

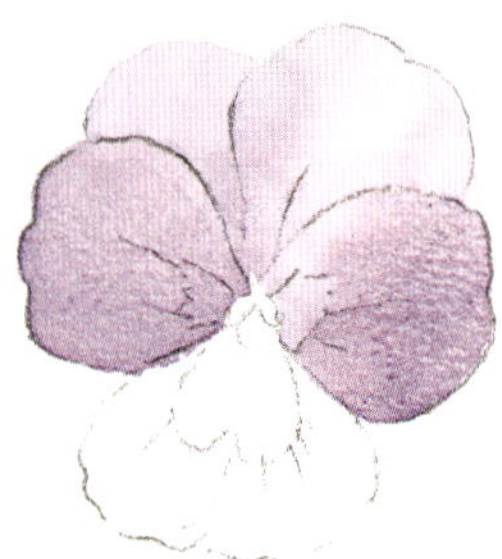

Step 2

Lay Down a Vibrant Purple Base

Mix a royal purple with Quinacridone Rose and French Ultramarine, adjusting warmer or cooler as desired. Apply a light, watery wash over the flower, leaving the center dot and bottom petal untouched. Use a thicker mix on the two center petals to make them stand out.

Scan to watch a video.

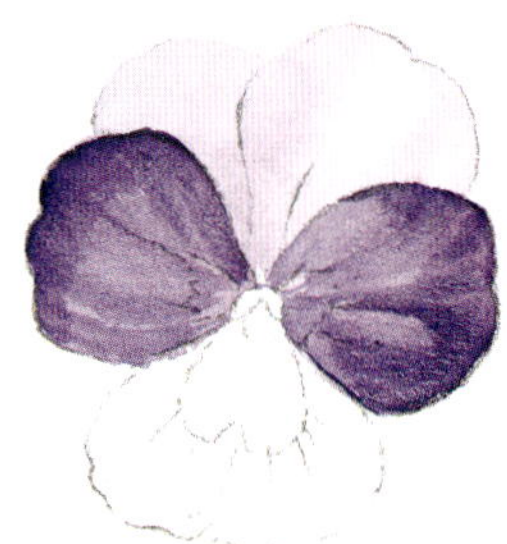

Step 3

Add Depth with Soft Petal Texture

While the middle petals are still damp, add a more concentrated mix of your purple along the outer edges. Then, using just the tip of your brush, gently pull the pigment inward to form soft ridges and natural petal texture.

Scan to watch a video.

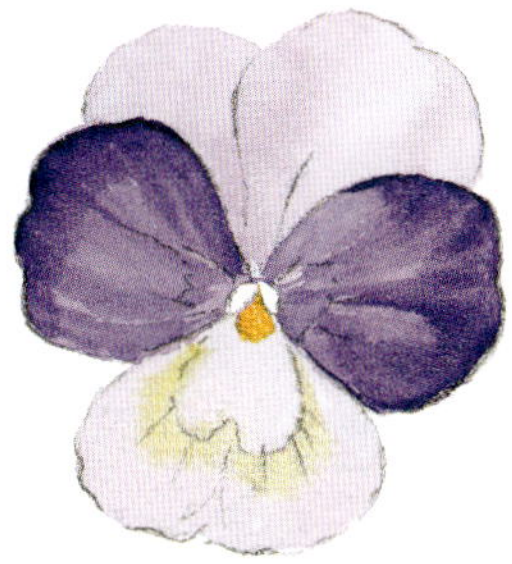

Step 4

Brighten the Center and Bottom Petal

Paint the flower's center with New Gamboge for a warm golden glow. Next, wet the bottom petal with clean water and softly add Hansa Yellow Light around the upside-down heart shape. Finish by glazing the remaining area of that petal with a diluted layer of your purple mixture.

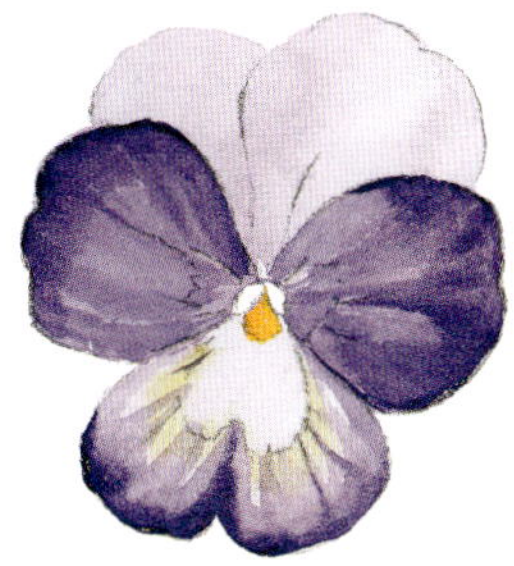

Step 5

Define Edges and Petal Veins

While the initial layer is still damp, switch to a thicker mix of your purple and gently define the edge of the petal. With a damp brush, soften the transition between light and dark areas to create smooth gradients. Lightly suggest petal veins using delicate, fine lines for added texture.

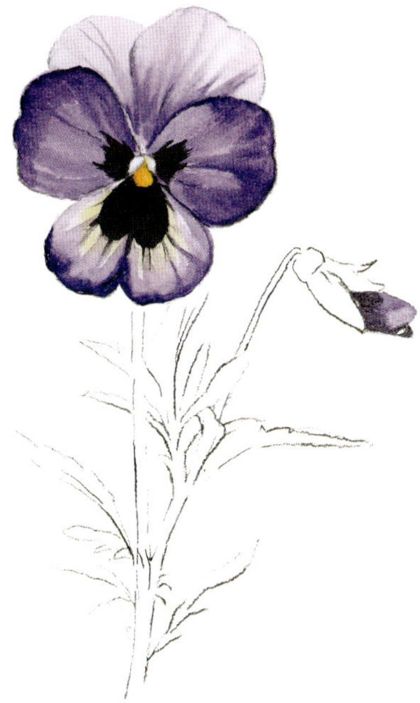

Step 6

Deepen the Shadows and Detail the Bud

Create a rich, nearly black purple by mixing Phthalo Blue with Pyrrol Scarlet. Use this bold shade to carefully define the flower's darkest shadows. For the flower bud, start with a light wash made from Quinacridone Rose and French Ultramarine. While it's still wet, drop in a touch of your creamier purple mix at the base to create dimension and depth.

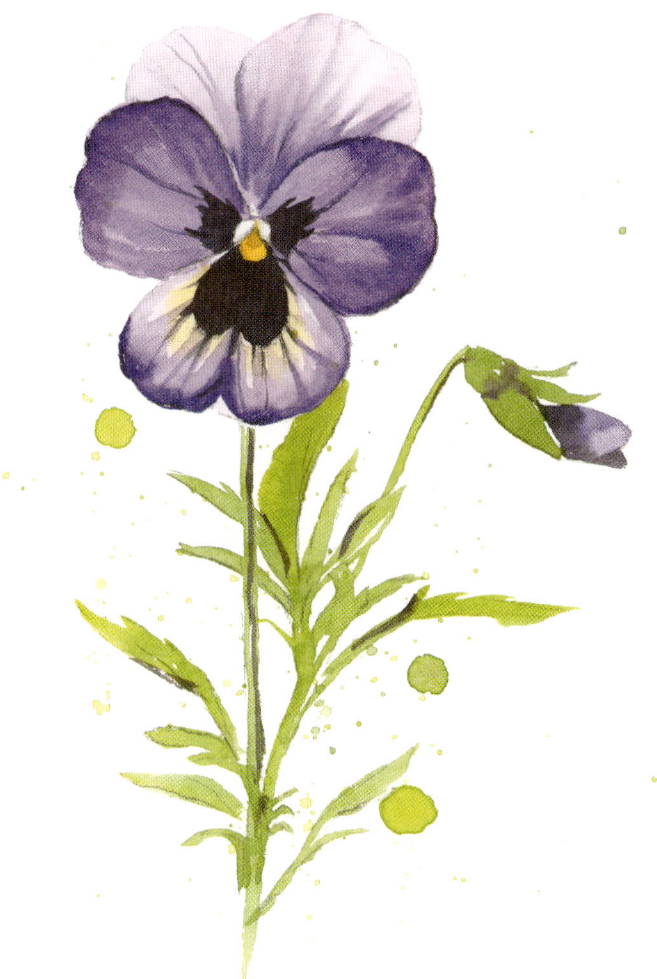

Step 7

Finish with Lively Leaves and Spatter

Finish by mixing Hansa Yellow Light with Phthalo Blue (GS) to make a fresh yellow green. Use this to fill in the leaves and stems. Then, with a hint of your dark purple, add subtle shading to select areas for contrast. For a playful final touch, load your brush with watery green and tap it gently to create a light spatter over the foliage. You can also paint a few larger droplets by hand to enhance the effect.

Pink Rose

Learn to paint a graceful rose by layering soft glazes and carefully building shadow shapes.

COLORS

Quinacridone Rose	Hansa Yellow Light	Pyrrol Scarlet	Phthalo Blue (GS)

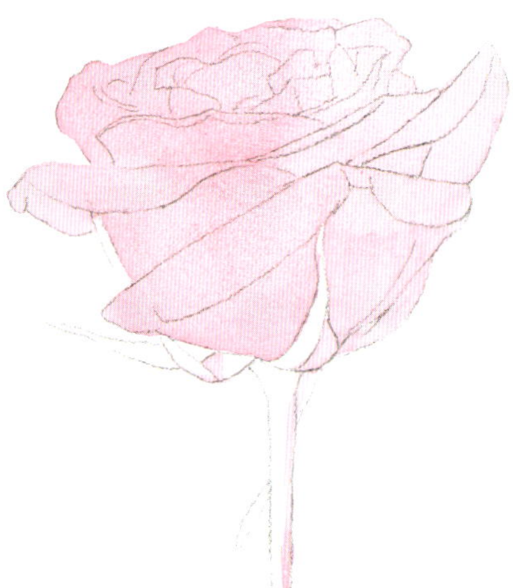

Step 1

Paint the First Wash

With a watery Quinacridone Rose, cover the entire flower in a flat wash, leaving the stem untouched. Work quickly so the color stays even.

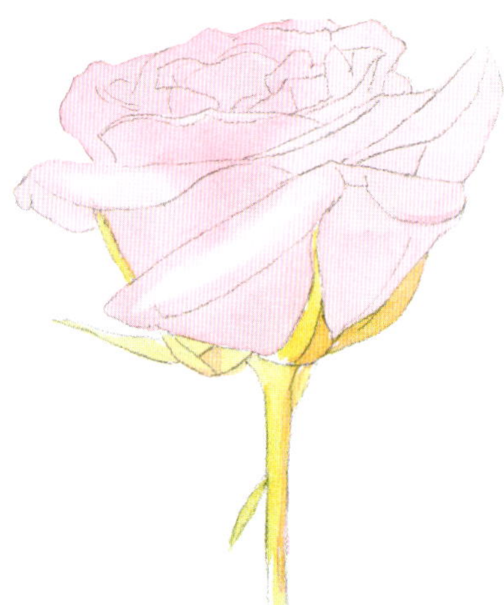

Step 2

Lift and Add the Stem

While the rose is still damp, use a clean, damp brush to gently pull out soft highlights on the broadest petals. Then paint the stem with creamy Hansa Yellow Light. Let everything dry before moving on.

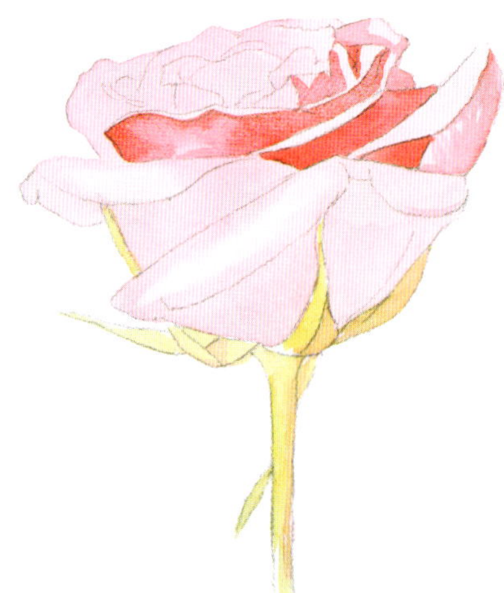

Step 3

Define the First Shadows

Mix Quinacridone Rose with Pyrrol Scarlet to make a richer pink. In a milky consistency, paint the shaded sides of the petals, leaving gaps for sunlit folds. This contrast of dark and light is what makes the flower look dimensional.

Scan to watch a video.

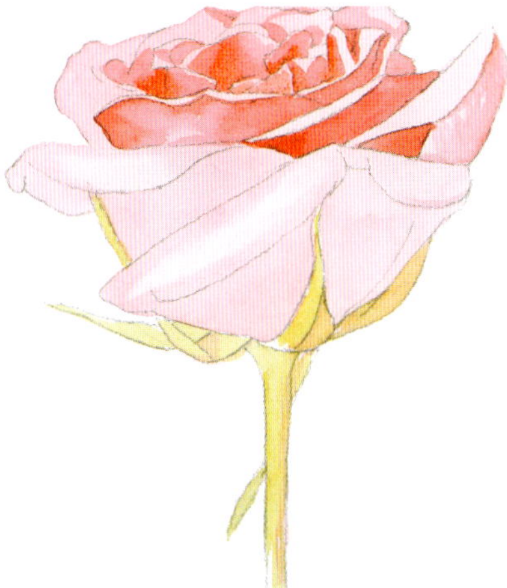

Step 4

Build Depth in the Center

The center may feel tricky because of its intricate folds. Take it one shape at a time. Darken the shadows but leave slivers of white and pink to show light catching on the curled petals.

Step 5

Shape the Larger Petals

On the broad side petals, lay down your pink mix, then quickly rinse and blot your brush. With the damp bristles, sweep along the edge to soften the transition from dark to light, creating a natural curve.

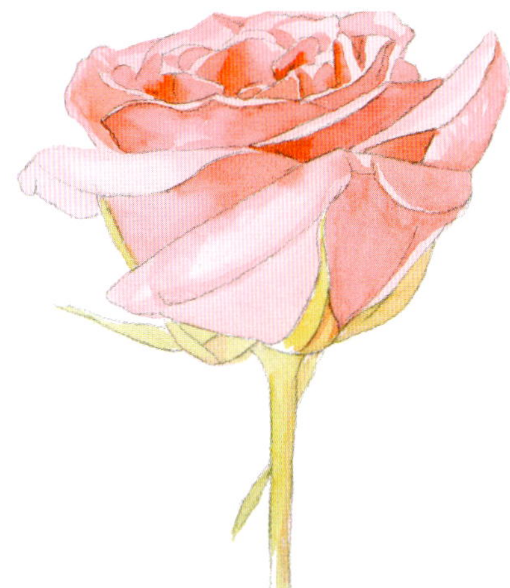

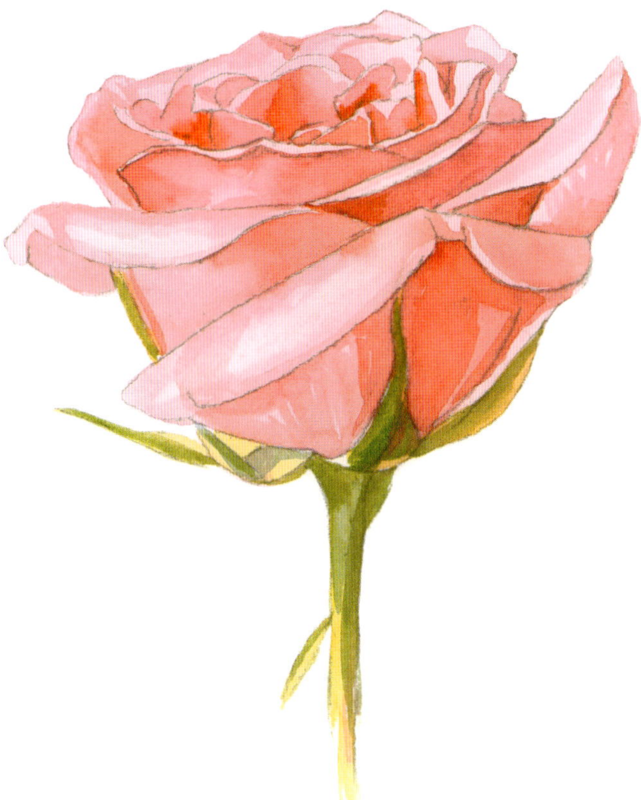

Step 6

Finishing Touches

Use more diluted pink on the petals facing the light, leaving their tops untouched for highlights and adding a few faint streaks for delicate texture. Then glaze Phthalo Blue (GS) over the yellow stem to create a soft green, and add any final touches—deepening shadows, refining folds, or strengthening highlights—to bring the rose to life.

Purple Iris

Embrace the art of patience in this luminous purple iris study. With only three primary colors, you'll build transparent layers, adding soft glazes and intricate details to reveal graceful structure and delicate beauty.

COLORS

Quinacridone Rose | French Ultramarine | New Gamboge

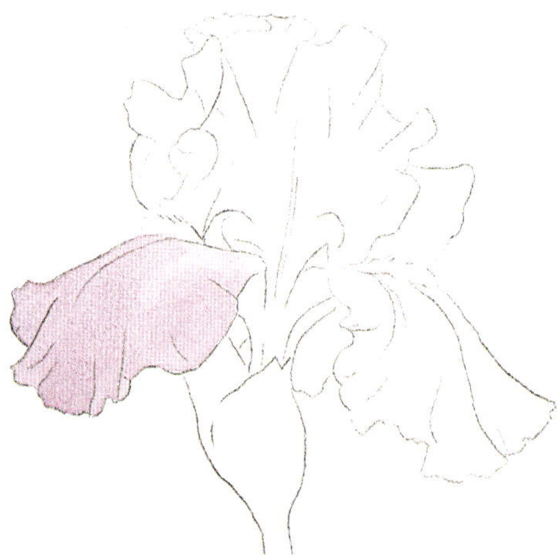

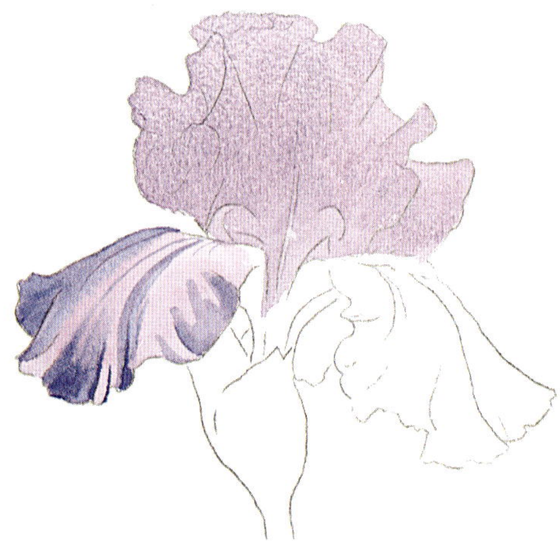

Step 1

Lay Down a Violet Base Layer

Mix Quinacridone Rose and French Ultramarine in a milky consistency to create a soft violet. Carefully fill in the first petal with this wash, keeping the edges clean and smooth.

Scan to watch a video.

Step 2

Add Rich Blue Shadows

While the base layer is still damp, drop in creamier French Ultramarine where the shadows and deeper folds of the petal appear. Use gentle, curved brushstrokes to mimic the petal's surface. While that petal dries, begin painting the violet base on the next one.

Scan to watch a video.

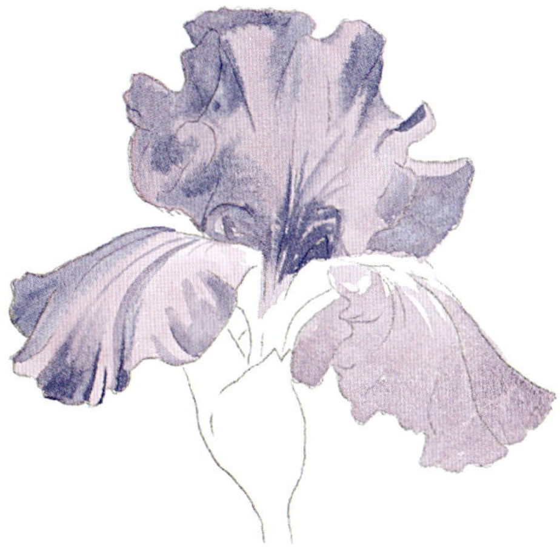

Step 3

Build Petal Texture, One Layer at a Time

Continue working one petal at a time, layering Ultramarine into the damp violet to create soft shadows and creases. This wet-on-wet technique builds natural-looking texture while keeping the petals soft and luminous.

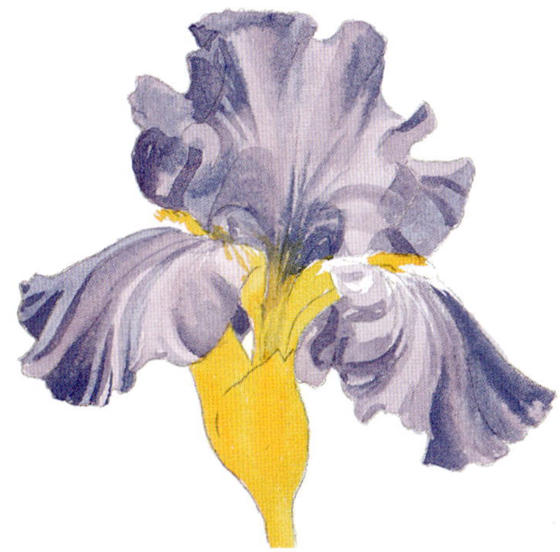

Step 4

Deepen the Petal Shadows

Once all three purple petals are dry, mix a darker violet using Quinacridone Rose and French Ultramarine. Use this to add final creases and folds, letting some of your original pale washes show through for contrast and luminosity.

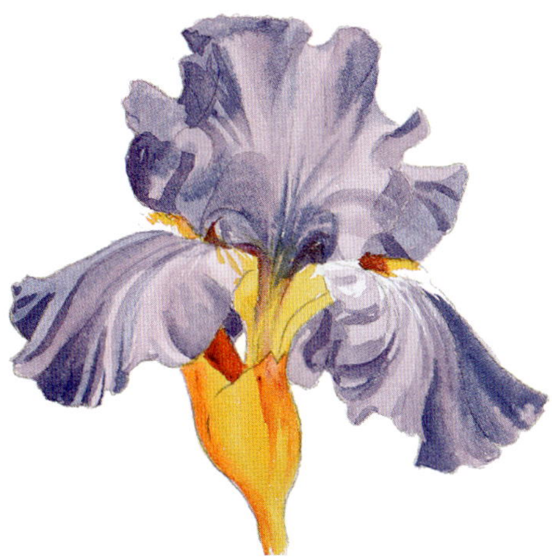

Step 5

Paint and Shade the Stem

Paint the stem with a milky wash of Gamboge Nova, keeping the edges clean so the bright yellow glows as a vibrant underlayer. Once dry, mix milky Quinacridone Rose and gently brush warm shadows along one side of the stem, softening the edges to create smooth gradients and a softly rounded form.

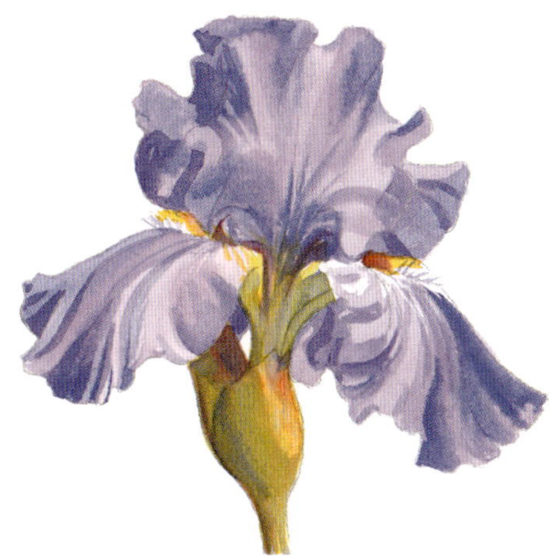

Step 6

Glaze with Blue to Shift to Green

Once the shadows are completely dry, glaze the stem with a thin wash of French Ultramarine using a wet-on-dry technique. This will subtly shift the color to a natural green and unify the tones.

Scan to watch a video.

Yellow Tulip

Paint a luminous spring bloom with glowing yellows and soft, blended shadows. This project will help you practice wet-on-wet color blending, subtle layering, and glazing with just two yellows and a touch of blue.

COLORS

Hansa Yellow Light | New Gamboge | French Ultramarine

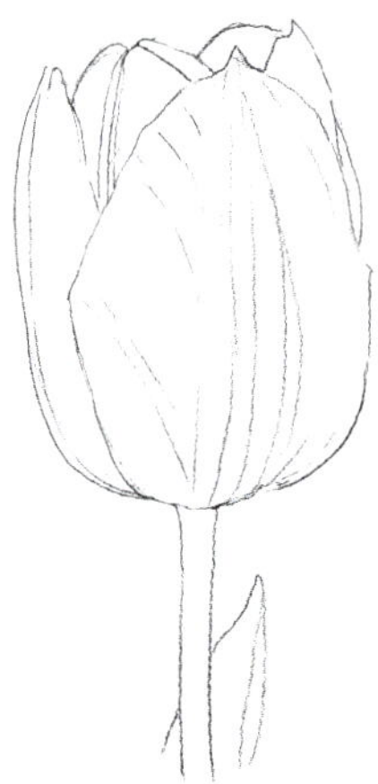

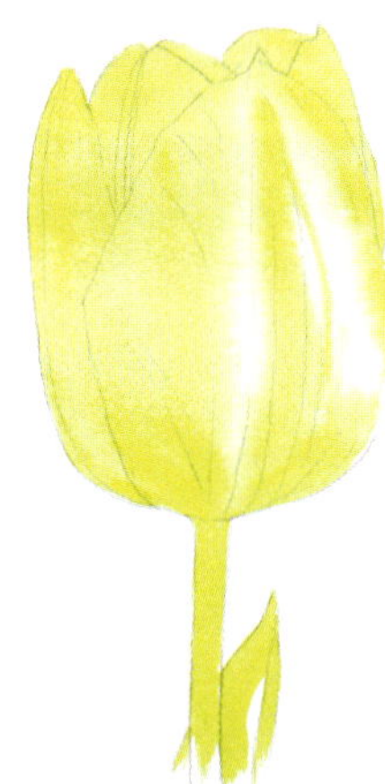

Step 1

Sketch Your Tulip

Begin by lightly sketching the tulip's rounded head with its large overlapping petals, making sure it dominates your composition. Let the petals feel slightly irregular. They should curve and overlap naturally, not look too stiff. Add a long, graceful stem and a simple leaf. Keep the drawing clean, but mark out a few highlight areas you'd like to preserve later.

Step 2

Paint the First Yellow Wash

Using a large soft brush, wet the inside of the tulip head and stem with clear water until the paper looks glossy but without puddles. Load up with creamy Hansa Yellow Light and paint across the entire flower, letting the color flow freely in the damp areas. Skip over the highlight zones you sketched earlier so they remain the untouched white of the paper. This first wash will give the tulip its luminous "glow from within."

Scan to watch a video.

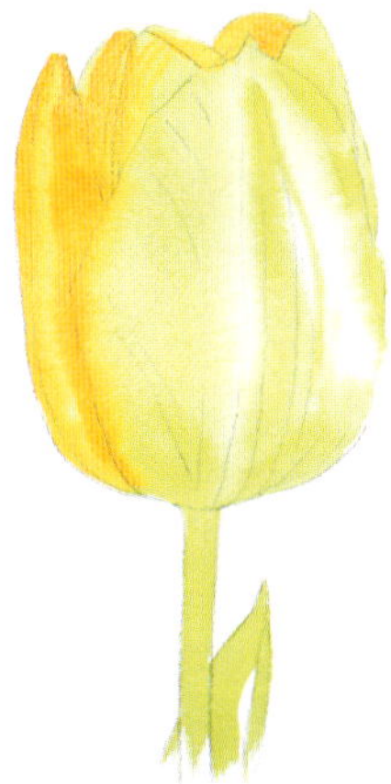

Step 3

Build the Warm Shadows

While the yellow wash is damp, switch to creamy New Gamboge and glaze it with gentle downward strokes along the left side and inner folds, following the petal curves. The damp paper will soften the strokes into natural shadows. Adjust your brush moisture—too wet causes blooms, too dry prevents smooth blending.

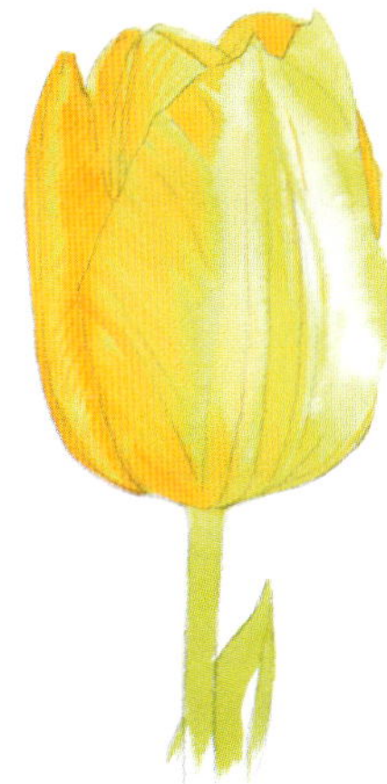

Step 4

Layer Petal Shapes

Once the first layers are dry, return with more New Gamboge to add subtle petal shapes. Vary the intensity: richer color for the shaded petals and lighter, diluted strokes for the ones catching more light. On the right-hand side, where the sun hits, keep your brushwork lighter and airier. This gentle shift in values—from deep gold shadows to soft lemon highlights—will help the flower feel rounded and alive.

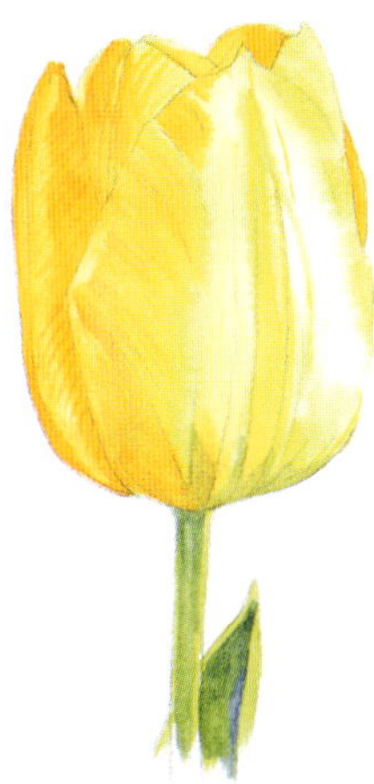

Step 5

Mix Fresh Greens for the Stem and Leaf

Mix a soft green by blending French Ultramarine with New Gamboge. Start with a thin watery version for the entire stem and leaf, then deepen the shadowed areas with a stronger, creamier mix. Keep your strokes smooth and vertical to match the direction of growth. To tie the stem and flower together, dilute Ultramarine into a pale blue and brush it lightly under the petals near the stem.

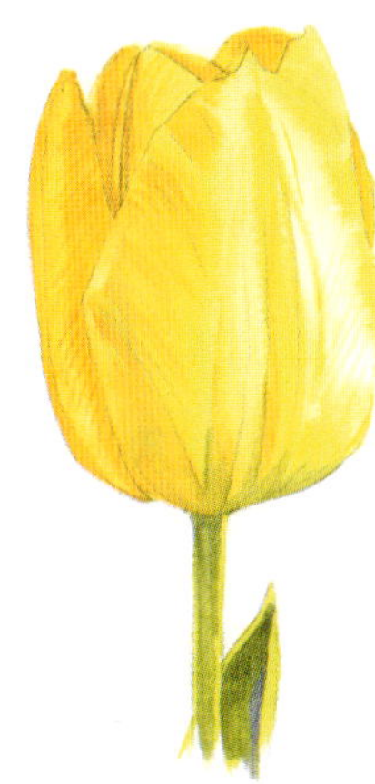

Step 6

Add Final Texture and Glazes

Now for the finishing touches! Use Hansa Yellow Light to streak a few delicate lines across the brightest petals, suggesting subtle veins. If the shadow side feels too pale, add one more transparent glaze of New Gamboge, carefully layered to avoid covering your highlights. Stand back and look. Your tulip should now have the fresh, glowing quality of a botanical study, simple but radiant.

Scarlet Zinnia

Paint a bold and cheerful zinnia bursting with warm yellows and fiery scarlet. This flower may look intricate at first glance, but by breaking it down petal by petal, you'll see it come together with ease.

COLORS

Hansa Yellow Light	Pyrrol Scarlet	New Gamboge	Phthalo Blue (GS)

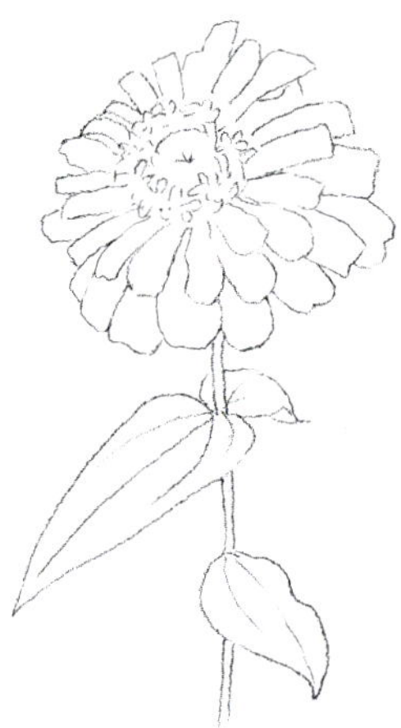

Step 1

Sketch Your Flower

Begin with a large round shape for the flower head and a straight stem extending downward. Add a smaller ellipse for the central disk, then sketch in the petals, letting them overlap and curve naturally. Include a couple of slightly uneven leaves to keep the composition lively and organic.

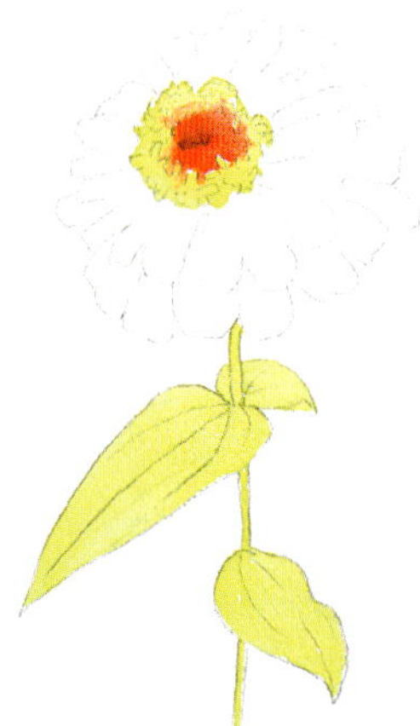

Step 2

Block in Yellow and Red

Paint the stem, leaves, and rim of the central disk with pure Hansa Yellow Light. Rinse your brush, then switch to milky Pyrrol Scarlet and paint the middle of the disk. Let the Pyrrol Scarlet softly touch the damp yellow so the edges melt together in a natural glow.

Scan to watch a video.

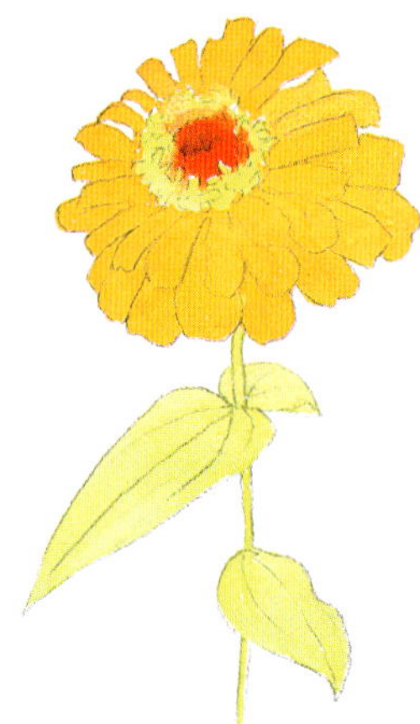

Step 3

Paint the Base Wash for the Petals

Using New Gamboge in a milky consistency, fill each petal with a flat wash, painting wet-on-dry. Be careful to stay within your pencil lines, but don't stress over perfection. Leave small white slivers between the most distant petals to suggest space and separation. Allow this layer to dry fully.

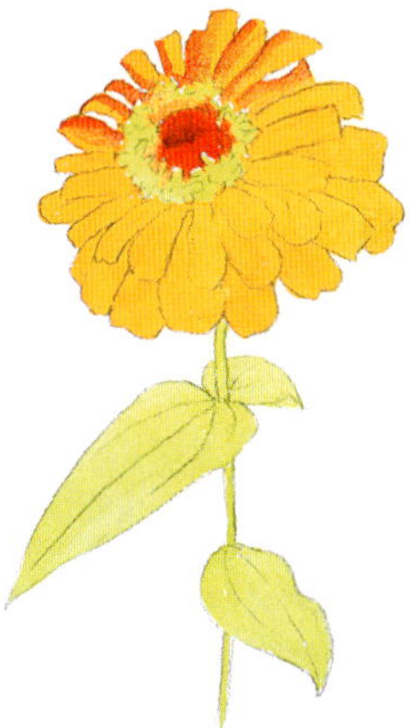

Step 4

Add Scarlet Accents

Working one petal at a time, load your brush with Pyrrol Scarlet and paint a stripe along the edge of the petal. Rinse and blot your brush, then swipe gently along the edge of that red to soften it into the yellow. This creates a seamless transition from glowing yellow orange to fiery scarlet.

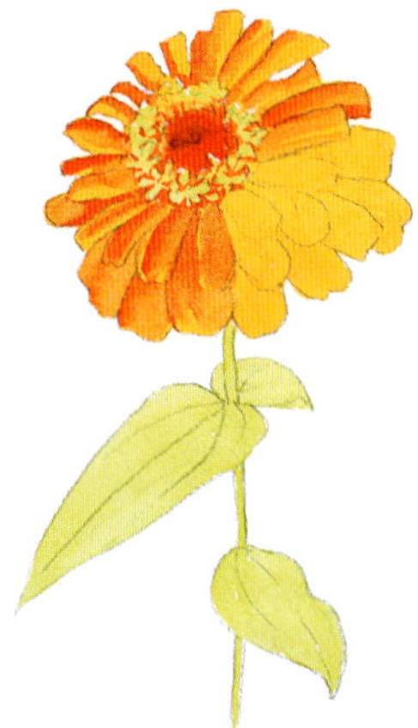

Step 5

Work Around the Flower

Continue this glazing process for each petal until the entire flower is full of vibrant blends. Add small dabs of scarlet between the yellow disk florets to create dimension in the center. The mix of strong reds and glowing yellows will begin to make the zinnia feel full and layered.

Scan to watch a video.

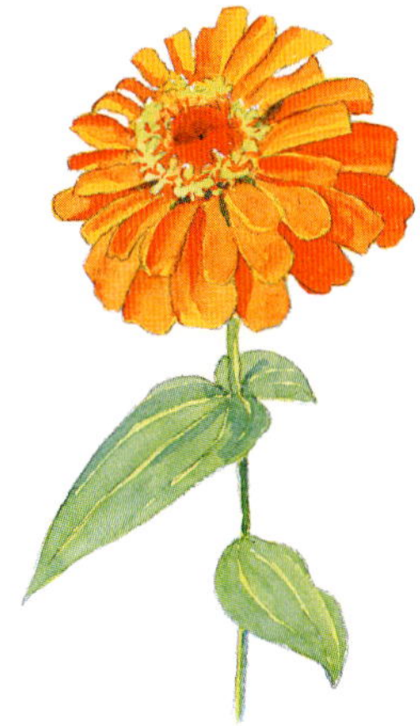

Step 6

Deepen Shadows and Glaze the Leaves Green

Use a thicker red to darken the petals that sit underneath, leaving thin slivers of yellow orange glowing along the edges. For the leaves and stem, glaze watery Phthalo Blue (GS) over the dried yellow base, letting the underpainting show through for natural highlights. Then mix Phthalo Blue with New Gamboge for an earthy green, adding just a few shadowed strokes to suggest veins and texture.

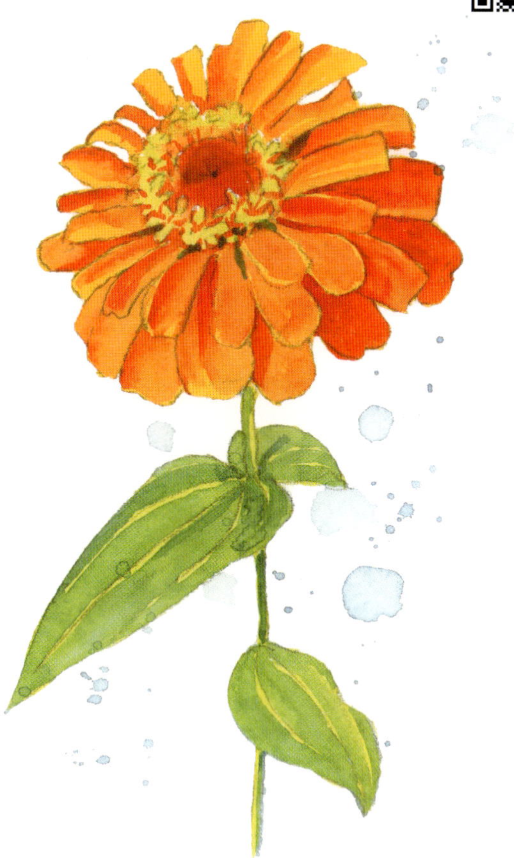

Step 7

Add Final Touches

With green still on your brush, dab in delicate shadows where the petals meet the disk to create depth. For a playful finishing touch, spatter watery Phthalo Blue lightly around the painting, echoing the freshness of a summer garden.

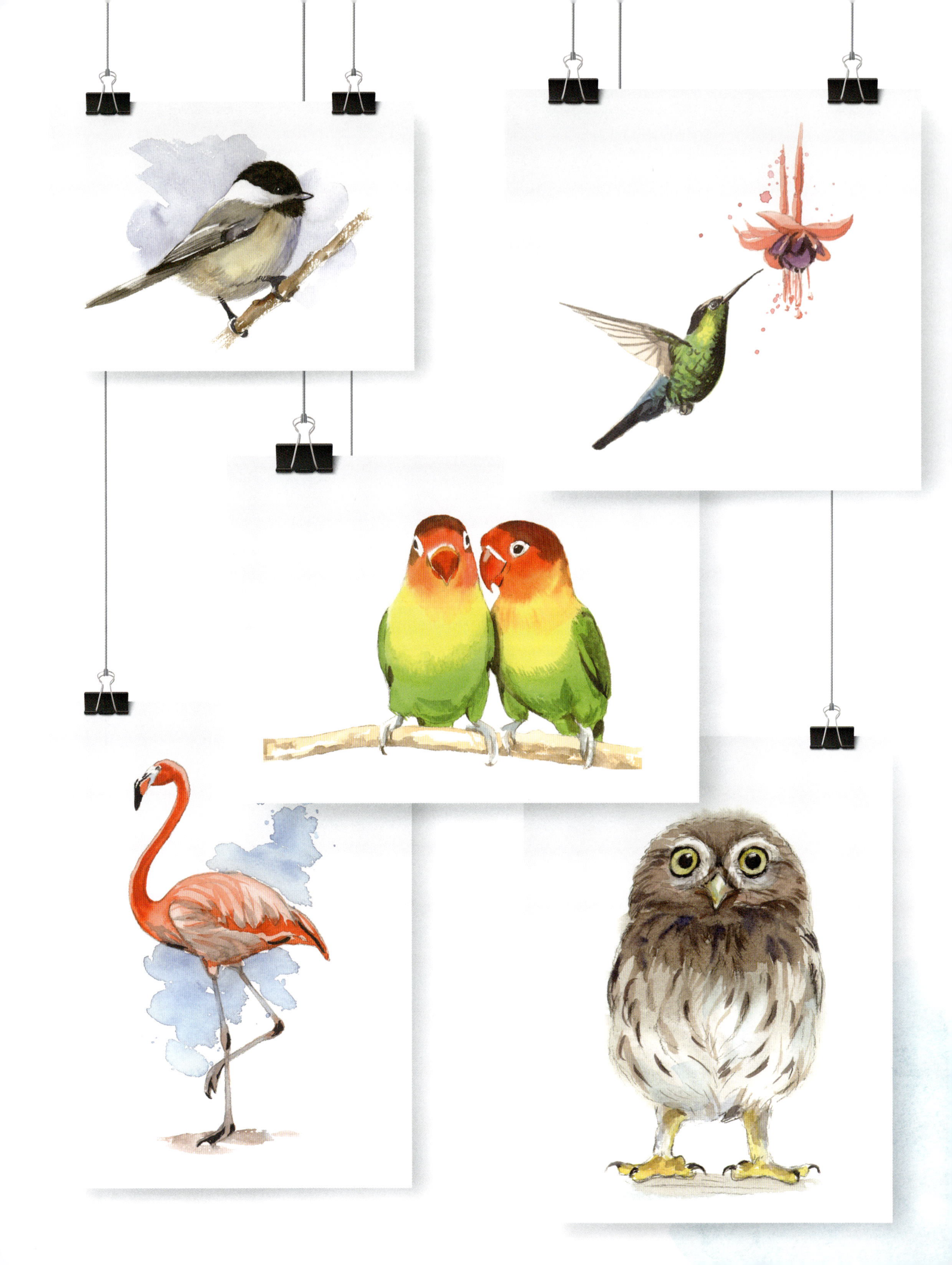

CHAPTER 5

20-Minute Birds

Birds are wonderful subjects for learning to sketch and paint. Built from simple shapes, they're easy to approach—yet their endless variety of color, texture, and personality makes them a joy to explore. Each one invites playful expression and creative interpretation.

Bold Kingfisher

Capture the striking colors of this exotic bird by layering primaries in bold, confident brushstrokes. With just a few well-placed details, you'll create the illusion of feathers and texture without overworking the piece.

COLORS

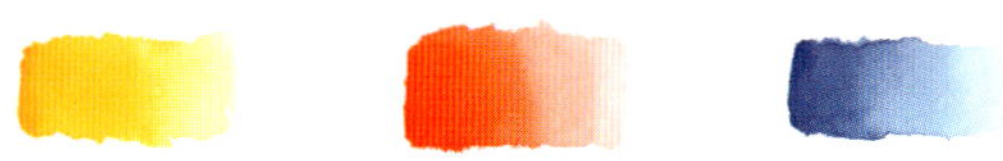

New Gamboge	Pyrrol Scarlet	Phthalo Blue (GS)

Step 1

Paint the Warm Belly

Sketch the bird then mix a pale orange by combining New Gamboge and Pyrrol Scarlet. Using wet-on-dry, fill the belly, the center of the face, and the lower beak. While it's still damp, drop in pure Pyrrol Scarlet along the front of the belly, the feet, and the beak for richer warmth and natural variation.

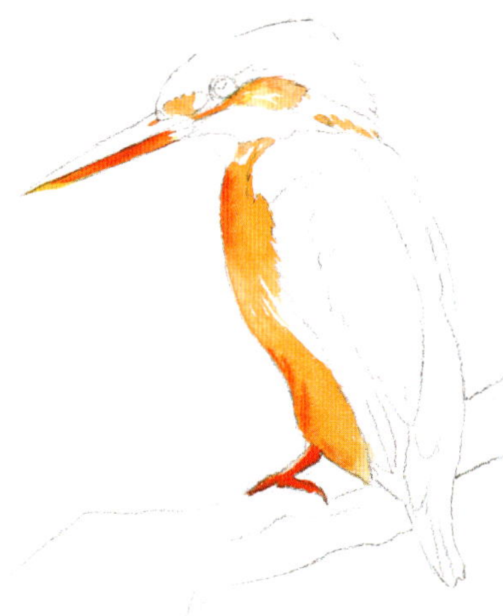

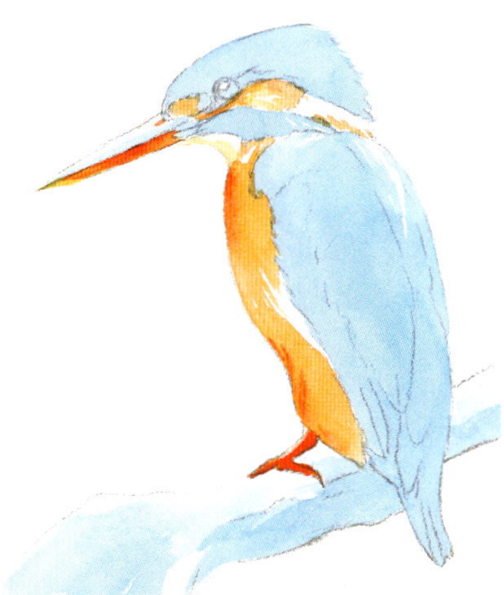

Step 2

Lay in the First Blue Wash

With watery Phthalo Blue (GS), sweep a cool base wash over the head, wings, and branch. Leave small gaps along feather edges and the branch to suggest glints of light. This loose underlayer sets the stage for the bold details to come.

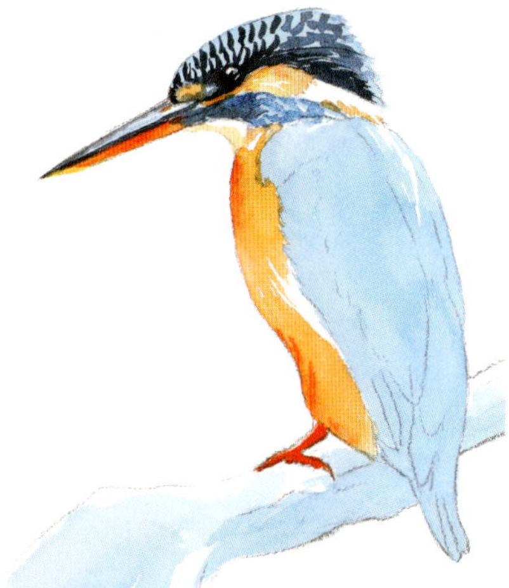

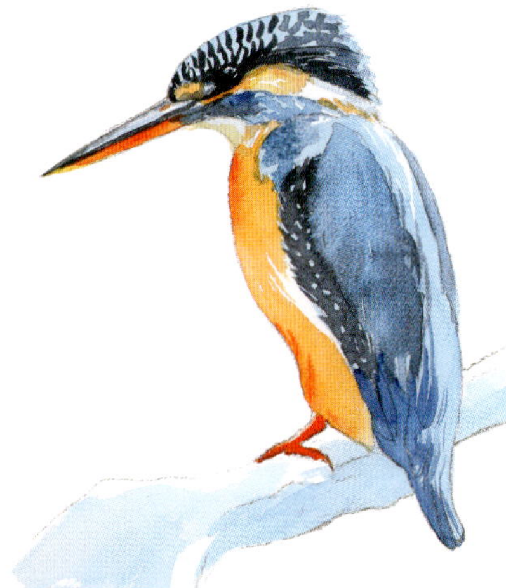

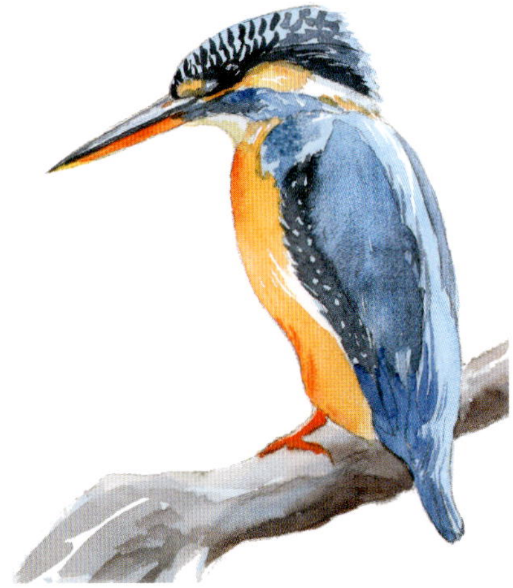

Step 3

Define the Head

Mix Phthalo Blue and Pyrrol Scarlet to create a dark, nearly black blue. Use short vertical dabs to paint the pinstripes on the head, leaving spaces between strokes for texture. Add the eye, preserving a crisp highlight, and then soften your mix with more water to paint the lighter feathers at the back of the head. Glaze the beak with this cool gray for added dimension.

Scan to watch a video.

Step 4

Add Wing Details

Strengthen the wing by painting a dark strip where it meets the belly. Negative paint around a few tiny dot shapes to suggest feather highlights. Then, sweep a watery blue wash across the wing with brushstrokes following the feather direction. At the tail base, use pure Phthalo Blue for a bold finishing touch.

Step 5

Paint the Branch

Shift your dark mix warmer by adding more Pyrrol Scarlet. Lay in a soft wash across the branch, then drop in a thicker, brownish gray at the base while it's still damp to create a natural shadow. Vary your strokes and colors slightly so the branch feels organic, not flat.

Step 6

Add a Playful Background

If you'd like, splash in a loose background of New Gamboge and Phthalo Blue. Let the pigments mingle on damp paper and touch in clean water to create blooming starburst effects—a fun contrast to the bird's sharp, graphic details.

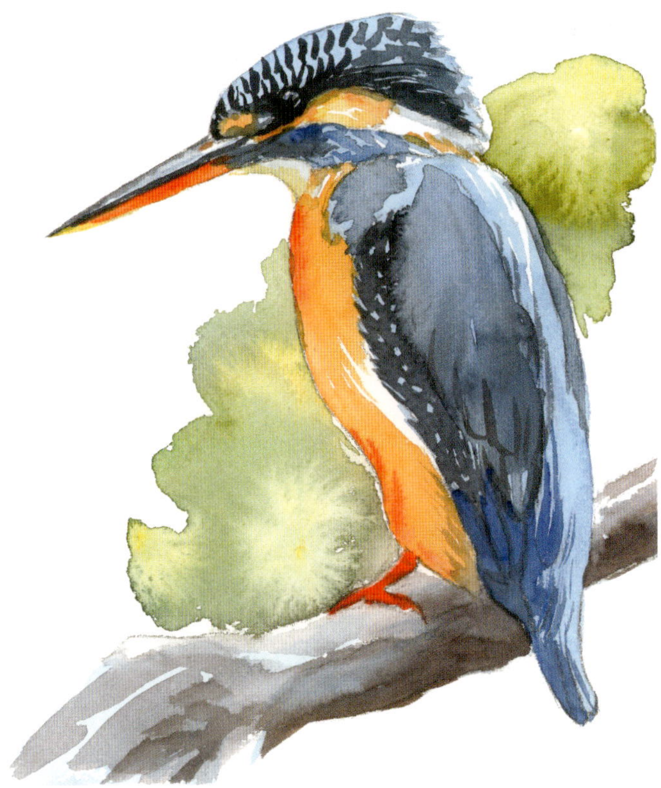

Backyard Chickadee

This cheerful songbird is a perfect balance of softness and detail. You'll use both wet-on-wet and wet-on-dry techniques to create a variety of textures, layering gentle washes with crisp accents.

COLORS

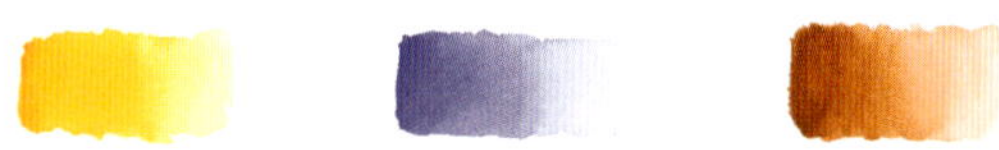

New Gamboge | French Ultramarine | Burnt Sienna

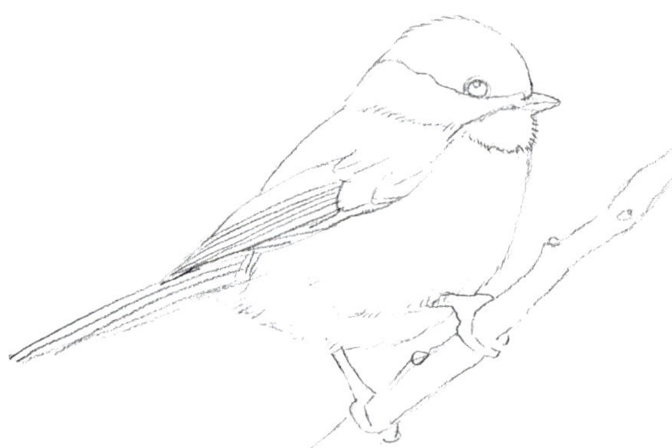

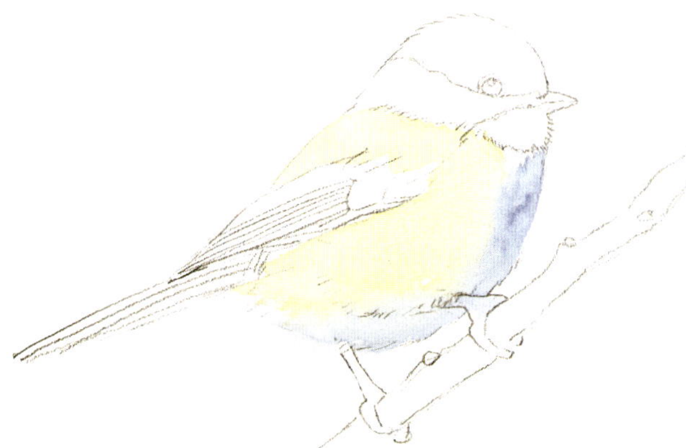

Step 1

Sketch Your Chickadee

Begin by drawing or tracing your chickadee, paying close attention to the key areas where dark and light feathers separate. Don't forget the angled, bumpy lines of the branch for texture, and be sure to mark the round highlight in the eye. This small detail will bring your bird to life later on.

Step 2

Add a Soft Base Wash to the Body

Start by applying a light wash of New Gamboge to the bird's back and side. Quickly mix up a light French Ultramarine wash and gently swipe it into the lower belly area just next to the yellow to create a cool, subtle shadow. Let the two colors meet and mingle softly for a natural gradient effect.

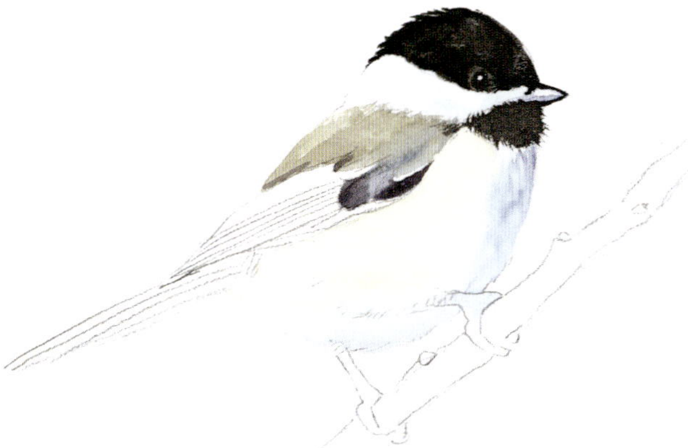

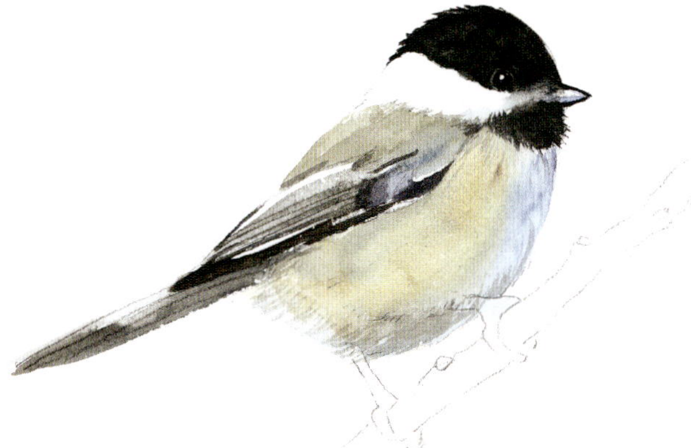

Step 3

Paint the Wing Shoulder and Black Cap

Mix Burnt Sienna, New Gamboge, and French Ultramarine into a warm gray and lightly brush it over the wing shoulder. Add more Ultramarine near the wing for a cooler medium gray. For the black cap and dark markings, use a thick 50/50 blend of Ultramarine and Burnt Sienna, carefully defining the darkest areas while preserving the white facial markings and eye highlight.

Scan to watch a video.

Step 4

Define the Wing and Tail Feathers

Mix a soft neutral gray using French Ultramarine and Burnt Sienna. Using light, directional brushstrokes, follow the natural flow of the feathers as you paint the lines of the wing and tail. Then, add a sheer wash of gray across the body and front of the head to gently deepen the form and give your chickadee more dimension.

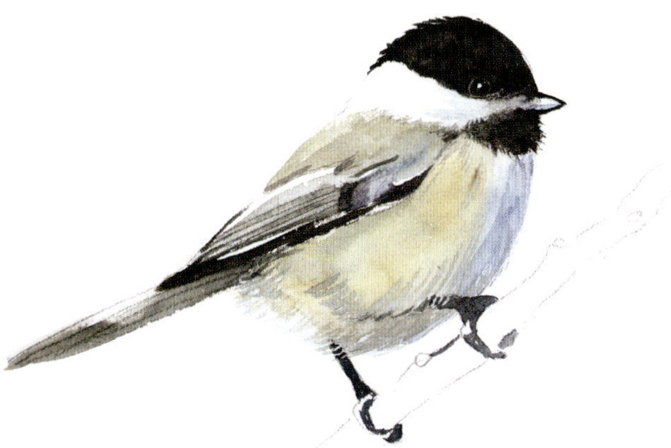

Step 5

Add Feet and Feather Texture

With a creamier mix of your gray (Burnt Sienna and Ultramarine), paint the feet, using negative painting to leave small highlights along the curved toes. This will help suggest shine and shape. Then, with a medium gray, apply soft, feathery strokes along the belly to add subtle detail and texture to the plumage.

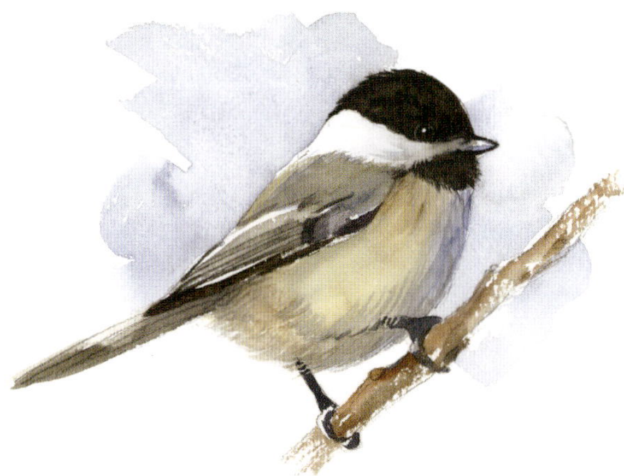

Step 6

Finish the Branch and Background

Use the drybrush technique and Burnt Sienna to paint the branch, letting the brush's broken texture mimic bark and roughness. Rinse your brush, then load it with watery French Ultramarine and loosely paint a splashy background. Feel free to let it run, bloom, and blend for a spontaneous, airy finish that adds movement and contrast to your composition.

Scan to watch a video.

Cuddling Lovebirds

Celebrate color in this cheerful lovebirds project! Use the full rainbow—from glowing yellows to deep reds and greens—to capture their playful charm.

COLORS

Hansa Yellow Light	Phthalo Blue (GS)	Pyrrol Scarlet

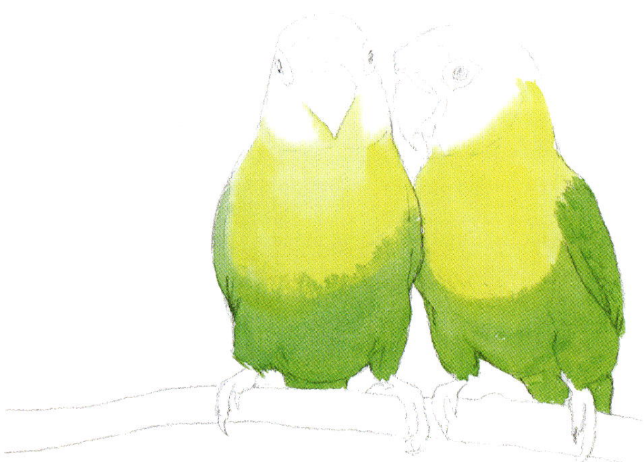

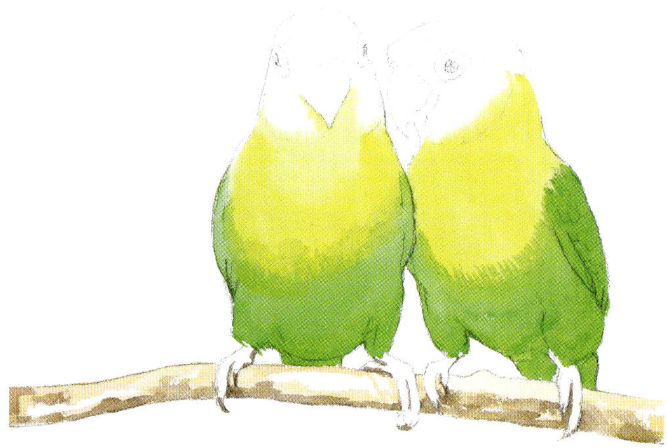

Step 1

Blend Yellow and Jungle Green

Sketch the birds and branch, then brush clean water over the birds' bodies, avoiding the beaks, tops of the heads, and feet. While the paper is still glossy, paint creamy Hansa Yellow Light into the centers of the birds. Then mix Phthalo Blue (GS) into the leftover yellow to make a bright jungle green, brushing it along the bellies, wings, and lower halves so the colors blend softly. Let dry completely.

Scan to watch a video.

Step 2

Perch Them on a Branch

Mix all three of your primaries into a watery, light brown for the branch. Paint gentle blobs of color along the top and bottom of the branch for texture and shape. Deepen the mix slightly and add a shadow along the underside of the branch, plus delicate dark claws on your birds' feet.

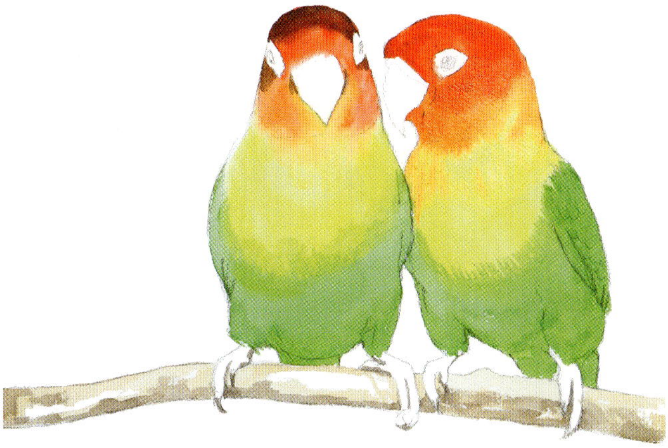

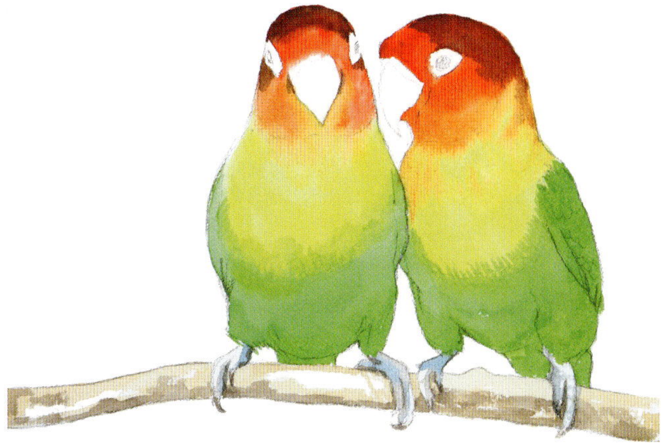

Step 3

Paint the Crowns

Lightly wet each bird's head and chest, avoiding the eyes and beak, then drop in creamy Pyrrol Scarlet at the top and blend downward with diluted strokes into the yellow for a soft orange glow. Mix a touch of Phthalo Blue (GS) into the red to create a dark brown, adding it damp-on-damp above the head and beneath the eyes for depth. Repeat on the second bird, using a fine damp brush to add soft, curved chest strokes for fluffy texture.

Scan to watch a video.

Step 4

Polish the Red Heads and Color the Feet

Add the final dark "cap" to the second bird's head using your Pyrrol Scarlet and Phthalo Blue (GS) mix. Rinse your brush and switch to a watery Phthalo Blue to paint the feet. Remember to leave some white paper showing along the tops of the feet to create highlights and a sense of rounded form.

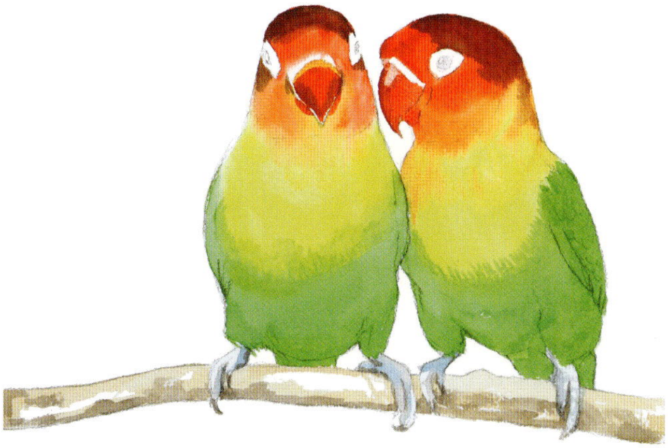

Step 5

Bring the Beaks to Life

Paint the beaks in pure Pyrrol Scarlet, avoiding the highlights to keep them shiny. Darken the undersides with a soft brown mix, blending while damp for smooth shading. Keep the brush slightly dry to avoid flooding these small areas.

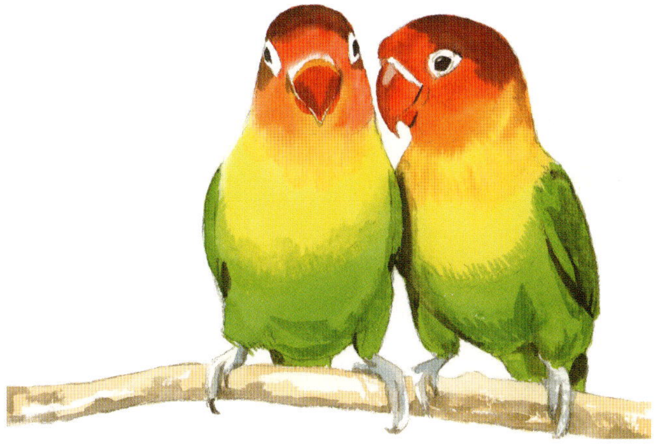

Step 6

Add Striking Dark Details

Mix a rich black using Pyrrol Scarlet and Phthalo Blue (GS). Carefully paint the eyes, preserving tiny white highlights for a spark of life. Use a less intense, diluted black to add soft shadows under the birds' wings and tails for a lovely 3D effect.

Scan to watch a video.

Flitting Hummingbird

Capture the dazzling energy of a hummingbird in motion. Blend vivid greens and shimmering blues to create iridescent feathers and a sense of movement that feels alive.

COLORS

Burnt Sienna	Pyrrol Scarlet	Quinacridone Rose	Hansa Yellow Light	Phthalo Blue (GS)	French Ultramarine

Step 1

Lay Down Warm Foundation Colors

Mix a watery Burnt Sienna and apply it to the wing, tail, feet, and top of the bird's head. Soften the edges and glaze a little more over the base of the wing and tail to gently deepen the value. Then, using a watery combo of Pyrrol Scarlet and Quinacridone Rose, paint the base layer of the trumpet-shaped flower with loose, confident strokes.

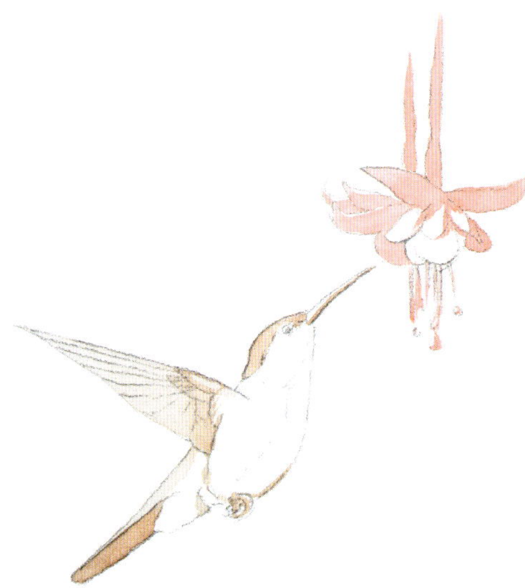

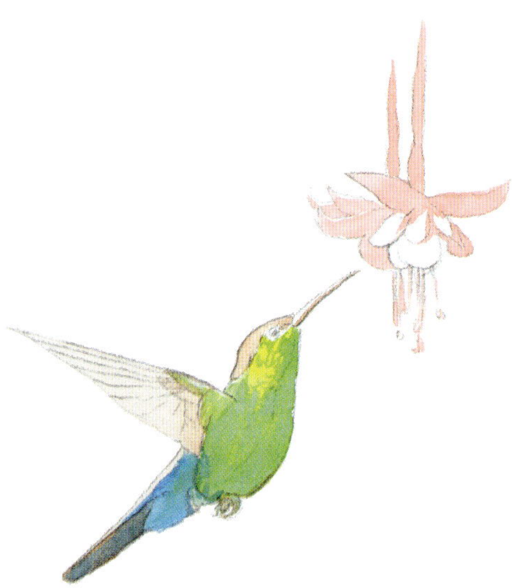

Step 2

Build the Glowing Green Body

Start by painting the bird's body and head with Hansa Yellow Light. While the surface is still damp, layer diluted Phthalo Blue (GS) over the throat and belly, letting it naturally blend into a luminous green. Leave the cheek area dry, then go back in with curved light blue brushstrokes to add a soft feathery texture. Finally, paint over the tail with a milky Phthalo Blue, even across the brown base, to unify the color and add vibrancy.

Scan to watch a video.

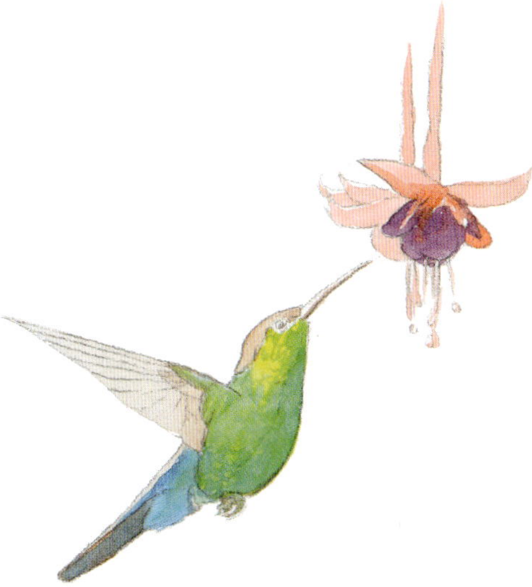

Step 3

Color the Honeysuckle

To bring the flower to life, mix French Ultramarine and Quinacridone Rose to create a lovely milky violet and apply it to the center of the bloom. Use watery Pyrrol Scarlet to brush in delicate shadows along the pink petals, giving them shape and softness.

Step 5

Define with Elegant Darks

Create a rich black by mixing Pyrrol Scarlet and Phthalo Blue (GS). With a fine brush, begin defining the hummingbird's eye, top of the head, underside of the beak, and tail feathers. Use a lighter version of this mix to shade the belly and layered feathers, using thin, curved strokes to suggest volume and softness.

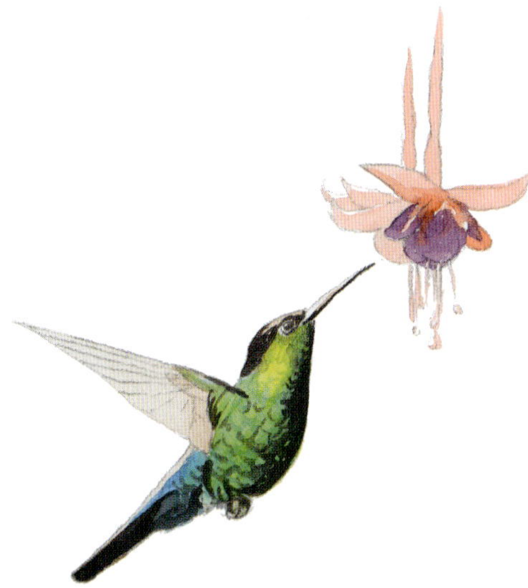

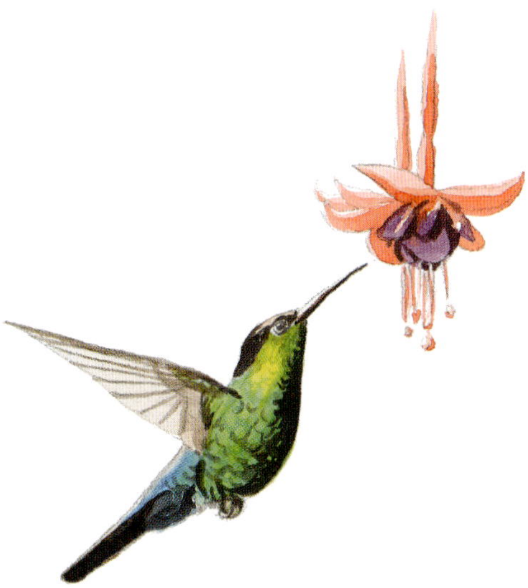

Step 5

Final Feather and Flower Touches

Mix a muted tone using Burnt Sienna with a hint of Ultramarine, then carefully define the wing feathers with subtle lines. Return to the flower with Pyrrol Scarlet and Quinacridone Rose, adding soft red shadows near the petals' base to enhance contrast and form.

Scan to watch a video.

Step 6

Spatter Some Magic

For a playful and energetic finish, load a brush with watery red (either Pyrrol Scarlet or Quinacridone Rose) and gently tap it over the background, letting the spatters dance around the flower. It's a lively touch that brings the whole scene to life!

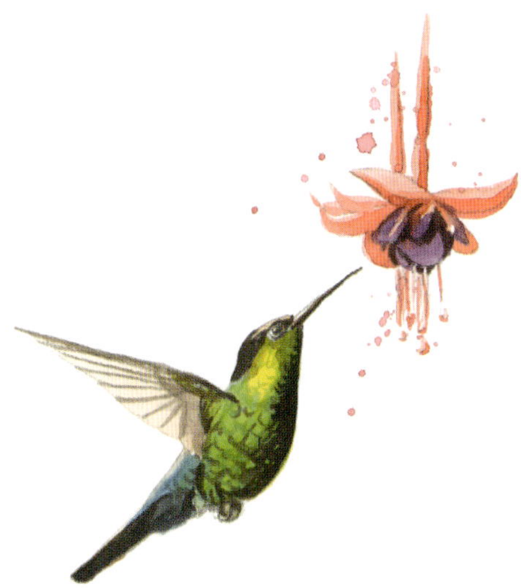

Little Owl

In this sassy little owl tutorial, you will practice painting soft base washes while layering expressive feather textures. Use confident, strategic brushstrokes to bring this inquisitive little bird to life!

COLORS

Burnt Sienna	French Ultramarine	Hansa Yellow Light	New Gamboge	Phthalo Blue (GS)	Pyrrol Scarlet

Step 1

Sketch the Owl with Balanced Proportions

Sketch or trace the owl, keeping in mind that the head is roughly one-third the height of the body. Be sure to make the eyes and legs symmetrical in both shape and size.

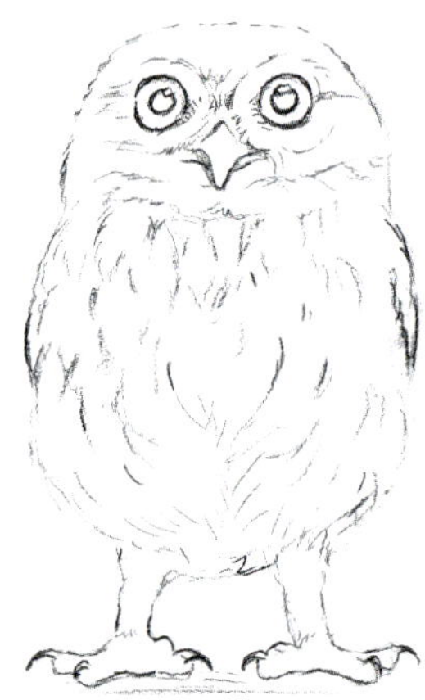

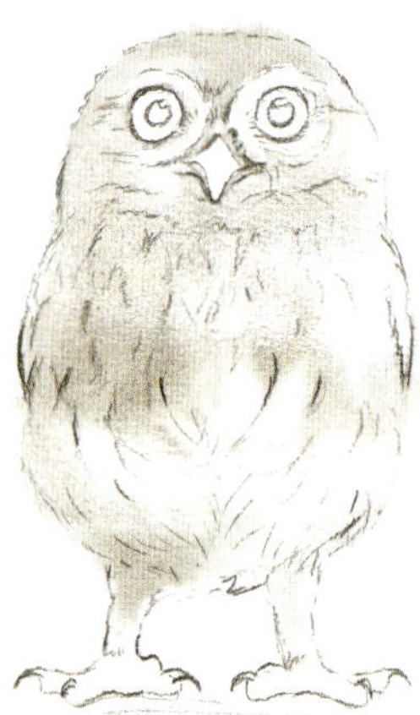

Step 2

Soften the Silhouette with a Fluffy Gray Wash

Wet the legs, eyes, beak, and extend the water a finger's width beyond the head and body. Mix a warm gray with Burnt Sienna and French Ultramarine, then, with a not-too-wet brush, gently apply it to the owl. The paint will softly bleed past the pencil lines, creating fluffy, downy feathers.

Scan to watch a video.

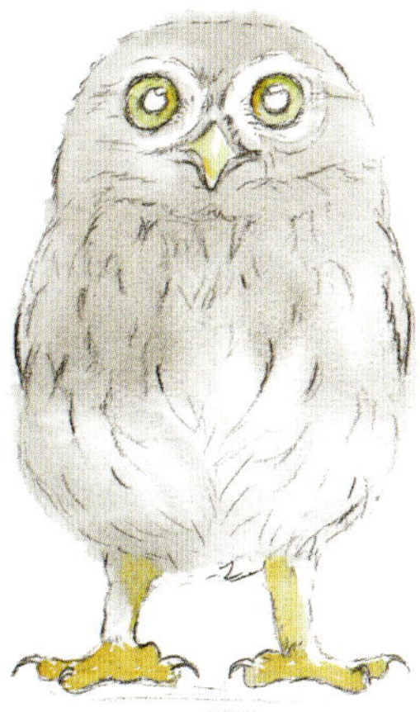

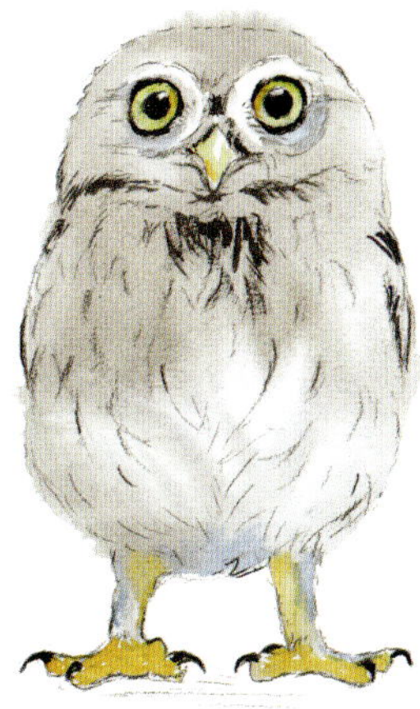

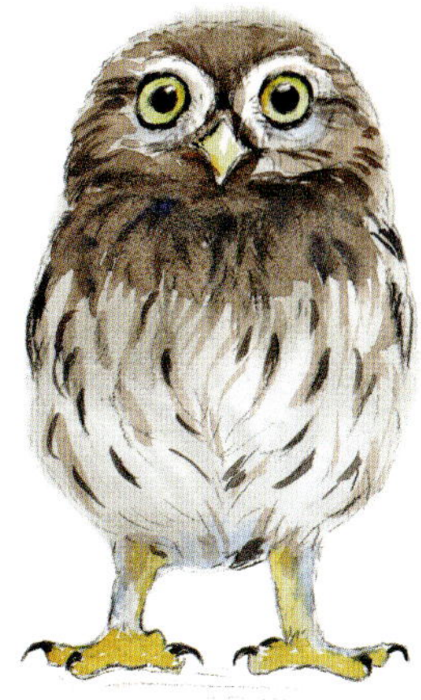

Step 3

Brighten the Features with Warm Yellows

Use Hansa Yellow Light and New Gamboge to paint the eyes, legs, and beak. Leave the center of the beak white to give it a shiny, curved appearance.

Step 4

Define the Darks and Add Depth

Mix a rich black using creamy Phthalo Blue (GS) and Pyrrol Scarlet. Use this black to paint the centers of the eyes, the dark rims around them, the claws, and the darkest feather details. Then, add a light touch of French Ultramarine to the underside of the belly, around the eyes, and on the legs.

Step 5

Feather the Head and Chest with Chocolate Browns

Create a chocolate brown by combining French Ultramarine and Burnt Sienna to a milky consistency. Fill your brush with this mixture and apply it to the head and breast area. While the paint is still damp, add touches of pure French Ultramarine for depth. To suggest soft feathers, twirl your brush on the palette to fan out the bristles, then use quick, curved downward strokes with the splayed tip.

Scan to watch a video.

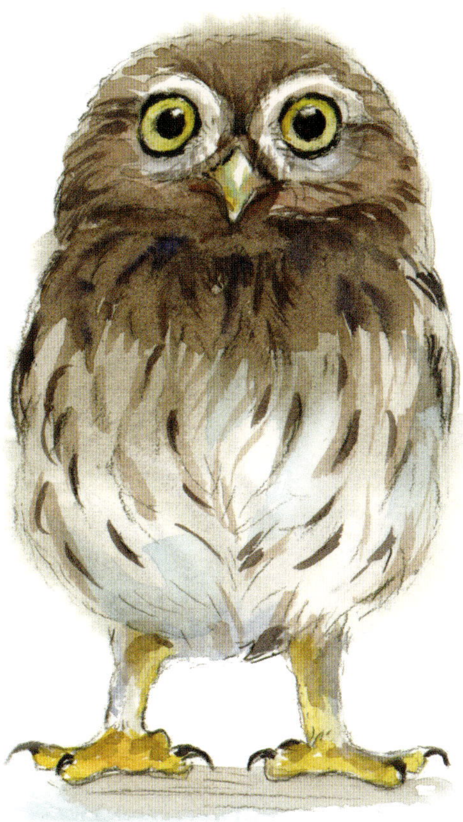

Step 6

Add Final Touches and Ground the Scene

Wrap up your painting with some playful finishing touches! Add light, watery strokes of Phthalo Blue (GS) to the owl's white belly and along the side of the beak for a hint of shimmer. Then, brush in a bit of soft brown on the ground to anchor your owl and bring the scene to life.

Purple Finch

Paint a sweet backyard bird with just four colors and loose, layered washes.

COLORS

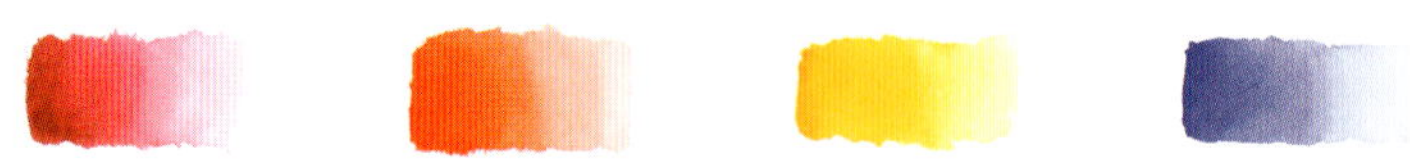

Quinacridone Rose | Pyrrol Scarlet | New Gamboge | French Ultramarine

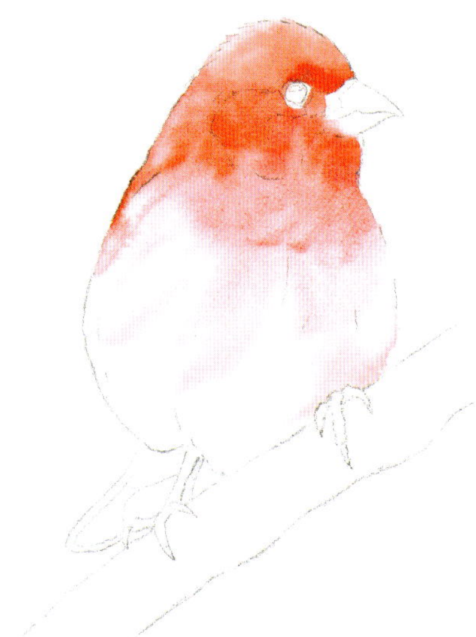

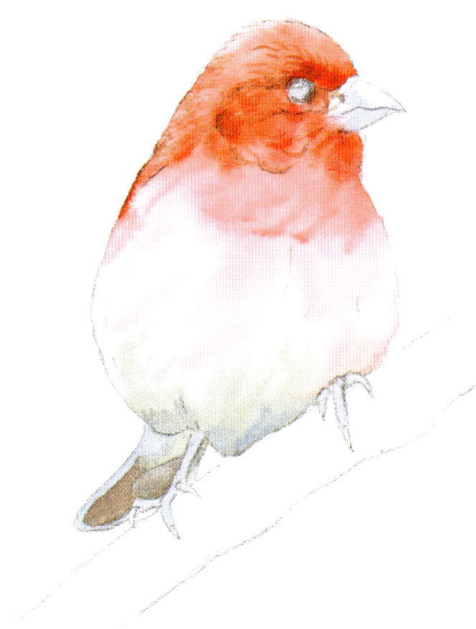

Step 1

Lay the Red Base

Wet the bird's body with clear water, avoiding the eye and beak. Drop in a 50/50 mix of Quinacridone Rose and Pyrrol Scarlet, starting with the darkest values above the eye and under the beak. Let the red fade into lighter pink halfway down the body with long, curved strokes suggesting fluffy feathers.

Scan to watch a video.

Step 2

Cool the Shadows and Add Details

Glaze a muted greenish-gray made from New Gamboge and French Ultramarine over the damp belly, deepening the blue near the branch for extra depth. Use a soft brown mixed from your three primaries to paint the underside of the tail, then let it dry. Next, add watery French Ultramarine to the feet, beak, and eye, preserving small highlights, and use your brown mix to place subtle feather marks around the head to define the skull and texture.

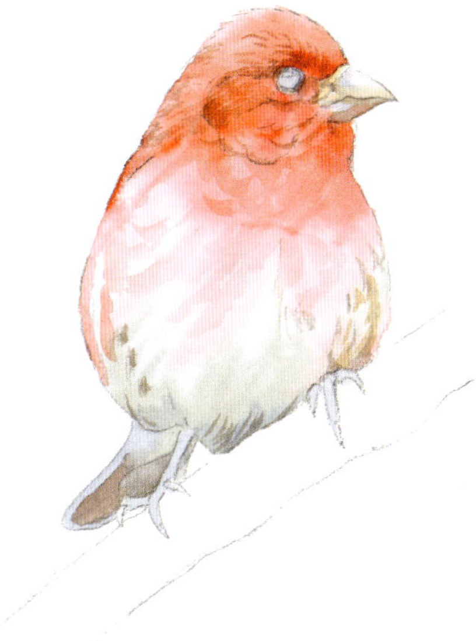

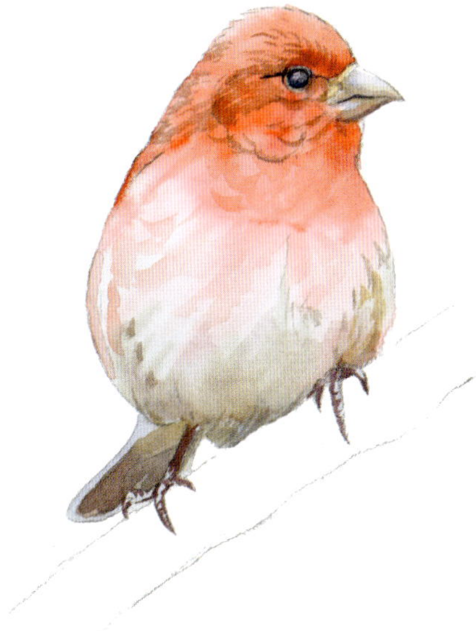

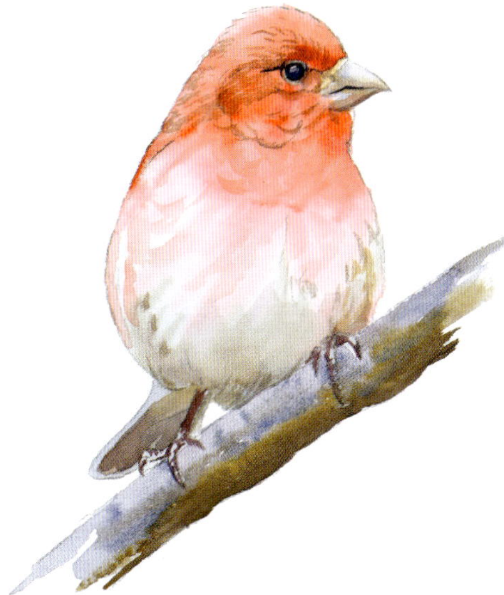

Step 3

Layer Soft Browns

On the dry breast and belly, add small comma strokes of diluted brown to suggest speckled feathers. Glaze New Gamboge in the middle of the beak, then shade the underside with a single stroke of watery Pyrrol Scarlet.

Step 4

Define with Darks

Mix a nearly black purple with French Ultramarine and Pyrrol Scarlet. Use this for the eye (negative painting around the highlight), the legs and toes, and a simple crease for the mouth. All of these facial details should be applied wet-on-dry.

Step 5

Paint the Perch

Brush French Ultramarine along the top of the branch, then switch to New Gamboge for the underside so the colors blend softly. While damp, add touches of thicker paint for bark texture.

Scan to watch a video.

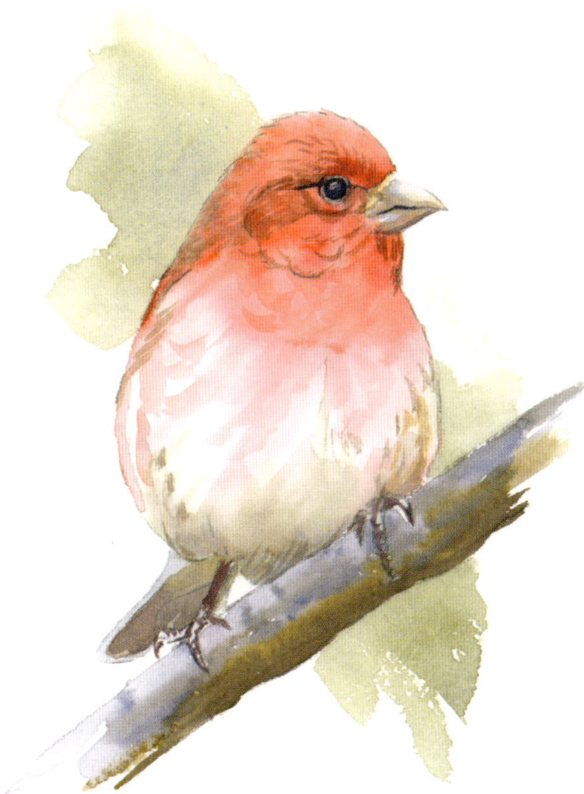

Step 6

Finish with Background Color

Loosely wash in New Gamboge and French Ultramarine around the bird for a fresh, atmospheric finish.

Red Cardinal

The brilliant cardinal, with its vibrant red plumage and lively song, brings warmth to any winter scene. This project captures its charm as you explore bold reds against a soft wintry blue background.

COLORS

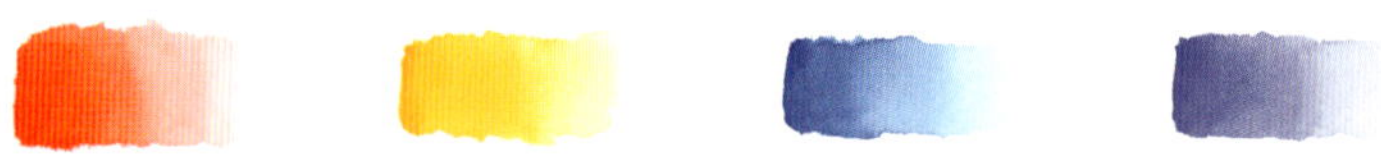

Pyrrol Scarlet	New Gamboge	Phthalo Blue (GS)	French Ultramarine

Step 1

Sketch Your Proud Cardinal

Capture the alert, vertical stance of the bird with its signature pointed crest and the angled branch it's perched on. Add key details like the highlight in the eye and the most important feather groupings so your painting has a strong foundation.

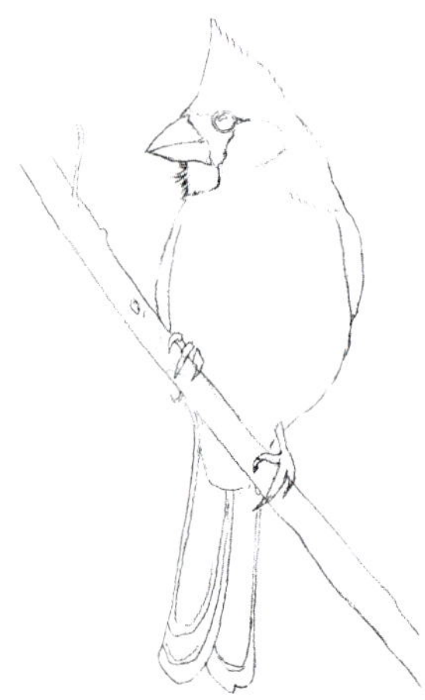

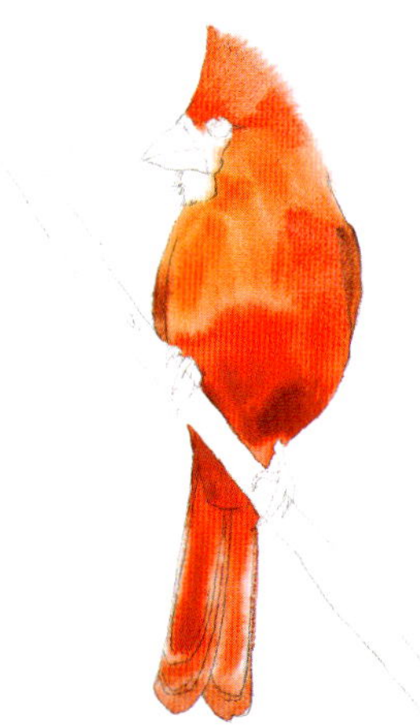

Step 2

Paint the Red Base Wash

Wet the whole bird, extending slightly past the crest for a soft edge. Drop in creamy Pyrrol Scarlet on the belly and tail, negative painting around a few feather edges to keep them fluffy. Add a touch of New Gamboge to warm the breast and keep the red strong on the wings. Splay the brush for natural feather texture. Finish with milky Pyrrol Scarlet on the head, letting it fade into the damp paper.

Scan to watch a video.

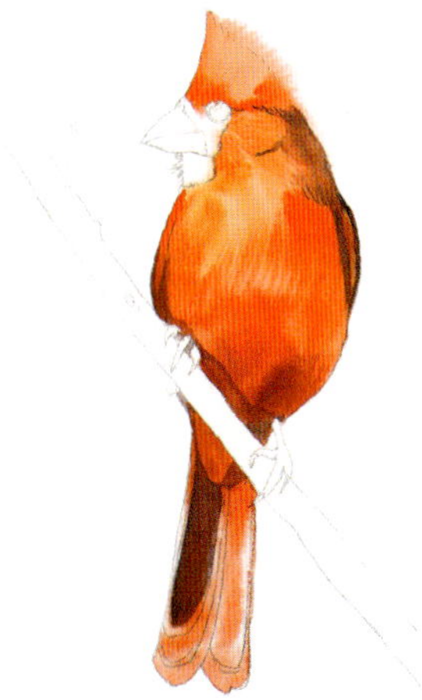

Step 3

Begin Defining the Darks

If your red base is still damp, that's fine; just be sure your brush is only lightly damp, with no extra water that could cause unwanted blooms. Create a deeper, warmer red by adding a touch of Phthalo Blue (GS) to your scarlet. Using this harmonious dark in a milky-to-creamy consistency, define the wing feathers, deepen the shadow under the belly between the feet, and enrich the tail feathers. With the tip of your brush, lightly suggest feather texture along the neck for added realism.

Step 4

Add a Beak, Feet, and Branch

For the feet, use a pale gray created from watery Pyrrol Scarlet and Phthalo Blue (GS). Paint the beak with a wash of watery scarlet, then add creamier red to mark the crease and give it dimension. Wash New Gamboge over the branch for a warm base color.

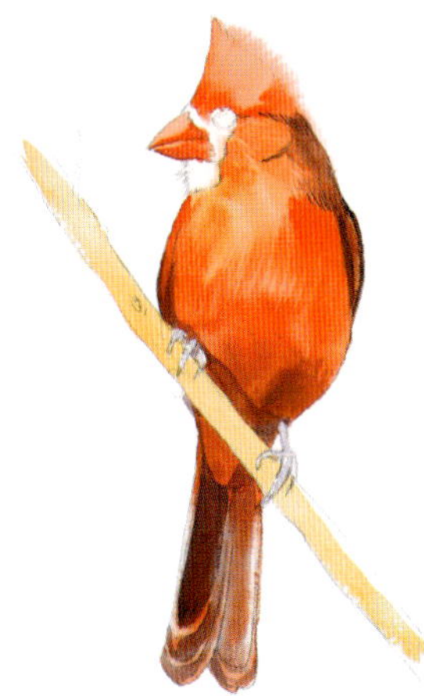

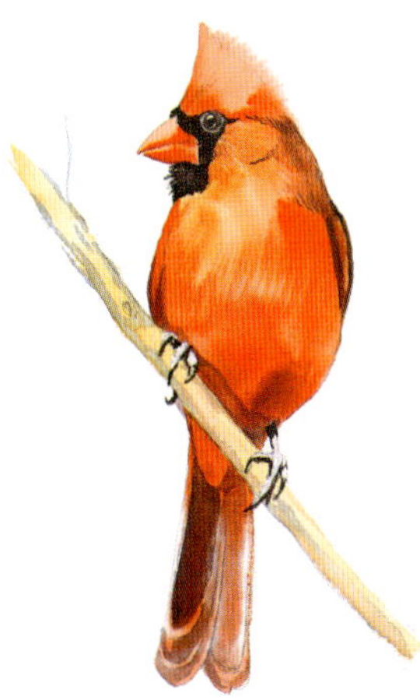

Step 5

Bring the Cardinal to Life with Details

Mix a rich black from Pyrrol Scarlet and Phthalo Blue (GS). Use it to paint the dark mask near the beak, the pupil of the eye, and the shadows around the feet. Avoid the highlight in the eye so it stays bright and lively. Keep the tops of the feet light to suggest sunlight. With a thinned version of your black, add subtle texture and shadow to the branch.

Step 6

Add a Cool Background for Atmosphere

Blob in some watery French Ultramarine behind the bird, letting the color bloom naturally for a soft, snowy feel. The cool blue will help the red cardinal pop while also adding a sense of depth and winter chill. Let this part be loose and expressive; it's your chance to make the scene uniquely yours!

Scan to watch a video.

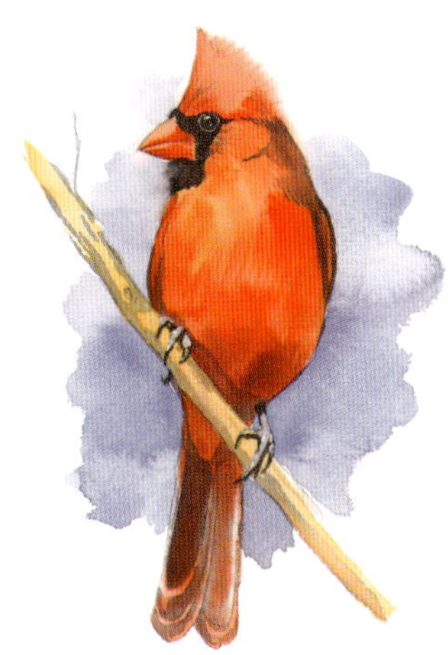

Spring Robin

Paint the cheerful European robin, a symbol of warmth and renewal, in this inviting tutorial. You'll explore the balance of bright orange breast feathers against soft brown-gray tones, learning to blend vibrant and neutral hues for a harmonious, lifelike result.

COLORS

Burnt Sienna	French Ultramarine	Hansa Yellow Light	Pyrrol Scarlet

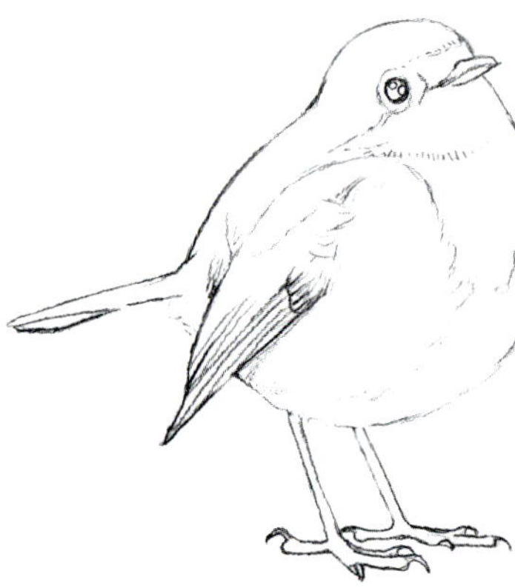

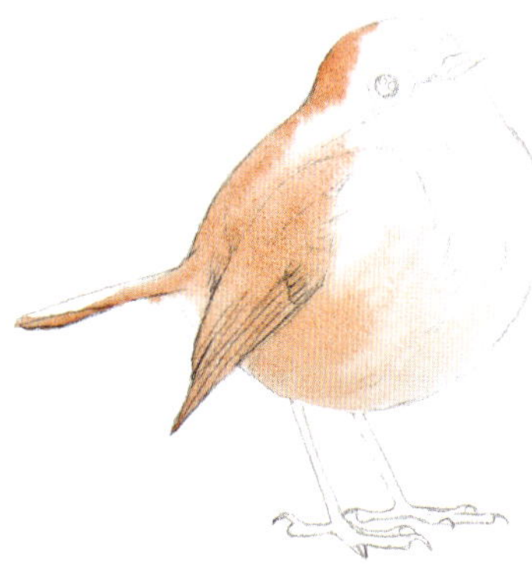

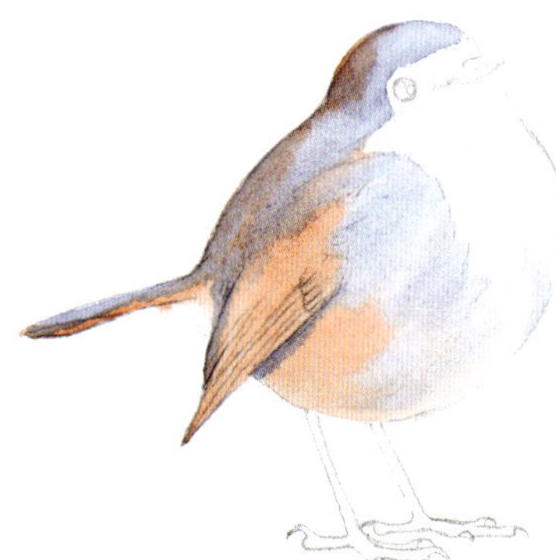

Step 1

Sketch the Bird's Perky Pose

Begin by sketching or tracing the bird, focusing on the plump body shape and the charming tilt of the head. Keep your lines light and clean to preserve the freshness of the final painting.

Step 2

Lay Down a Soft Burnt Sienna Base

Wet the bird, avoiding the face, breast, and legs. While glossy, wash milky Burnt Sienna over the back, tail, wings, and underbelly. Feather the edge upward as it nears the breast to create a soft transition into the lighter chest.

Step 3

Add a Touch of Blue

While the Burnt Sienna wash is still damp, brush a milky French Ultramarine over the head, back, tail, and breast, but avoid the wings for now. Make sure the moisture on your brush matches the dampness of the paper.

Scan to watch a video.

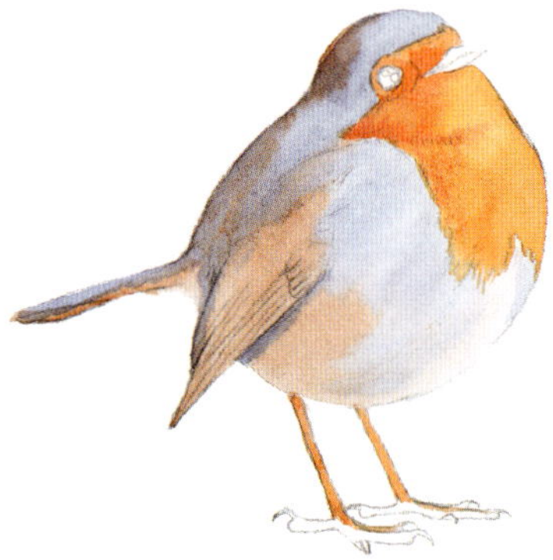

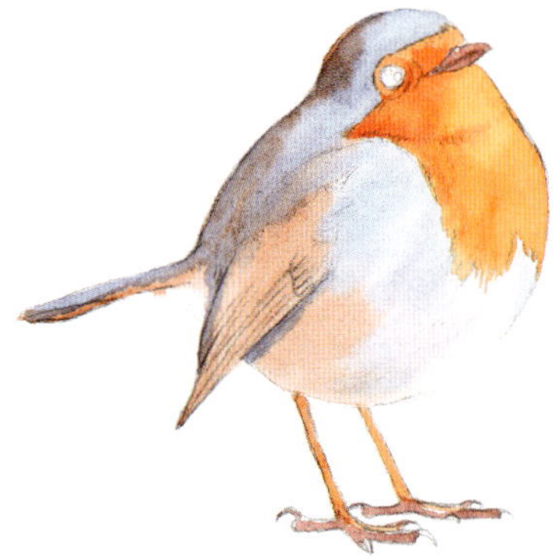

Step 4

Paint the Vibrant Orange Breast

Mix Hansa Yellow Light and Pyrrol Scarlet to create a glowing yellow orange. Paint the breast area in a smooth wash. While the paint is still damp, deepen the color near the eye and shoulder by dropping in more Pyrrol Scarlet. This will add natural shading and make the head feel more rounded.

Step 5

Detail the Beak and Feet

Create a soft red violet by mixing Pyrrol Scarlet with a touch of French Ultramarine. Use this to paint the beak and feet, leaving tiny highlights—especially on the top of the beak and toes—to suggest reflected light and form.

Step 6

Refine and Finish with Final Touches

Mix a creamy dark neutral using a 50/50 blend of French Ultramarine and Burnt Sienna. Use this mix to paint the eye, beak, claws, and any final dark feather details, being careful to leave highlights where needed. If the bird needs more depth, mix a medium gray from the same pigments and glaze over shadowed areas. To suggest feather texture, splay the bristles of your brush and apply quick, dry brushstrokes with your gray mix. This adds subtle realism and softness to the form.

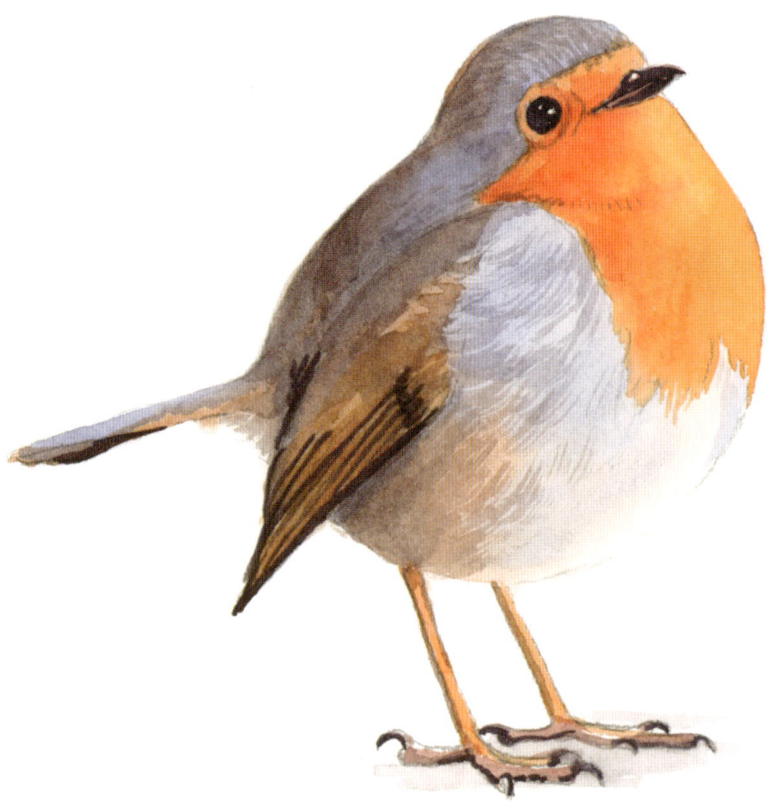

Scan to watch a video.

Tall Flamingo

Practice glazing, lifting, and delicate brushwork as you bring this graceful flamingo to life with just two colors!

COLORS

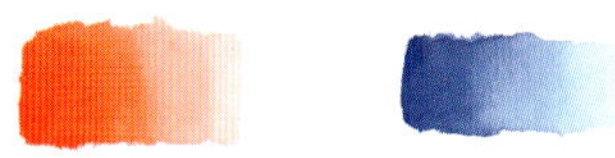

Pyrrol Scarlet

Phthalo Blue (GS)

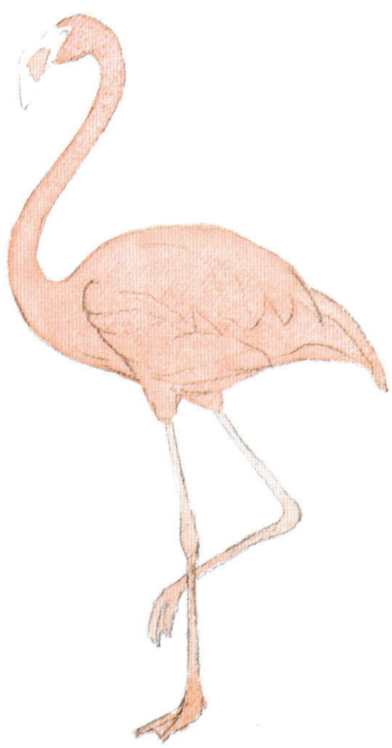

Step 1

Lay in the Pink Base

Cover the entire bird with a flat, watery wash of Pyrrol Scarlet, keeping the beak's white areas clean.

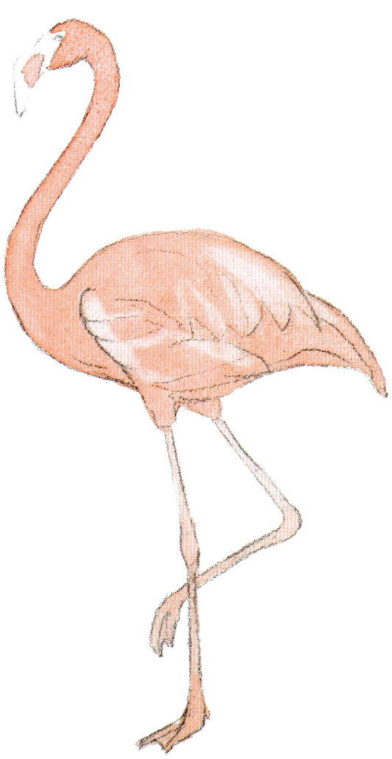

Step 2

Lift Highlights While Wet

While the first wash is still damp, use a clean, slightly damp brush to lift out soft highlights. Focus on the wing shoulder and feather edges to suggest light catching the bird's form.

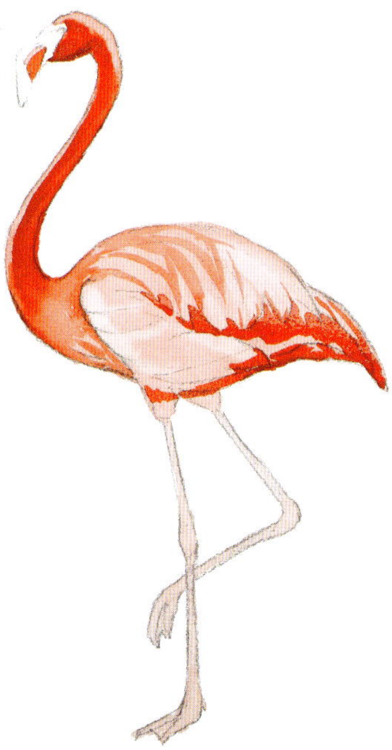

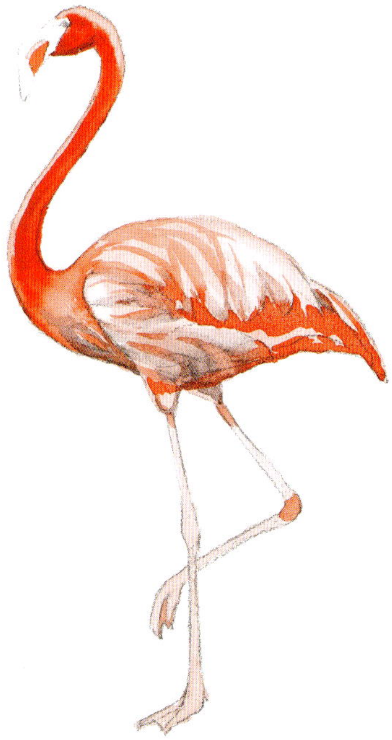

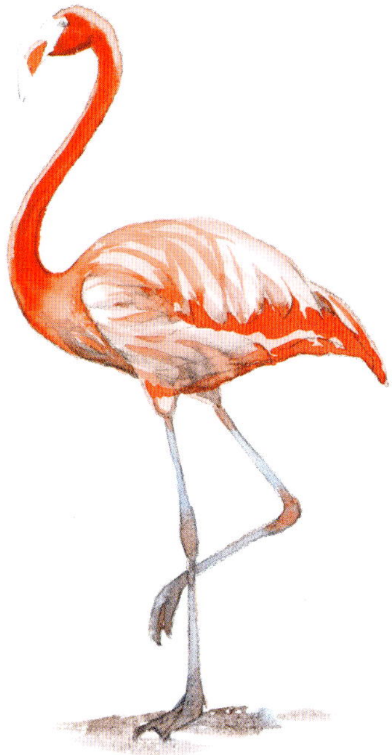

Step 3

Deepen the Red Feathers

Glaze creamy Pyrrol Scarlet over the neck and the darkest feather areas. Leave a narrow strip of the lighter wash along the neck's curve to suggest sunlight. With the remaining paint in your brush, add gentle curved strokes to build feather texture on the back.

Step 4

Add Subtle Shadows

Mix a pale purplish gray from Pyrrol Scarlet and Phthalo Blue. Use this soft shade to paint shadows under the body and along the underside of the neck. Add a few deeper red accents with milky Pyrrol Scarlet, especially around the leg joints and wing edges.

Scan to watch a video.

Step 5

Paint the Legs and Ground

Glaze the legs with a watery wash of Phthalo Blue for a cool contrast. Then, use your red-blue mix to loosely paint a soft ground shadow so the bird feels anchored to the page.

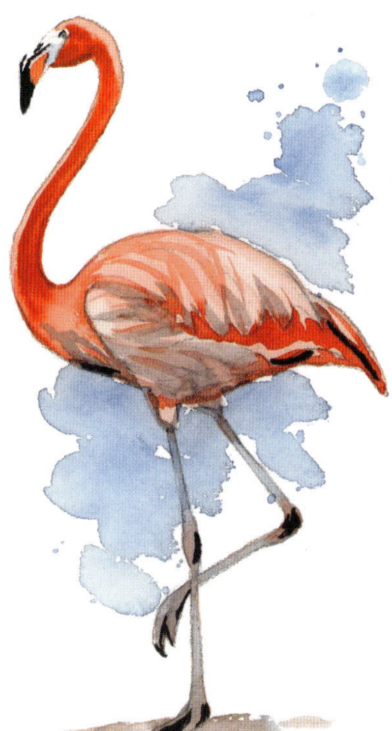

Step 6

Define Details and Add Blue Splashes

Mix a creamy black from your two colors and, with a fine brush, paint the beak tip, small round eye, and a few dark accents on the feathers and legs. Then finish with playful strokes of pure Phthalo Blue in the background, using loose, blobby motions to keep the piece fresh and whimsical.

Tropical Toucan

Enjoy experimenting with a rich variety of color mixes using just three primaries and Burnt Sienna in this exotic bird painting!

COLORS

Hansa Yellow Light | Phthalo Blue (GS) | Pyrrol Scarlet | Burnt Sienna

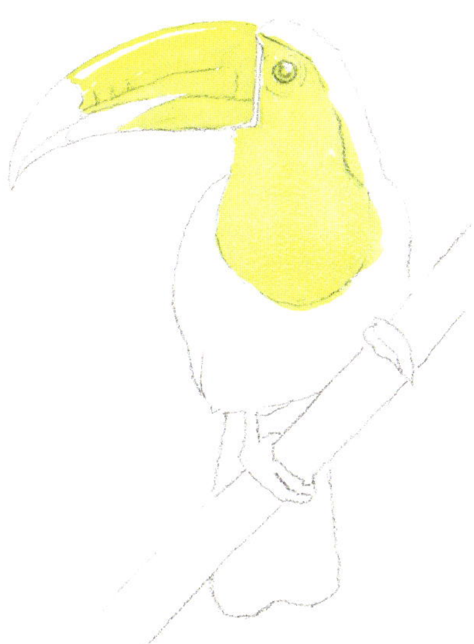

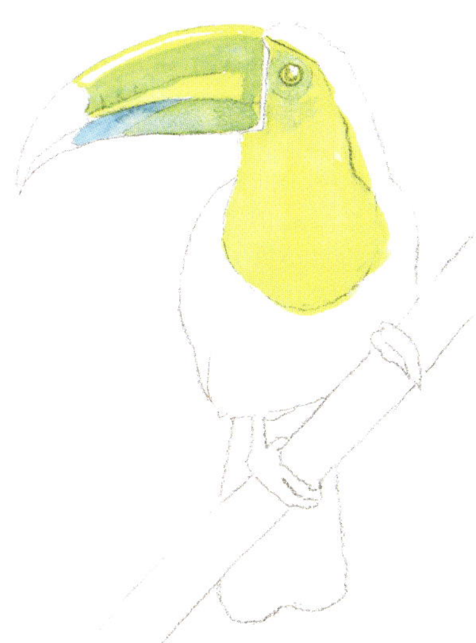

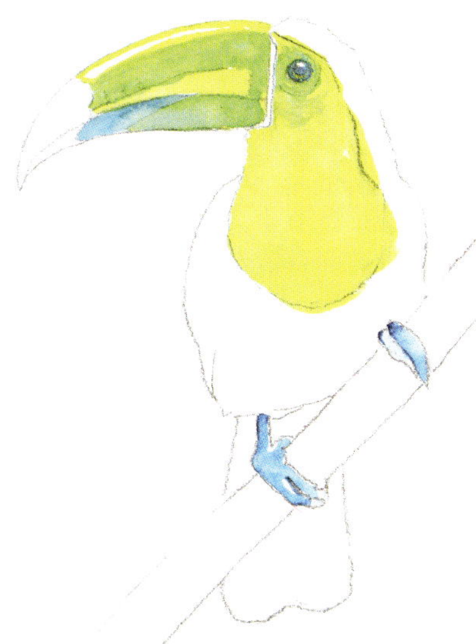

Step 1

Lay in the Yellow

Paint the breast and central beak area with pure Hansa Yellow Light. Let it dry completely before moving on.

Step 2

Glaze in Green

Brush a watery tint of Phthalo Blue (GS) over the yellow areas at the top and bottom of the beak, and around the eye. This creates a bright light green glaze.

Step 3

Add Blue Accents

Use milky Phthalo Blue for the feet and eye. Leave tiny slivers of white between the toes and a small highlight in the eye for sparkle.

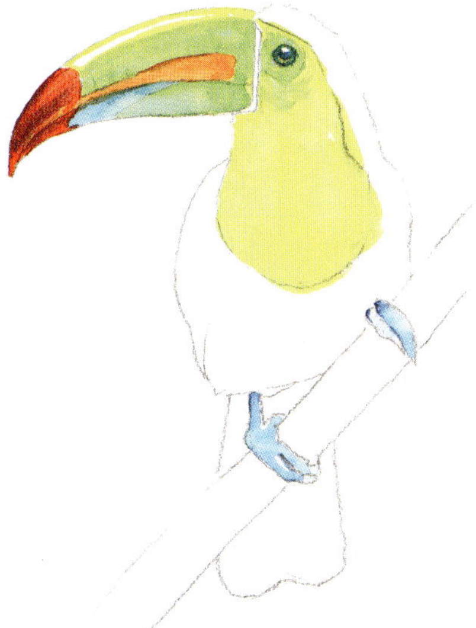

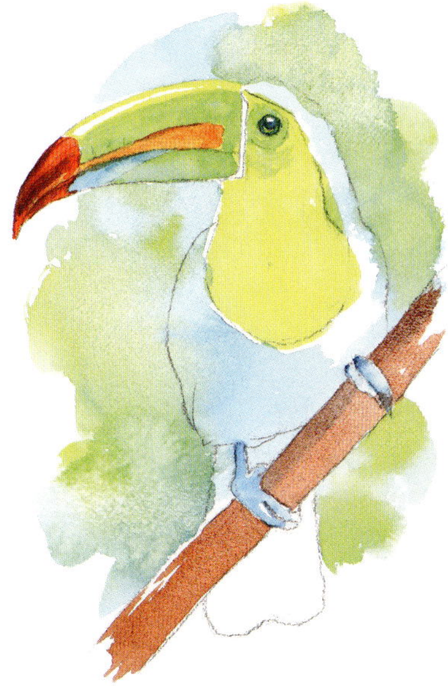

Step 4

Add a Pop of Red to the Beak

Layer Pyrrol Scarlet over the yellow strip to turn it into orange, then apply a stronger Scarlet wash on the beak tip. Deepen the outer edge with a touch of blue to give it roundness and form.

Step 5

Paint the Background and Branch

Choose any colors you like for a loose, watery backdrop. Cool tones (Phthalo Blue and Hansa Yellow Light) recede in space and make the bird pop against the background. Use Burnt Sienna to block in the branch with broad, simple strokes.

Scan to watch a video.

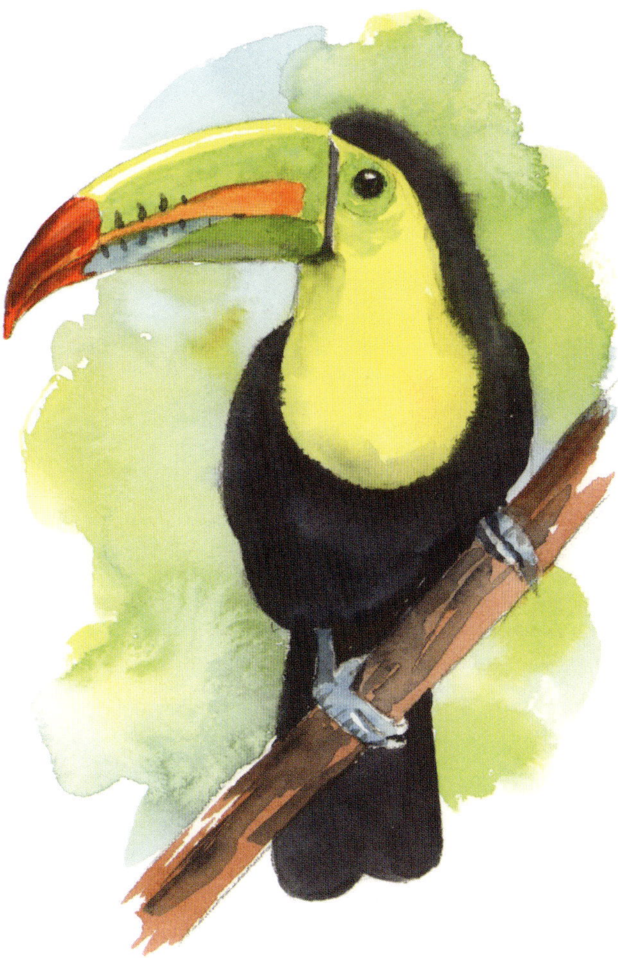

Step 6

Finish with Black

Mix a deep black from Phthalo Blue and Pyrrol Scarlet. Use this to paint the toucan's glossy feathers and small beak markings. With a thinned version, add texture to the branch and shading to the feet. Deepen the eye one last time, then add any final touches to complete the painting.

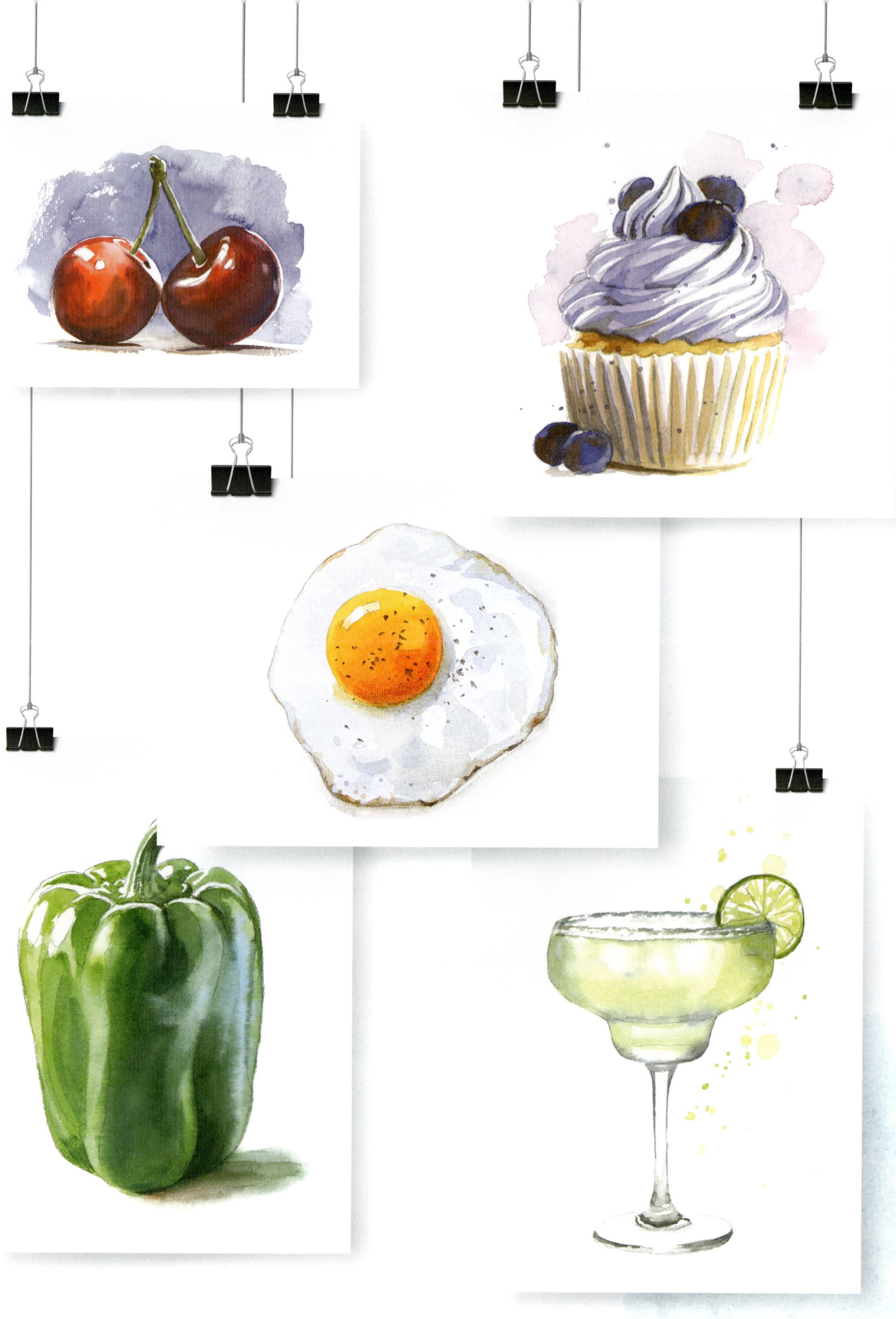

CHAPTER 6

20-Minute Still Lifes

A still life can be anything—a bowl of fruit, a favorite mug, or a trinket from your desk. These familiar objects invite you to explore color, shape, and texture, revealing how even the simplest things can become beautiful through your brush and imagination.

Bird's Nest

Capture the cozy complexity of a bird's nest with warm browns, golden glows, and airy overlapping strokes. By layering color and leaving gaps, we'll suggest the intricate weave of twigs and grasses without getting bogged down in detail.

COLORS

New Gamboge | Burnt Sienna | Phthalo Blue (GS)

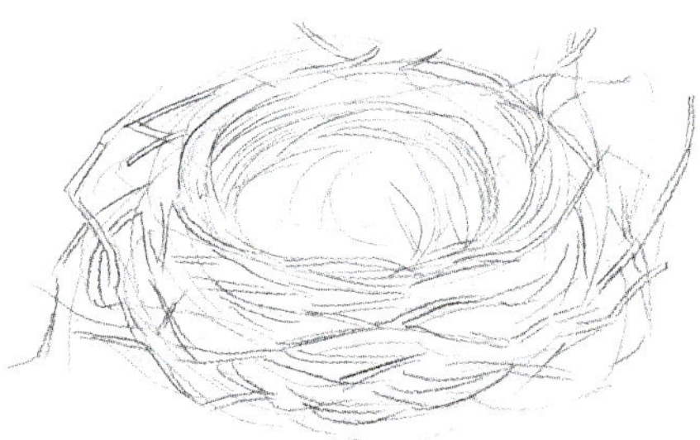

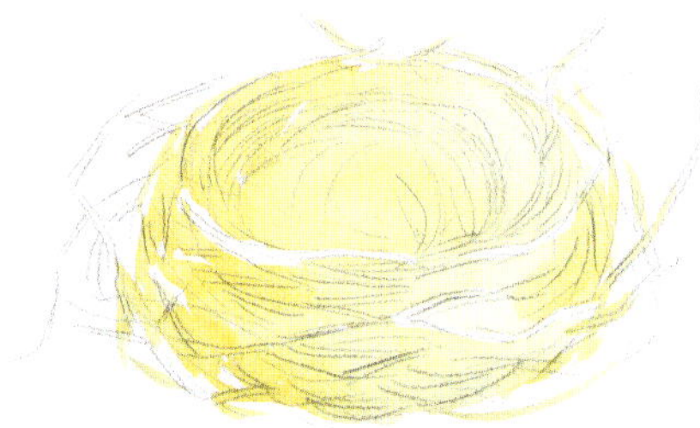

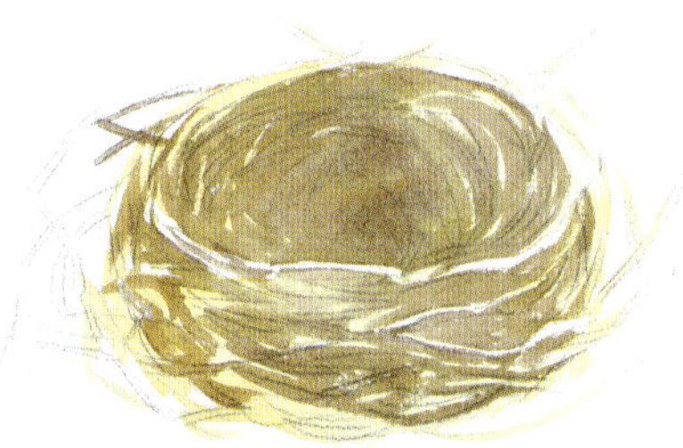

Step 1

Sketch the Nest

Lightly sketch a horizontal oval for the nest's base. Add intertwining lines and loose twigs to suggest the woven structure. Keep it organic—slightly uneven edges make the nest feel more natural.

Step 2

Lay a Golden Base

Wash the nest with New Gamboge, leaving the very outermost strands untouched so they can stay lighter. Use negative painting to skip over a few twigs and stems, building instant variety and depth.

Step 3

Add Warm Brown Layers

Mix Burnt Sienna with a touch of Phthalo Blue for a rich brown. With curved, nestlike strokes, darken the interior and tuck a few darker strands into the outer edges. Leave open spaces between strokes to keep the weave light and textured.

Scan to watch a video.

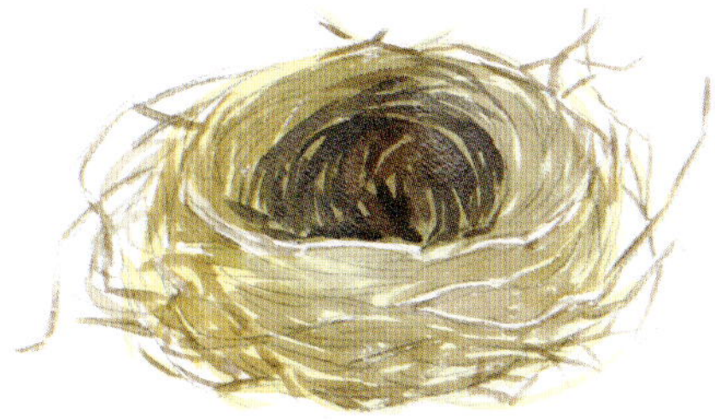

Step 4

Deepen the Bowl

Create a near-black by adding more blue to your brown. Use this to paint the shadowy depths at the nest's center, using curved C strokes to mimic overlapping twigs. Let your brush skip in places so it looks woven, not solid. Use this dark mix to add stray grasses flicking outward from the rim, giving the nest an airy, irregular edge.

Scan to watch a video.

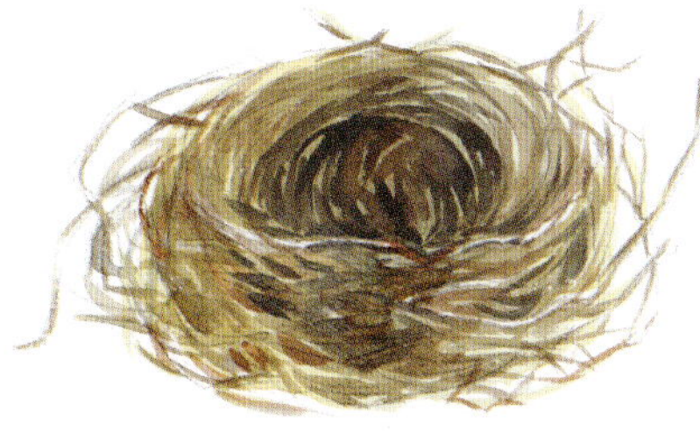

Step 5

Weave in More Variety

Glaze more twigs using alternating warm browns (more Burnt Sienna) and cooler browns (leaning blue). Work in layers, letting each one dry slightly before adding the next. Always leave slivers of light peeking through. This broken texture is what makes the nest look convincing.

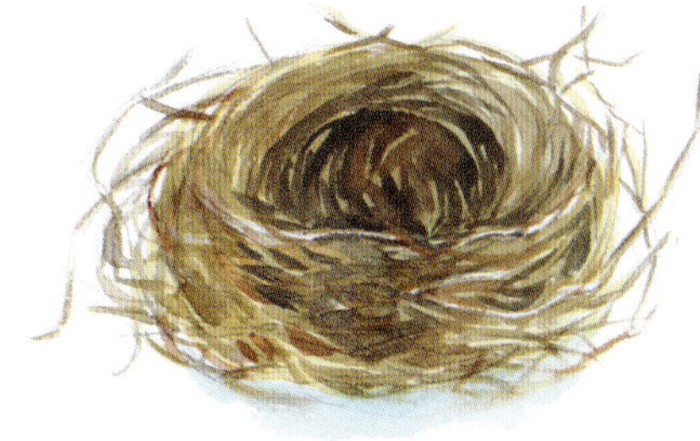

Step 6

Ground with a Shadow

Mix a watery wash of Phthalo Blue and paint a soft cast shadow beneath the nest. Feather out the edges with a clean damp brush so it settles naturally into the page.

Step 7

Finish the Nest

Once everything is dry, evaluate your painting. If needed, glaze a diluted brown wash over the interior to unify the layers while leaving the outer strands light. Add a few last wispy strokes for loose grasses, and the nest will feel complete.

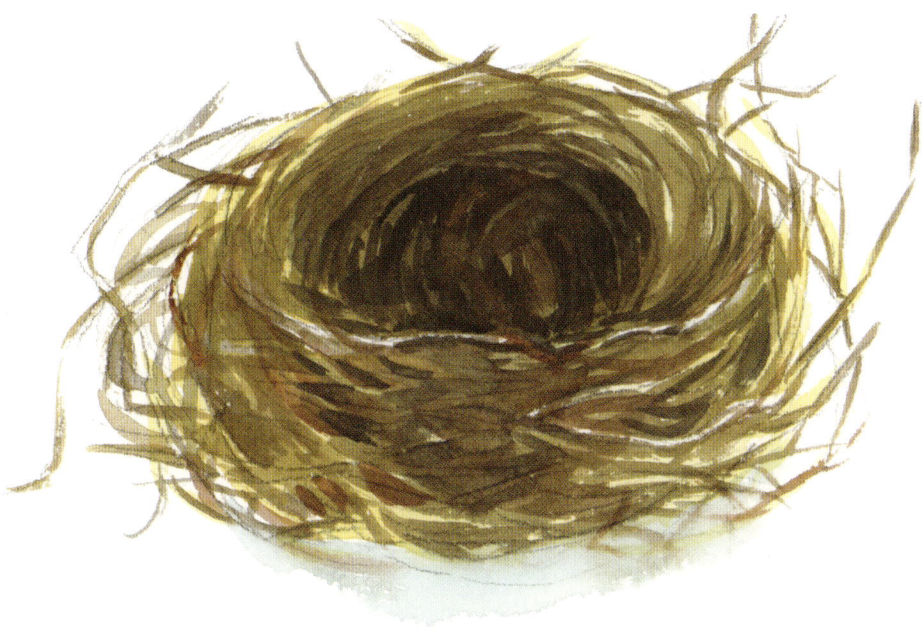

Tip

The charm of this subject lies in suggestion, not precision. Let your brushstrokes stay lively, and resist the urge to overfill every gap.

Blueberry Cupcake

Practice glazing and wet-on-wet techniques to paint a dessert so rich you'll almost want to taste it!

COLORS

French Ultramarine	Quinacridone Rose	New Gamboge	Burnt Sienna

Step 1

Start with a Violet Wash

Mix a milky violet from French Ultramarine and Quinacridone Rose. Wash this over all the shadowed areas of the cupcake, painting carefully around the highlights on the berries, frosting, and cup. This underpainting sets up the form and helps you map out your lightest lights.

Scan to watch a video.

Step 2

Add Touches of Golden Yellow

Rinse your brush well before picking up New Gamboge. With a milky consistency, paint the cake beneath the frosting. Then use upward strokes to tint the folds of the paper wrapper, adding warmth and a hint of transparency in the shadows.

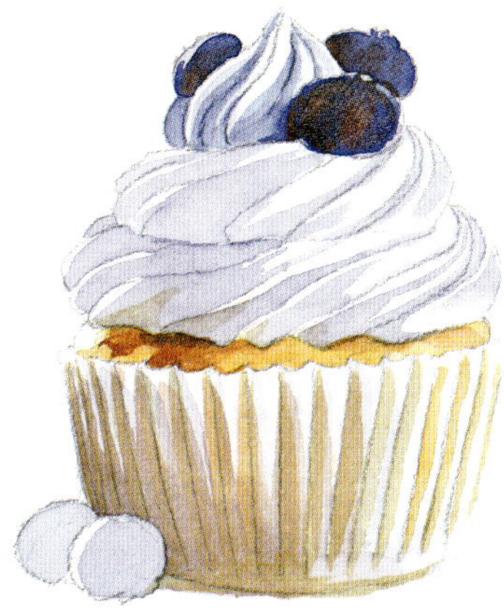

Step 3

Build Shadows with Burnt Sienna

Glaze a light tint of Burnt Sienna across the left side of the cupcake—on both the cake and the paper. This deeper layer strengthens the shadow side and helps establish a clear light source.

Step 4

Paint the First Blueberries

Use a creamy wash of French Ultramarine for the berries. While the paint is still damp, drop in Burnt Sienna to create a darker, more natural blue. At the same time, use milky Ultramarine to begin deepening the folds and creases in the frosting.

Scan to watch a video.

Step 5

Shape the Frosting

Glaze another layer of Ultramarine mixed with a touch of Quinacridone Rose over the frosting. With thoughtful, curved brushstrokes, carve out shadows between the swirls, being careful to preserve the untouched paper for sparkling highlights.

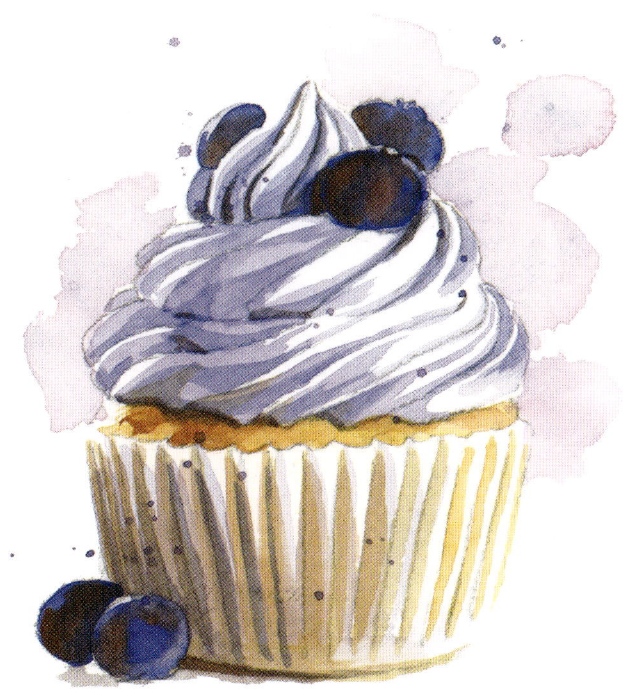

Step 6

Finish Blueberries, Shadows, and Background

Paint the bottom berries with the same Ultramarine-and-Sienna method, preserving a highlight on the foremost berry, and use your darker mix to define the paper cup's folds and add a soft curved shadow beneath the cupcake. Then finish with a playful background by mixing a watery red violet from Quinacridone Rose and French Ultramarine, blobbing and spattering it loosely around the cupcake to create lively contrast that makes the dessert pop.

Cherries

Explore the contrast between soft wet-on-wet blends and crisp, reflective highlights as you paint deep reds so vivid and juicy, you'll be tempted to reach out and taste them.

COLORS

French Ultramarine	Pyrrol Scarlet	Burnt Sienna	Quinacridone Rose	Phthalo Blue (GS)	New Gamboge

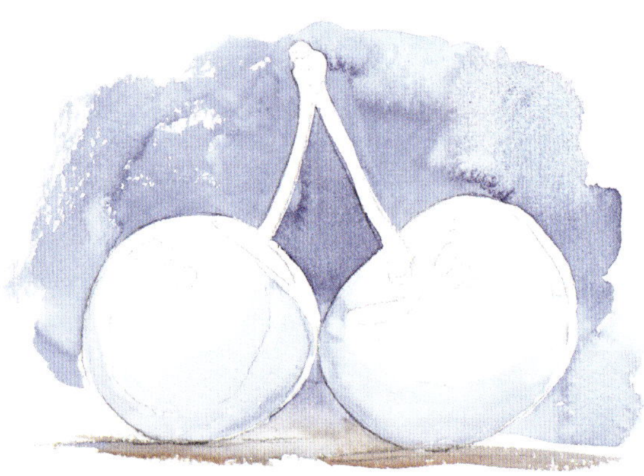

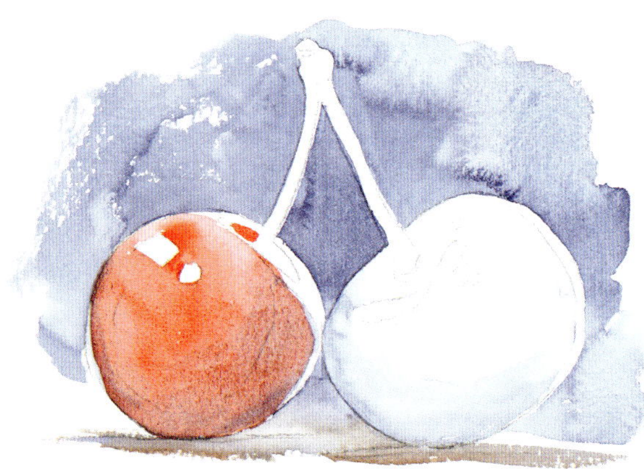

Step 1

Paint the Cool Background and Shadows

Sketch the cherries, then mix a milky French Ultramarine with a touch of Pyrrol Scarlet for a soft violet blue. Paint it wet-on-dry around the cherries to define the background and use the same mix for the curved cast shadows. Add a hint of Burnt Sienna at the base for grounding, and let everything dry.

Scan to watch a video.

Step 2

Lay Down the First Cherry Wash

Mix a watery blend of Pyrrol Scarlet and Quinacridone Rose. Fill in the first cherry with this wash, carefully painting around the highlight shapes. Near the stem base, dab in a slightly more saturated Pyrrol Scarlet to suggest the gentle dip at the top of the cherry.

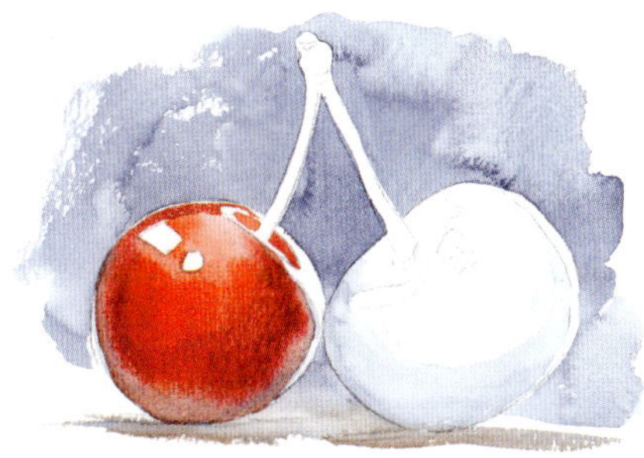

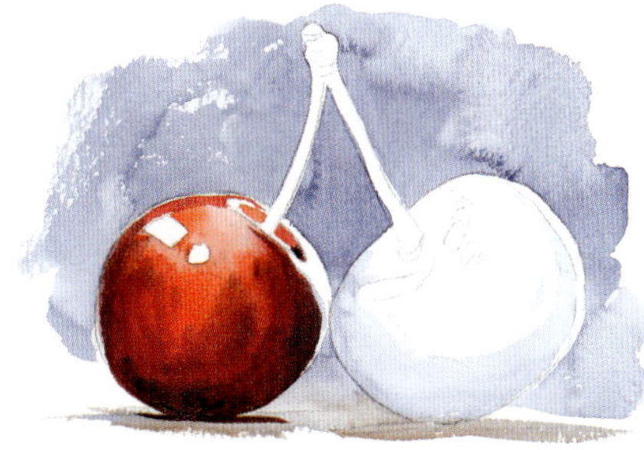

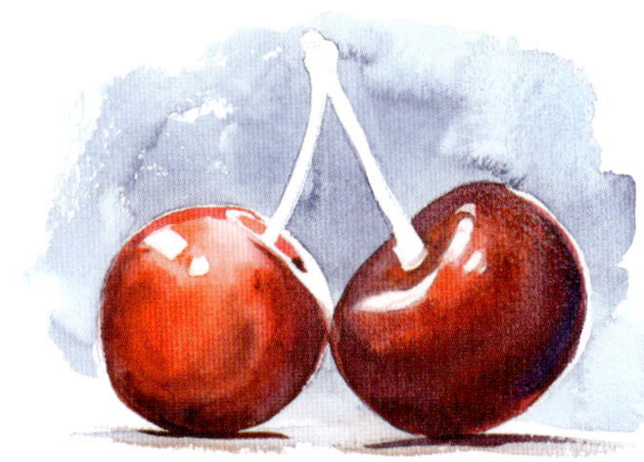

Step 3

Deepen the Color While Wet

While the cherry is still damp, quickly switch to a creamier mix of Pyrrol Scarlet and Quinacridone Rose. Gently brush this into the center of the cherry using the wet-on-wet technique. Leave some lighter areas untouched, especially near the top, to preserve the glow and enhance the sense of form.

Step 4

Add the Core Shadow

Prepare a thick mix of Phthalo Blue (GS) with Pyrrol Scarlet. Using a curving motion of your brush, drop this deep shadow into the base of the cherry. Work quickly and resist the urge to over-brush. Let the pigment settle naturally into the damp layer for a soft, organic transition.

Step 5

Paint the Second Cherry

Repeat the same process (Steps 2–4) for the second cherry using the wet-on-wet method. To make this cherry feel deeper and richer, cover more of the form with your Phthalo Blue and Pyrrol Scarlet mix. For added dimension, introduce a hint of pure Phthalo Blue to the darkest side on the right. This cool tone makes the form recede and glow.

Scan to watch a video.

Step 6

Paint the Stems and Final Touches

Mix an earthy green by combining New Gamboge with French Ultramarine. Pull your brush toward you on the palette to form a sharp point, then carefully paint each stem. If possible, leave a sliver of white paper along the top edge of the stems for a highlight. Finish with subtle refinements: lift a small highlight on the darker cherry using a clean, damp brush, gently dabbing the paper. These small adjustments will bring your painting to life.

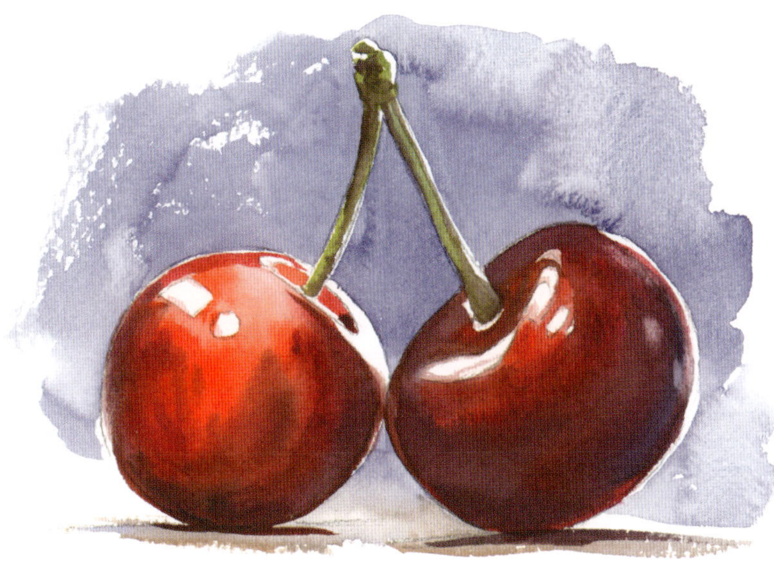

Conch Shell

Embrace the spirit of the coast in this radiant conch shell tutorial. Discover the interplay of warm and cool hues within the shell's smooth interior, then complete your seaside masterpiece with loose, expressive background washes.

COLORS

Pyrrol Scarlet	Quinacridone Rose	New Gamboge	French Ultramarine

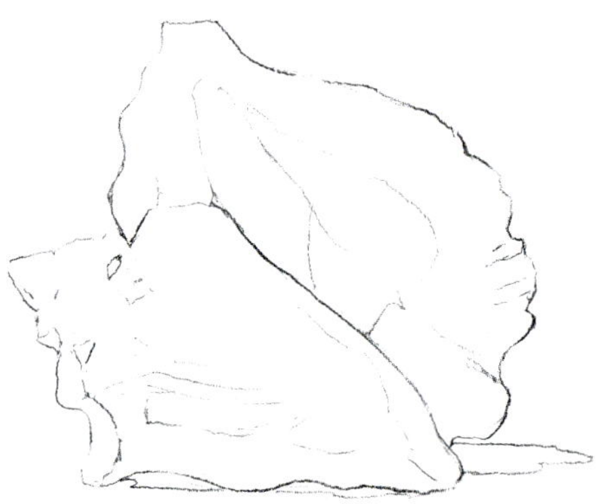

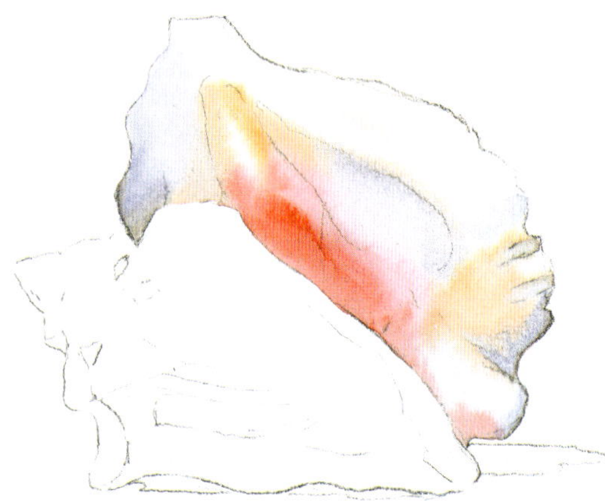

Step 1

Start with a Simple Shell Sketch

Trace or freehand the outline of the shell, keeping your lines clean and light as a foundation for the vibrant color to come.

Step 2

Paint the Luminous Inner Shell

Use clean water to thoroughly wet the area inside the pencil lines of the inner shell. The surface should look glossy but without any pooling. Next, mix a rich, creamy blend of Pyrrol Scarlet and Quinacridone Rose and apply it to the bright pink sections. While the paper is still damp, drop in touches of New Gamboge and French Ultramarine, letting the colors mingle naturally and create beautiful, soft transitions.

Scan to watch a video.

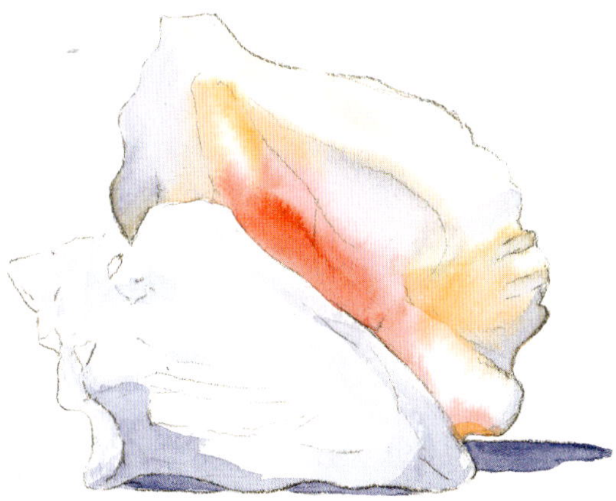

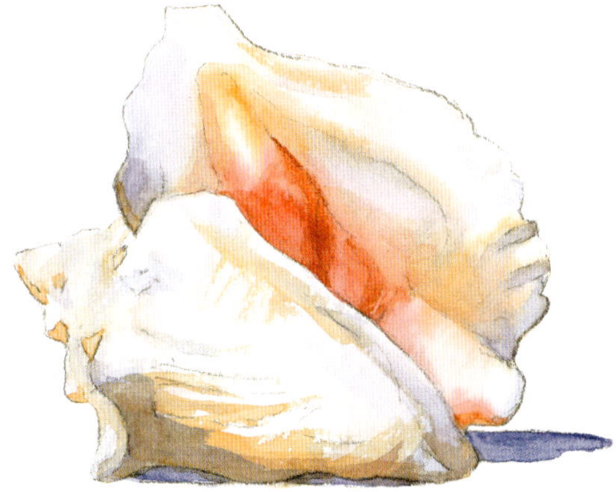

Step 3

Add Gentle Shadows and Structure

Use a diluted wash of French Ultramarine to gently paint the light shadows across the textured, bumpy surface of the shell. For the deeper shadows along the underside of the conch, switch to a more concentrated blue to add depth and contrast.

Step 4

Glaze Warm Tones and Add Texture

Mix New Gamboge with Pyrrol Scarlet to create a warm orange hue. Lightly glaze this over the shadowed areas, then use drybrushing to add a textured, sun-kissed tan across the shell's surface. If the top portion of the shell has dried by now, go back in with a second, deeper layer of your Pyrrol Scarlet and rose mix to intensify the interior and add dimension.

Scan to watch a video.

Step 5

Finish with a Fun Background (Optional)

You can leave your painting as a clean, minimalist piece with a white background or have some fun suggesting a beachy setting! I painted a soft, sandy base using a flat wash of Pyrrol Scarlet and New Gamboge, then added touches of pure French Ultramarine in the background. While the blue is still damp, drop in clean water to create blooms and movement, giving your scene a lively, coastal feel that almost dances off the page.

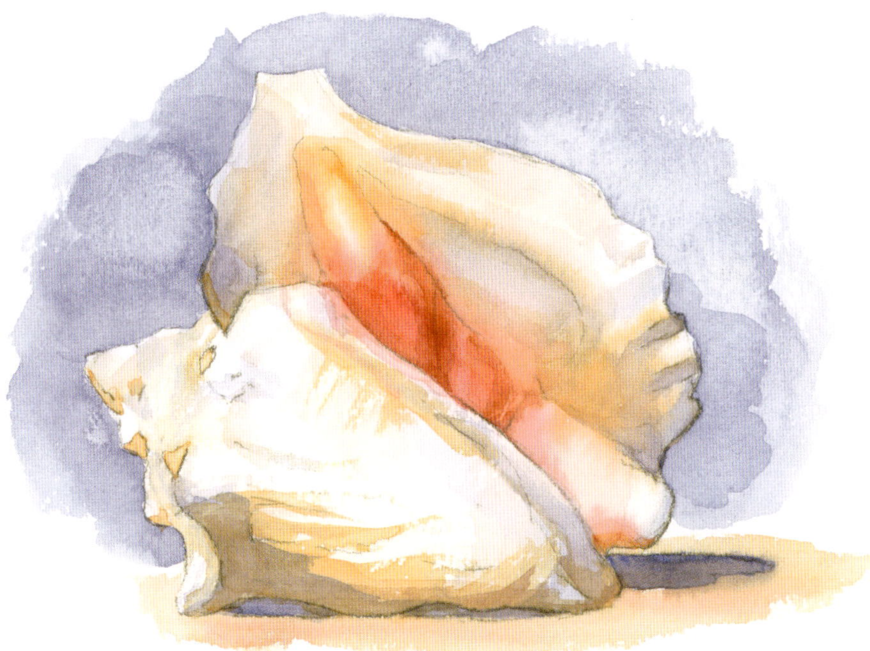

Espresso Cup

Paint a cozy porcelain cup with depth and shine using just three colors.

COLORS

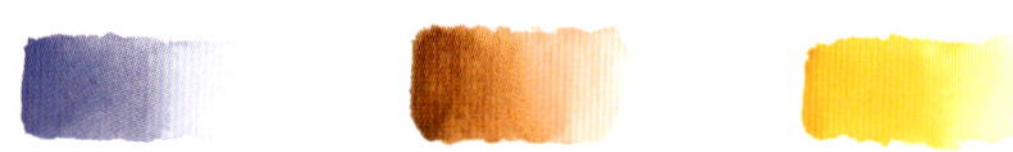

French Ultramarine | Burnt Sienna | New Gamboge

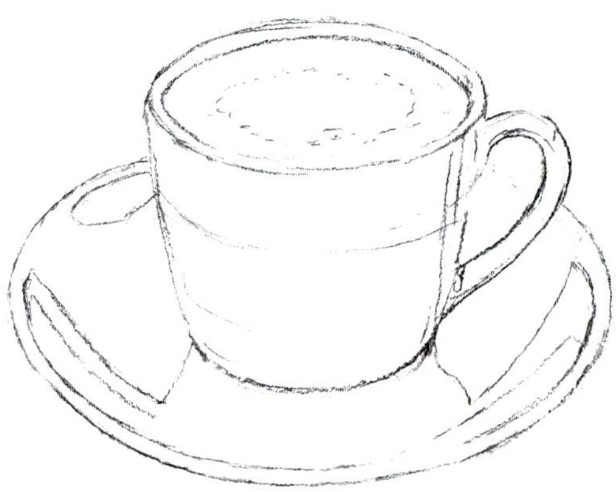

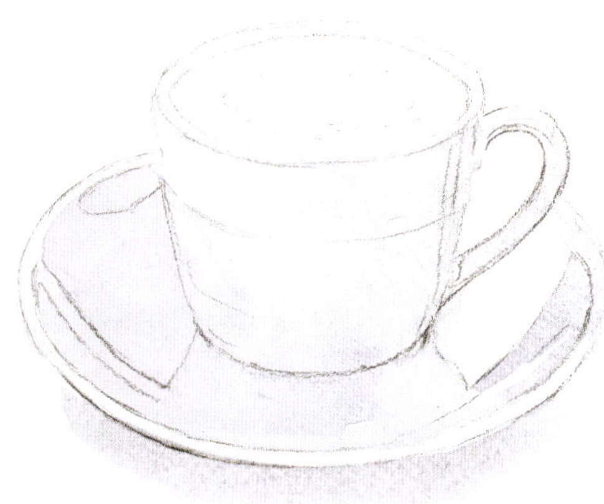

Step 1

Sketch the Cup and Saucer

Begin with the large ellipse of the saucer, then float a smaller ellipse above it for the mouth of the cup. Connect the two with slanted sides, then add a graceful, curved handle. Lightly sketch a few highlight shapes on the cup to remind yourself where to leave the paper white.

Step 2

Lay in the First Wash

Mix French Ultramarine and Burnt Sienna into a watery 50/50 neutral gray. Paint this wash smoothly across the cup and saucer, leaving your highlight areas untouched. With the same mix, add a soft shadow beneath the saucer. To keep it natural, rinse and blot your brush, then feather the lower edge of the shadow so it fades gently into the paper. Let everything dry fully before moving on.

Scan to watch a video.

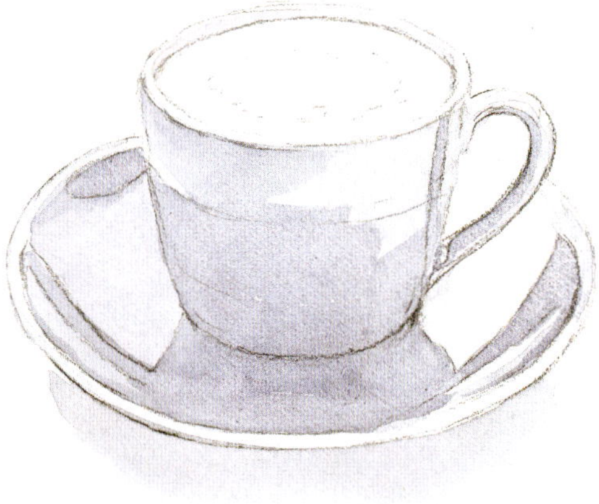

Step 3

Build Subtle Depth

Using the same gray, glaze a second layer on the shadowed side of the cup and the underside of the saucer. Pay attention to the reflected shapes where the cup meets the saucer. This small detail helps make your porcelain look shiny and dimensional. Let it dry.

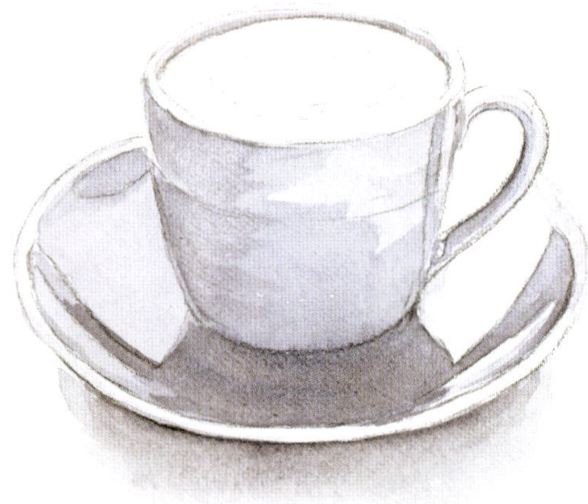

Step 4

Deepen the Shadows

Glaze on a final layer of gray to strengthen the darkest areas, especially beneath the saucer and in the cast shadow. With your brush loaded in a milky consistency, curve your strokes gently along the left side of the cup. This little curve instantly makes the porcelain look rounded and three-dimensional.

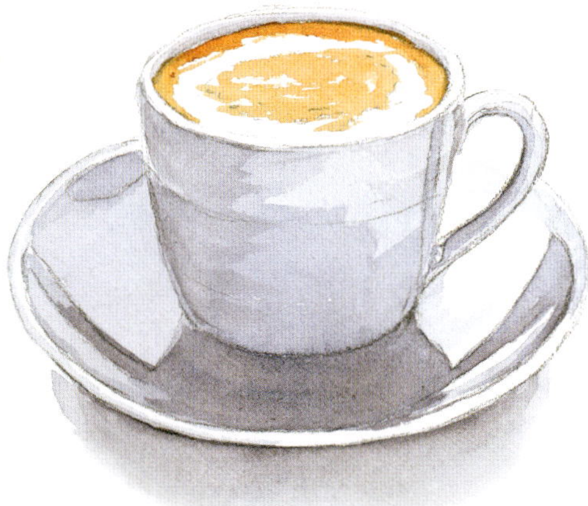

Step 5

Pour the Coffee

Mix a warm espresso tone with New Gamboge and Burnt Sienna in a milky consistency. Paint it inside the cup's rim, following the curved ellipse for accurate perspective. Add a few loose strokes for variation, leaving a small white oval as the foamy highlight.

Scan to watch a video.

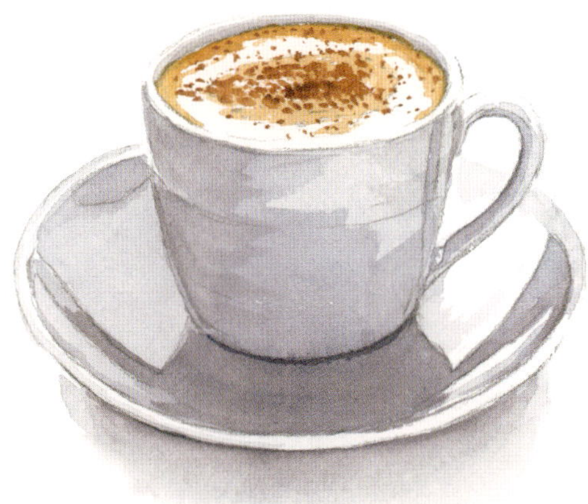

Step 6

Add the Finishing Garnish

For a playful touch, load your brush with creamy Burnt Sienna and tap in tiny, irregular dots across the foam. Keep them random and varied in size so it feels like a natural dusting of cacao rather than a polka-dot pattern. This subtle detail makes your drink look truly café-worthy!

Fried Egg

Explore the beauty of simplicity in this over-easy egg study. Use a balance of bold and delicate washes to capture the glowing warmth of the yolk and the soft translucence of the white.

COLORS

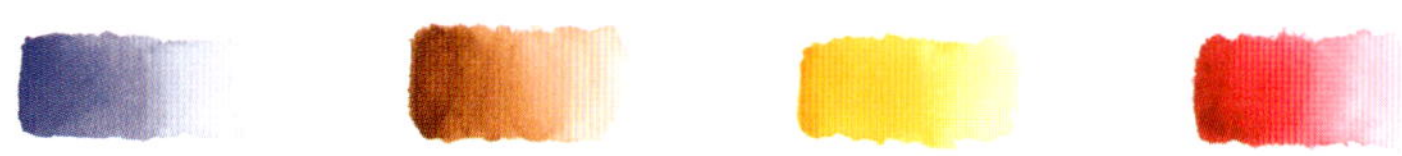

French Ultramarine | Burnt Sienna | New Gamboge | Quinacridone Rose

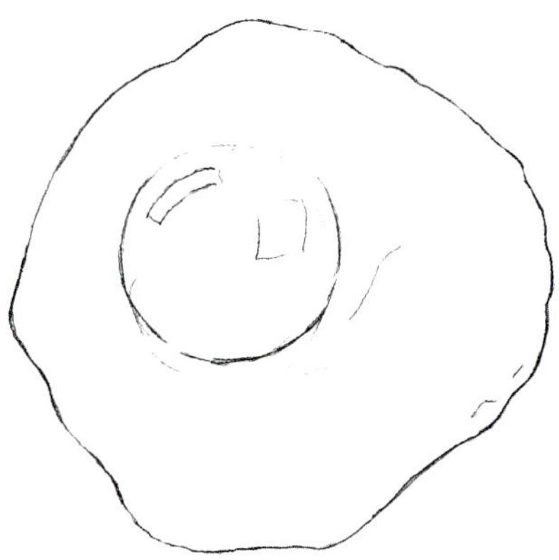

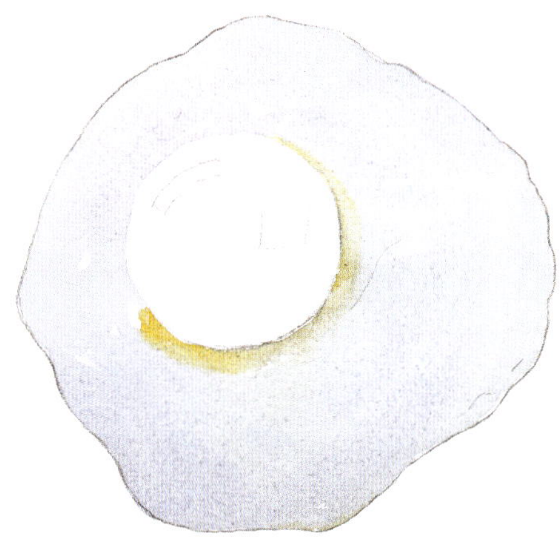

Step 1

Sketch a Simple Fried Egg Shape

Don't worry if you're not confident in your drawing skills—*this part is easy and fun!* Start by drawing a loose, wiggly shape for the egg white—think of a blobby amoeba. Next, add the yolk: a more rounded circle that's just slightly off to one side. You can freehand it or trace around something circular (like a bottle cap) to keep it neat. Finish by lightly sketching a few curved highlight shapes inside the yolk, following the curve of the circle to help it feel round and glossy.

Step 2

Paint the Egg White with Subtle Color and Glow

Mix a watery French Ultramarine with a touch of Burnt Sienna for a cool gray and lightly wash it over the egg white, leaving a few highlight slivers. While damp, blot your brush and drop in a bit of New Gamboge near the yolk's edge to suggest reflected color.

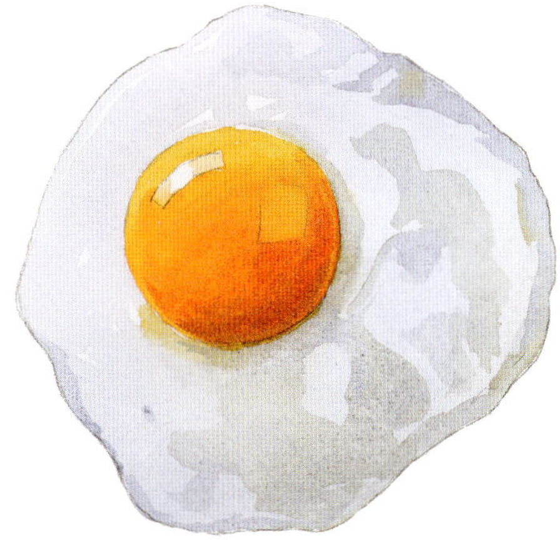

Step 3

Add the Yellow Egg Yolk

Paint the yolk with creamy New Gamboge, leaving the brightest highlight. While damp, mix in a bit of Quinacridone Rose to create a warm orange for the shadow side. With a lightly dampened brush, blend a middle transition between dark and light, avoiding the secondary highlight and keeping the damp-on-damp blend smooth.

Scan to watch a video.

Step 4

Add Soft Shadow Textures to the Egg White

Mix a very watery combination of French Ultramarine, Burnt Sienna, and a touch of New Gamboge to create a soft, neutral gray. Using this diluted mix, glaze a few loose, organic shadow shapes over the egg white to suggest subtle surface texture. Focus these shadows mostly on the right side of the egg, keeping the left side lighter to preserve the sense of light direction and form. Keep your brushstrokes soft and irregular—think gentle blobby patches, not hard lines—for a natural, realistic look.

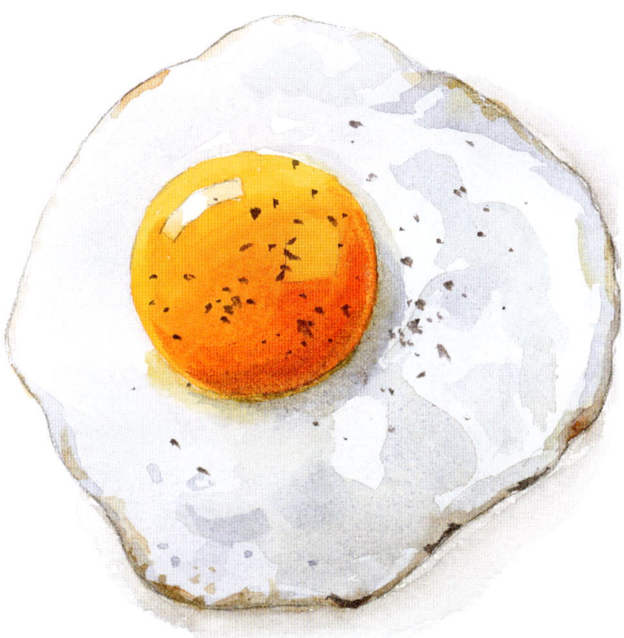

Step 5

Finish with Crispy Edges and a Sprinkle of Pepper

Time for the final touches! Use a slightly stronger mix of your Burnt Sienna–Ultramarine mix to paint a crispy, textured edge around parts of the egg white to suggest delicious browning. Then, add a subtle shadow along the right side to ground the egg and give it depth. For the perfect finishing detail, sprinkle in some tiny pepper specks; just a few flicks of dark paint across the top will bring the whole piece to life with texture and contrast.

Scan to watch a video.

Green Bell Pepper

Paint a vibrant, glossy pepper using negative painting and wet-on-wet blending with just three colors.

COLORS

Phthalo Blue (GS)	Hansa Yellow Light	Pyrrol Scarlet

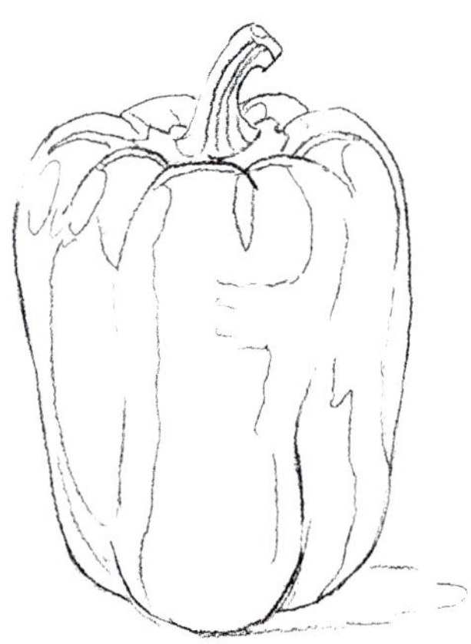

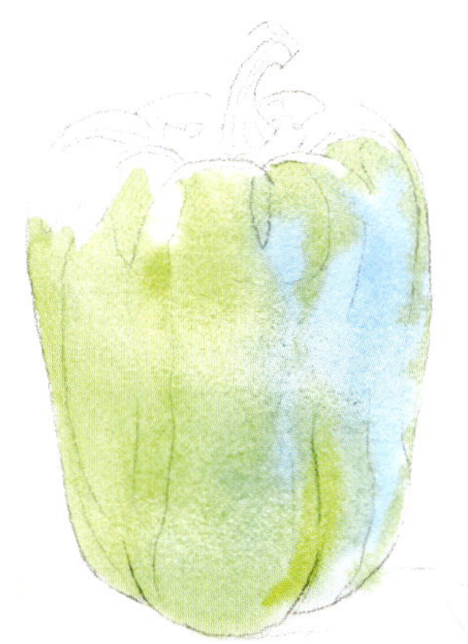

Step 1

Sketch the Vegetable

Draw a rounded pepper shape standing upright. Mark out your brightest highlights so you can avoid them when painting.

Step 2

Paint a Light Base

Wet the pepper with clean water, leaving the top and highlight areas dry. Brush in milky Phthalo Blue (GS) along the right side, then switch to Hansa Yellow Light for the left. If your brush still carries a hint of blue, let it mingle with the yellow for a fresh lime-green base wash.

Scan to watch a video.

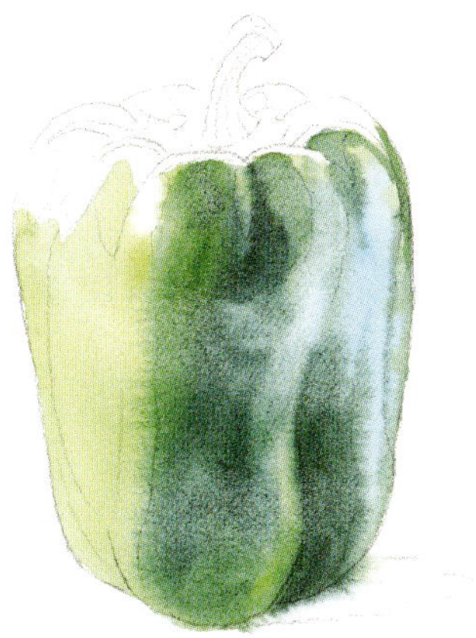

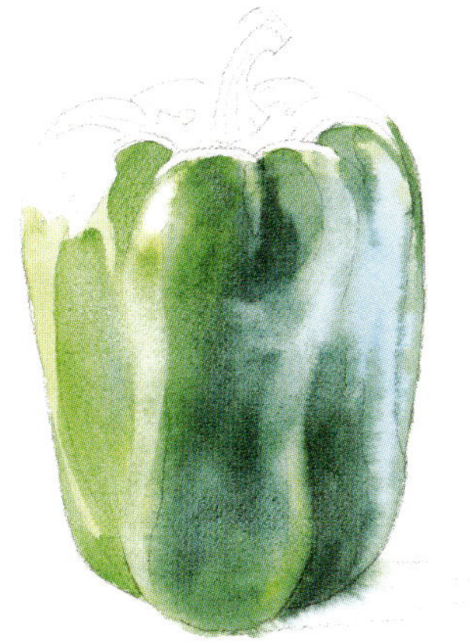

Step 3

Soften Shadows Wet-on-Wet

While the paper is still damp, mix a deeper green with Phthalo Blue, Hansa Yellow Light, and a touch of Pyrrol Scarlet. Paint this into the shadow side in a creamy consistency, negative painting around your highlights and lighter blue areas. The damp surface will soften your edges naturally.

Step 4

Refine the Light Side

As the paper begins to dry, layer medium greens onto the highlighted side. Match the wetness of your brush to the paper so your strokes blend smoothly, defining the pepper's curves without losing its shine.

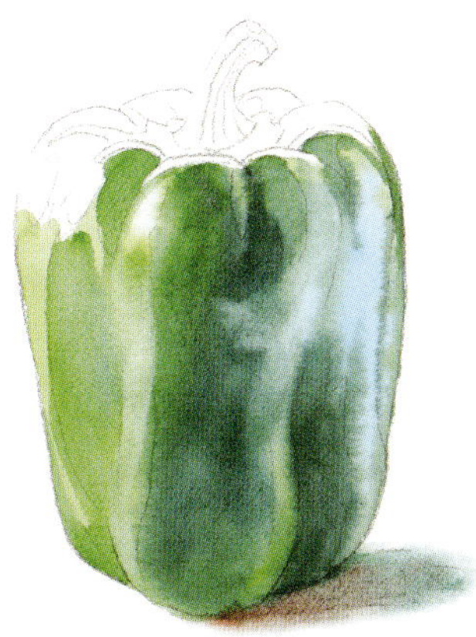

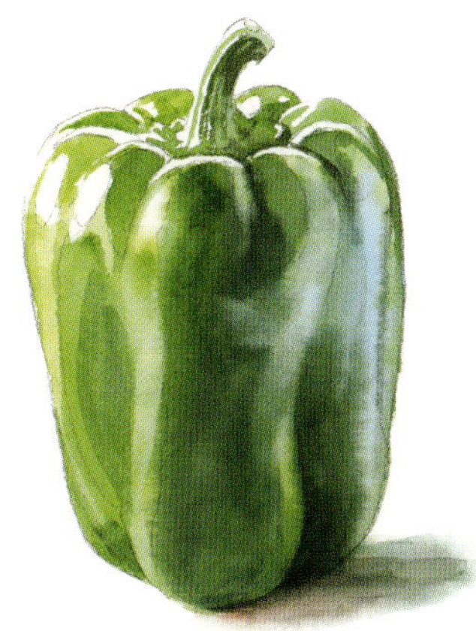

Step 5

Add a Ground Shadow

Mix Pyrrol Scarlet with a little green for a natural shadow beneath the pepper. Place it just to the right of the base, then soften the edges with a clean, damp brush so it fades into the page.

Step 6

Finish the Top

Use a medium green (Phthalo Blue and Hansa Yellow Light) to paint the top details wet-on-dry. Leave your highlights intact to show the rounded bulges. Darken the creases and stem base with your rich green mix for depth and realism.

Scan to watch a video.

Refreshing Lime Drink

Glassware makes a wonderfully tricky subject, with its crisp, geometric edges contrasted by the loose, organic shapes of whatever it holds. In this lesson, we'll tackle that balance using just three primaries to paint a refreshing, colorful beverage.

COLORS

Hansa Yellow Light	French Ultramarine	Pyrrol Scarlet

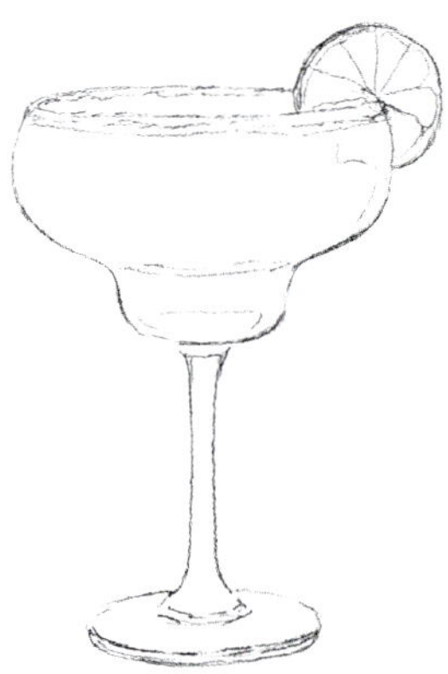

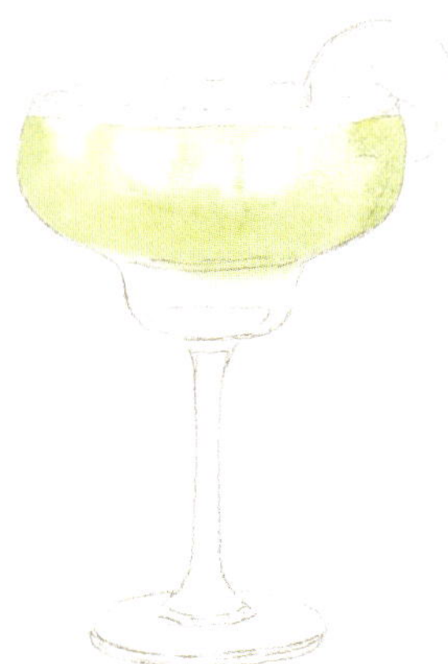

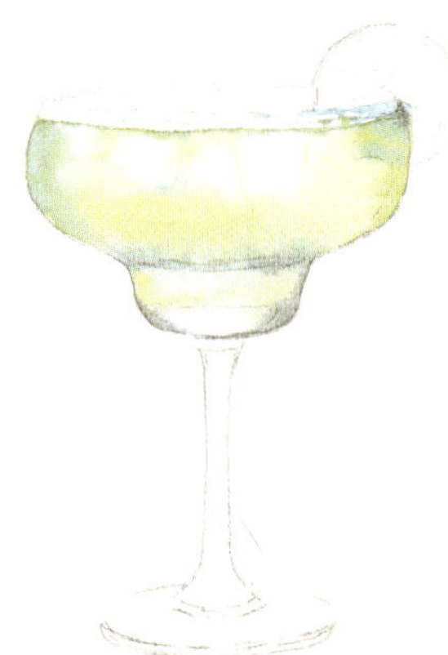

Step 1

Sketch the Glass

Begin with the basic glass shape. The bowl should be about twice as wide as the base, with symmetrical curves that flow elegantly into the stem. Add a lime wedge perched on one side for balance and character.

Step 2

Paint the Lime-Tinted Liquid

Wet the cup interior with clean water until the surface is glossy. Drop in a milky mix of Hansa Yellow Light with just a hint of French Ultramarine for that zesty lime-green glow. Leave a few bright gaps in the center so they read as sparkling ice cubes.

Step 3

Blend Soft Shadows While Wet

While the surface is damp, deepen the outer edges and base with Ultramarine to suggest the glass curve. Use the same blue for dotted sugar crystals under the lime. Mix Ultramarine and Pyrrol Scarlet for a soft gray shadow beneath the cup, softening the edge with a damp brush.

Scan to watch a video.

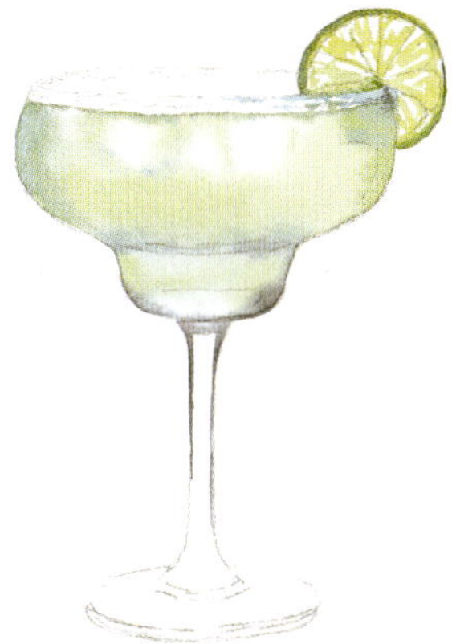

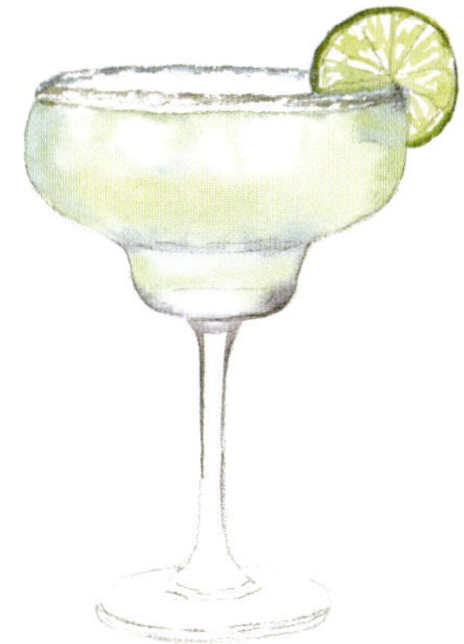

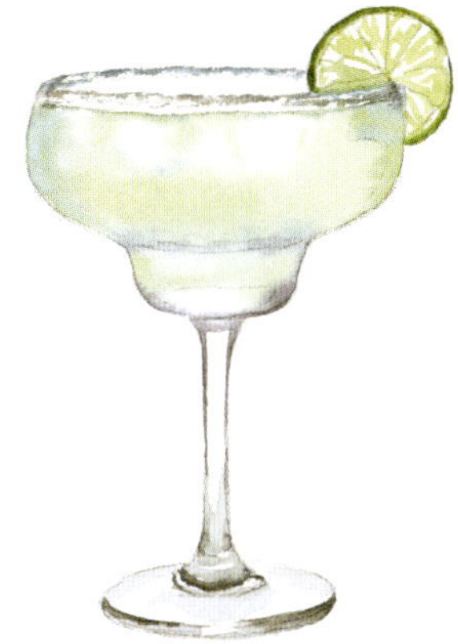

Step 4

Garnish with a Lime

Mix Hansa Yellow Light with a trace of Ultramarine for the juicy inner “spokes.” Outline the outer ring of the lime with a creamier version of the same mix. With your gray blend, lightly outline the stem, keeping the linework delicate to preserve the glassy effect.

Step 5

Create the Sugary Rim

Reload your gray mix, blot your brush, then drag it drybrush style across the rim to mimic the uneven sparkle of sugar. Keep it loose and irregular for a natural look.

Step 6

Finish the Stem and Base

Prepare two grays: one creamy, one watery. Use the darker mix for the curves and accents at the base, and the lighter wash to suggest reflections along the stem and bowl. This balance of values captures the transparent quality of glass.

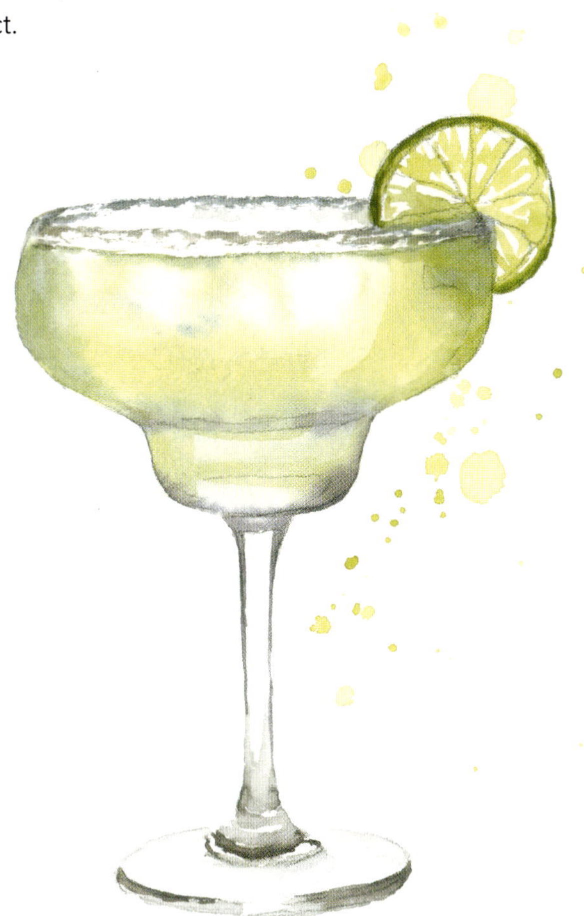

Step 7

Add Festive Spatter

For a playful finishing touch, flick bright yellow or lime green spatter around the painting to suggest lights and celebration!

Strawberry Cheesecake

Explore the reds and pinks of your palette as you paint glossy strawberries and silky glaze. With just a few intentional brushstrokes, you'll capture shine, texture, and the irresistible appeal of a perfectly plated treat.

COLORS

Pyrrol Scarlet | Quinacridone Rose | New Gamboge | French Ultramarine

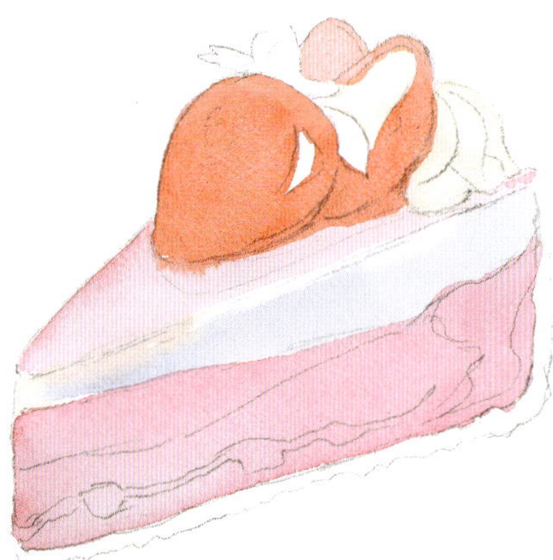

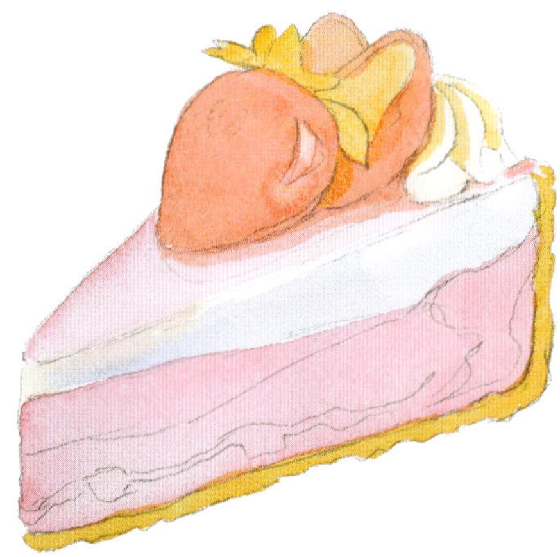

Step 1

Lay Down a Light Base Wash

Begin with light washes of all four colors. Paint the cheesecake body with watery Quinacridone Rose, using a paler mix on top. Wash the strawberries with delicate Pyrrol Scarlet, leaving highlights. Lightly tint the whipped cream with New Gamboge, and add a subtle French Ultramarine wash to the thin "white" top edge.

Scan to watch a video.

Step 2

Warm Up the Crust and Leaves

Using a milky mix of New Gamboge, paint in the cheesecake's crust and the green tops of the strawberries. Add soft warm shadows to the whipped cream for extra dimension. With watery Pyrrol Scarlet, sweep a stroke along the bottom edges of the strawberries to suggest a glowing red reflection shimmering on the shiny cheesecake surface.

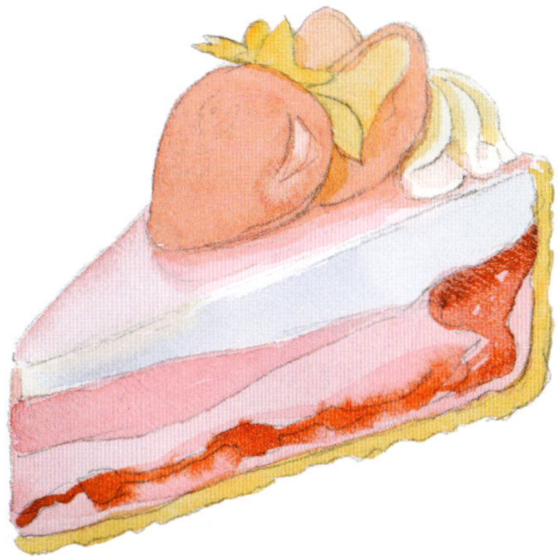

Step 3

Add a Juicy Layer of Jelly

Apply a thin second coat of Quinacridone Rose to the mid-section of the cheesecake slice. For that delicious strawberry jam layer, load up your brush with rich Pyrrol Scarlet and paint a textured, bumpy squiggle along the bottom edge of the slice to mimic glistening strawberry jam embedded in the dessert.

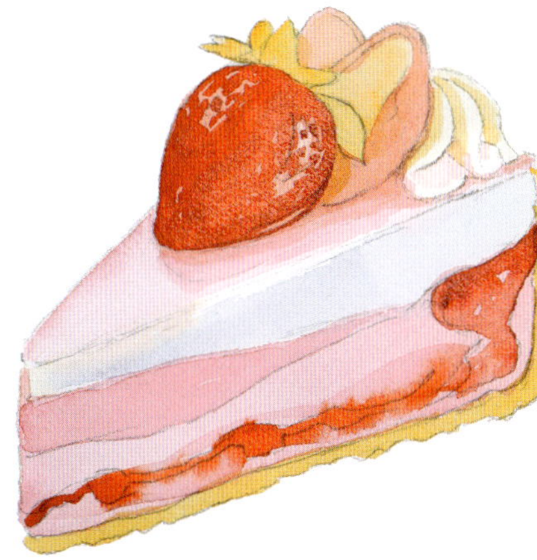

Step 4

Paint the Plump Strawberry on Top

Grab some more creamy, vibrant Pyrrol Scarlet and paint the main strawberry sitting atop the cheesecake. Keep the tip of your brush fine and controlled, carefully painting around tiny highlights to preserve a juicy shine. Add small dots within the highlights to suggest strawberry seeds for a touch of realism.

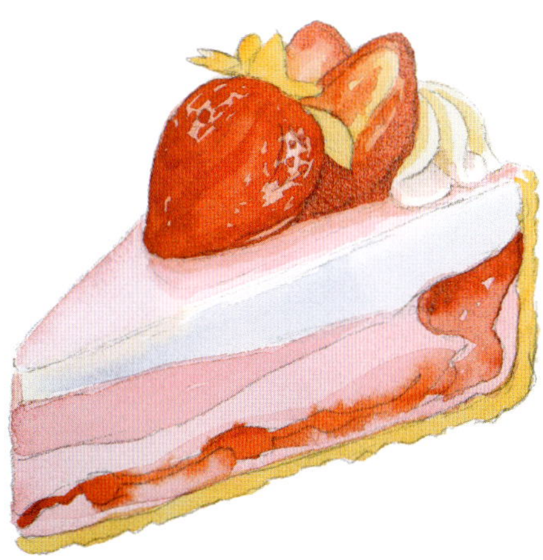

Step 5

Paint the Cut Strawberries

Next, paint the two halved strawberries with Pyrrol Scarlet, blending lighter values in the centers to create a soft, juicy interior. Deepen the color with thicker, darker paint at the base to build depth and show off the slices' shape.

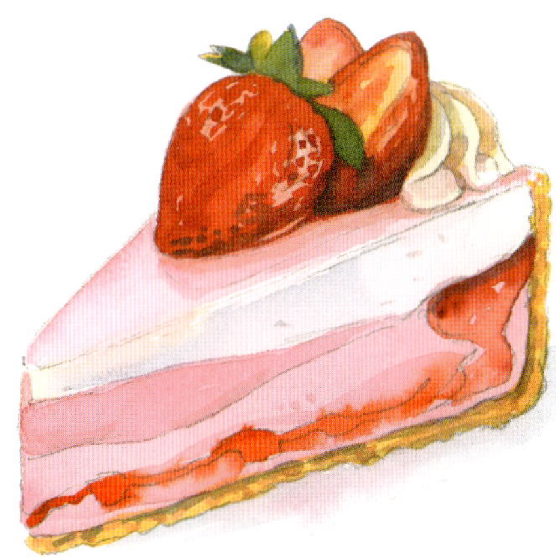

Step 6

Finish with Leaves and Final Details

Mix an earthy green with French Ultramarine and a touch of New Gamboge to paint the leaves and deepen strawberry areas with subtle seed details. Create a soft blue gray from Ultramarine, New Gamboge, and a hint of Quinacridone Rose, adding textured shadows to the crust and a light shadow beneath the cheesecake. Finish with tiny speckles in the filling for extra realism.

Well-Loved Baseball

Bring this timeless baseball to life by shading from light to dark and shaping it into a convincing sphere. Finish with a cast shadow that gives it weight and presence—almost as if it's ready to roll off the page.

COLORS

Burnt Sienna	French Ultramarine	New Gamboge	Pyrrol Scarlet

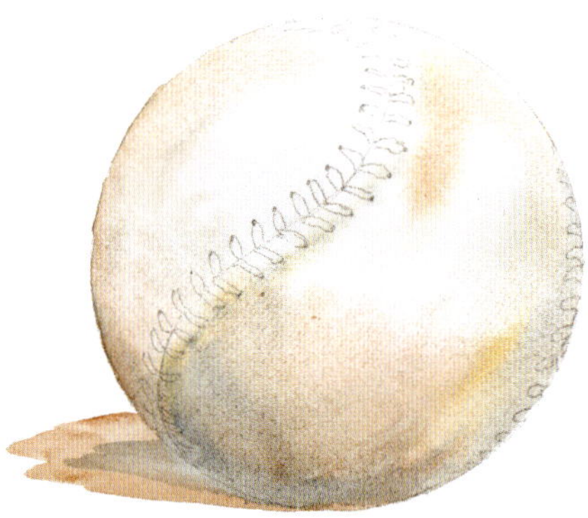

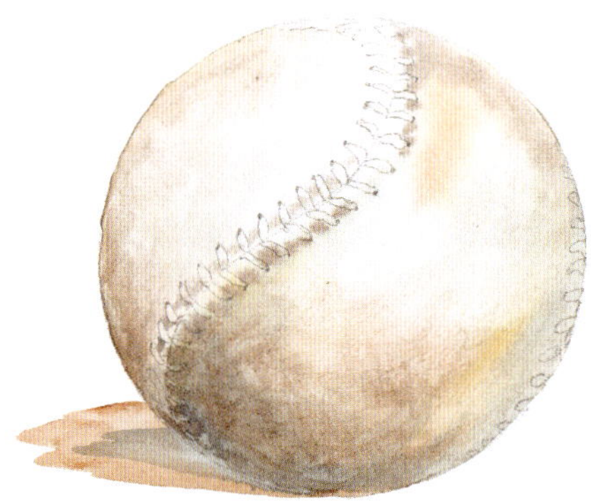

Step 1

Lay a Wet-on-Wet Foundation

Sketch the baseball, then brush clean water evenly inside the baseball shape, staying carefully within your pencil lines. While the paper is still glossy, drop in milky Burnt Sienna, concentrating more pigment at the bottom for shadow and form. Add small touches of French Ultramarine and New Gamboge for lively color variation and a weathered look. Finish with a loose cast shadow on the left.

Scan to watch a video.

Step 2

Build Rough Texture and Form

While the first wash is still damp, deepen the color by layering more Burnt Sienna in a rough, cross-hatching motion. Concentrate this textured color along the bottom, top, and under the stitching lines to begin sculpting the baseball's roundness and well-worn surface. Let the entire painting dry completely before moving on.

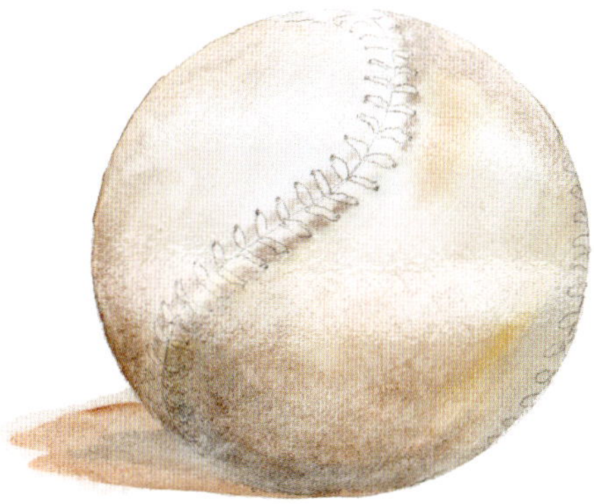

Step 3

Smooth and Soften the Surface

If any areas feel too blotchy or harsh, don't worry. Once dry, gently rewet the ball with clear water. This trick helps soften transitions and smooth out uneven patches, giving your baseball a more polished look.

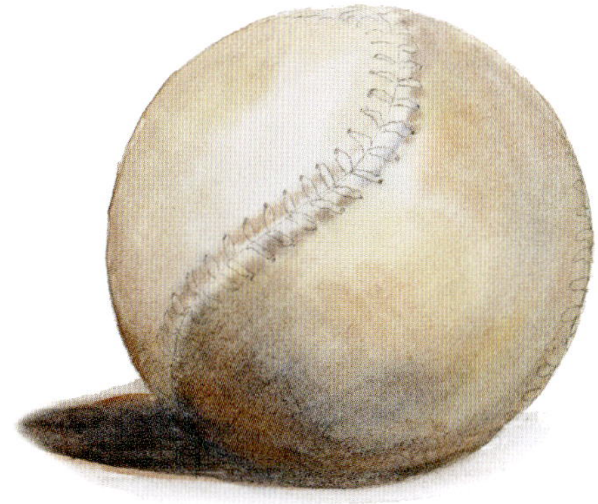

Step 4

Deepen Shadows

On glossy-wet paper, dab a creamy Burnt Sienna and French Ultramarine mix into the bottom of the ball to build soft, dark dimension without pressing too hard. Then use a richer 50/50 blend of the same colors to paint the cast shadow on the ground, letting its edge merge gently with the ball for a natural, lost-edge effect under strong light.

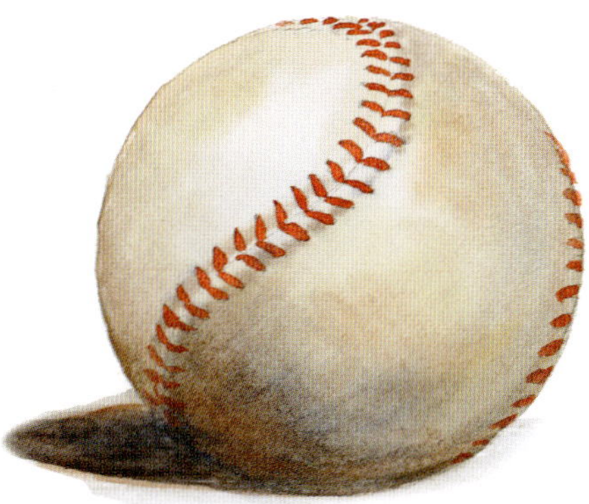

Step 5

Stitch on the Signature Red Threads

Now for that classic baseball detail! Use pure Pyrrol Scarlet to paint each stitch along the S curve you sketched earlier. Think of each stitch as two tiny leaves side by side, adjusting their size as they curve around the ball's form to create a sense of perspective.

Scan to watch a video.

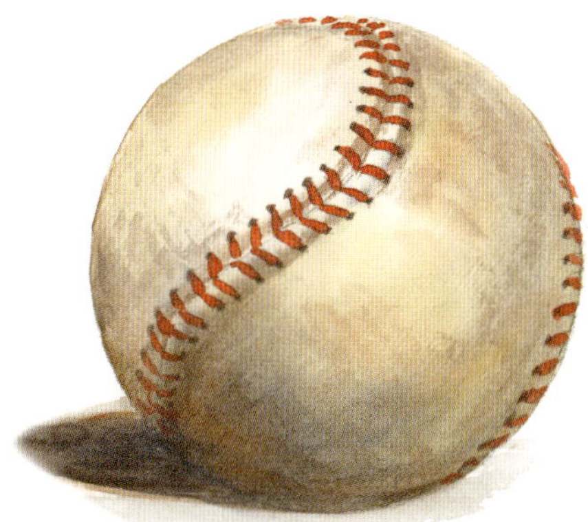

Step 6

Add Character with Final Textures

Re-mix your dark blend and dot tiny holes at the base of each stitch for realism. Add a light Burnt Sienna sweep through the stitching curve for dimension. Finish with a dry brushstroke of slightly damp Burnt Sienna to create rough, broken textures that suggest a well-worn baseball.

Traceable Templates

I have provided templates of all the projects in the books that you can use to jump-start your paintings. You can also download and print these templates using the QR code below or visiting https://www.quarto.com/files/20MinuteWatercolor. See page 26 for tips on transferring images.

Scan to download reference photos and traceable templates for all of the projects in the book.

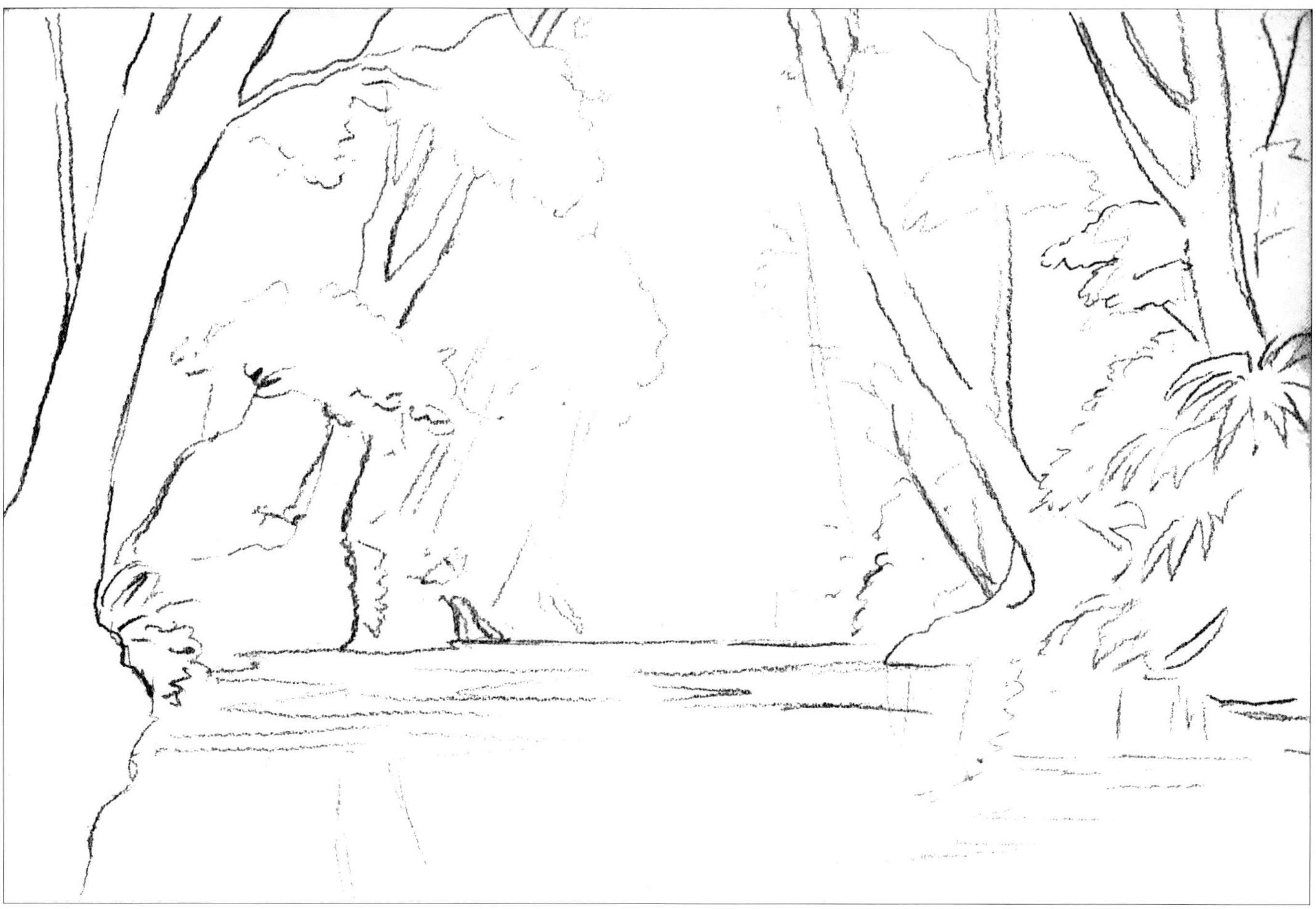

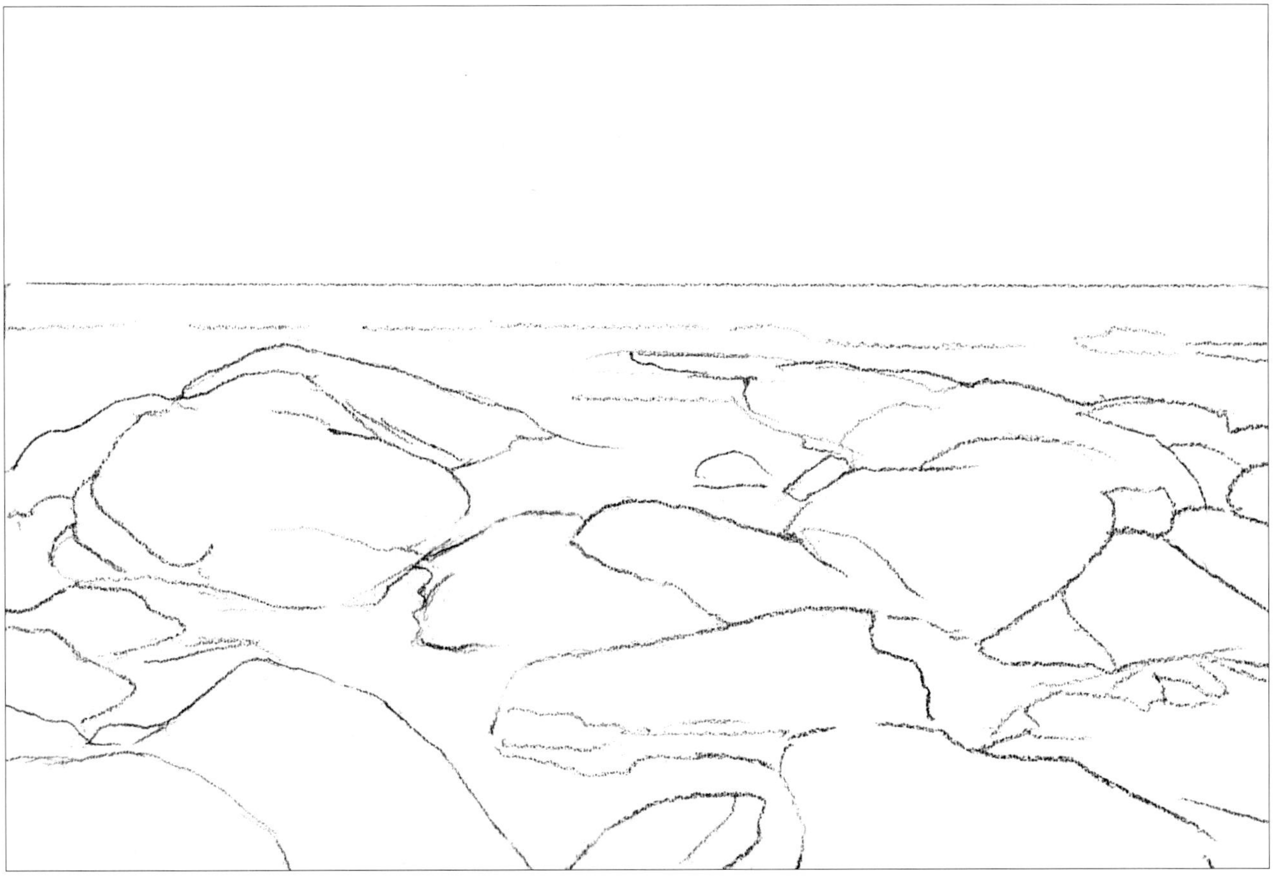

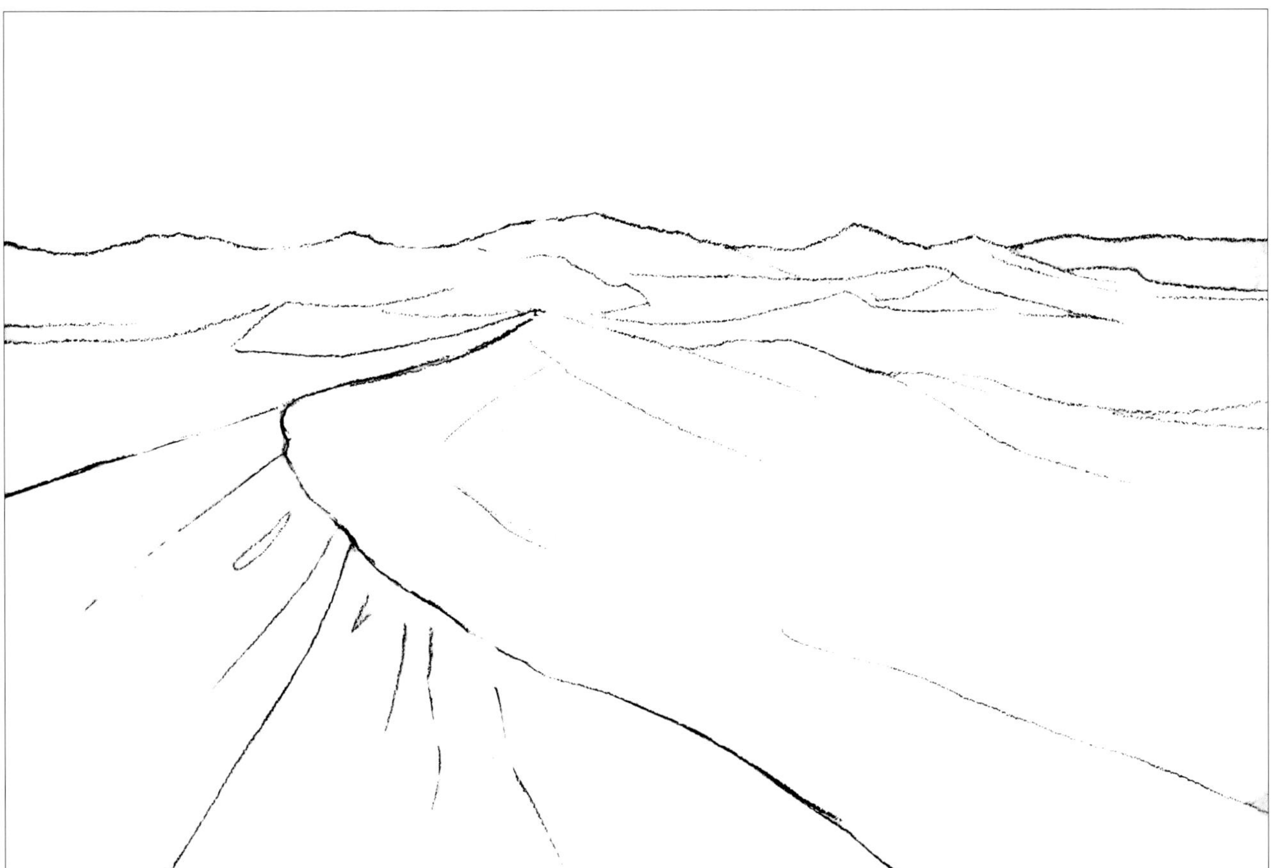

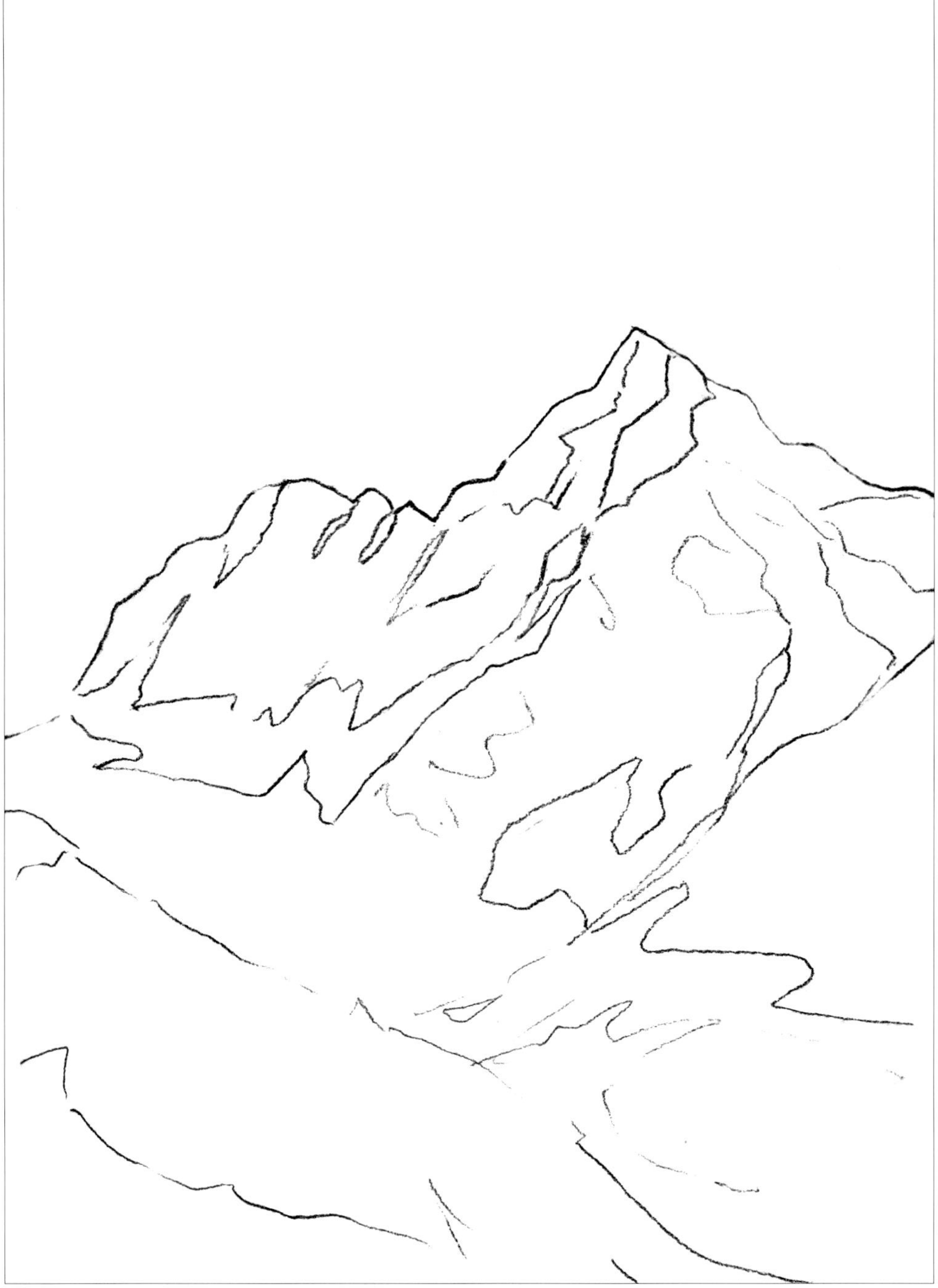

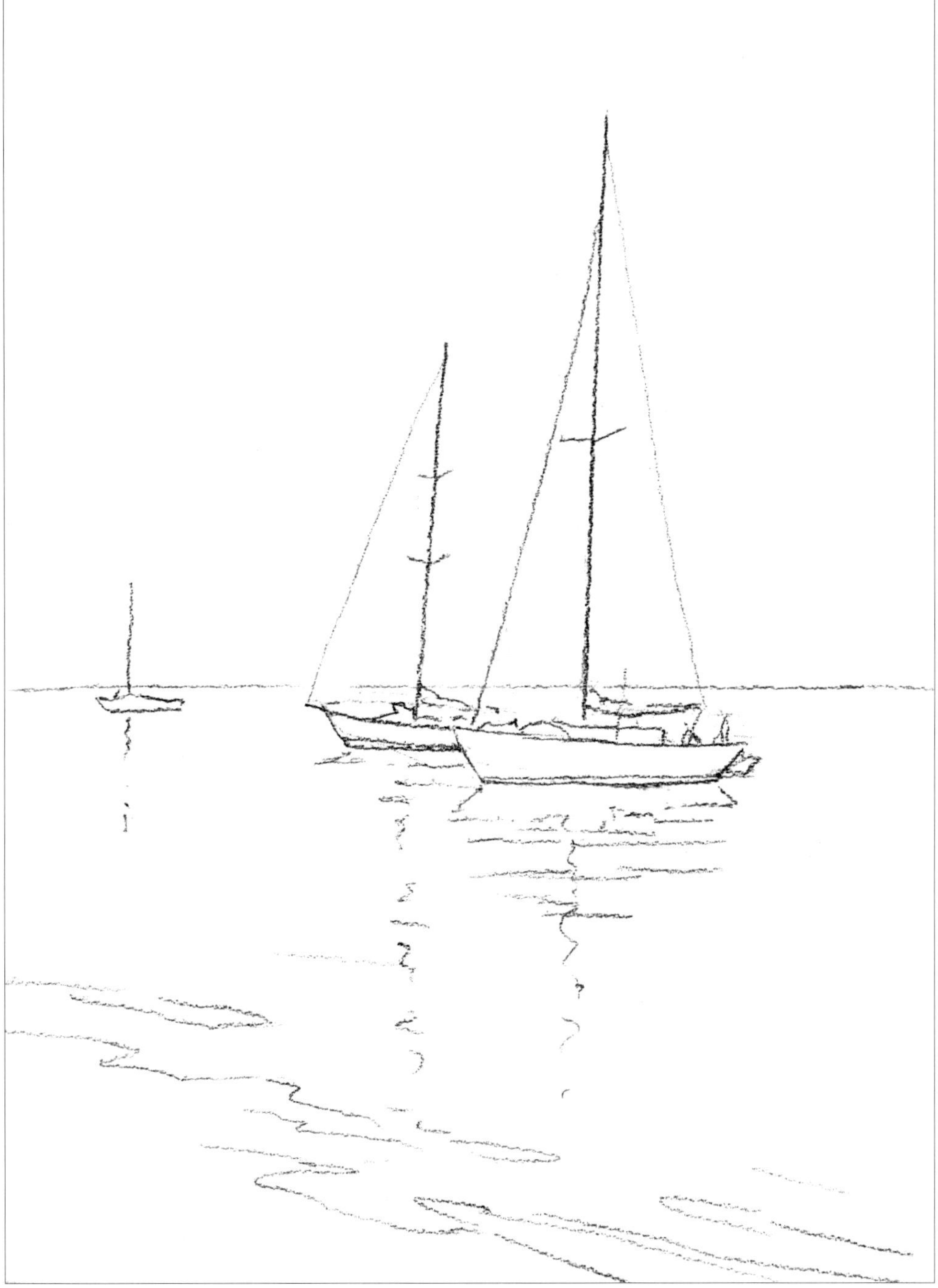

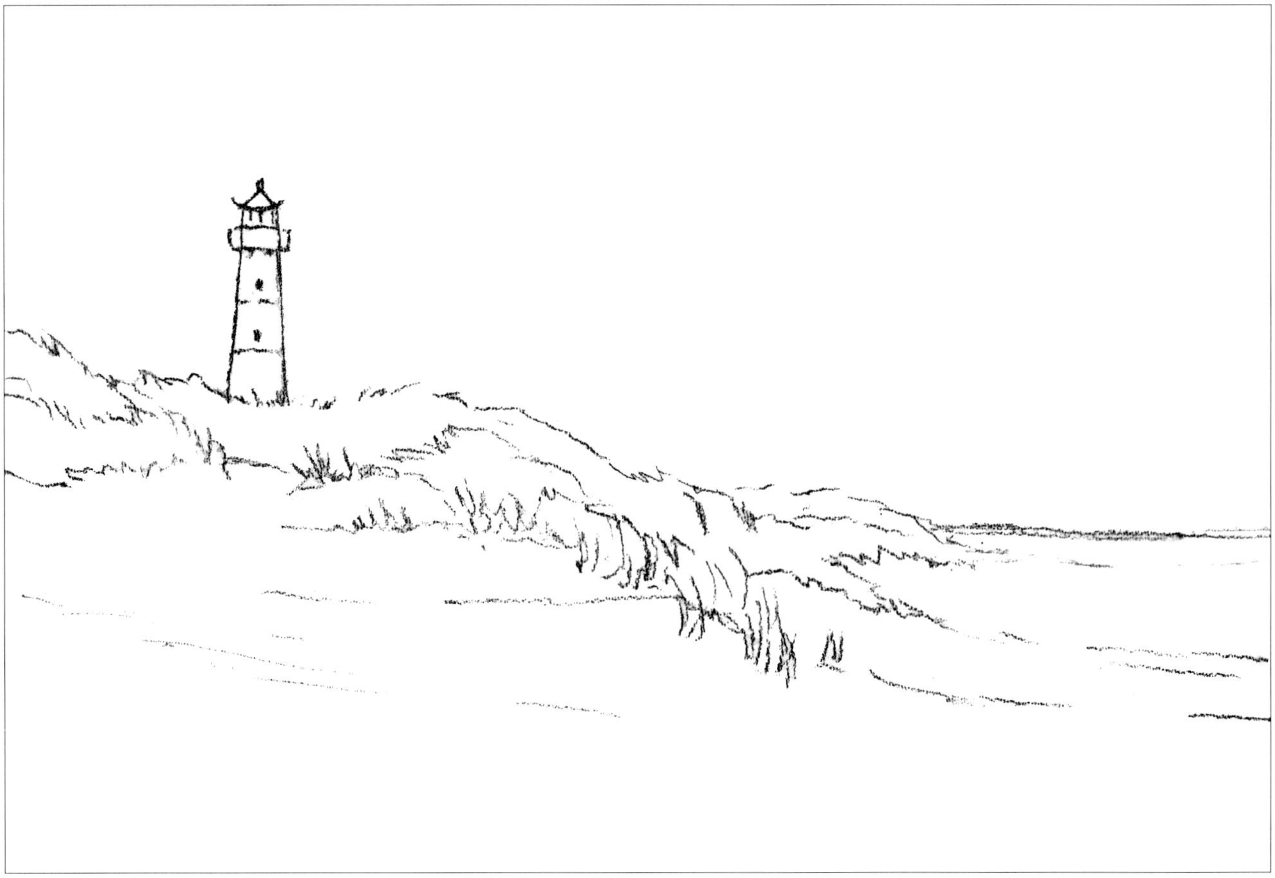

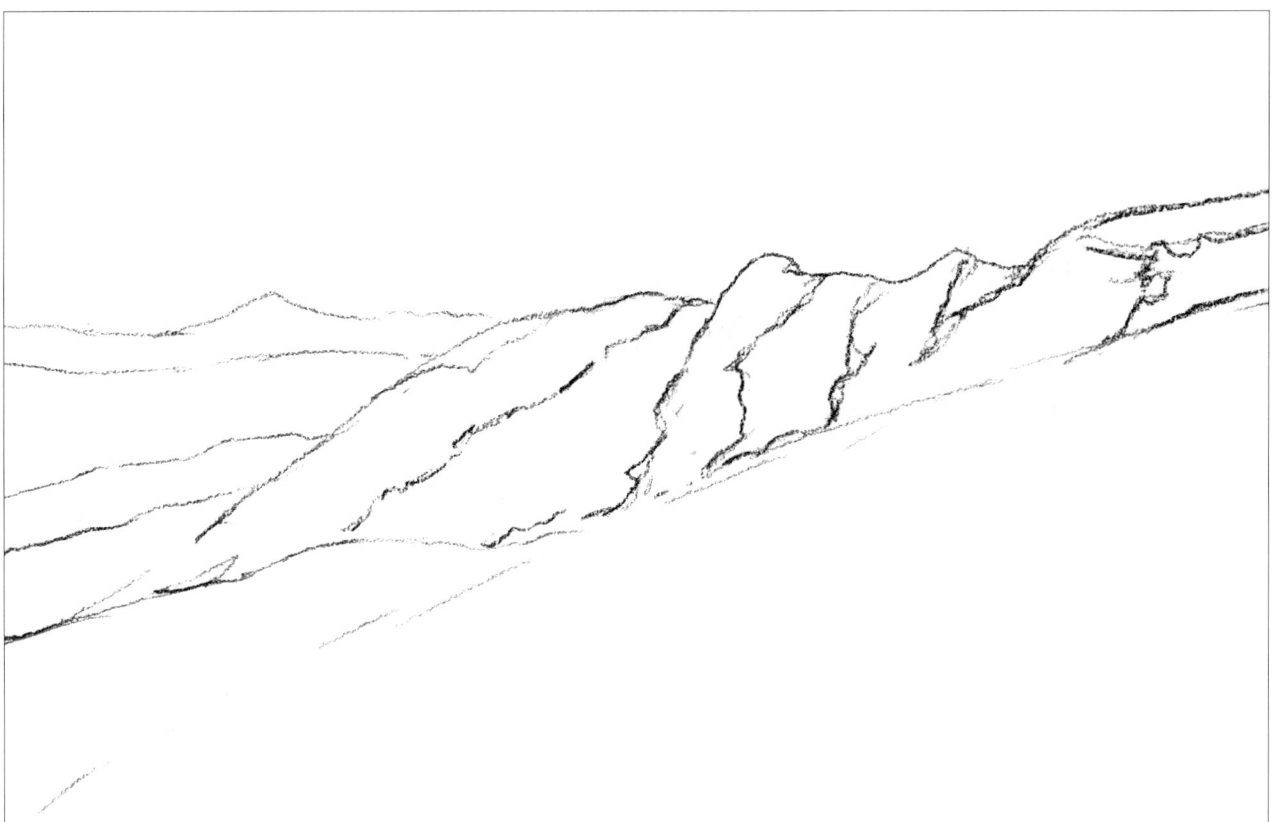

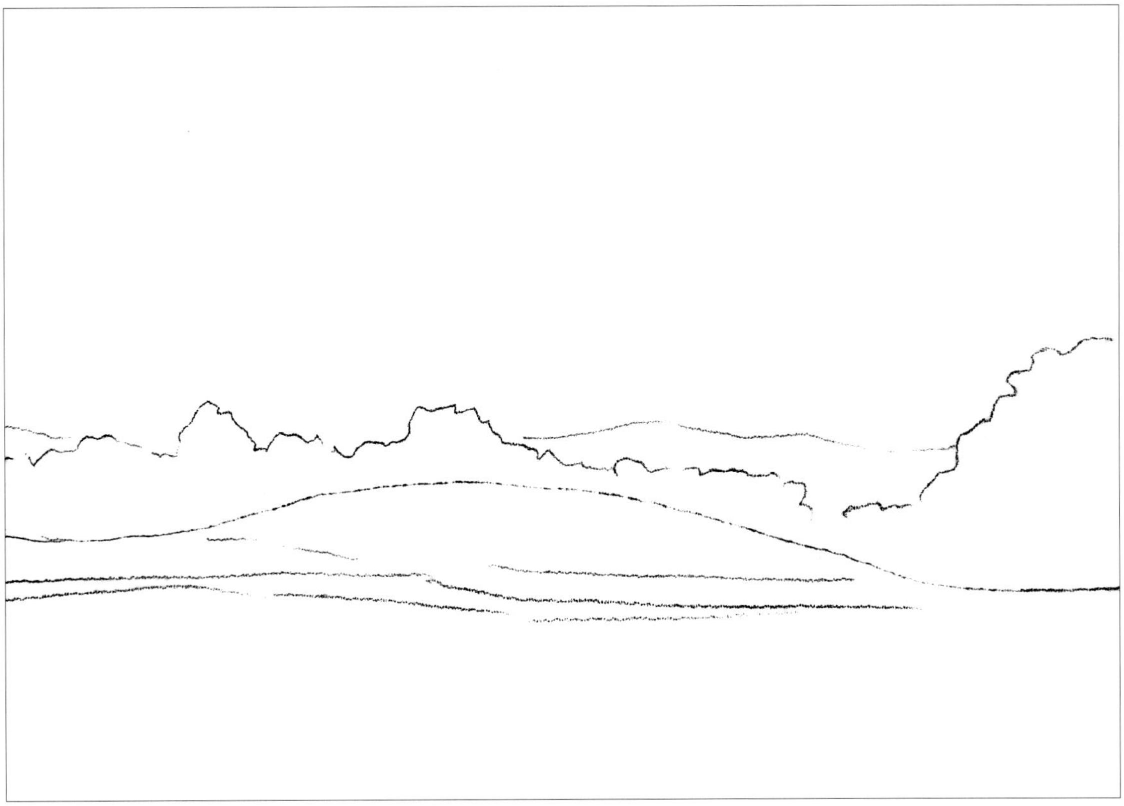

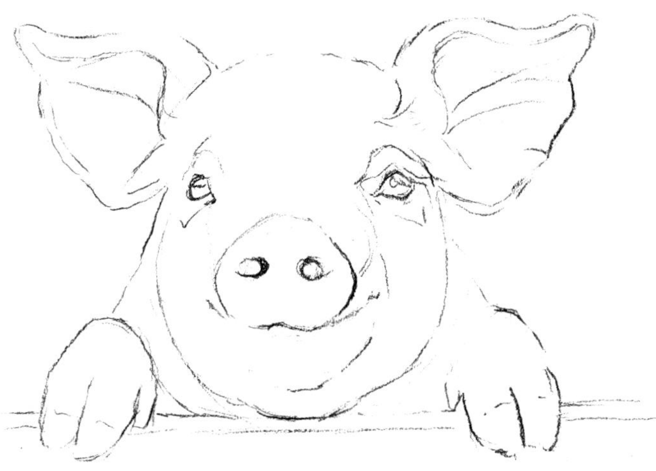

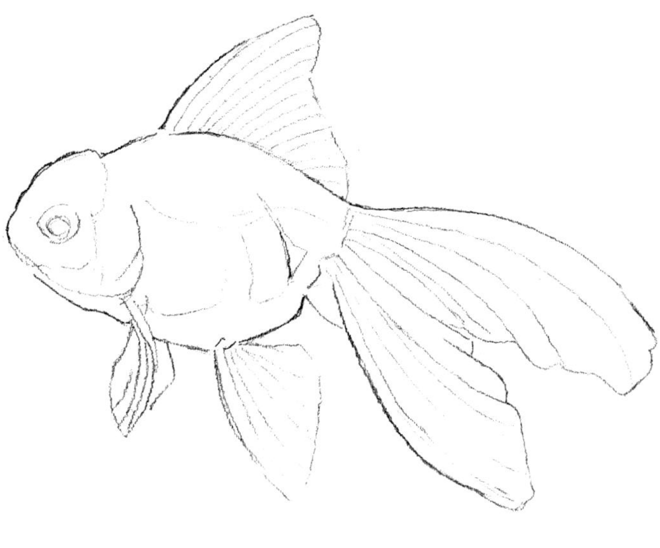

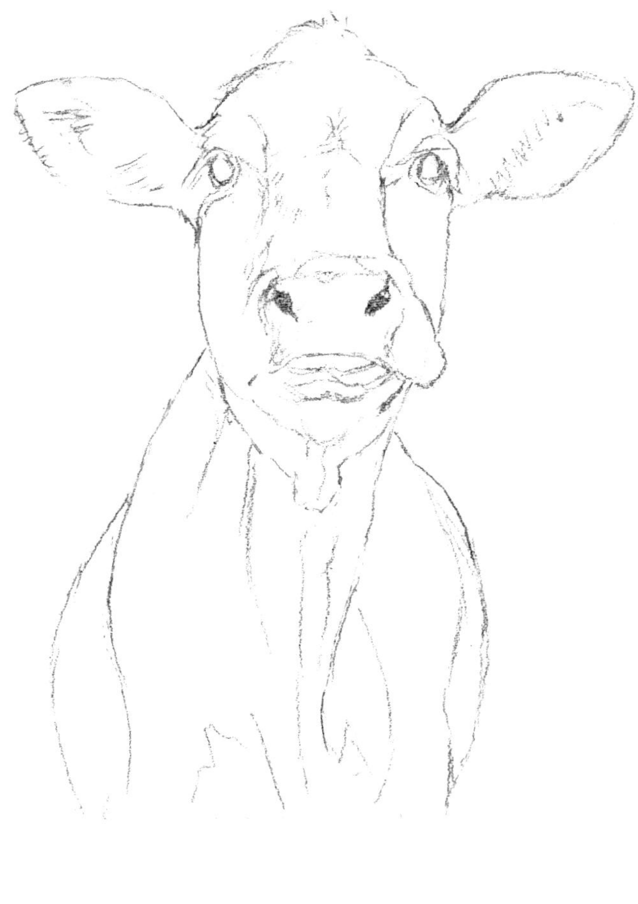

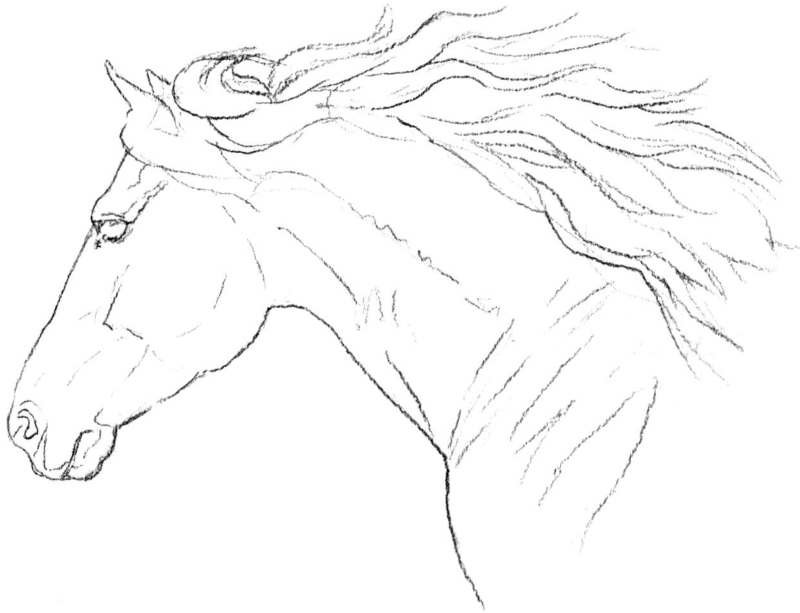

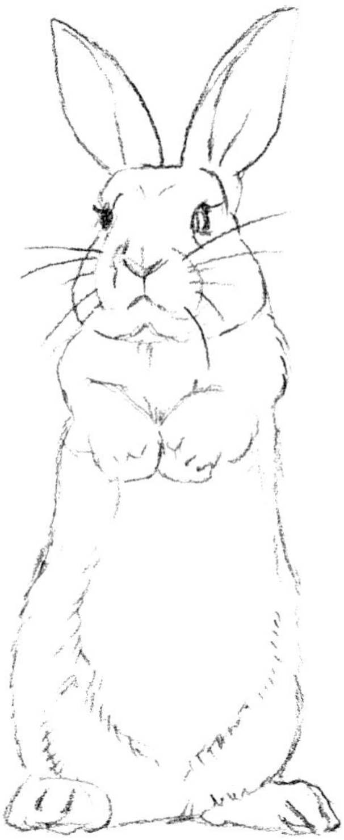

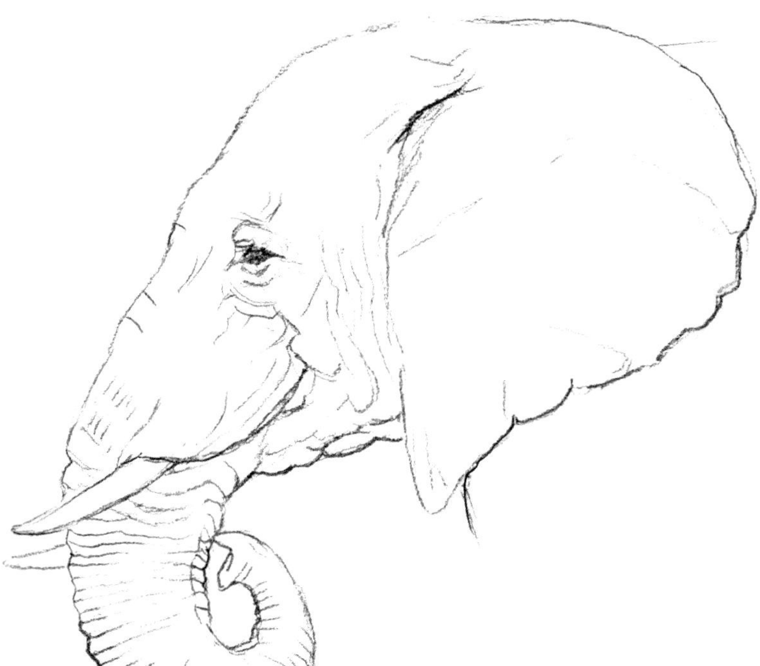

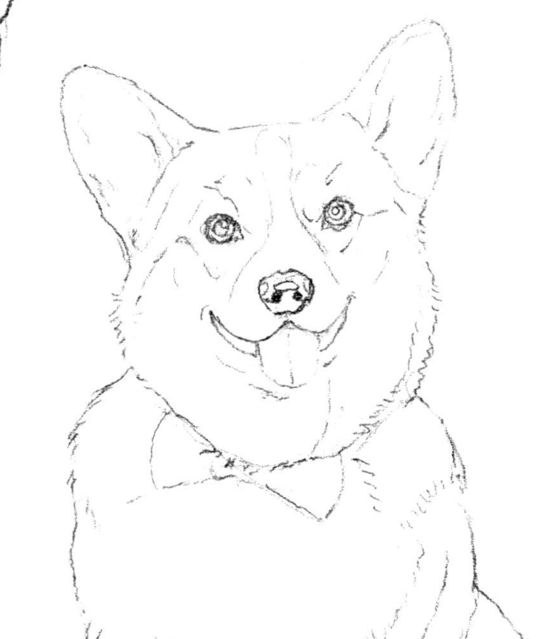

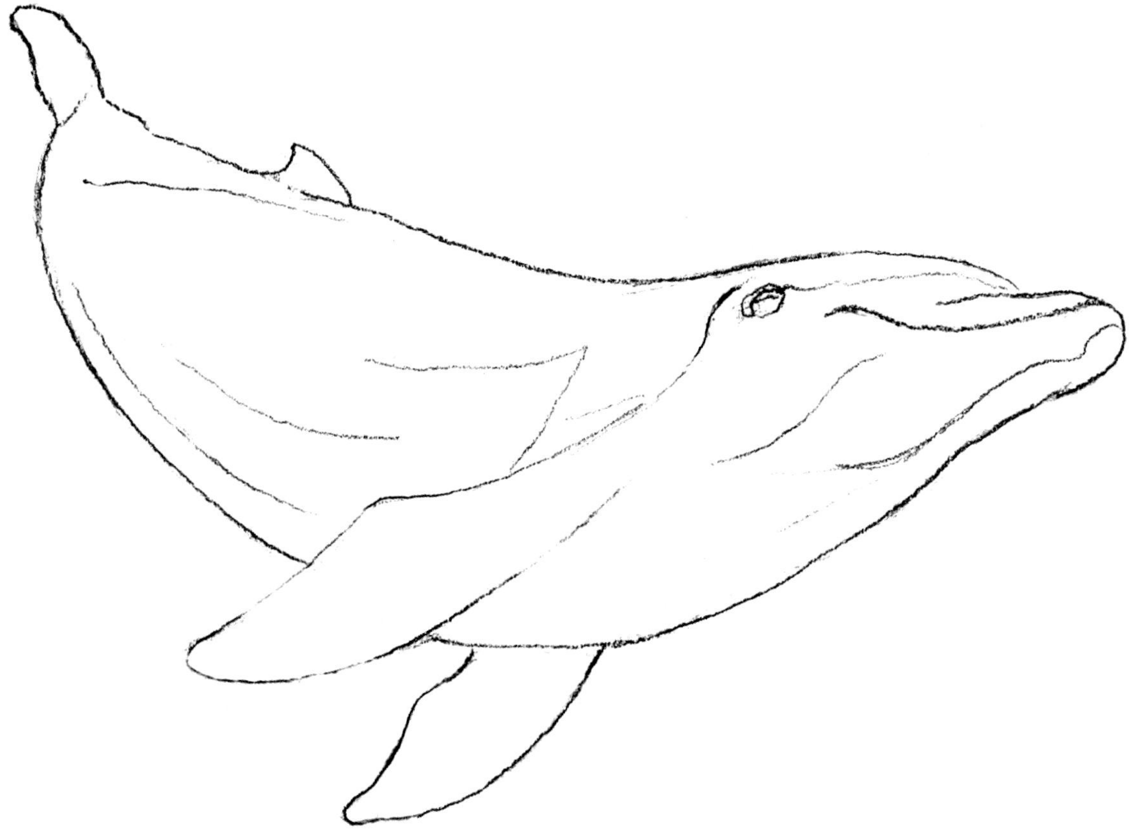

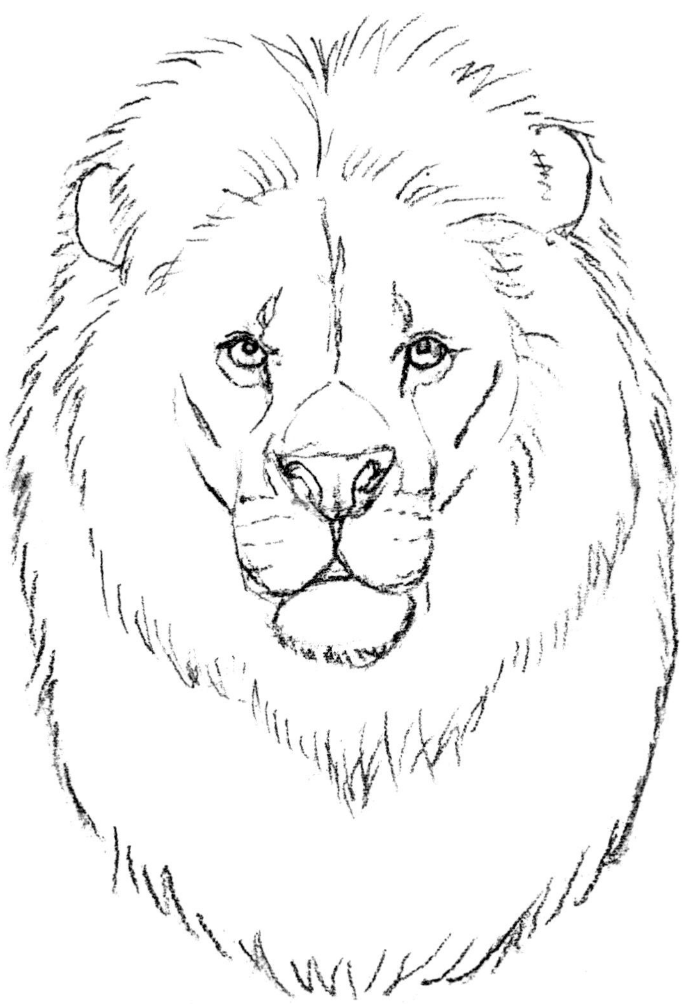

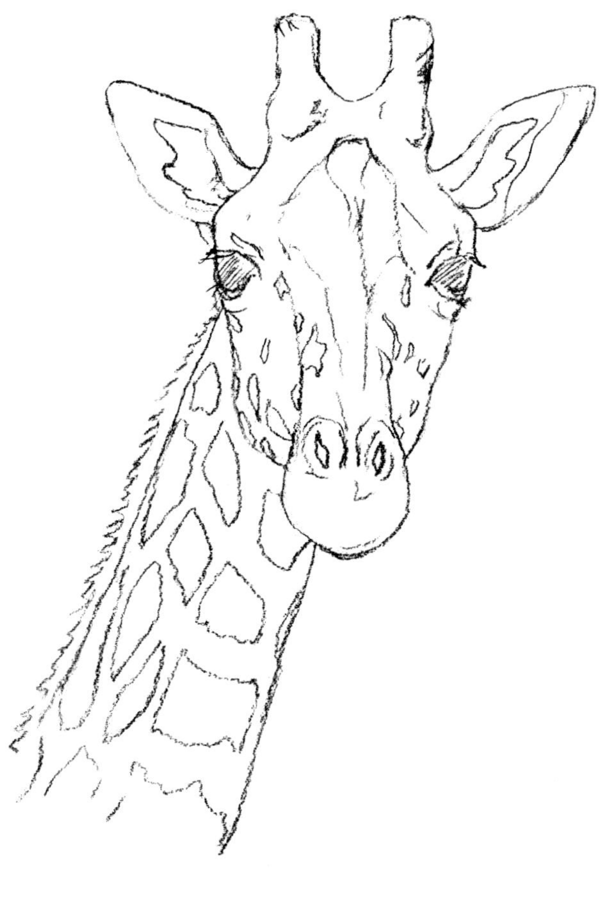

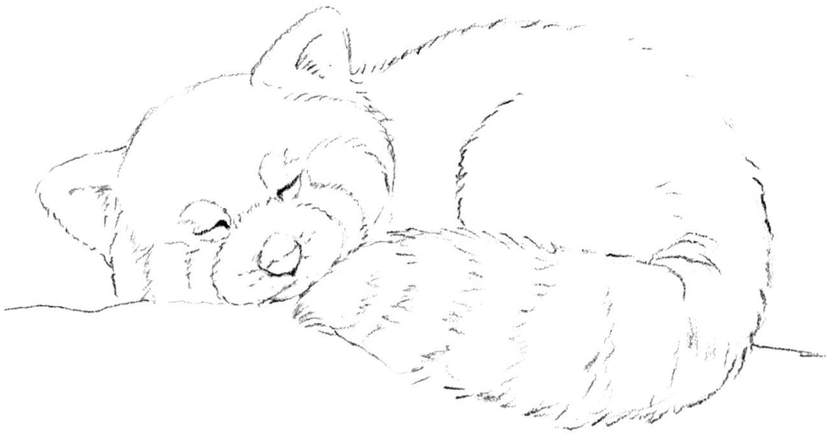

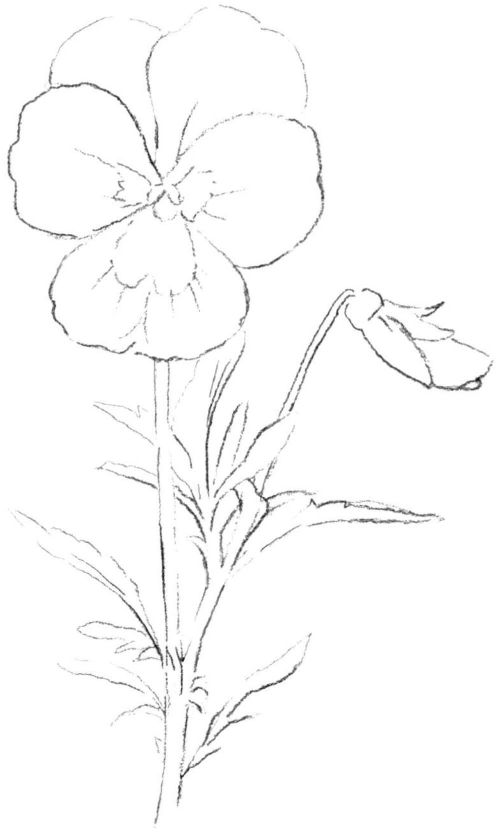

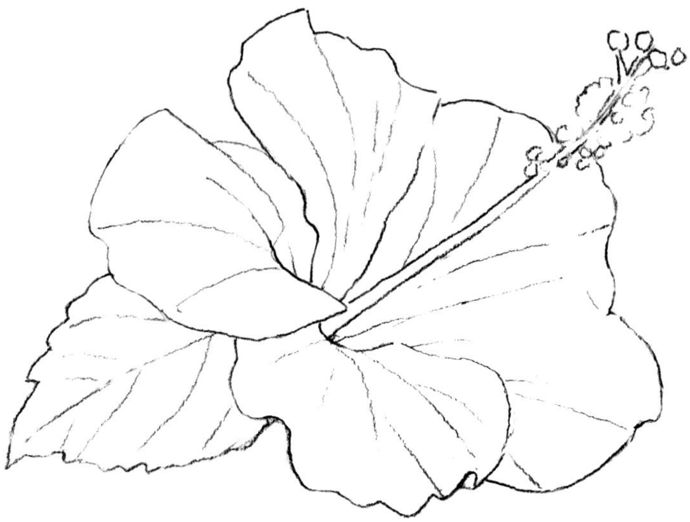

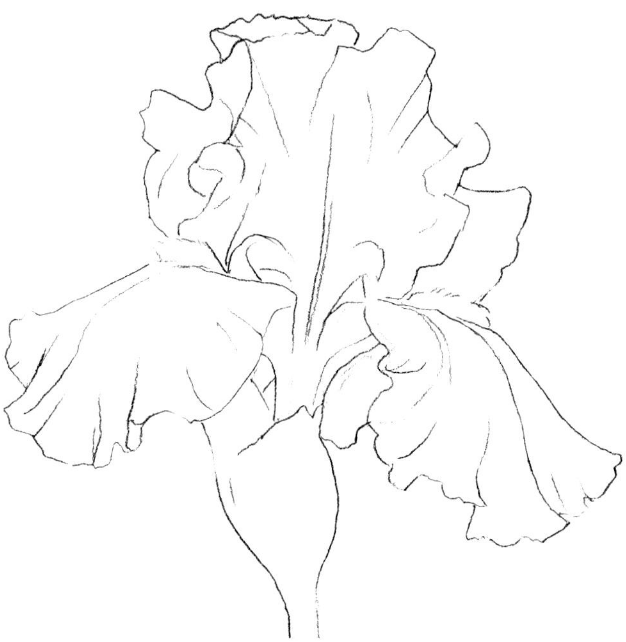

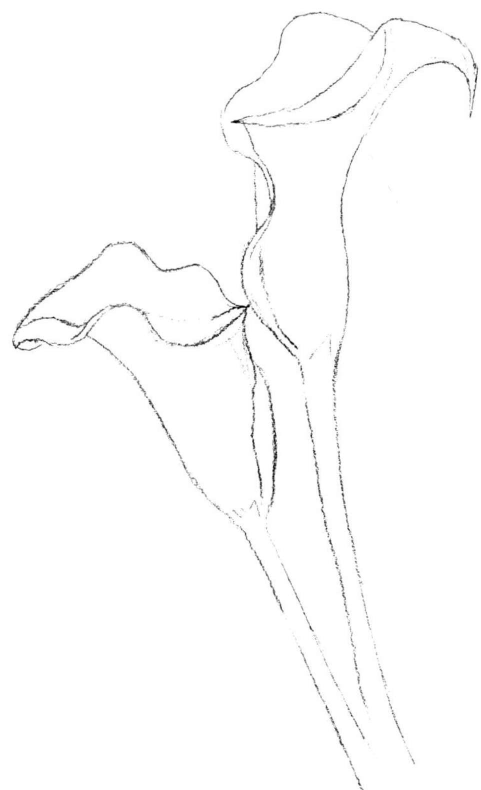

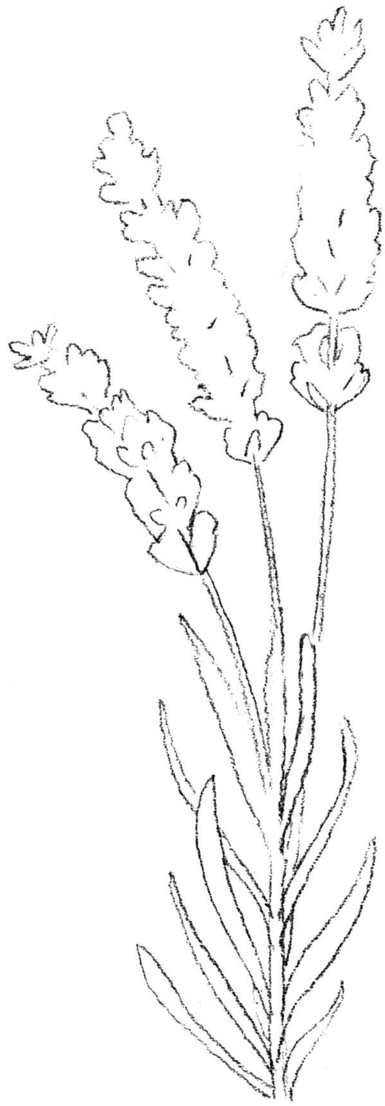

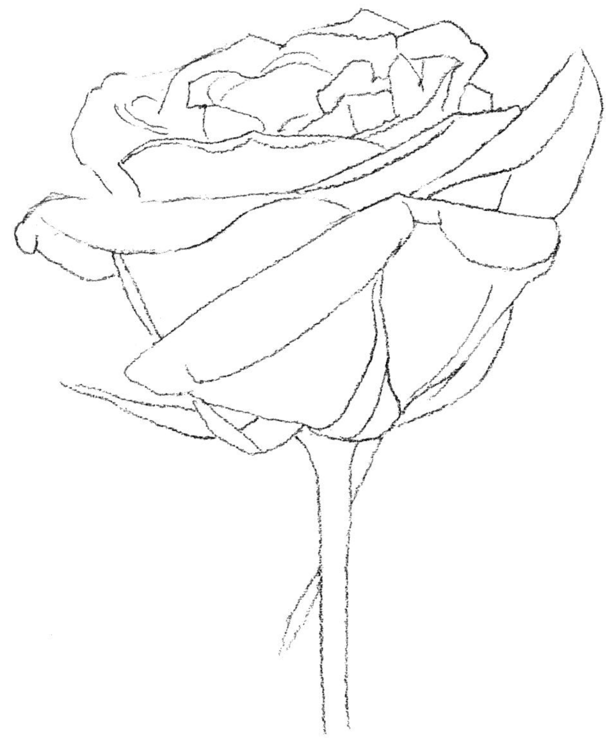

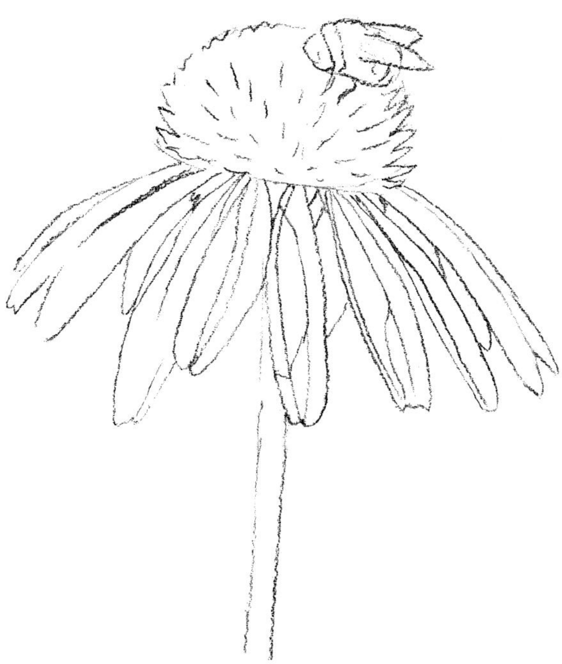

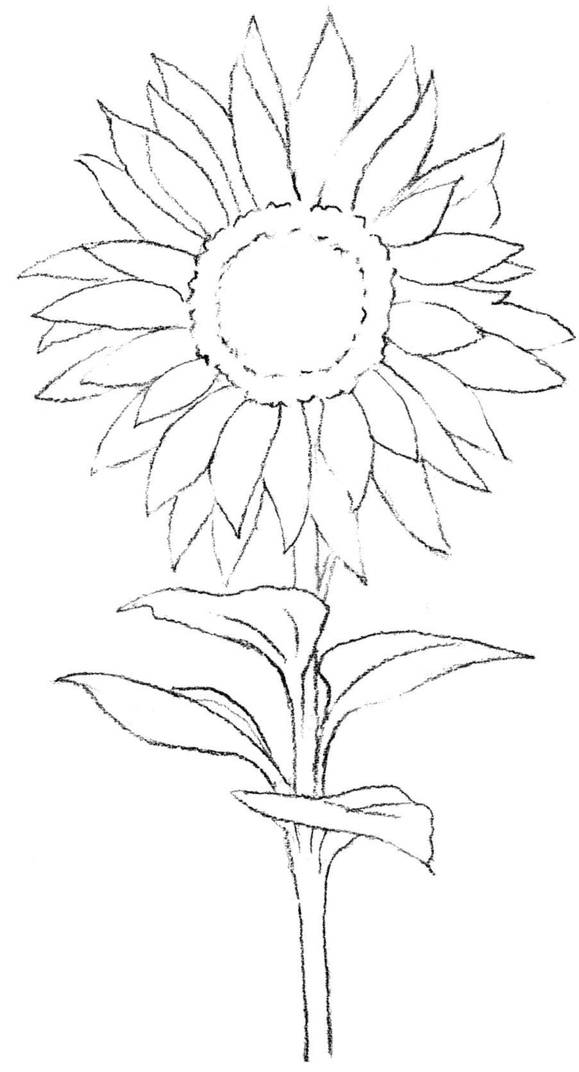

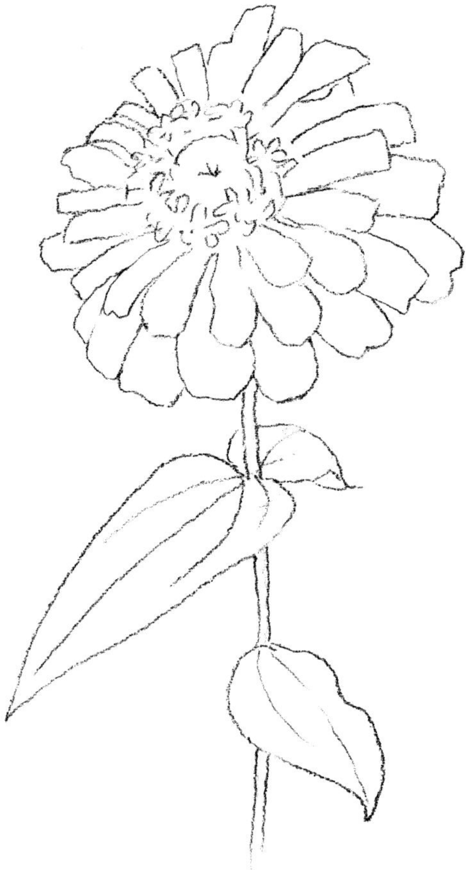

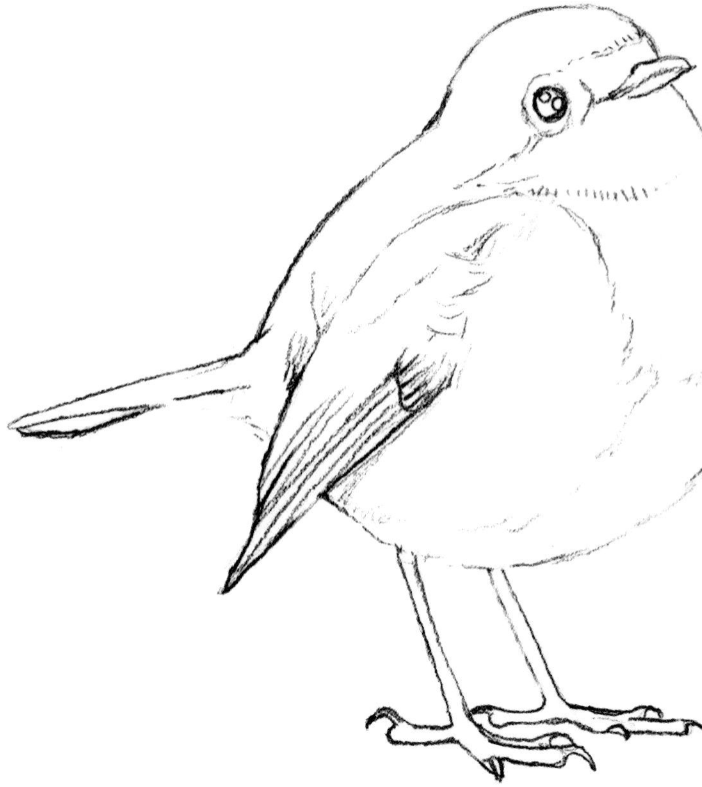

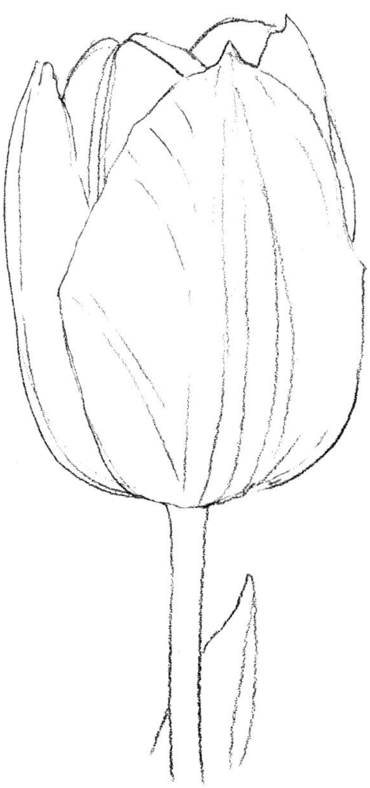

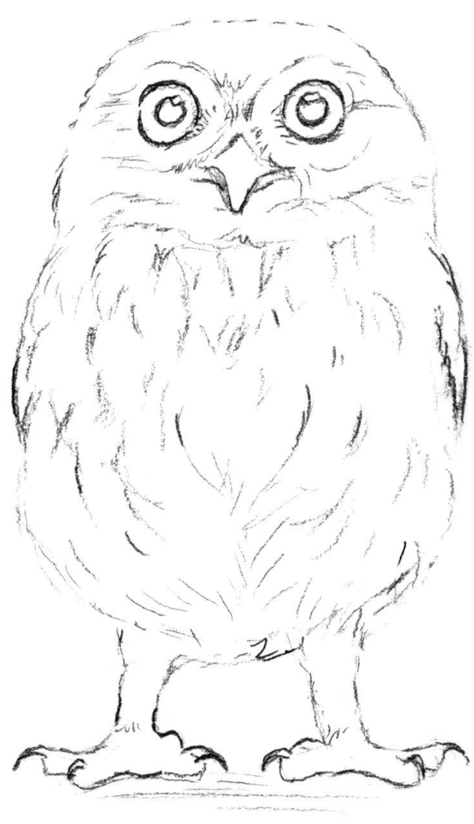

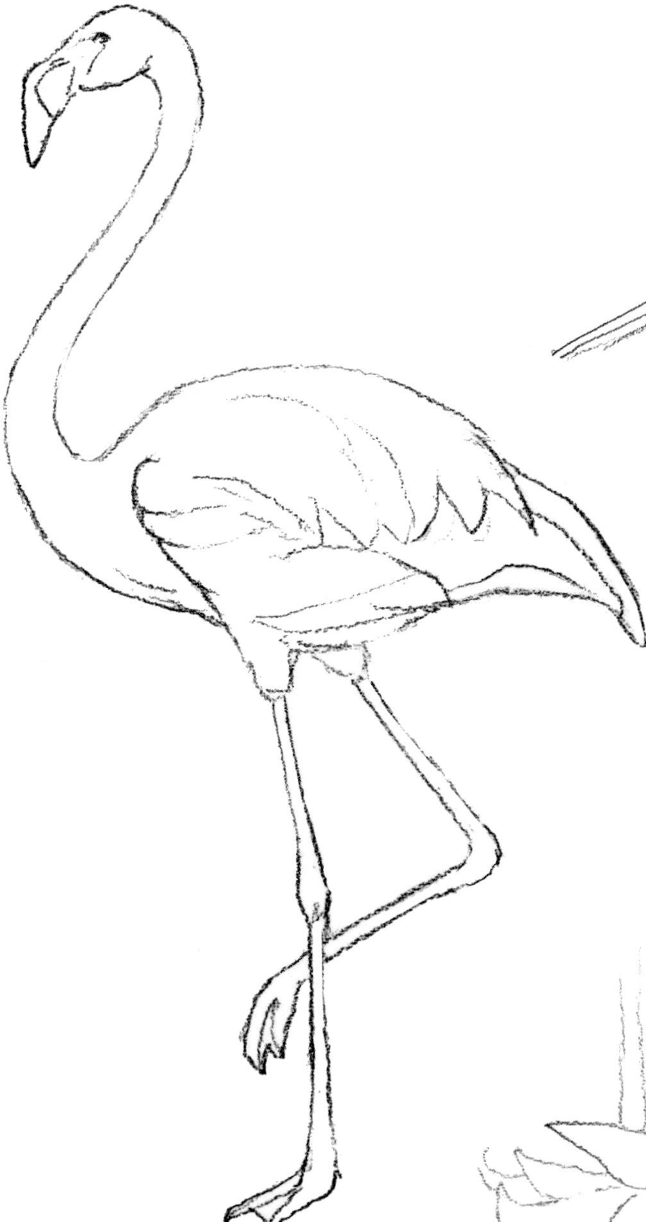

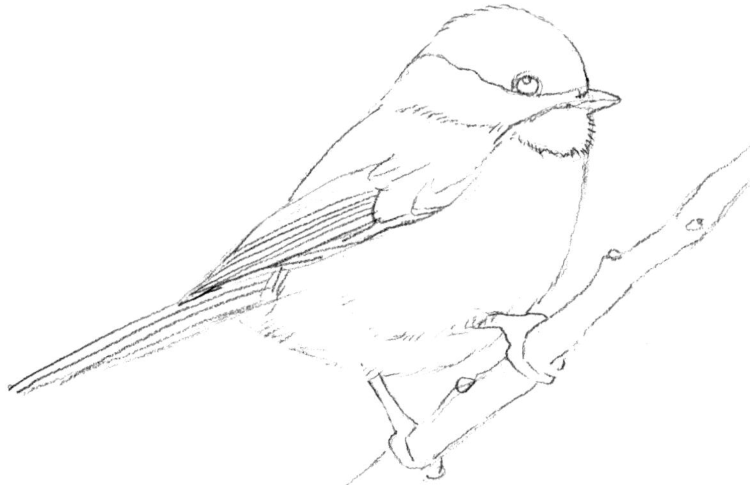

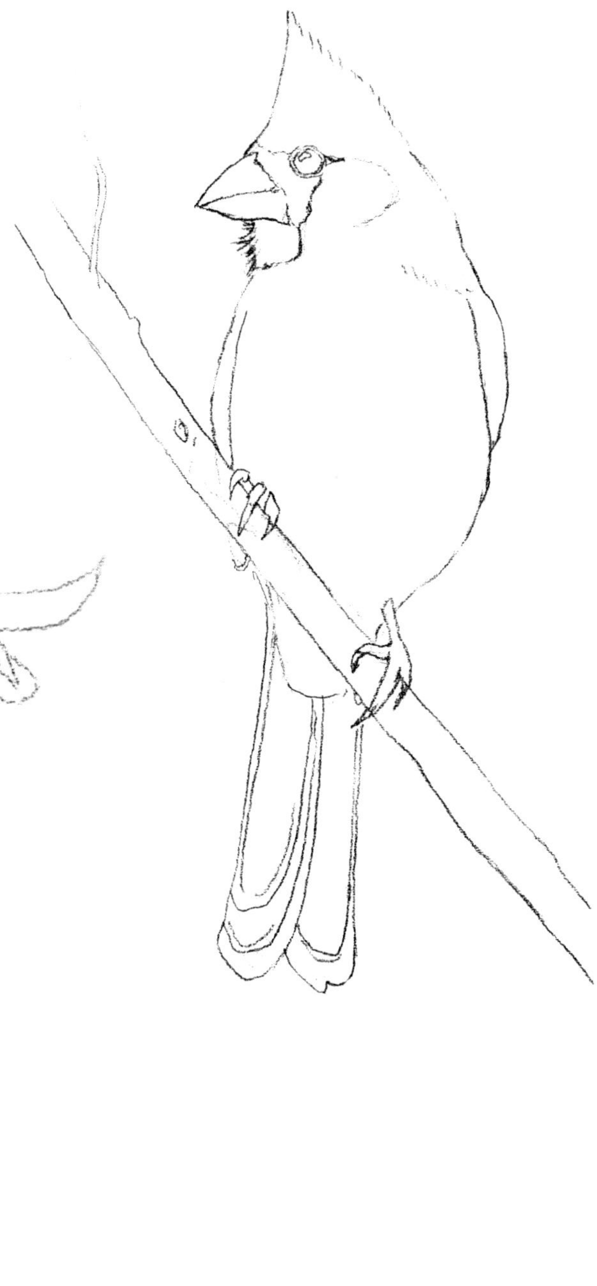

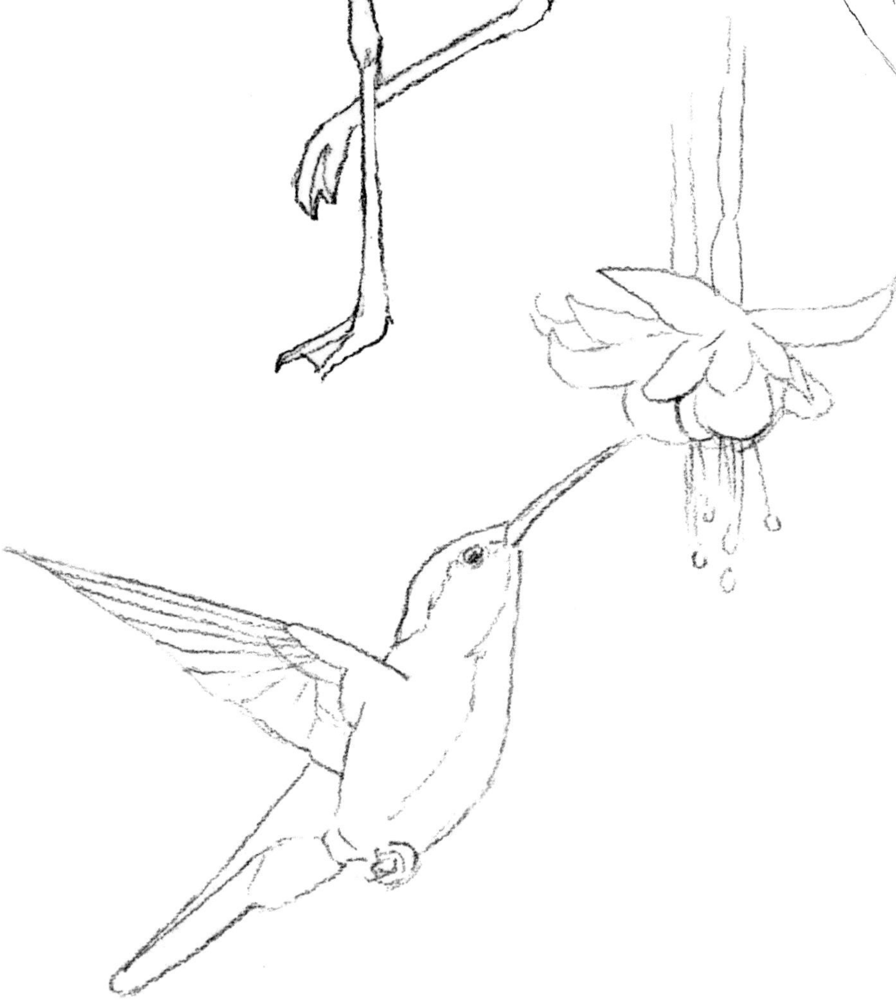

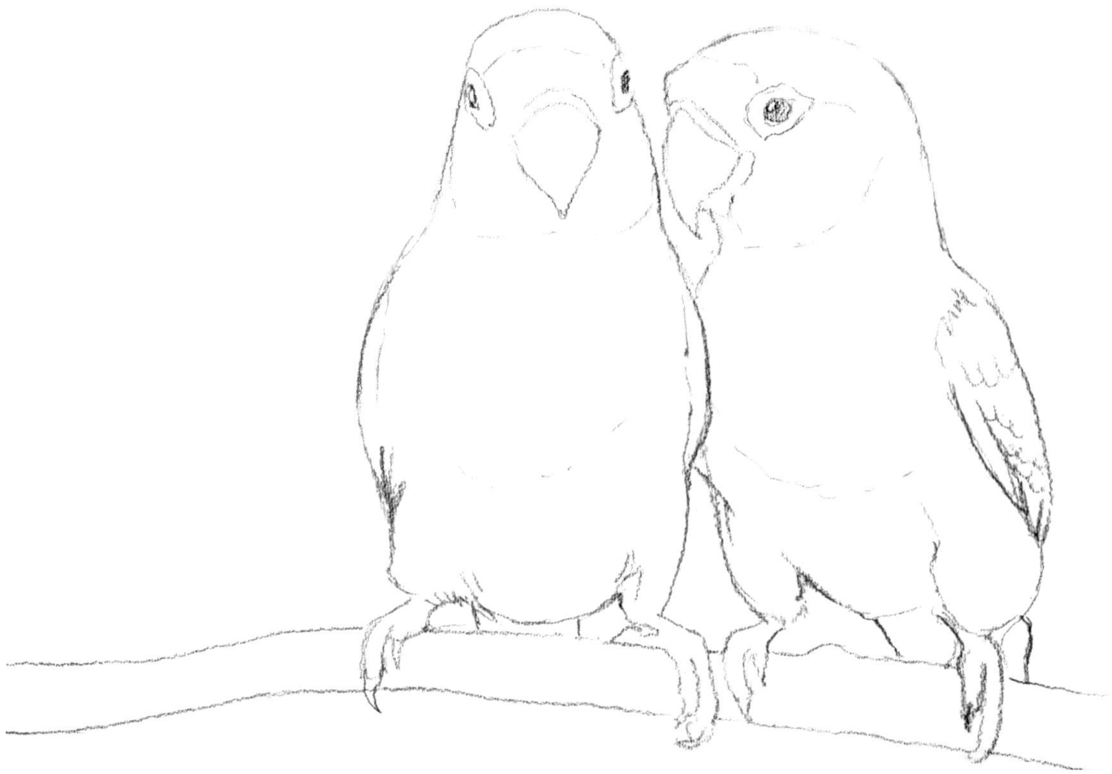

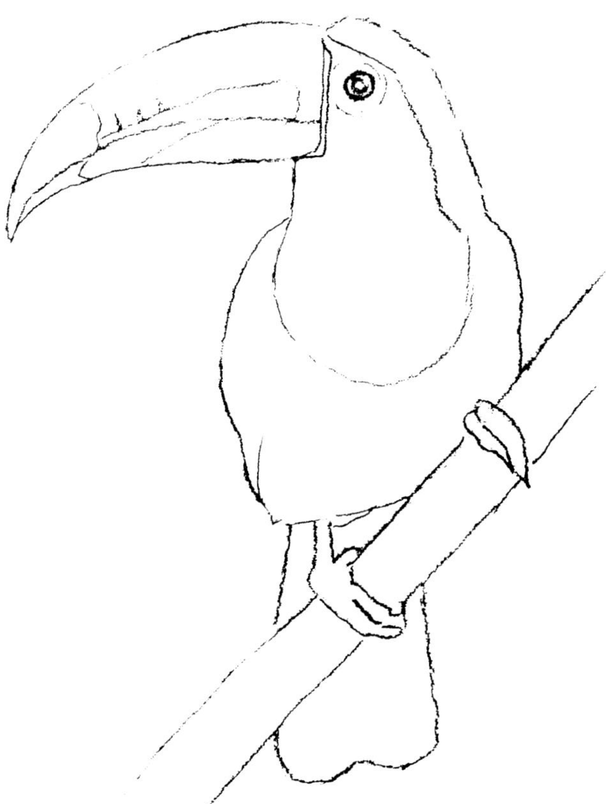

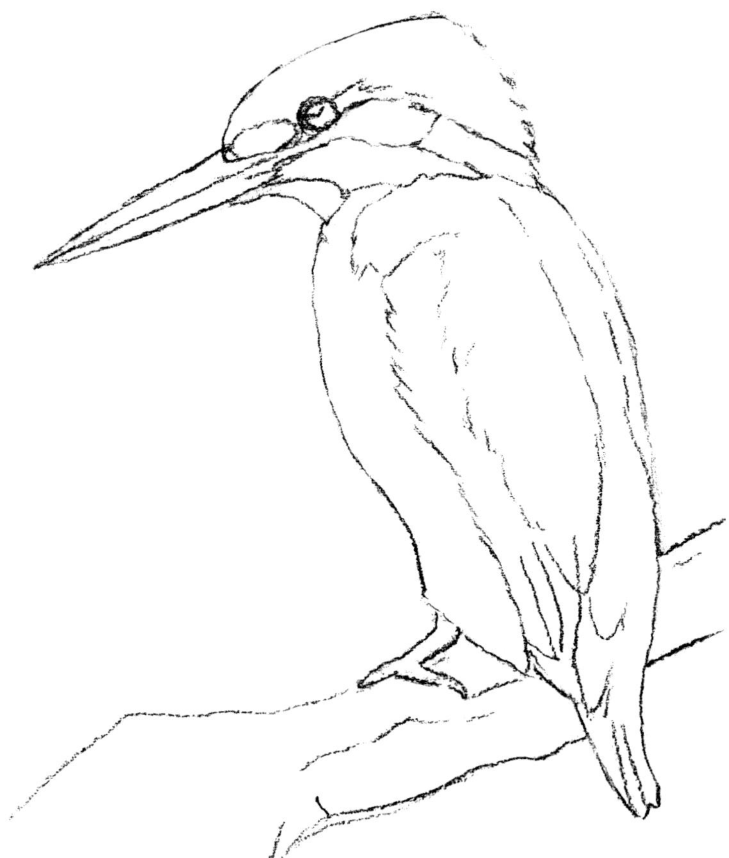

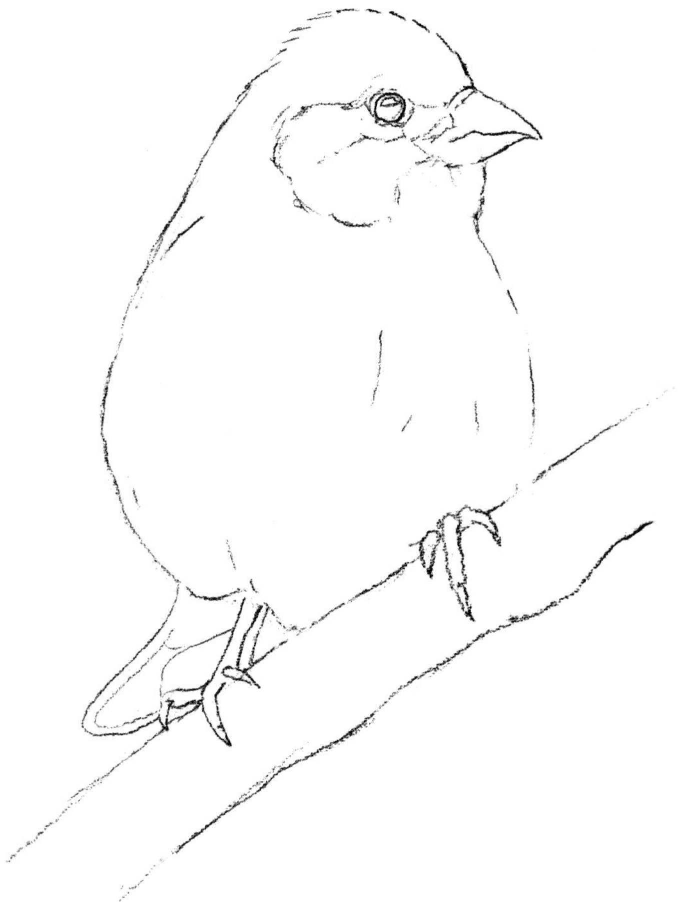

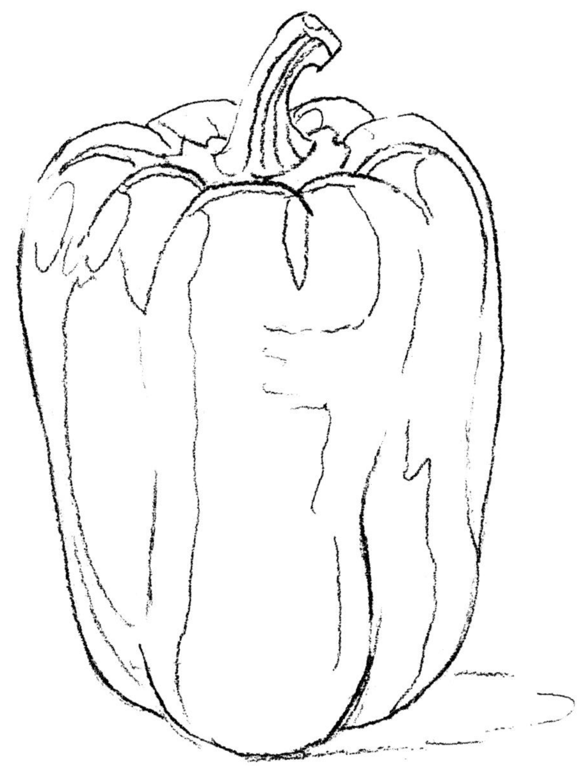

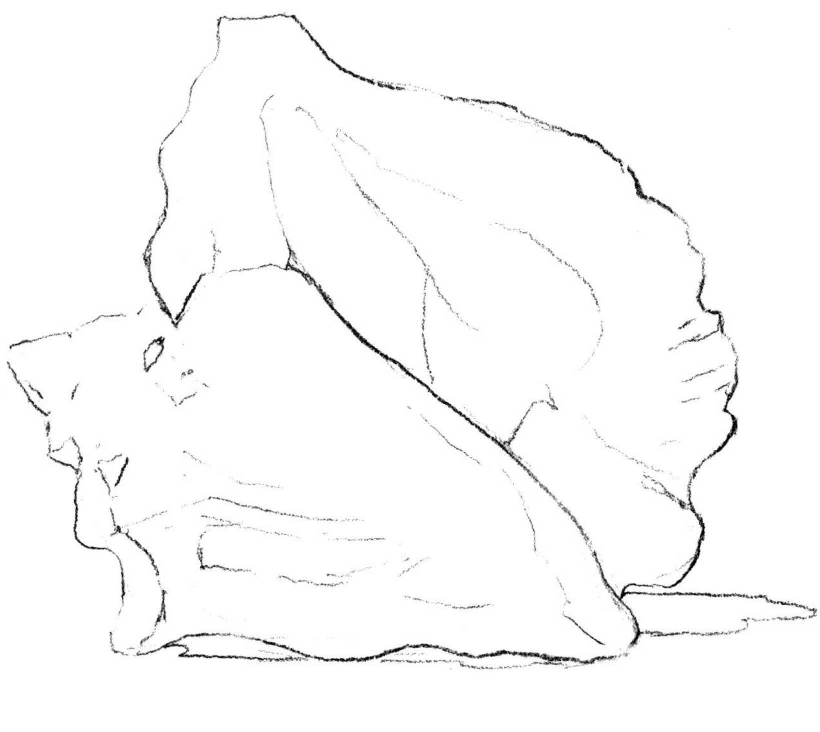

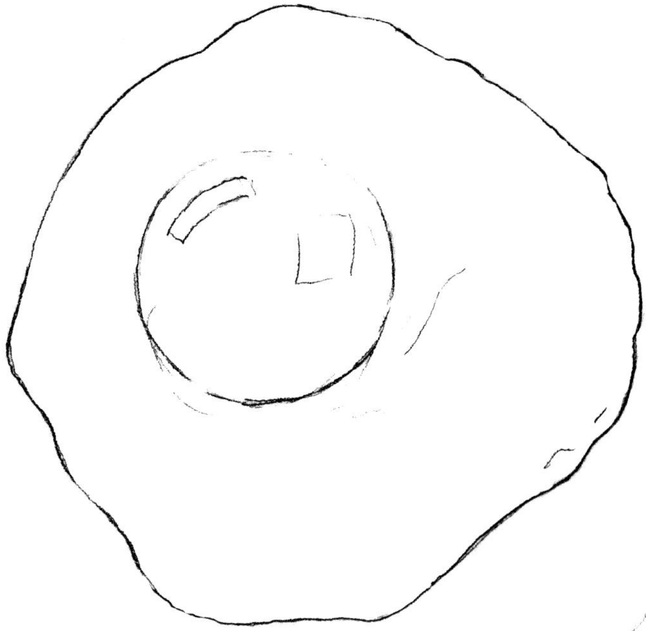

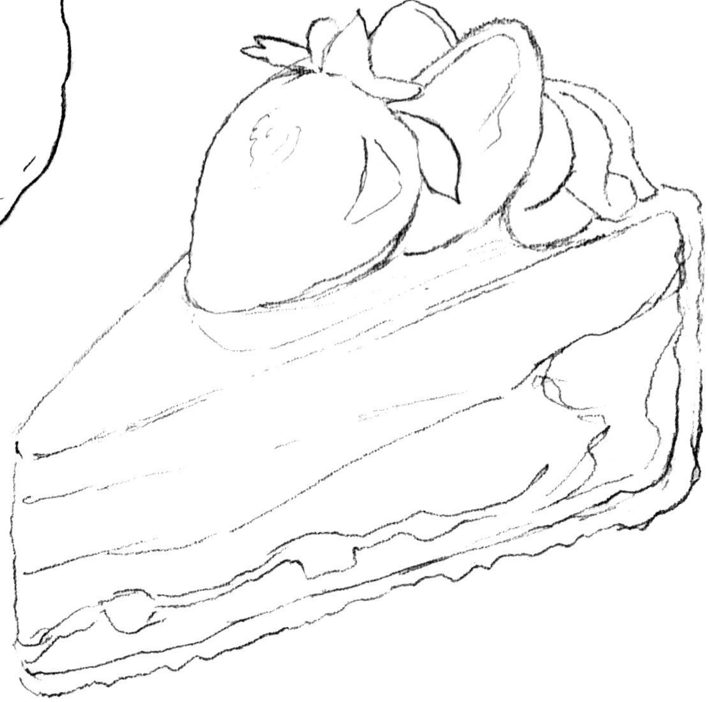

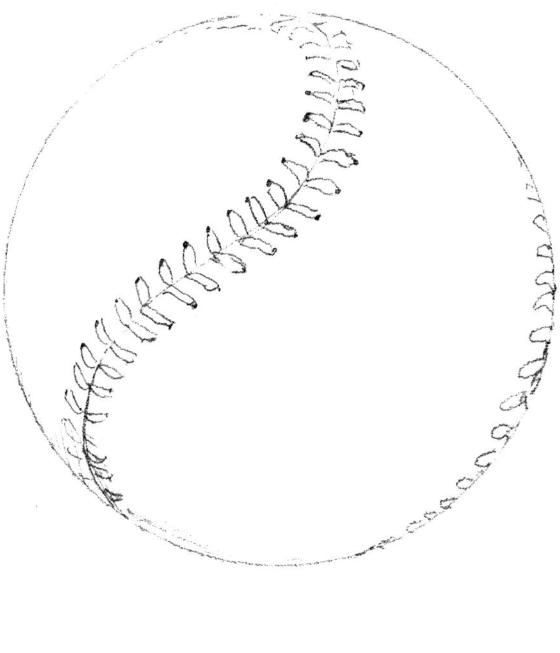

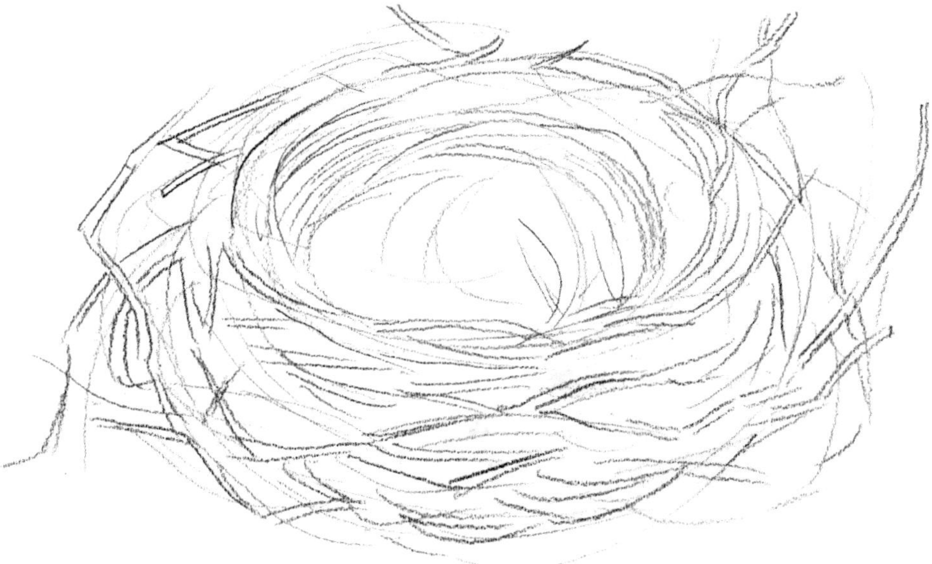

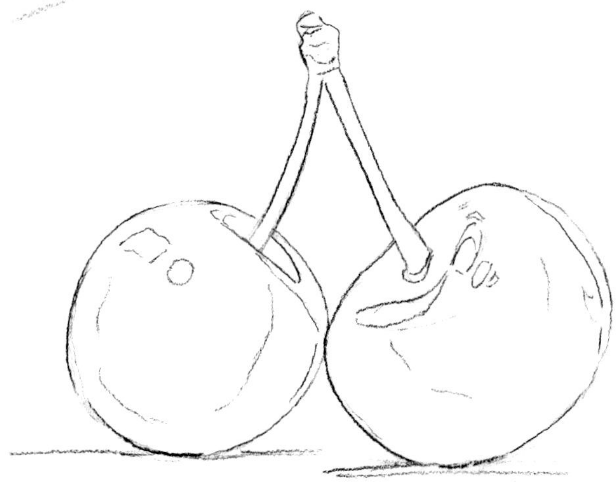

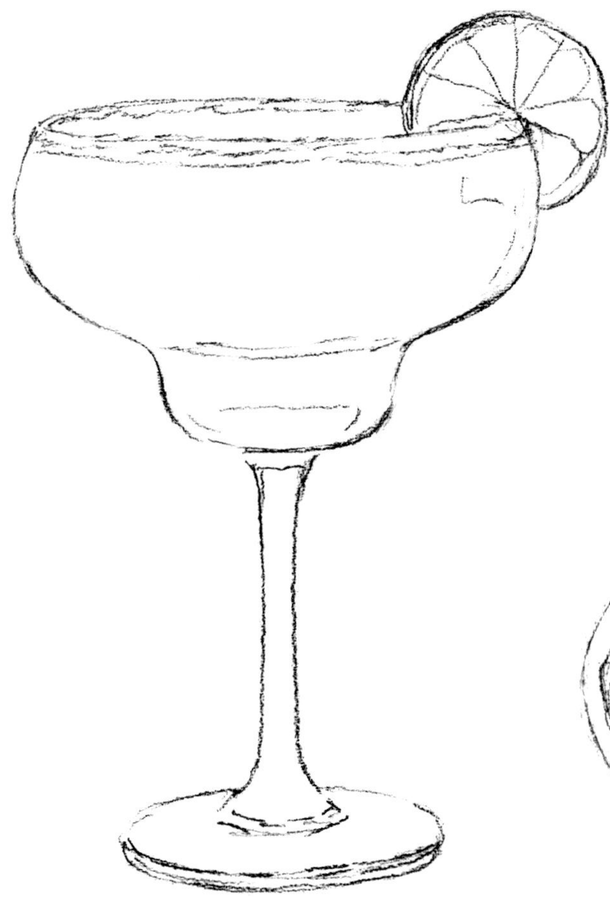

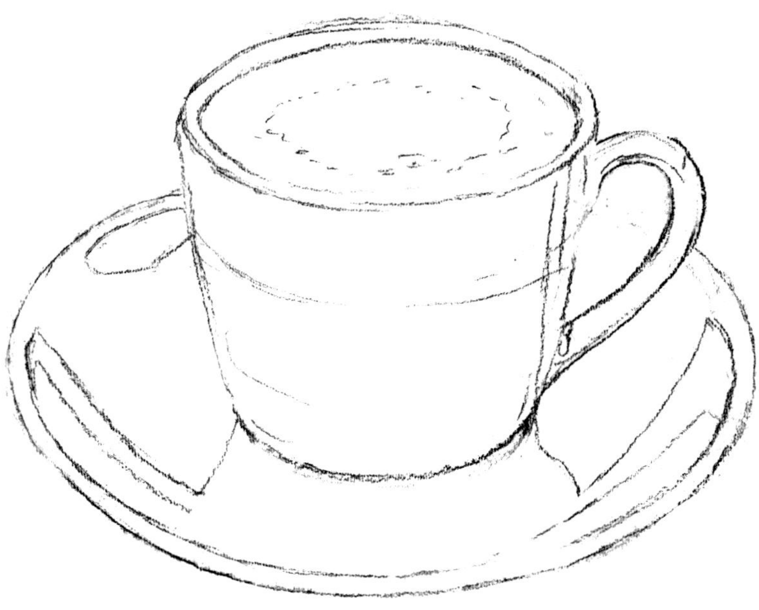

About the Author

Emily Olson is a Colorado-based artist, plein air painter, YouTuber, and passionate outdoor enthusiast. Originally from Wisconsin, she began her teaching journey through music, studying both music and art in college, and spent ten years teaching piano before transitioning to a full-time art career.

In 2019, Emily launched her YouTube channel, where she shares in-depth watercolor tutorials, product reviews, and painting tips. She also founded Watercolor Mastery, an online school dedicated to providing high-quality instruction for her students. As a lifelong learner, Emily constantly explores new paints, surfaces, and techniques, aiming to inspire her students with a spirit of curiosity and exploration that she believes is essential for artistic growth. She is the author of *Paint the National Parks.*

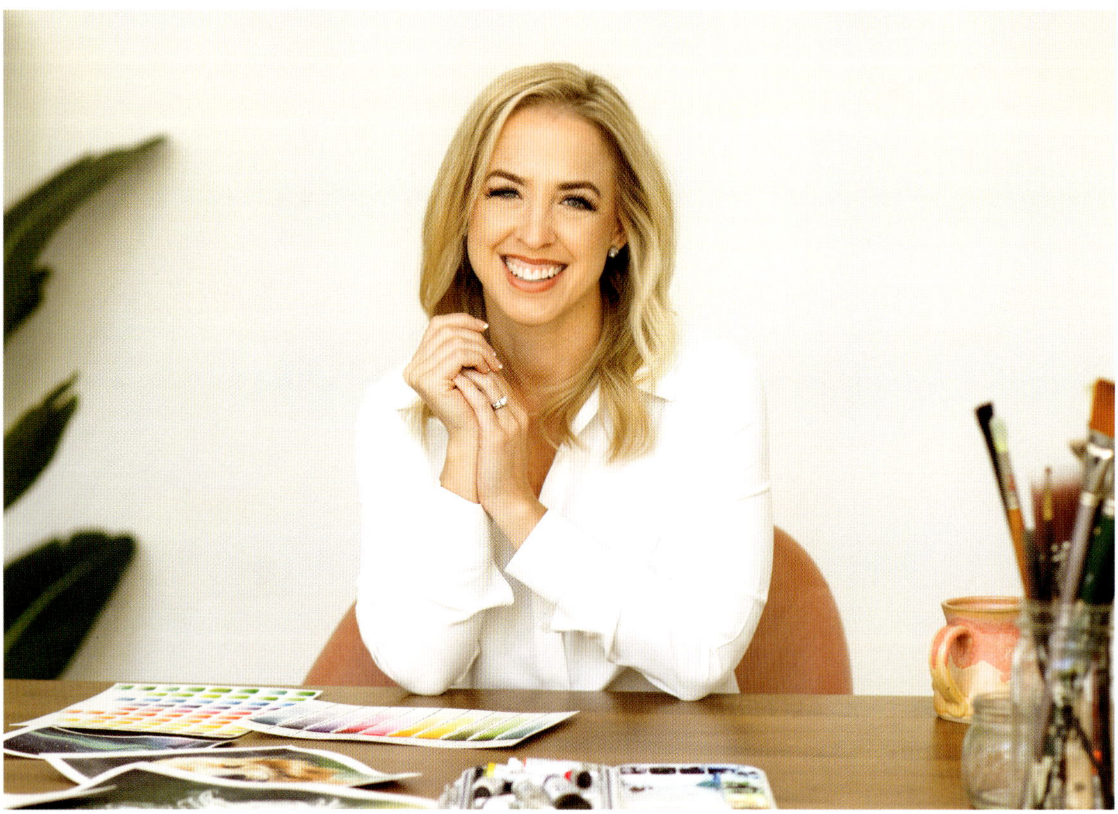

Index